CONTEMPORARY
ARMENIAN AMERICAN DRAMA

A scene from Joyce Van Dyke's *A Girl's War,* New Repertory Theatre (2003).
Director Rick Lombardo; Bobbie Steinbach as Arshaluis Sarkisian (*foreground*) and
Mason Sand as Seryozha Sarkisian; photo by Craig Bailey.

CONTEMPORARY
ARMENIAN AMERICAN DRAMA

AN ANTHOLOGY
OF ANCESTRAL VOICES

EDITED BY
NISHAN PARLAKIAN

COLUMBIA UNIVERSITY PRESS

NEW YORK

COLUMBIA UNIVERSITY PRESS WISHES TO EXPRESS ITS
APPRECIATION FOR ASSISTANCE GIVEN BY THE PUSHKIN
FUND TOWARD THE COST OF PUBLISHING THIS BOOK.

Columbia University Press
Publishers Since 1893
New York   Chichester, West Sussex
Copyright © 2004 Columbia University Press

Library of Congress Cataloging-in-Publication Data
Contemporary Armenian American drama : an anthology
of ancestral voices / edited by Nishan Parlakian.
        p. cm.
    Includes bibliographical references.
    ISBN 0–231–13374–X (cloth : alk. paper)
    1. American drama—Armenian American authors. 2.
Armenian Americans—Literary collections. 3.
Armenian Americans—History.   I. Parlakian, Nishan,
1925–
PS508.A7C66 2004.
812′.5080891992—dc22

                                        2004050160

Columbia University Press books are printed on
permanent and durable acid-free paper.
Printed in the United States of America
c 10 9 8 7 6 5 4 3 2 1

This publication was made possible by
a generous grant from the Dolores Zohrab
Liebmann fund.

This volume is dedicated to the memory of Barbara Bejoian, one of our playwrights—wife of Newell Thomas and mother of two young children, Casey and Ian—who passed away shortly before publication.

CONTENTS

PREFACE

In putting this anthology together, it was gratifying to learn that a number of produced and published contemporary Armenian American dramatists had written plays on their ethnic interests. For more than half of the last century it seemed that the theatrical marketplace eschewed plays with Armenian themes or that Armenian American dramatists, small in number, had few if any ethnic plays to offer the theater. In time, however, the best of our playwrights began to command professional attention for their ability to create dramas with universally appealing plots and characters (Armenian or otherwise). One need only point to dramas by writers such as Saroyan, Ayvazian, and Arzoomanian (included in this volume) who drew praise for their works on Broadway and in various prestigious regional theaters throughout America. Even at the time of this writing, two works herein are having staged readings and presentations in Boston, New York, and Philadelphia, drawing accolades from critics and the general public.

It was a pleasure for me, in preparing this volume, to review the theatrical activities of Armenians during the past century in the United States and, even earlier, in the homeland. It became very clear that Armenians had an abiding interest in theater, as we know it today, as far back as the mid-nineteenth century, when modern Armenian drama began to manifest itself. The freedom of the theater in the early twentieth century—with the birth of Armenia after World War I—however, became circumscribed with the Sovietization of the new nation. Under communism, playwrights lacked the freedom of unfettered expression because of governmental censorship. In America early in the last century, Armenian American writers, despite hearing their parents' dramatic tales of Turkish depredations, seemed more often than not to favor writing about them in the novel and story genres rather than in plays. It has been argued that the excitement of the theater, with its potential to galvanize mass audiences by creating "unacceptable" propaganda against Turkey, would have threatened the well being of Armenian "hostages" still uneasily residing there. Powerless, Armenians had little if any voice to command attention in the halls of international justice. But in the last thirty years—with significant action on the part of Armenian lobby groups in this country, who have demanded world attention to past Armenian tribulations and new favorable scholarship on that subject—our writers began giving both joyous and doleful expressions of their ethnicity, past and present, through dramaturgy.

As I fulfilled the quota of plays for this volume, others of high quality by new dramatists came to my attention suggesting, perhaps, that more publications of this order will be welcomed in the future.

My interest in Armenian and Armenian American drama began with a request in 1972 from the Diocese of the Armenian Church (Eastern), headed by Archbishop Torkom Manoogian (now the Patriarch of Jerusalem), to serve as artistic director of the Diocesan Players. I thank the patriarch once again for his confidence in me and for setting me on a new and exciting course. I am indebted to the Delores Zohrab Liebmann Fund for again supporting my efforts in publishing our significant dramas. The attention of M. Haigentz, Esq., fund administrator, was both remarkably patient and solicitous. The cooperation of editorial director at Columbia University Press, Jennifer Crewe, and her assistants was essential to the formulation of this volume. The comments of the various authors and the sound advice of Aram Arkun of the Diocesan Zohrab Center and Aris Sevag, managing editor of the *Armenian Reporter*, were highly useful. A number of friends helped me assess the importance of Armenian drama in the homeland. Dr. George Dermksian had much to report on his association as an actor with Elia Kimatian, one of the earlier directors of Armenian ethnic theatre in this country, and he put me in touch with 102-year-old Sooren Papazian, who reported on Kimatian's work as a stage director in Turkish Armenia. Anne Vardanian, actor and theater scholar, also gave me her professional view of ethnic theater activity during the mid-twentieth century. Other stage enthusiasts acting in ethnic theater here, too numerous to name individually, informed me of their lively theatrical experiences in the homeland or the near east. In particular, Setrak Terpanjian, a member of the Diocesan Group, gave witness to his theatrical work in Istanbul. Dr. James Tashjian, a former editor of the *Armenian Review*, reported on the publication of plays (or lack thereof) in that journal. And Dr. Dickran Kouymjian, holder of the Armenian Chair at California State University, Fresno, was helpful in connecting me with the Saroyan Foundation. There are others who assisted in the creation of this volume, some with technical expertise and others with knowledge of the background of this work. Finally, I owe much to my wife Florence, for bringing stability into our lives as I moved toward the consummation of this work.

NOTE ON
"ARMENIAN"
TRANSLITERATION

In the plays that follow, the playwrights include in
their dialogue brief expletives or short phrases in
"Armenian" transliterated into English. These id-
ioms are not critical for understanding the plays and
are meant to enhance the ethnic ambience of the
mise-en-scène. Transliteration from the Armenian,
however, is often imperfect because each Armenian
American writer speaks the dialect of his or her forebears, and these various ancestors may have origi-
nated from different homeland regions. Phonetically, their dialects might be dissimilar, and there is no
one definitive method of transliteration for all of
them. An English-speaking reader can have difficulty deciphering the sound of the Armenian language
because many phonemes in the original have no
counterpart in English (and vice versa). Fortunately
herein, except perhaps for simple expletives, the
meaning of the transliterated Armenian phrase is
given in English in square brackets. In the case of
one play, the author suggests in parentheses that the
phrase following can be spoken in Armenian. And
in that piece, as in every one of the plays, the feeling
for Armenian ethnicity is suggested by allowing de-
liberate misuse of English grammar, syntax, and vo-
cabulary by characters in the homeland or first generation immigrants in America.

CONTEMPORARY
ARMENIAN AMERICAN DRAMA

INTRODUCTION

NISHAN PARLAKIAN

The contemporary full-length Armenian American dramas and the brief curtain raiser of this volume were created in English largely by artists of Armenian extraction during the last third of the twentieth century. Newspaper accounts and reviews and recommendations from literary colleagues and playwrights helped in finding them. There was no effort to select works on the basis of genre. As it turned out, the dramaturgy herein represents admixtures or blends of farce, comedy, tragicomedy, and tragedy. Perhaps the best overall description of genre for most of our plays would be the term "*drame*," a work generally of serious theme, but lightened by relevant humor.

Although our experienced dramatists have written on various subjects of general interest, the plays here specifically reflect the shared or common experiences in Armenian group and family life in Armenia, Turkey, and America. These include the joy of being with kith and kin in a free society in which Armenians can practice their faith and enjoy their ethnic customs; the turmoil and travail of transplantation from the Anatolian homeland to the diaspora; the feared dissolution of Armenian racial identity through assimilation; the loss of hegemony over ancestral lands; and the chaos and agony associated with the genocide of the Armenian nation.

In the years preceding our contemporary period, if Armenian Americans wrote plays on the themes noted above, they seemed to have been few and far between and rarely achieved notable public recognition. But for the most part, after the first wave of Armenian immigration and even to the present, it is noteworthy that the same motifs emerged mainly in prose and poetry. These literary forms remain, to this day, the dominant genre of literary expression for Armenian American writers, several critically admired ones in the last century being Leon Surmelian (novel, *I Ask You Ladies and Gentlemen*, 1945); Marjorie Housepian (novel, *A House Full of Love*, 1957); Diana Der Hovanessian (poetry, *How to Choose Your Past*, 1978), Nancy Kricorian (novel, *Zabelle*, 1998), and Peter Balakian (memoir, *Black Dog of Fate*, 1999).

Early in the last century, fledgling writers, the offspring of immigrant parents, put pen to paper to "connect" with the literary world through fiction and poetry that often imitated abundant examples in journals and magazines. Indeed, these writers aspired for literary recognition by submitting their works for publication to such periodicals. This is not to say that zealous beginners eschewed the dramatic form completely, but they anticipated that recognition in that genre required stage production, more often than not, before publication. This tradition—production before publication—dates back in English drama to the Elizabethan and Jacobean eras, most obviously typified by Shakespeare's dramatic output, especially in quarto form.

It is germane to note, also, that dramatic writing requires an aptitude quite distinct from writing stories and poems. In his essay "The Three Voices of Poetry," T. S. Eliot discusses the three variant writing forms as they applied to his *verse* composed as lyric poetry, story or epic, and drama. Early in his career, Eliot observes, he wrote lyrical poems and verse epics and only later found his way to crafting verse drama such as *The Cocktail Party* and *The Confidential Clerk*. He explains how he *developed* from writing in the first or lyric voice (poems in which the writer addresses himself or one other person), to the second or epic voice (verse epics or stories in which the writer addresses a reading audience or reads his work out loud to a group), to the third or dramatic voice (verse plays in which the author is *"everywhere present and everywhere invisible"* [italics mine]). In short, a play most often depicts characters with various points of view that often create conflicts through face to face argument resolved in a climax and denouement giving us the drama's theme *without necessitating the author's presence in the action as a spokesman.*[1] The lesson for the neophyte writer is that poetry and stories more often than not *require* the author's presence by way of his personal thoughts, sentiments, and opinions. In drama, for the most part, that presence is lacking. In no manner does this argument ascribe superiority to writing in any one of the voices over another. Homer's epic greatness is not diminished by similar themes developed in the soaring tragedies of Aeschylus, Sophocles, and Euripides; Shakespeare's sonnets by themselves define him as a major poet.

For the skilled Armenian American storyteller and poet, artistic recognition came expeditiously from three exceptional "ethnic" publications of the early and mid-twentieth century, namely *Ararat*, *The Armenian Review*, and *The Armenian Weekly* (previously called *The Hairenik Weekly*), whose readership was not limited solely to Armenians. Apart from inspiring younger generations to write and contribute, the excellence of the published material went a long way in establishing the viable presence of Armenians in America.

James Mandalian, editor of the *The Review* and *The Weekly*, was eulogized by Lawrence Terzian in *Ararat* in 1974 as having promoted

> with unfailing zeal, the discovery of new writers who will vitalize all communications. . . . More than anyone else in Armenian-American letters, he was the single receptive editor, the mentor, for a group of short story writers in English just emerging in the 1930s and early 40s. In this golden period of the American short story . . . he published and enthusiastically supported the first writings . . . of William Saroyan, Leon Surmelian, Jessamyn West, [and] A.I. Bezzeride.

Edward J. O'Brien, editor of the annual *Best Short Stories* "consulted *The Hairenik Weekly* for his yearly selection of good writing and included [it] in the company of *Story, Esquire, Atlantic Monthly, New Yorker, Southern Review,* and *Harper's Magazine,* for publishing the greatest number of 'three asteriks' stories of distinction for the year 1939." For these published young artists, Terzian's observation concludes, the "writing process . . . was both an intense Americanization and a hyphenation of cultures."[2]

In a 1969 anthology of selected works from *Ararat*, which dated back to its inception ten years earlier, Jack Antreassian, its founding editor, noted the need for the periodical. He observed in his introduction that "in spite of their long life as a nation, Armenians remained a mystery to much of the world, with very few having an awareness of their history, geography, even of their existence." He invited non-Armenian contributors to submit their works to avoid the impression "that Armenians were talking only to Armenians." "Our community had concerns other than Armenian," wrote the editor, "and anything that was to be of interest to them had to be of their world. Similarly our history and culture could have meaning to non-Armenians only if they were relegated to an environment real to them." What inspired the new generation of Armenian American writers to submit works to *Ararat* was exactly the hope that the world beyond Armenian readers would recognize them. A score of *Ararat* stories, Antreassian informs us, "have been cited in Martha Foley's annual anthologies as among the best published in America. Our poetry, fiction and articles have been subsequently reprinted in books and anthologies. Young writers have gone from our pages to gain general recognition of their work."[3]

Following up in equally sanguine terms, Leo Hamalian, editor of *Ararat* after 1969, in his introduction to the twenty-fifth anniversary issue of selections from *Ararat* since its inception (1959–1985) reaffirmed the eloquence and high quality of writing in the journal. "Such a gathering of writers," he observed, "creates a sense of national literature, with one foot in Armenia and the other abroad." As he concludes, Hamalian throws a spotlight on the state of Armenian American playwriting when he regretfully remarks that, owing to space limitations, some short plays previously published in *Ararat* by Mary Morabito, Raffi Arzoomanian, Rene Bartev, and William Saroyan could not be included.[4]

The bibliography in the second part of the twenty-fifth anniversary issue (which listed all printed material from the journal's inception) revealed several more plays. Under the "Dramas" section the works of two of the four dramatists above—Saroyan and Bartev—do not appear. All told, the special issue gives us ten playwrights to be credited with fourteen short plays for volumes one through twenty-five (consisting of one hundred issues). A section on drama and theater is mainly given over to articles and reviews.[5]

If plays in *Ararat* were scant, they were surely wanting in *The Review* and *The Weekly*. Dr. James Tashjian and Mr. Tatul Sonentz-Papazian, who were associated with the latter two from their earliest publication years (1930s and 1940s), in an interview in 2002 asserted that there was no drama to speak of in the journals. Dr. Tashjian, having researched materials available to him as a former editor of the *Review* after Mandalian, informed me that his predecessor had published two plays: *A Dachik for Hairig* by Armen Banklian and *The Last Mohigian* by Nishan Parlakian in the years 1958 and 1959.

Evidently, *The Review* and *The Weekly* were largely interested in articles, poetry, and fiction, and apparently playwrights had few if any inducements to submit dramatic works through advertisements, contests, or special drama issues. On the other hand, the *Ararat* board, having a cross-section of members with various literary interests, saw the need to increase play submissions with the incentive of publication in a special drama issue. I was the assigned editor, and I wrote of these efforts in my introduction in 1993:

> The Ararat Board several years ago decided that its past efforts at publishing Armenian American playwrights were too small and concluded that a special drama issue would help bring our dramatists to the attention of theatrical markets. The problem, of course, was space. The full-length play has been the usual format for writers interested in commercial production, but one such play would have taken up the whole issue. For that reason, a search was made of the Armenian-American talent pool and a significant number of short plays were turned up.[6]

Of twelve published plays, three were clearly ethnic Armenian in content, a sign, however, that before 1993 there was some general interest in playwriting among second generation Armenians.

Having ascertained that writing in the dramatic mode lagged behind poetry and fiction, we cannot simply ascribe the phenomenon to the journals mentioned above. What incentive or inspiration was there for the offspring of Armenian immigrants to write plays in English? This question may be addressed relevant to three points:

1. The availability of stage productions with American drama groups.
2. The inspiration of immigrant parents acquainted with homeland theater.
3. Ethnic theater influences on second-generation artists working in English.

1. AVAILABILITY OF STAGE PRODUCTIONS FOR ASPIRING PLAYWRIGHTS

I suggested earlier that to write plays one must have a sense of or feeling for the special metier or "voice" of theater. That talent alone, however, is not the final mark of his abilities. He must have access to sizable audiences, knowledgeable in theatrical art, to appreciate and assess his work. Such audiences are readily available in large urban centers. A cliché that has a good deal of truth in it is: It is almost useless to try to attain "real" theatrical success without "making it in the Big Apple" or "on Broadway." Lacking appropriate direction, a new writer would be at a loss finding the "route" from initial inspiration to stage production. Early in the twentieth century, there were few opportunities for playwrights to find professional-level productions in off-Broadway, off-off-Broadway, and regional theaters, most of which became available after midcentury. Local amateur dramatic groups in small urban centers were less apt to attain theatrical excellence with untried plays. Armenian immigrants, however, tended to live in larger cities where they found abundant work for a livelihood. Fortuitously, sizeable metropolises also feature institutions of higher learning with drama departments and private acting schools (such as the Actors Studio, the Neighborhood Playhouse and the H. B. Studio in New York City and Second City in Chicago) offering serious theater-arts study for interested second-generation students. And occasionally in such centers, students formed drama groups idealistically hopeful of creating "stage-worthy" communal creations.

One such group called Drama Lab, for example, was established in 1948 in New York by City College and Columbia University students. Having had considerable theatrical experience in their respective institutions, most members acted, some directed, and others created scenery and lighting. Importantly, they kept business books since, as professionals, they sold tickets for their shows. Two members of the group, veterans of World War II, wrote plays. One had collaborated on a Broadway hit called *Stalag 17*, a war play; the other dealt with losing the peace in a defeated Germany through the covert resurgence of Nazism portrayed in his play *Their Hills Are Scarred*, ultimately his Columbia master's thesis. Scenery for the drama was built in the basement of producer Christopher Jaffe's parents' home.

Dr. Jaffe, a refugee of the war was impressed by the energy of the group but wondered about the efficacy of the activity. On opening night, at the play's climax, the hero shouted the heartrending genocidal question about the incineration of six million Jews: "Were they garbage?!" At intermission, the good doctor came up the theater's central aisle and whispered to the playwright: "You've got some play there." For certain one Russian American Jew and one neophyte Armenian American playwright learned what a staged drama could eloquently say about ethnic holocausts.[7]

2. IMMIGRANTS AND INHERITED THEATER CONNECTIONS

Armenians transplanted from Turkey and the Caucasus to America in the early twentieth century were familiar, to varying degrees, of Armenian drama. Many knew that modern Armenian culture and particularly drama found expression during the nineteenth century in the high population centers of Constantinople and Tiflis. With understandable pride, some could cite that the theater of the Roman period in the ancient Armenian capital cities of Artashat and Tigranacerta boasted theaters of considerable size modeled after those of ancient Greece and that Euripides' *Bacchae*, was staged in 53 B.C. by King Artavazd II (55–34 B.C.), who wrote several worthy tragedies himself, none of which, however, survive.[8]

From the classical age through the medieval period, no scripts (if there were any) of Armenian plays are extant. Theatrical activity continued with the improvised representations of Armenian mythical heroes and ancient gods by the *gusan*, or minstrel, an itinerant performer who entertained with animated speech and actions to the accompaniment of music. The Armenian *gusan* brings to mind the itinerant "theater" of the bards or troubadour singers of the *dolce stil novo* in medieval southern Europe as well as the bands of roving actors of the Italian *commedia dell' arte* of the sixteenth through eighteenth centuries.[9] The pagan subject matter of the *gusan* was reprehensible to the clergy after the Christianizing of Armenia in the early fourth century. But in time the clergy themselves created brief theatricals based on church rituals, giving to the faithful visual reinforcement of biblical events. (Here again this clerical activity seems an earlier parallel to the miracle and morality plays of the Church in late medieval Europe.[10])

A repertory of Armenian plays, however, had its beginning not in the Armenian church but through the proselytizing efforts of the Jesuits in the seventeenth century. By the early nineteenth century, the Armenian Catholic Mekhitarists on the island of San Lazzaro, Venice, truly a publishing house of literary, educational, and historical books, began creating and staging plays on religious and biblical themes.[11] They also produced secular tragedies on Armenian history and farces depicting the lower strata of Constantinople life, the likes of which were to be seen later in the century in *The Honorable Beggars* by Hagop Baronian. The movement of Mekhitarist school drama to Constantinople, capital of the Ottoman Empire, clearly marked that metropolis as one of the two major centers of Armenian theater. Mekhitarist-schooled dramatists Mukugerditch Beshigtashlian and Tovmas Terzian wrote plays in the 1860s on nationalistic themes.[12] The cosmopolitan nature of the city, implies D. M. Lang, made supportable "the first regular Turkish-language theater," founded by an Armenian named Hagop in 1870, as well as an Armenian opera.[13] Furthermore, semi-improvisational dramatic fare such as *orta oyunu* (literally, the play or game in the middle), which were performed in the open on streets and squares or in coffee houses, may have contributed to Baronian's creation of written comedy.

The second large city where modern Armenian drama burgeoned was Tiflis (Tbilisi, Georgia). E. Allworth observes that the development of the new drama there was not necessarily dependent on continuity from "an imposing original base or a borrowed one . . . and relates more to contemporary forces than to continuity with the distant past."[14] At the turn of nineteenth century, Iranian control of Tiflis/Tbilisi gave way to Russian governance. The new presence brought with it Russian influences in theater and the arts generally. Allworth informs us that the "founding of a Russian drama theater in Georgia, in 1845, the authorities' lenience in allowing local plays to be performed for a while uncensored, financially supporting productions, and other assistance, gave the contemporary creative arts in Tbilisi both practical and esthetic stimulation."[15] Khatchatur Abovian, author of *Theodora, or a Daughter's Devotion* (1841), written in the Armenian vernacular and in the dramatically sentimental style of his teacher, the first head of the Nersisian School, Arutiun Alamadian, is said by scholars to have been the father of the new Armenian drama. It is Abovian's student Gabriel Sundukian, however, who made the greatest literary impact on the modern Armenian theater, starting with his comedy *Sneezing at Night is Good Luck* (1863). Sundukian, schooled in Turkish, Arabic, and Persian at the university in St. Petersburg and a translator at the chancellery of the Russian viceroy in Tbilisi, "responded to the enthusiasms of the time for fresh theatrical literature. It cannot be coincidental that a permanent, professional Armenian theater was established at Tbilisi in exactly the year Sundukian ventured into dramaturgy."[16] His comedy-dramas such as *Khatabala* (1866) and *The Ruined Family* (1873) as well as other notable plays are about the improprieties, follies, and foibles of society. *Bebo* (1871), about the wealthy bilking the downtrodden in society, is as venerated by knowledgeable Armenians as *Hamlet* is by anglophones and is reprised often in Erevan at the Sundukian Memorial Theater and in the diaspora.[17]

As the nineteenth century ended, two formidable playwrights, Alexandre Shirvanzade and Levon Shant, appeared on the literary scene, the former born in Azerbaijan (1858), the latter in Constantinople (1869).[18] Both went abroad to Europe, Shirvanzade (the first time was 1907 to 1910) to Paris to avoid unrest in the Caucasus and Shant to pursue higher education in Germany and later to become a theater manager in Paris. Before his departure, Shirvanzade had written his first play,

Princess (1891), as well as his masterpiece, *For the Sake of Honor* (1904). For fear of harsh media reception, the latter was first performed on December 10, 1904 not in Tiblisi, the political capital of Georgia and the cultural center of the entire Transcaucasian region, but in Baku, Azerbaijan, where it was enthusiastically received. A month later it opened in Tbilisi and was subsequently performed throughout the Caucasus and in Constantinople. By 1911 it had posted more than 300 performances, a record unprecedented in Armenian theatrical history. When *For the Sake of Honor* and *Bebo* were produced by the Diocesan Players in the 1970s under the direction of Nishan Parlakian, in the Kavookjian Auditorium under St. Vartan Cathedral in New York City, they played to packed houses numbering in the several hundreds, all of whom knew of them as superlative works of dramatic art.

Shant's playwriting career began in Paris with several realistic plays (1901–1904) influenced by Neitzschean philosophy assimilated during his graduate studies in Germany. On his return to the Caucasus, he served as a principal of the Gayanian Girl's College in Tbilisi and as a teacher at the Armenian school of Erevan. By 1908 he began the writing of historical dramas, chief among them being *Ancient Gods*, which, when staged in Tbilisi in 1913, overwhelmed the theater world with its theme on the eternal conflict between hedonistic abandonment and the life of the spirit. An opulent dramatic tour de force, it combined expressionistic and symbolic stage décor, a huge cast of human and mythical characters, and language rising at times to lyrical versification. *Ancient Gods* is another of the masterpieces of Armenian theater that many educated Armenians regard proudly as a capstone of their literature.

With due respect accorded the genius of Hagop Baronian in the rise of modern Armenian drama in Constantinople, Allworth notes that "the new medium failed to develop there so rapidly or so well as in Tbilisi."[19] In any case, the sense that their drama was an ascendant literary force in the two capitals could not have been lost on the Armenian populace of Caucasia and Anatolia. Many educated and culturally curious Armenians living in smaller cities, without access to professionally staged dramas, had available accounts and reviews of them in newspapers and copies in book form.[20]

In a recent study of Ottoman Armenian education from 1853 to 1915, Pamela S. Young reinforces the view of a well-educated and literate middle class by tracing the development of an Armenian schooling system throughout Turkey, which included "the establishment of charity schools, increasing support for the education of women, and the evolution of the formal curriculum" based largely on western models. "In addition to formal classes, active participation in the theater [and] music societies . . . underscores the importance of informal activities in the construction of identity."[21] From interviews with theater participants in Armenian ethnic theater in the United States in the past century (to be covered further on) and according to Young's scholarship, there was theatrical activity in Tbilisi and Istanbul high schools, as well as in those in provincial cities such as Erzerum and Kharpert. Setrak Terpanjian, a leading actor of New York's Diocesan Drama Group in the

1970s, recently (May 2003) spoke of his Armenian high school acting experiences in Istanbul in the 1960s. And currently, eyewitness centenarian Sooren Papazian stated unequivocally that Elia Kimatian, had a flair for stage directing during his early years in Turkey. He observed that Kimatian left the village of Havav, near the town of Palu, and migrated to Kharpert, Turkey, to direct plays not only in various schools but also in large homes. Another actor-director, Mugerditch Noorian, had acted at an early age in *Arshak II*, in his native Sivas, Turkey. Noorian immigrated in the early 1900s to Providence, Rhode Island, and, while still without employment, performed in that city's Lernayin Taderakhoump (Mountainous theater group) along with Elia Kimatian (also a new immigrant). For a brief while Noorian went to New York to act in and direct *Black Earth* for Ike (Morning), a group of dramatists from his native Sivas.

We can be certain that a number of talented native Armenians brought to this country a knowledge of theater. Theatrical experience was surely passed on to second-generation Armenian Americans who, by acting in the Armenian language, kept it and the heritage of theater alive. Some Armenian theater artists active in English language theatricals in the past century most likely knew of and participated in Armenian theater.

3. IMMIGRANT CONNECTIONS WITH ETHNIC THEATER IN THE UNITED STATES

Theater activity itself was not a primary concern of the initial wave of Armenian immigration struggling for existence in the New World; hard work was, according to historians David Marshall Lang and James H. Tashjian. The latter, writing about early Armenian immigrants aptly observed that "industrial authorities and government labor spokesman . . . declared that the Armenian workman is among the most industrious of workers. The story of the Armenians in America is full of Horatio Alger stories, and the Armenian immigrant has learned the valuable lesson that the surest way to advance in a chosen field is through pure, unadulterated, honest, unstinting hard work."[22] Massachusetts drew new immigrants to its shoe factories, woolen mills, machine-casting plants, and barbed-wire production works; New York State, to its shirt and collar factories and aluminum-casting operations; Michigan, to its automobile-assembly plants; and Pennsylvania, to its coal mines. Theater activity under such arduous labor conditions was extremely difficult to sustain, observed Charles A Vertanes in 1954:

> Even artists with professional backgrounds had to reconcile themselves to the lowly circumstances of immigrant communities and to carrying on their work on the crumbs of time left over from the main occupations imposed upon them by a cruel fate of earning a livelihood in most humble and arduous pursuits.[23]

True there seemed to be little time for artistic pursuits but that time, well spent, allowed Armenian theater and culture in America to flourish in large measure as we shall see.

To more properly gauge how we came ultimately to the dramaturgy in this volume, it would be fitting to trace the history and social context of drama among Armenians in the New World. That history is mapped out generally by Nishan Parlakian in "Armenian-American Theatre," a chapter in *Ethnic Theatre in The United States,* edited by Maxine S. Seller.[24] This history refers to Armenian theatrical groups in the United States as early as the beginning of the twentieth century in cities such as New York, Hartford, New Britain, Chicago, Los Angeles, and Boston. Worcester, which holds the oldest Armenian community in Massachusetts, had a drama group as early as the first decade of the twentieth century (circa 1909). P. K. Thomajan gives an account of his experiences with it:

> Certainly, the most memorable event of my childhood memories of the Armenian Church were the Sunday night melodrammers [*sic*] given by the theatrical group on the rude stage downstairs. It had a painted front curtain of sad Myre Hayastan [Mother Armenia] weeping at the foot of Mount Ararat—it was a real tear jerker and charged with incendiary patriotism. Productions alternated between domestic farces and blood and thunder killer-dillers about Armenians being cruelly persecuted by the Turks who were later made to bite the dust by our heroes armed to the teeth. Boos, howls, screams, and shouts, accompanied every crisis. Of course, all dialogue was in Armenian, a further incentive to acquire some knowledge of the mother tongue. After the attacked Armenians had been heroically revenged, gun smoke filled the hall and it was the sweetest perfume.[25]

In 1899, however, there was a performance of the historical Armenian drama *Arshak II* in a grander setting, at New York City's Carnegie Hall. Despite that auspicious event and the theatricals of various amateur groups in New York, Armenian theater showed its strongest presence after the First World War, that is, after the expulsion of Armenians from their Anatolian homeland and their subsequent flight to America, Europe, and elsewhere in the Middle East. Dramatic presentations often dealt with the struggles and hopes of the new immigrants and later included the works of the best Armenian playwrights as well as non-Armenian pieces.

ZARIFIAN, KIMATIAN, AND NOORIAN AND THE ARMENIAN ART THEATER

The formation of drama groups was highly important to early Armenian immigrants seeking to preserve their national identity, for it bound members together as an ethnic group in a way that only theater can. Two Armenian immigrants of the first decade of the last century, Mugerdich Noorian and Elia Kimatian, performed in Providence for a number of years and joined forces in 1920 to form an acting group called Knar (Lyre) in New York City. There they awaited the celebrated Shakespearean actor and director Hovhannes Zarifian, who came from Armenia in 1921 to head the Hai Arvest Taderakhoump, The Armenian Art Theater, which created a renaissance in Armenian drama in New York City during the 1920s and 1930s. The group performed all its plays in the Armenian language, although some selections in its repertory included non-Armenian plays such as *Sherlock Holmes*, *Secrets of the Harem*, *The Robbers*, *The Devil*, *Trilby*, *The Trial of Mary Dugan*, *Topaz*, *Kean*, and many Shakespearean plays. Zarifian traveled to Armenian population centers throughout the country, not only those in the nearby Northeast but also in California and Michigan, using local talent in smaller roles to avoid the cost of transporting and supporting home members of his group on the road. For his shows at home, he often utilized vacant Broadway Houses such as Hampden's Theater, The John Golden Theater, and the Longacre Theater, rented for three hundred dollars for a Sunday-only performance. Unlike Armenians today, who are completely fluent in English and go to American theater and movies, Armenians then needed to experience not only their own but also world drama in their native language. However, it surely was not lost on aspiring theater artists seeking opportunities in American theater—nor on audiences—that with appropriate material it was not that difficult to have regular access to the "professional stage" in English, though never on Sunday.

After the passing of Zarifian in 1937, it was not until the outbreak of World War II that Kimatian formed his Theater Lovers Group, composed of young, English-proficient, American-born Armenians acting in Armenian, though their grasp of the language was not at the level of the early Zarifian players. No doubt some of these children of immigrants, heading toward full maturity by the mid-twentieth century, were acquiring an appreciation for a beckoning English-language theater.

In the nineteen-year career of his group in New York City, Kimatian's repertoire consisted of only two non-Armenian plays. The others were popular works from the Armenian modern-classic repertoire or his own works and adaptations. In the latter category, he came close to universal interests in 1946 with his *Victims of War*, about intermarriage between Armenians and Americans, and his dramatic version of Franz Werfel's best-selling novel *The Forty Days of Musa Dagh*. With the latter, it should have been patently clear to viewers and artists that that best-seller in English might have made a stir on the regular American stage.

THEATER SPONSORED BY RELIGIOUS, CULTURAL, AND BENEVOLENT ORGANIZATIONS

With Kimatian gone from the New York scene by 1961, the Sevan Theatrical Group emerged under Angel Havagimian in 1964. Noorian directed several plays under its banner. His last effort came in 1970, coinciding with the demise of Sevan, whose former members began a workshop at the Diocese of the Armenian Church of America (Eastern). By 1971 the workshop became the Diocesan Drama Group. Nishan Parlakian became its artistic director in 1972 at the behest of Archbishop Torkom Manoogian, diocesan primate (now the patriarch of Jerusalem). The group produced the works of the most celebrated Armenian dramatists and, for variety, Saroyan's *Hello, Out There* in *Armenian* and Souren Bartevian's tragedy on the genocide, *The Eternal Flame*.

In addition to Armenian-language stage productions, the primate (recognized as a poet and musicologist in his own right) asked various artists to contribute their theatrical talents by presenting plays in English, giving anglophones (American and Armenian) an appreciation of Armenian art and culture. To that end in the 1970s and 1980s, the diocese sponsored English-language productions of Saroyan's *Hello, Out There* and *Armenians* in 1974; Rolleri and Antaramian's *The Armenian Question* in 1977; Parlakian's translation of *For the Sake of Honor* in 1978; and Balakian's *Home* in 1988. The diocese also established an annual One World Festival (in St. Vartan's Park at Thirty-fifth Street and Second Avenue in New York City, adjacent to the conical, gold-roofed Armenian Cathedral), during which Armenian food was available and the featured theatrical entertainment was ethnic dancing in full costume, including performances by the notable Antranig Armenian Dance Ensemble. If not all of America, then surely New York and the Northeast were learning more about Armenians through the work of the Armenian Church.

Paralleling diocesan theatrical activity, Herand Markarian in 1967 formed the Masis Theatrical Group of the Armenian Cultural Association. Markarian produced not only fine plays from the Armenian repertoire but also his own, a few of which dealt with timely problems confronting the Armenian community. The most important of these was *Polarization* in 1977, an examination of two major Armenian problems. According to *The Armenian Weekly*, one of these, illustrated through an Armenian family in New York, concerned their "struggle to preserve their identity and still adapt to the American life-style."[26] *Polarization* also exposed the dangerous political and church schisms vitiating the strength and harmony of the Armenian community.[27] Because Markarian felt that drama was the weakest branch of Armenian literature, he brought variety to his offerings by staging translated foreign plays. After writing a number of significant plays in Armenian, Markarian wrote the first version of his contribution to this volume in English for his daughter to stage as her Barnard College graduation project. Upon being enlarged later, it had a significant run off-Broadway. By this time, there was no question that the theatrical torch was passed on from Armenian to English.

THE AGBU AND SATAMIAN

In the late seventies the Ardashad Theatre Company, sponsored by the Armenian General Benevolent Union (AGBU) and organized by Krikor Satamian, set up shop in New York City, utilizing the same stage as the Diocesan Players, the Kavookjian Hall, beneath the Armenian Cathedral. Satamian came from civil-war-torn Beirut and brought his theatrical experience as an actor and director at Britain's London School of Film and the Bristol Old Vic to plays like Goldoni's *The Liar* and Chekov's *The Bear*, which had been unknown to most Armenian audiences. Ardashad, like the two older groups, toured New York and the northeastern United States. With the relaxation of U.S. immigration quotas in 1965, the flow of Armenians from Beirut and Soviet Armenia increased because of intolerable conditions related to civil war and civil rights in their home countries. Obviously, Armenian communities in the diaspora became the destination of migrants, most especially Glendale, a suburb of Los Angeles whose Armenian population has risen to over a half million. A few years after the shift of the Armenian population's density to the West Coast, the Diocesan Drama Group suspended activities, and the Masis Company seemed somewhat less visible in the east. But the Tekeyan Cultural Association's newly formed "Mher Megerditchian" Theatrical Group began presenting a play each year in New York and New Jersey. It has garnered a following among ethnic theater enthusiasts as well as fine reviews that pay particular attention to its ability to tour with full scenery throughout the Northeast.

The AGBU's contributions to Armenian ethnic theater through the multiple talents of Krikor Satamian have been considerable. Satamian took Armenian ethnic theater not only to various cities in the United States but also to Armenian communities as far off as Argentina. He readily welcomed performing artists from Armenia and often performed with major homeland stars such as Mher Megerdichian in Baronian's *Brother Balthazar*. Eventually the AGBU felt the burgeoning Armenian population of California would benefit from Satamian's art and in 1980 moved him to their center in Los Angeles. Satamian has again and again shifted from versatile performances in Armenian to appearances in English-speaking roles in films such as *Chic Peas*, about the lives of new Armenian immigrants, and *Pedestrian*, written, produced, and directed by Jason Kartalian. Several years ago he appeared in the Los Angeles area in a reprise of Raffi Arzoomanian's *The Moths*, which had premiered at the Mark Taper Forum twenty years earlier.

THE ARMENIAN STUDENTS ASSOCIATION

The Armenian Students Association has supported the dramatic activities of its members from time to time. One of the first of these efforts came more than a half century ago when Nishan Parlakian joined several other young Armenian Americans to stage plays in English. He served as artistic director for four years and in the last of them (1954) finally established a group focus by staging plays written by Armenian Americans William Saroyan, Archie Minasian, and himself. Saroyan himself ventured to communicate with the group, advising the director that when staging the now classic *Hello Out There*, the actor playing the jailed prisoner, incarcerated falsely for rape, temper his reading of the first line of the play—namely, the words of the title.

There is no question that some of these ASA theater group members (all of whom spoke Armenian well)were, as early as the mid-twentieth century, looking for favorable acknowledgment from English-speaking audiences. They rented the noted off-Broadway Master Theater at 103rd Street and Riverside Drive (later the permanent home of the Equity Library Theater), paid stage designers, and built scenery. In addition to Nishan Parlakian's continued association with English-speaking theater, the leading man of the Saroyan work, Buck Kartalian (father of the film artist mentioned above), appeared on Broadway and later in several Hollywood films, including a notable role in *Planet of the Apes*. Anne Boranian Vardanian, Kartalian's costar, went on to teach drama in California, where she acted and directed for numerous English speaking groups and received both a master's and a doctorate for translations of Levon Shant's major plays, including his masterpiece, *Ancient Gods*.[28]

EDUCATIONAL, ENTERTAINMENT, AND SOCIAL ASPECTS OF ARMENIAN ETHNIC DRAMA

In her study of ethnic theater in the United States, Maxine Seller, having closely compared and contrasted essays by twenty knowledgeable ethnic contributors, came to some general conclusions regarding a more or less similar pattern of development in most of these theaters. What has been covered above concerning Armenian theater in America seems to fit her conclusions. Like the theater of many ethnic groups, such as the Finns, Swedes, Yiddish, and Italians, for example, Armenian theater was at its peak in the first third of the last century. There is no doubt that new immigrants heard the best dramatic Armenian uttered by actors such as Noorian, Kimatian, and especially Zarifian, all of whom had come over, so to speak, on the same boat with them. Seller's general observation, that immigrants, "deprived of opportunities to learn about their own culture through poverty, isolation, or political oppression . . . arrived in the United States hungry for exposure to their native language, histories, and literature,"[29] fits the Armenian case only partially since, as we have shown, there was a considerably high level of literacy among transplanted Armenians. But it would be true to say for them that "ethnic theater was . . . an important agent of Americanization." All the non-Armenian plays of the Armenian Art Theater that were "adopted and translated from the American stage introduced immigrants to many aspects of mainstream culture."[30]

Entertainment was always a primary end of ethnic theater. Seller emphasizes the new immigration's need for tragic and comedic fare of all sorts: "diversion, excitement, and glamor." Very appropriate for Armenians purged from Turkey is the observation that immigrants could even "express the grief they felt at leaving

friends and family behind, perhaps forever, and facing the frustrations and disap-
pointments of American life."[31] The variety of offerings by the Armenian Art Theater included comedies and tragedies from world drama and Shakespeare in the
famed Mahseyan Armenian translations.[32]

Finally, ethnic theater activity became a focal point for immigrant communal
life, especially for those who came together to rehearse, build scenery, and discuss
future offerings. The theater was a kind of social center in the Armenian experience, akin to men's clubs where Armenian Americans drank bitter demitasses of
coffee and played *tavloo* (backgammon), and, just as in Saroyan's *Armenians*, discussed the possible assimilation and disappearance of Armenians. Other parallels
to the social aspect of theater included the women's church auxiliaries, which often planned the decorations for the altar and baked *choreg* (sweet bread sticks) and
ethnic pastries for faithful churchgoers to consume at the end of the service and
mass. Sunday theatrical presentations by the Diocesan Players, for example, were
always followed with a dinner prepared and served by the auxiliary for the players
and faithful fans. Since Armenian Americans of the second generation were not
just spectators but often contributors to ethnic theater events, it was not lost upon
them that they were getting an education in how the theater works. The excitement of theater itself served as an inducement to extend their dramatic interests
into non-Armenian, venues where they found favorable contacts for future involve-
ment in American theater.

DECLINE AND RESURGENCE OF ARMENIAN
AMERICAN THEATER

Seller's general observation is that ethnic theater abated, between 1925 and 1950, in
some measure because of the quota laws of 1924 restricting immigration. Audiences
presumably shrunk owing to Americanization, the geographic dispersion of immigrants as they attained affluence, and the competition of radio, film, and the
emerging medium of television. Though the Armenian Art Theater held its own
from 1921 until 1937, it was by all accounts an economic struggle for Zarifian during the Great Depression. When Kimatian gave New York the Theater Lovers,
consisting mostly of talented amateurs gleaned from the progeny of the first immigrants, he played not on professional Broadway stages but in the auditoriums of various colleges, high schools, halls, and hotels. The group produced essentially one
play a year, usually on one day, whereas Zarifian, with the assistance of several professionals, had previously had as many as a dozen plays to offer each year. Diminished talent, fewer offerings, and reduction of audience size all constituted a cal-
culable if not critical decline for Armenian ethnic theater.

But despite the reduction of audiences, Armenian theater, like those of other
national groups, had a resurgence after World War II, especially in the 1960s and
1970s, owing partly to the Hart-Celler Immigration Act, which led to massive new

immigration and an increase in ethnic populations, including Armenians.[33] When AGBU established Satamian and his group in California in 1980 to service the burgeoning Armenian population there, Armenian theatrical activity further increased.

ARMENIAN ETHNIC IDENTITY FULLY ASSERTED AT THE APPROACH OF THE NEW MILLENIUM

If Armenian ethnic identity seemed somewhat attenuated because of the relatively small number of Armenians in the United States in the first half of the twentieth century, it nevertheless firmed up as many among them, by diligence and application, succeeded economically and socially. There were new social forces at play in America that gave incentive to all minority groups to assert themselves as being, so to speak, 100 percent of their ethnicity and 100 percent American.

> The 1960s, 1970s, and 1980s saw a renaissance in Armenian culture in New York and other cities in the United States. One reason for this renewed interest in Armenian culture was the focus on ethnicity given to the nation by the black civil rights movement begun in the 1960s. The effect was a diminishing of the melting-pot concept of Americanism and an effort on the part of government to foster ethnic programs with federal funds. Being American did not mean dissolution of ethnic backgrounds anymore.[34]

For Armenians, this new ethnic elan allowed them to focus their attention on matters that were often on their minds and often repressed as they made their way in America. The most serious of these was their concern with the genocide perpetrated against the Armenian race in Turkey and the need for justice in an international context. Surely the Armenian sentiment was no less serious than that of African Americans who in their own way had suffered genocide two centuries before.

By the 1970s and 1980s, Armenian Americans still wrote on various aspects of ethnicity, but frequently the writing contained polemical ideas (though these were generally far less voluble than the incensed ethnic tirades of the contentious black dramatist Le Roi Jones [Immamu Amiri Baraka]), which can be seen as mild propaganda concerning Armenian ethnicity, identity, and the genocide. The general population of Armenians, including writers, were becoming aware of Michael Hagopian's library of genocide-survivor testimony on videotape. Their hopes were raised for the admission of genocidal guilt by Turkey through the lobbying efforts of the newly formed Armenian Assembly and the Armenian National Committee of America in the 1970s, which drew attention to the well-known Armenian Question. They supported the plans for an Armenian Genocide Museum in Washington. They were inspired by the genocide scholarship of Vahakhn Dadrian (Armenian), Taner Akcam (Turkish), Israel Charney (Jewish), Richard Hovanissian (Armenian), and others. They applauded the work going on in Holocaust studies centers at Yale and Drew universities and the Zoryan Institute. They found strength in the mounting ratification of bills by the legislative bodies of many nations that formally recognized the great genocide. They gloried in the strengthened Armenian voice expressed through the growing numbers attending Martyrs Day commemorations in New York's Times Square and in other major American cities. In the wake of increased Armenian American sociopolitical activity, artists and writers expressed what may have seemed heretofore as being too contentious.

HOMELAND DRAMA

Early in the twentieth century in the Soviet Republic of Armenia, there were apparently no performances of plays on the Armenian Question that could serve as models for writers in America. Under Soviet domination from Stalin on through Brezhnev (1982), it would hardly have been possible for the Armenian Republic, let alone its artists, to take a stand that the central Soviet government might consider politically incorrect. Controversial stances that might affect the balance of power in the Caucasus, which involved the Soviets, Turkey, Azerbaijan, and Georgia in relation to Armenia, as well as international issues, were generally taboo subjects in the arts—especially in an actively censored theater—and were strictly the concern of the Soviet Politiburo. Gradually, however, signs of politicizing on small and large stages in Armenia manifested themselves.

With the passing of Brezhnev, Soviet policy allowed more latitude for artistic expression during the subsequent Krushchev regime. After the lackluster leadership of Yuri Andropov (1982–1984) and Chernenko Konstantin (1984), the accession of Gorbachev as general secretary in 1985 brought about a more permissive theatrical atmosphere, owing in part to the general secretary's policies of glasnost and perestroika. (This led ultimately to the breakdown of the USSR and the separation of the Armenian Republic from the union in 1991). Between 1990 and 1992, with the coming of a free Armenia, small showcase theaters similar to New York City's off-Broadway and off-off-Broadway houses proliferated.[35] Concomitantly, there was a growth of dramatic offerings dealing with political agendas both domestic and international.

Established in 1982 in the basement of a building near the Matenadaran (Library of ancient manuscripts), toward the end of the profligate eighteen year Brezhnev ascendancy, the Camera (Chamber) Theater, seating less than a hundred, felt secure enough to satirize the central government. It staged the mini-extravaganzas *Haik* and *Brave Nazar*; the former poked fun at governmental corruption and celebrated the Armenian nation's religious spirit and its language. At its climax, Haik, the mythical progenitor of the Armenian race and hero of the piece, points to the communist red flag as he shouts into a microphone, "We have come to God too late!" Following this, at the denouement, the cast recites the Armenian alphabet in a reverberant chorus booming forth through loudspeakers as the stage lights black out, leaving every spine tingling.

Brave Nazar, in style and imagination nothing like the burlesque farce extravaganza of 1924 by Terenig Demirchian about a cowardly ne'er-do-well's chimerical rise to kingship, nevertheless is about the greatness of high office thrust upon a mediocrity by the propagandistic spin of the media.[36] The farce is an obvious spoof on Gorbachev's unexpected rise to power. At the final curtain, the general secretary and his wife sit side by side, smiling broadly and ironically waving a goodbye to the audience.

Other "off-Broadway-type theaters"—The Malian Kino, The On Wheels, The Experimental, and The Gavit—were not yet into current politics. But the latter theater's *For the Sake of Gigos*, a play about the misrule of Armenia through the ages, could have served governmental dissidents as a piece of political activism.

Large government-sponsored theaters also essayed into politics. *Unfinished Monologue*, by Perch Zeituntsyan, written in 1981 toward the end of the Brezhnev era and still in repertory in 1990 at the Sundukian Theater, fortuitously had avoided serious, if any, censorship despite its content, which dealt, in part, with the immorality and red tape of communist governance. The best play of that season, according to Levon Hakhvedian, Armenia's chief drama critic at the time, was *Your Last Haven*, by Zora Harutyunian, which was also concerned with governmental corruption—so intense that it pressed Armenians into evacuating the homeland for resettlement elsewhere.

In *The Great Silence* (1984; produced 1990), and *All Rise, the Court Is in Session* (1988), Zeituntsyan aspires for transnational political recognition of the genocide. The former play, a tragedy about the imprisonment and murder of the nationalist poet Daniel Varouzhan, has the immediacy of name appeal to Armenians. A consummate craftsman, Zeituntsyan increases the dramatic tension from scene to scene through taut discoveries. Among them, the most poignant are Varouzhan's arrest and incarceration on 24 April 1915 and then his touching farewell to his wife followed by the climax in which this spiritual voice of Armenia is silenced along with those of three hundred other intellectuals at the brutal hands of Turkish gendarmes.[37] *All Rise, the Court Is in Session* has more immediate universal appeal. It dramatizes the 1921 Berlin trial of Solomon Tehlerian, in which he is acquitted of the murder of Talat Pasha, mastermind of the 1915 Turkish genocide of Armenians. In the United States the Pasha killing was dramatized in Armenian by Herand Markarian, a playwright represented in this volume. Courtroom drama, be it in film, television, or on stage, generally has receptive American audiences—a hint, perhaps, to translators that both Tehlerian plays might do well on the commercial American stage.

Playwright Zeituntsyan, having family in California, spends considerable time there. He has had three of his plays translated into English in recent years, including *Unfinished Monologue* which was produced (2001) in English by Aramazad Stepanian in his own translation at his Armenian Theater Company in Los Angeles.[38] Hopefully Zeituntsyan's two genocide plays will soon follow. Drama written in Armenia is having an influence on Armenian American audiences and readers, not only with the production of Zeytuntsyan's play, as mentioned, but also its publication in an excellent translation in the recent Columbia University Press volume on modern Armenian drama mentioned earlier. A formal cross-pollination between Armenian and American theater has already begun as we shall see.

AMERICAN RECOGNITION OF HOMELAND ARMENIAN DRAMA

The coming of the new millennium has brought about an auspicious theatrical interchange between the Armenian government and the United States. In September 2002, Armen Khandikian, head of the Dramatic Theater of Erevan, Armenia, was invited to direct a play entitled *To Forget Herostratus*, concerning the conflict between an individual and the state, at the Riverside Theater in Bristol, Pennsylvania, reciprocating that company's production in Armenia during the summer of 2001. Twenty-four years earlier (in 1979), on a two-month theater visit in Erevan, I saw Khandikian's *Herostratus* at the Dramatic Theater. It appeared then to be a veiled political comment regarding the governance of Armenia under communism. But how could that have been, at a time when state-supported theater could only exist, Ishkhan Jinbashian writes, "as long as it conformed to pre-Glastnost Soviet ideological correctness."[39] As a guest of the communist government at the time, I had already observed the official censorship committee in action at a dress rehearsal of a play and assumed that any direct subversive material in *Herostratus* must have been attenuated or there would have been no opening. The production in Bristol, says Jinbashian, is in a new English translation and "based on [Khandikian's] own adaptation of the . . . original," making it a significant democratic conjunction between the United States and Armenia.[40] The current theatrical exchange can prove especially effective with a play that demonstrates to Americans that a Middle Eastern nation espouses the efficacy of democratic governance over arbitrary despotism. The theatrical interchange may prove a boon to many Armenians if it can help influence current laggard U.S. policy that declines to call the Turkish extermination of a million and a half Armenians a genocide, notwithstanding the mountain of evidence proving the position.

The inaction has been viewed by some as a disparagement of Armenia's national integrity and by others as a blow to the Armenian sense of identity. In a recent article, Florence Avakian digests the ideas of Seta Dadoyan (of the American University of Beirut) in a speech made at Columbia University on the effect of the genocide and its importance in regard to Armenian self-definition. "In the Middle

East, the Armenians who are a minority and are at a distance from the majority culture are not in an advantageous situation. For Armenians, the persistence to survive is now a 'counter-action' to the Genocide and a new mechanism of opposition."[41]

This is not to say that Armenians generally lack a sense of group or "racial" identity. The genocide did not create a mass of fractionalized people in spirit and soul. On the contrary, it brought a "nationless" nation into being, with vibrant ethnic connections to a worldwide diaspora. In the absence of totally independent governmental leadership, (1914 to 1918 and then 1920 to 1991), Armenian identity did not dissolve. The single most significant force for the cohesion of the Armenians historically has been the unifying power of the Armenian Apostolic Church, which made the nation proud to have been the first in the world to accept Christianity (A.D. 301). The matter of variant faiths (Christian/Moslem) has relevancy to the genocide. So has the false Turkish argument that the Armenians acted as a subversive fifth column, siding with the Russian enemy threatening its borders during a war. But no single point dominates in the matter of Turkish denial. Armenians still await the judgment of an international court on a question of honor and justice that all nations seek.

The theater (and today one would include film), with its immediacy of impact, Alexis de Tocqueville (1805–1859), that astute observer of the early American republic, informs us, is the clearest indication of the spirit and direction of a nation. The official state-to-state interchange of drama between America and Armenia gives one a sense that second- and third-generation Armenian American playwrights and homeland dramatists combined will help demonstrate the commonality of democratic goals between the two nations. This allows us to hope that the plays of this volume, dealing not only with genocide but even more with the joys and travail universally known to all transplanted people in the United States, may effect an additional force of democratic symbiosis between America and Armenia. Surely then, as a reflection of the Armenian spirit, the theater should be encouraged to continue monitoring it both in the homeland and the diaspora.

RAFFI ARZOOMANIAN

Ellis Island 101 by Raffi Arzoomanian, a minor classic, is the brief curtain raiser for this volume. It concerns America's renowned gateway where those "yearning to be free" come, and where the accepted find joy, the rejected sorrow. It also serves as our dramatic "doorway," through which we pass metaphorically into a land where our playwrights are free to speak for their forebears in the seven dramas that follow it. This short work describes the struggle for entrance into the United States by two Armenians, an elderly woman who has been rejected for illiteracy several times and a highly educated, hypersensitive, middle-aged professor who hopes to contribute to his adopted country as a teacher. Each character in his or her own way fails an entry requirement. Both are to be sent back to the oblivion of a "home-

land." Both will try for entry again. The perceptive observation of reviewer Patrick Collins is that "the author . . . gives us a play of poignancy and supreme irony," affirming "the resiliency of the human spirit."[42] How often have we heard the stories of immigrants who had their burning hope for sanctuary smothered by rejection, at the gate of democracy, by an inadvertent cough thought by customs to be a manifestation of tuberculosis? And how often has hope been reanimated with an incomprehensible Sisyphean will? The old woman's situation bursts into bathos as we learn that her two sons, residents in the United States, pass Liberty Island back and forth by ferry in New York City's upper bay, shouting encouragement to their mother during this time of evaluation, truly a farcical exercise in futility. The tension of the customs interrogation in *Ellis Island 101* is reminiscent of a similar scene in Elia Kazan's film *America, America*, in which an Irish customs inspector, unable to grapple with the Armenian name "Ohanness" in a passport, changes it arbitrarily to Joe Arness. The name and passport have been given to a Greek friend by an Armenian going to America on the same ship. Knowing that he is dying of consumption and will not gain admission to America, the Armenian commits suicide by jumping into the sea, leaving his passport to his Greek friend. The irony of the piece lies partly in the moral imperative it suggests: the need for freedom supercedes the passion of ethnicity. When first-generation immigrants complain about the assimilative nature of America, they forget that the lack of liberty in the homeland was often the glue that bound them in their ethnicity.

WILLIAM SAROYAN

In his *Armenians* (1971), William Saroyan became the first Armenian American to unambiguously write, in dramatic form, about the plight of the newly formed Armenian nation in 1918 and the diminution of national identity after the slaughters of 1915. David S. Calonne observes, however, that Saroyan dealt with the second of those themes, which he terms "exile and estrangement," more than three decades earlier in his first play, *My Heart's in the Highlands* (1940), based on an earlier short story (1936).[43] This progression exemplifies how a writer's mode of expression moves from the second voice (story) to the third voice (drama), as discussed earlier with reference to T. S. Eliot's essay "The Three Voices of Poetry." The action of the play centers on a homeless, dying Scottish vagabond, Jasper MacGregor, who enters the life of a family headed by Ben Alexander, an impoverished poet. Calonne notes that the family is Armenian, for Armenian is spoken by Ben and his mother, "adding a deeper dimension to the theme of exile."[44] On the basis of that understanding, he concludes, "we now respond to MacGregor's homelessness within the context of Armenian estrangement in America." Abetting that argument in his *Obituaries*, written long after the play, Saroyan parallels the Scottish and Armenian yearning for homeland, with the following observation: "Jasper MacGregor, or Kaspar der Krikor, it comes to the same thing, you know, and highlands are highlands, whether in Scotland or Armenia."[45] There is, however, a probability that the general reader, unschooled in modern Armenian history, would not specifically link the play to "Armenian estrangement in America" despite its deeply moving action. A clear-cut statement from Saroyan on Armenian exile and estrangement in America comes a third of a century later in *Armenians*.

The 1974 production of Saroyan's *Armenians* at the Diocoese of the Armenian Church is in all respects a paradigm of ethnic writing for contemporary Armenian American playwrights—more for the inspiration of its poignantly eloquent thoughts and sentiments and its masterfully differentiated characters than for its plot. Taking place in Fresno, California, it deals with "the anguished reaction of certain Armenian-Americans to the report that their newly created democratic homeland in 1920 has been divided between the Turks and the Russians."[46] The play's characters heatedly express themselves about many topics highly significant to the Armenian psyche, among them the breaking away of immigrant Armenians from the mother church—established by St. Gregory the Illuminator in A.D. 301—to follow Christ in the Protestant faith. Further disquietude gnaws at them in the local patriotic club, where the feeling that another massacre similar to the one in 1915 is about to "recur and again they will be relegated to the role of voiceless, powerless onlookers. . . . All that can be left for them to do is to keep the spirit of Armenia alive. That is the hope that Saroyan offers Armenians in his bitter-sweet ending. Beyond that the author sounds a universal warning against the forces of genocide and assimilation that destroy nations and ethnicity."[47]

Though Saroyan was in his early teens during the time of the play's action, the characters he resurrects are individuated by their appearance, by what they say about themselves, by what others say about them, and by their actions. Father Kasparian of the Armenian Apostolic Church has an openness of personality, feeling comfortable, in a sense, as the leader of the true church for Armenians. He works hard from morning till midnight and occasionally recommends a sip of cognac to abate the accumulated stresses of the day. One imagines him as a man of open gestures of the hands and arms. Reverend Papazian of the Armenian Congregational Church seems peevish and the pain in his ankle manifests itself in the grimness of his face. He has disdain for Father Kasparian's air of authority and denigrates him for his inability to speak English. The Presbyterian Reverend Knadjian is easygoing and reconciled to the fact that since his wife is an Englishwoman, he is unable to make his children love Armenia. Later, in the patriotic club where men come to relax over a card game of *scambile* and a cup of coffee, Dr. Jivelekian, a Harvard medical school graduate and a confident healer of great wit tells a farmer asking for a free diagnosis: "Your back hurts. You've been lifting heavy boxes, so of course it hurts. I've told you, rest your back. You're not satisfied with that. What will make you happy, sir?"[48] The gesturing, the body attitudes, and the movement are simple to visualize. Generally speaking, the whole drama invites the reader to imagine bodies in action, especially in the second act, in which ordinary men from Moush, Bitlis, Dikranakert, and other ancestral cities rise to high eloquence over the life and death of the Armenian race. There are no overt stage instructions written into the play, but any director worth his salt would have no difficulty in utilizing the whole stage (as a painter his whole canvas) by creating variety of movements based on psychologically sound blocking or choreography. Edward Setrakian's 1974 staging was received favorably by audiences and critics to the apparent puzzlement of Saroyan himself, who did not attend any performances. Deprecating the production, based on an audio, he observed that it was "off base." He thought Setrakian had allowed the actors to "get too shrill, a bogus trick. Armenians are not shrill."[49]

Kouymjian, editor of *William Saroyan: An Armenian Trilogy*, informs us that *Armenians*, along with *Bitlis* and *Haratch*, were written during the last decade of Saroyan's career and were concerned essentially with "his ethnic origin . . . and the problem of being forced to live in exile."[50] Surely the thoughts and sentiments on Armenian ethnicity in the *Trilogy* are most profound and rise to a universal level, addressing the question of ethnicity for all people. In that regard, one would do well to consult Kouymjian's introduction to his volume for an in-depth analysis. There the editor also touches on the esthetics of dramatic writing, observing that "in later years, Saroyan regarded theater as a more direct vehicle for communicating ideas and reflections than story or essay."[51] There can be no quarrel with that view, and one could add that Saroyan must have had a good sense of that theatrical power in some of his early plays. Of the *Trilogy* plays, *Armenians* stands out (like *The Time of Your Life*, 1939) as a stage-worthy drama, metaphysical at times, but charged with brilliant dialogue and inherent movement. In fact, Kouymjian informs us that Saroyan knew of its inherent theatricality "in offering the play and preparing notes for the premiere."[52] *Armenians* was produced only once. It should be resurrected in this age when Armenians still seek justice in the "court" of the civilized nations of the world. It sets an example of profound thought and near-poetic utterance in dramatic form for all playwrights dealing with their ethnicity.

NISHAN PARLAKIAN

In Nishan Parlakian's *Grandma, Pray for Me*, Deacon, head of an Armenian family living in an American urban center, has no apparent concern about the loss of Caucasian Armenia under the firm yoke of the Soviet Union at the outbreak of the Second World War. He is a transplanted Armenian from the Anatolian plateau. He is a tree whose roots withered, in part, when wrenched from their rich original soil and set into the apparently infertile earth of America. The branches of his life are gnarled. Little seems to have gone right for him in the new land. He is tormented by the menial work he labors at. He tries to rationalize the necessity of his marriage to his wife Diamond, whom he impregnated before marriage, making him an abject sinner in the sight of God. If his marriage had not made his son Mickey legitimate, the young man's characteristics as a poet-philosopher would have marked him a true copy of Deacon. Adding to his sorrow is the fact that Agate, the woman

Deacon was promised to in the homeland, was lost to him when the genocidal purges from Turkey started. Nevertheless, she too found her way to America and, of all ironies, has lived on the floor above with her daughter Pearl and a sickly husband who has since passed away. Deacon's thoughts are heavy, profound, and almost always given vent lyrically.

Though Mickey has "inherited" his father's sense of futility in a world that seems to malfunction, the father cannot comprehend the parallel nature of their temperaments. He presses upon his son the irksome labor that the father abhors on the occasion of the lad's birthday party, urging him to return to the job he quit and insisting that idealistic thoughts must give way to practical thinking about earning a living. In an impassioned plea to his son, Deacon cries out with the zeal of his youth in the homeland:

> I was a philosopher-poet, that's what I was. And I looked for meanings. Oh, oh! I remember my golden days. You hear me? I used to run to the tops of hills, barefoot, and look at the sky. I used to stand panting with blood beating in my temples and a cool breeze brushing my face. And with each beat I was aware! Bump! Bump! Bump! Aware do you hear, that there was something I had to know. And I looked hard into the sky until my eyes filled with tears.[53]

In truth Deacon has fallen away in some measure from his Christian faith, and the spiritual leadership of the family is left to Grandma. Failing in health, blurred of vision, she reads her large-print Armenian Bible daily, giving her son, daughter-in-law, and grandson the hope for a better future. Subtly she encourages Agate's daughter Pearl to wait patiently for Mickey to ask for her hand in marriage. In this way she heals the wounds of the past. Agate's sorrow that fate wrenched Deacon from her life and Diamond's alienation from him for his "spiritual bigamy" are ameliorated with the melding of the two families.

In her appraisal of the play, Anne Paolucci observed that *Grandma* "is also an interesting 'document,' for it preserves the flavor of Armenian family life while dramatizing the inner conflicts of transplanted individuals, the immigrant experience characteristic of our multi-ethnic society, combining 'strong local color' and 'unconscious universality'—the two features (as T. S. Eliot reminds us) found in all landmark literary works."[54] In a more parochial mode, critic Adam Adamian hoped that many people would attend the play—"to see the grandeur and desperation of the Armenian heart . . . and be comforted by the fact that it is deathless."[55]

BARBARA BEJOIAN

In *Dance Mama, Dance*, Barbara Bejoian gives us a view of the Armenian immigrant community in Watertown, Massachusetts, which the character Lucene Arevian Kinsor abandoned with her infant daughter Anne when gossip about her grew intolerable after her husband Krikor secretly "deserted" her to fight for the liberation of Armenia from the yoke of Soviet communism. Her marriage to Krikor, a true love match, had been frowned upon by many in the Watertown community because of his membership in the active Revolutionary Party, in contrast to her ties with the more conservative Democrats. James Tashjian informs us that both of these Armenian political parties avowed their goal was the liberation of Armenia from Soviet domination, noting, however, that the Tashnag (Revolutionaries) were the stronger group, while the Ramgavars (Democrats) displayed ambiguities in the fight against communism.[56] Bejoian is our only writer who alludes to the dichotomy between these Armenian political factions, which has been a severe divisive force vitiating the social and political power of the world's Armenian population of some seven or eight million.

Accompanied by her daughter, Lucene has returned to Watertown to pay her respects at her mother Violet Arevian's funeral. Isolated in "exile" in New Hampshire, the visit has a positive impact on Anne (baptized with the Armenian name Ani), who has been denied connections with her ethnic roots. The young woman is intrigued by Armenian customs, hospitality, and food in a vibrant ethnic setting. A budding amorous relationship with a young Armenian man adds even more excitement to her visit. Why had her mother kept her from all this joy? Slowly, the reasons become manifest when Lucene, looking over her mother's effects, discovers letters to her by Krikor attesting his love and concern for her and their daughter. Pressured by her husband, Violet had not forwarded any of the mail to her daughter in New Hampshire, ostensibly to put an end to her politically maladroit marriage. In the healing process for mother and daughter, it is the local priest's aged sister, Tawkoohee Manian, who presses Lucene for understanding vis á vis the Armenian community's past prejudices and argues that Anne be allowed to discover her Armenian heritage. The final, climactic mother-daughter confrontation reveals the truth about her father's alleged desertion and death. When Tawkoohee exerts her will to bring Lucene and Anne back to their ethnicity, she encapsulates the essentials of being Armenian with objective correlatives. One "smells" the divine scents of her Armenian culinary arts, especially the baking of *choreg* (sweet breadsticks). The play's universe is uniquely Armenian, with the talk of *sarma* (stuffed grape leaves), the making of *bastegh* (pureed grape juice dried flat and covered with powdered sugar). Armenian music both popular and liturgical envelopes many scenes, along with ethnic dancing, making Bejoian's play a total Armenian experience. Apart from the significant issue of the fractionalization of Armenian political power, Bejoian brings forward, as in no other drama in English by an Armenian American, the importance of Armenian women historically. She does this by reflecting three generations of Armenian culture in the lives of three women: "the oldest in the community, a younger woman trying desperately to forget her Armenian roots, and that woman's daughter, who wants to discover the heritage her mother has denied her."[57] By doing so, Bejoian allocates a place for Armenian women in the pantheon of national heroes who fostered the continuity of the Armenian race by their courageous sacrifices, including, of course, their suffering and death in defending their families and their nation during the barbaric massacres of the early twentieth century.

LESLIE AYVAZIAN

Some of our dramas reflect the genocidal past of Armenians and the difficulties of regenerating life in America. But in two plays herein a female character, dissatisfied with the status quo in America, is impelled by an inner impulse to return to the present-day liberated but beleaguered homeland. *Nine Armenians*, by Leslie Ayvazian, is one of these plays. The oldest daughter of a close-knit Armenian family, Ani, is currently in jail in Nevada for taking part in a protest against America's nuclear program. Upon her release and return home, she announces at the funeral of her grandfather (Pop) that she will pursue a humanitarian cause she has carelessly neglected, namely the salvation of an Armenia in desperate need.

Her announcement is somewhat surprising since, during the opening scene in which she does not appear, her family seems to have little if any awareness of her intentions. Her father, John, mother Armine, younger sister Virginia, and younger brother Raffi are leaving the home of John's elderly parents, Non (Marie) and Pop (Vartan), after a delightful dinner. The parting is taking a rather long time as they fill their car with all sorts of uneaten Armenian food. Rapid-fire dialogue is interspersed with interesting problems of the family. Through the hurried, light talk, however, Pop's dictums on the perilous condition of Armenia give us foreshadowing of what is to come. Armenians are freezing in the winter for lack of fuel, waterless for most of each day, and without electric power for sufficient light at night. These shortages are partly the result of the blockade of the landlocked country by Turkey and Azerbaijan, its hostile Muslim neighbors. We also learn that Pop, a Christian cleric, is a man of considerable erudition and the author of several books.

As the first scene ends, Pop dies unexpectedly. At his funeral service, his son John observes that "many of us were baptized by him, married by him, as he stood at this pulpit, in this church. I think of this and I think of the church he built in one night in Casaria. . . . The church he built with his father, in one night, from sundown to sunrise, because the Turkish laws forbid the construction of a Christian house of worship."[58] Ani follows her father with a poignant eulogy of her own, in which she tells of her grandfather's educational stories and his efforts to teach her about the Armenian massacres and their family's forced march through the Syrian desert without food or water until they dropped dead. The drama takes on special significance when she vows to go to Armenia to witness for Pop.[59] Ayvazian's dramatic structure is adroit. By utilizing ironic reversals, she creates the mixture of mirth and sorrow that is so often true in our own lives.

While Ani is packing for her trip, Non gives her, among other things, Pop's inscribed new book and an urn with his ashes, which are to be interred in Casaria. At the airport her father John continues to have doubts about Ani's trip. She does not speak Armenian, he says, and wants to go to a place where it is so hard to live because the blockaded nation lacks the necessities for adequate living. But she is adamant in her desire to go and witness and declare to the world the injustices inflicted on the Armenian nation.

Ayvazian creates highly poignant scenes in the middle course of the drama, in which Ani's experiences in Armenia are related by letters home. As she writes on one side of the stage she talks out what she is composing, and her grandmother and father on the other side continue, in their dialogue, the contents of her letter when she is silent. When Ani returns home, saturated with the sorrows of Armenia, she comes to realize with the help of her grandmother that Armenians worldwide must work for the restoration of the Armenian nation and race. By her example, her own mother becomes imbued with the spirit of going to Armenia to become another witness of the unjust tribulations Armenia is being subjected to.

As in our other plays, there is important exposition relating to genocidal atrocities that intensifies the drama as in scene 14. There, Non tells Ani of what horrors befell Pop's mother during the genocide.

> They were walking, Ani, down the roads to the desert. They were walking to their death. Holding their children, vacant eyed. Collapsing, bleeding, walking down the roads into the desert, where they died. And their children died. The Turks made the women walk. And the Turks stopped them to rape them. Cut them. Dismember them.[60]

Exposition can often prove an obstacle when it mires the forward movement of action and plot. Having wide theatrical experience as both an actor and playwright, Ayvazian has found the proper balance between the revelation of necessary background and the introduction of discoveries and ironic reversals that create exciting theater. In short, wittingly or not, she adheres to the time-honored Aristotelian precept that plot is the soul of a play and, one might add, it is essentially that aspect that, when brought to a logical climax and denouement, gives the audience the central thought of the work. In this case, that core principle might well be that talk itself does not solve problems; only actions do.

HERAND MARKARIAN

Levels of psychological trauma brought on as a result of violent Turkish depredations during the massive 1915 genocide have never been formally assessed. Those Armenians who somehow lived through the wanton rapes, pillaging, beheadings, heinous tortures, immolation of villagers massed in churches, and waterless, foodless treks through the Syrian desert finally to find a life in America were legion.

Sometimes the telling of their tragedies to loved ones was sufficient to neutralize the effect of psychological trauma. And yet there were those who could not engender the psychic energy to attain catharsis by telling all when that "all" dealt with extremely personal matters. Sometimes making a choice, on a death march, about the distribution of crumbs garnered for food and withheld from loved ones wracked the conscience of many a survivor. Not unique were stories such as the one of a girl of nine and a younger brother trekking through the Syrian desert to Aleppo. The girl was "adopted" by a Christian Arab family, and when her brother came begging to the family barn where she worked, she feared giving the hungry boy a handful of bulgur.[61] How many might well have preferred death in the killing desert tracts than having to relive again and again the horror of how the dead of the past died. Neuroses would have been the least of the many emotional traumas prevalent among the first Armenian immigrants to this country.

Herand Markarian's *Mirrors* is unique among our several plays because it concerns testimony heard directly in the context of psychological trauma. The author states in his introduction that Old Teny, the drama's central character, is a tormented soul. "As strong as she has portrayed herself throughout her life (living alone, supporting herself, not asking for any help), she breaks down when a lost fragment of her life, her brother, enters her reality."[62] Hospitalized under the care of Dr. Jim Brown, she is induced with the aid of a new drug to relive and confront the genocidal horrors she experienced and repressed. We must assume with the playwright that, in the course of time, new therapeutic treatment will mentally mend Old Teny. And if it does not, she will continue to be living proof of the devastation of the genocide close to a century after its perpetration.

Mirrors was based on the experiences of Markarian's mother, "whose stories of the Armenian Genocide, she had heard as a child." The author expanded a shorter form of the work "to include the agony of those people I had known in my childhood and whose countless stories still haunt my conscience." In this work Markarian eloquently transmits to his audience the cries of his ancestors for justice and by leaving Old Teny with the possibility of recovery leaves us with the hope that in time the Armenian nation will find its just peace.

WILLIAM ROLLERI AND ANNA ANTARAMIAN

In *The Armenian Question* by William Rolleri and Anna Antaramian, the testimony about the Genocide is not an artist's re-creation but the facts themselves as mouthed and recorded by actual survivors on interview tapes stored at the Diocese of the Armenian Church of America (Eastern), where the play was first presented in 1977.

To be able to reproduce the actual depositions of genocide survivors, the authors created what might be termed a "courtroom drama" in a Paris setting. What is at issue in the adjudication to follow? Our authors have conceived of a debate in which Turkey is making application to an international committee of the United

Nations for surplus food to mitigate the effects of a famine that will devastate the world within a few years.

Obviously the need for food is greater than the projected supply. What nations merit relief and how much? Surely those having records of humane relations with their own people and the nationalities within their own borders, as well as with other nations in the world. Furthermore, a needy nation must submit correct census figures to prove the extent of its need. Turkey, of course, has not been given favored status by the International Monetary Fund nor given admission to the European Union because of its poor civil rights record and inhumane treatment of its minorities. In addition, are its census figures elevated owing to the unaccounted loss of population? How can the Turkish representative for their petition prove his nation deserving with the forthcoming testimony of Armenian genocide survivors?

These living victims sit at a table ready to testify about the inhuman treatment the Armenian people suffered at Turkish hands during the 1915 genocide. At a table on the other side of the stage sits the Turkish government's chief representative. Despite the infirmities of age as they near the ends of their lives, the survivors shuffle to the witness chair to rasp out their horrendous stories. Although their eyewitness testimony is devastating, or perhaps because of this, our authors, allow the Turkish advocate to offer salient rebuttals. These, coming by way of Turkish cross-examination, however, are injurious and often incomprehensible to the survivors. The reliability and accuracy of the census figures that the Turkish application for relief is based on can be brought to question, as can Turkey's mistreatment of present-day Armenian and Kurdish minorities. When all is said and done, the survivors' testimony of the inhuman depredations inflicted on them and their kin is literally gut-wrenching. The result as to food allocations will need further adjudication, but the case, at least for the audience of *The Armenian Question*, has been made with devastating effect.

To get Turkey to admit its culpability for the Armenian genocide during the sovereignty of the Ottoman Empire, the Armenian cause may best be served by "courtroom" dramas (as we have observed before) such as *The Armenian Question* in which testimony becomes a significant part of the action placed in a believable context. The drawback here may be the Turkish counter-arguments, some of which have specious elements that are seemingly relevant in the immediacy of the moment. But they come to naught in the full light of scholarship and the eyewitness testimony of non-Armenian observers such as U.S. Ambassador Henry Morganthau and especially the eloquent German Armin Wegner (and his photographs), who was in the midst of the carnage as it went on.

JOYCE VAN DYKE

To complete this review of our dramatic octology, we turn last to Joyce Van Dykes's *A Girl's War*, which deals with the issue of the Armenian majority in the enclave of

Karabagh fighting for separation from Azerbaijan to end the state-sponsored depre-dations being inflicted on them. The action begins at a photo shoot in New York City where Anahid Sarkisian (Anna), age thirty-one, is modeling. For all intents and purposes, she is one of the "girls" that modeling agencies assign to jobs. She makes good money and apparently has no serious concerns. But then quickly enough we are introduced to the girl's heart-rending thoughts, emotions, and sense of guilt. This state of mind overwhelms her when, in a daydream, her mother Ar-shaluis (living actually in war-torn Karabagh) appears to remind her of the struggle of the Armenian people under Muslim Azeri and Turkish rule and in particular of their suffering in the present Karabagh conflict. In doing so, she summarizes the eras of historical torment suffered by the Armenian race. Anna, the "girl," affected emotionally by the "encounter" with her mother, falls into a heated argument with her photographer and former lover, Stephen. This is followed by a wrenching dra-matic discovery, by phone, that her younger brother Seryozha (like her older broth-er earlier) was killed in an enemy assault in Karabagh. Despite her mixed feelings about the usefulness of a "girl" in her birthplace, she is impelled like the proverbial homing pigeon to fly back to Martarash, her native village in the disputed enclave. There, a series of ironies occur, not the least of which is that she falls in love with Ilyas Alizade, an Azeri whose family has been known to her family for years when the Muslim and Christian population in Martarash lived together in neighborly peace. Not long after, Stephen Wellington, her photographer, along with Tito, his assistant, visit the Sarkisians on assignment in the general region.

Ilyas, who has ostensibly deserted from the Azeri Army, is suspected by the Sarkisians of being a terrorist who has been planting land mines throughout the town, one of which kills an old friend of the family. For this Anna and mother Ar-shaluis hold him prisoner to be turned over to the Armenian Fedayeen (guerilla) Army for trial. But in another reversal, Anna optimistically begins to doubt her lover's guilt and hopes he is innocent as he claims. With Arshaluis covering him with her sniper's rifle, he finally admits that he set the landmines, believing that Anna could never really love him. Knowing he will be tortured and killed by the Armenian *fedayeen*, Ilyas seizes Tito for a shield, holding him close with a knife to his body. Arshaluis, an excellent shot, sends a bullet into Ilyas, who in dying mor-tally stabs the innocent Tito. Van Dyke's climax is shockingly apt, and the denou-ment clarifies the theme of the drama. How many must die needlessly before peo-ple learn to live with each other? A girl out of harm's way in America, for the sake of familial love, returns to her birthplace with the noblest intentions and is swal-lowed up in the fury of war—a girl's war—in which idealism and the immediate imperative of kill or be killed constantly clash, with apparently no resolution. The view is reminiscent of Aeschylus's treatment, in the *Orestian Trilogy*, of the chain of vengeful retaliatory bloodletting through the three plays dealing with the aftermath of the Trojan War. Van Dyke acknowledges the constant dilemma of war and de-struction in Armenian history and hopes that the forces of love and sensibility (manifested in this drama by a "girl") will one day end Armenia's periodic crises.

CONCLUSION

The plays within this volume and similar ethnic dramas would be welcome to all Anglophones interested in America's multifaceted ethnicity. They would be appreciated by audiences as individual productions or in ethnic theater festivals supported by government agencies such as the National Endowment for the Arts, as well as with the sponsorship of private organizations such as the Guggenheim Foundation, the Carnegie Corportaion, and several Armenian organizations mentioned earlier. Already, Armenian films have moved in this direction, as is evident from those appearing in the New York Armenian Film Festival at New York University in June of 2002, during which "genocide, contemporary Armenia, Diaspora . . . prehistory and modern history . . . [and Armenia's] torment and triumph . . . are explored by conventional and experimental filmmakers." Represented at the festival were works by Atom Egoyan (such as *Exotica* and *The Sweet Hereafter*), whose recent epic *Ararat* opened at the Cannes Film Festival in 2002.[63]

The dramatic form seems best for "teaching" and influencing people. Audiences sitting shoulder to shoulder in a kind of galvanic contact can create huge numbers of converts to a cause in a short time. It is the definitive and immediate contact between writer and audience and the immediacy of understanding and appreciation communicated through applause that make playwrights generally, and those represented here especially, ply their craft.

NOTES

1. T. S. Eliot, "The Three Voices of Poetry," (New York: Cambridge University Press, 1954).

2. See Lawrence Terzian, "In Memoriam," *Ararat*, no. 56 (Winter 1974): back cover.

3. Jack Antreassian, "Ararat—the Early Years," introduction to *Ararat: A Decade of Armenian American Writing*, ed. Jack Antreassian (New York: Armenian General Benevolent Union, 1969).

4. Leo Hamalian, "The View from Ararat," introduction to *Ararat* 26, no. 1, "25th Anniversary Issue" (Winter 1985): 5.

5. See Hamalian, "The View from Ararat," 6.

6. See *Ararat*, "A Quarterly, Special Issue: Drama," *Ararat* 34, no. 136 (Autumn 1993): 3.

7. Nishan Parlakian, "Their Hills Are Scarred" (master's thesis, Columbia University, 1950); performed at The Master Theater, New York, 1949.

8. Nishan Parlakian and S. Peter Cowe, eds., *Modern Armenian Drama: An Anthology* (New York: Columbia University Press, 2001), ix–xi.

9. On *commedia dell'arte*, see Sheldon Cheney, *The Theatre* (New York: Tudor, 1947), 188.

10. On miracle and morality plays, see Cheney, *The Theatre*, 171.

11. Parlakian and Cowe, *Modern Armenian Drama*, x–xi.

12. Parlakian and Cowe, *Modern Armenian Drama*.

13. D. M. Lang, *The Armenians* (London: George Allen & Unwin, 1981), 3.

14. Edward Allworth, introduction to *Evil Spirit*, by Alexander Shirvanzade, trans. Nishan Parlakian (New York: St. Vartan Press, 1980), xv.

15. Allworth, introduction to *Evil Spirit*, xiv.

16. Allworth, introduction to *Evil Spirit*, xvi.

17. Vartan Ajemian, "A Word on the Fiftieth Anniversary of the Theater," preface to *Sundukian Memorial Theater, 1922–1972* (Erevan: "Hayastan" Publicatons, 1972); a record of all Sundukian plays produced at the theater between the dates in the title.

18. For an account of Shirvanzade's life, see Nishan Parlakian, introduction to *For the Sake of Honor*, trans. Nishan Parlakian, (New York: St. Vartan Press, 1976). For an account of Shant's life, see Levon Shant, *Ancient Gods*, trans. Anne B. Vardanian (Laverne, Calif.: Laverne University Press, 1987).

19. Allworth, introduction to *Evil Spirit*, xvii.

20. See introduction to *For the Sake of Honor* (note 18), p. xiii.

21. See Pamela J. Young, "Knowledge, Nation, and the Curriculum: Ottoman Armenian Education, 1853–1915," Ph.D. diss., University of Michigan, 2001), quotation taken from dissertation abstract.

22. James H. Tashjian, *The Armenians of the United States and Canada* (Boston: Hairenik Press, 1947), 6–7. See also Lang, *The Armenians*, 126–27.

23. Charles A. Vertanes, "Introductory Outline of the Armenian Theater," in *Two Thousand Years of Armenian Theater* (New York: Armenian National Council of America, 1954), 12.

24. Maxine S. Seller, ed., *Ethnic Theatre in The United States* (Westport, Conn.: Greenwood Press, 1983).

25. P. K. Thomajan, *Worcester Memories* (Leominster, Mass.: Eusey Press, 1983), 94–95.

26. Melinie J. Karakashian, review of *Polarization*, by Hrand Markarian, *The Armenian Weekly*, 11 June 1977.

27. Karakashian, review.

28. See Shant, *Ancient Gods*, trans. Anne Vardanian, in *Modern Armenian Drama: An Anthology*, ed. Parlakian and Cowe (New York: Columbia University Press, 2001), 186–253.

29. Seller, ed., *Ethnic Theatre*, 6.

30. Seller, ed., *Ethnic Theatre*, 6.

31. Seller, ed., *Ethnic Theatre in The United States*, 8.

32. See Nishan Parlakian, "Shakespeare and the Armenian Theater," *Council on National Literatures: Quarterly World Report* 5, no. 4 (October 1982): 5–10.

33. See Seller, ed., *Ethnic Theatre*, 12.

34. See Nishan Parlakian, "Armenian-American Theater," in *Ethnic Theater in the United States*, ed. Maxine Seller (Westport, Conn.: Greenwood Press: 1983), 31. Also see Pierre Papazian, "No Man Is an Island . . . ," *Outreach* (a publication of the Prelacy of the Armenian Apostolic Church of America) 2, no. 9 (January 1980): 5.

35. Nishan Parlakian, "Armenian Theater: An Update," *Council on National Literatures World Report* 6 (1993): 14.

36. Parlakian, "Armenian Theater: An Update," 31.

37. Parlakian, "Armenian Theater: An Update," 30

38. See also Perch Zeytuntsyan, "Born and Died," trans. S. Peter Cowe, and "The Saddest of Sad Men," trans. Daniel Weissbort, in *Two Plays*, by Perch Zeytuntsyan (Los Angeles: April Publishing 2001).

39. Ishkhan Jinbashian, "Armen Khandikian Makes Directing Debut in Pennsylvania," *The Armenian Mirror-Spectator* (Watertown, Mass.), 7 September 2002.

40. Jinbashian, "Armen Khandikian."

41. See Florence Avakian, "Prof. Dadoyan Tackles Myth Versus Reality of Armenian Identity at Columbia U. Lecture," *The Armenian Mirror-Spectator* (Watertown, Mass.), 22 June 2002.

42. Patrick J. Collins, "The Absurd as Accessory," a review of *Four Plays*, by Raffi Arzoomanian, *Ararat* 22, no. 3 (Summer 1981): 72.

43. David Stephen Calonne, *William Saroyan: My Real Work Is Being* (Chapel Hill: University of North Carolina Press, 1983).

44. Calonne, *William Saroyan*, 77.

45. Calonne, *William Saroyan*, 77.

46. See Nishan Parlakian, "Saroyan's *Armenians*," review, *Ararat* 16, no. 3 (Summer 1975): 26–27. See also Dickran Kouymjian, ed., *An Armenian Trilogy* (Fresno: California State University Press, 1986), especially the introduction and front material.

47. Parlakian, "Saroyan's *Armenians*," 27.

48. Kouymjian, ed., *An Armenian Trilogy* (containing the text of *Armenians*), 67.

49. Kouymjian, ed., *An Armenian Trilogy*, 9.

50. Kouymjian, ed., *An Armenian Trilogy*, 2.

51. Kouymjian, ed., *An Armenian Trilogy*, 2–3.

52. Kouymjian, ed., *An Armenian Trilogy*, 38.

53. Parlakian, Nishan, *Grandma, Pray for Me*, act 2, this volume.

54. Anne Paolucci, afterword to *Grandma, Pray for Me*, by Nishan Parlakian (New York: Griffon House, 1988).

55. Adam Adamian, "I Saw the Grandeur of the Armenian Heart," review of *Grandma, Pray for Me*, by Nishan Parlakian, *The Armenian Reporter*, 24 March 1988.

56. Tashjian, *The Armenians of the United States and Canada*, 37.

57. *The Armenian Mirror-Spectator*, press relaease, 6 May 1989.

58. Leslie Ayvazian, *Nine Armenians*, scene 2.

59. Ayvazian, *Nine Armenians*, scene 2.

60. Ayvazian, *Nine Armenians*, scene 14.

61. The story was told only once to the editor by a genocide survivor.

62. See *Mirrors*, introduction, this volume.

63. See *The Armenian Mirror-Spectator*, "The New York Armenian Film Festival," 29 June 2002.

REFERENCES

Adamian, Adam. "I Saw the Grandeur of the Armenian Heart." Review of *Grandma, Pray for Me*, by Nishan Parlakian. *The Armenian Reporter*, 24 March 1988.

Ajemian, Vartan. "A Word on the Fiftieth Anniversary of the Theater." Preface to *Sundukian Memorial Theater, 1922–1972*. Erevan: "Hayastan" Publicatons, 1972.

Allworth, Edward. Introduction to *Evil Spirit*, by Alexander Shirvanzade, trans. Nishan Parlakian. New York: St. Vartan Press, 1980.

Antreassian, Jack. "Ararat—The Early Years." Introduction to *Ararat: A Decade of Armenian American Writing*, ed. Jack Antreassian (New York: Armenian General Benevolent Union, 1969).

Avakian, Florence. "Prof. Dadoyan Tackles Myth Versus Reality of Armenian Identity at Columbia U. Lecture." *The Armenian Mirror-Spectator* (Watertown, Mass.), 22 June 2002.

Ararat. "A Quarterly, Special Issue: Drama." *Ararat* 34, no. 136 (Autumn 1993).

Calonne, David Stephen. *William Saroyan: My Real Work Is Being*. Chapel Hill: University of North Carolina Press, 1983.

Cheney, Sheldon. *The Theatre*. New York: Tudor, 1947.

Collins, Patrick J. "The Absurd as Accessory." A review of *Four Plays*, by Raffi Arzoomanian, *Ararat* 22, no. 3 (Summer 1981): 71–73.

Eliot, T. S. "The Three Voices of Poetry." New York: Cambridge University Press, 1954.

Hamalian, Leo. "The View from Ararat." Introduction to *Ararat* 26, no. 1, "25th Anniversary Issue" (Winter 1985): 5–6.

Jinbashian, Ishkhan. "Armen Khandikian Makes Directing Debut in Pennsylvania." *The Armenian Mirror-Spectator* (Watertown, Mass.), 7 September 2002.

Kouymjian, Dickran, ed. *An Armenian Trilogy*. Fresno: California State University Press, 1986.

Lang, D. M. *The Armenians*. London: George Allen & Unwin, 1981.

Paolucci, Anne. Afterword to *Grandma, Pray for Me*, by Nishan Parlakian. New York: Griffon House, 1988.

Papazian, Pierre. "No Man Is an Island. . . ." *Outreach* 2, no. 9 (January 1980): 5.

Parlakian, Nishan. "Armenian Theater: An Update." *Council on National Literatures World Report* 6 (1993): 14–40.

——. Introduction to *For the Sake of Honor*, trans. Nishan Parlakian. New York: St. Vartan Press, 1976.

——. "Saroyan's *Armenians*." Review. *Ararat* 16, no. 3(Summer 1975): 26–27.

——. "Shakespeare and the Armenian Theater." *Council on National Literatures: Quarterly World Report* 5, no. 4 (October 1982): 3–13.

——. "Their Hills Are Scarred." Master's thesis, Columbia University, 1950.

Seller, Maxine S., ed. *Ethnic Theatre in The United States*. Westport, Conn.: Greenwood Press, 1983.

Shant, Levon. *Ancient Gods*. Trans. Anne B. Vardanian. Laverne, Calif.: Laverne University Press, 1987. Reprint, in *Modern Armenian Drama: An Anthology*, ed. Nishan Parlakian and S. Peter Cowe, 186–253. New York: Columbia University Press, 2001.

Tashjian, James H. *The Armenians of the United States and Canada*. Boston: Hairenik Press, 1947.

Terzian, Lawrence. "In Memoriam." *Ararat*, no. 56 (Winter 1974): back cover.

Thomajan, P. K. *Worcester Memories*. Leominster, Mass.: Eusey Press, 1983.

Vertanes, Charles A. "Introductory Outline of the Armenian Theater." In *Two Thousand Years of Armenian Theater*, 2–13, 27–30. New York: Armenian National Council of America, 1954.

Young, Pamela J. "Knowledge, Nation, and the Curriculum: Ottoman Armenian Education, 1853–1915." Ph.D. diss., University of Michigan, 2001.

Zeytuntsyan, Perch. "Born and Died," trans. S. Peter Cowe, and "The Saddest of Sad Men," trans. Daniel Weissbort. In *Two Plays*, by Perch Zeytuntsyan. Los Angeles: April Publishing 2001.

RAFFI ARZOOMANIAN

ELLIS ISLAND 101

To Elmas Arzoomanian
dearest mother, dear friend, and surviving grace

THE PLAYWRIGHT

In 1965 Ralph Arzoomanian received his Ph.D. in
dramatic art at the University of Iowa. After a year as
a Yale fellow, he went on to Lehman College of
CUNY and was a professor of theatre for thirty-five
years until his retirement in 2002. His full-length
plays, *The Coop* and *The Moths* were published in
his anthology *Four Plays* and were produced in New
York and Los Angeles, the former at the Actor's Playhouse and the latter at the Mark Taper Forum. *The
Moths* received a second production in Los Angeles
in 1999. His one-act play *The Tack Room* was included in the volume *Best American Short Plays of
1992*.

 Ellis Island 101 is loosely based on a true story
that was told to the author by his late mother Elmas.
The male character was added to give the play
counterpoint. *Ellis Island 101* appeared in several
collections, including *Four Plays*, published by the
Armenian General Benevolent Union's Ararat Press,
and has been produced at various theatres here and
abroad—and more than once within the main
building on Ellis Island.

THE PLAY:
BRIEF BUT BRILLIANT

In its action and characterizations, *Ellis Island 101*
may be taken simply as a metaphor of life on a see-

saw. But the deeper image is closer to life in purgatory, where the nearby torch light of the Statue of Liberty continually makes moths of humans, luring them to the gate of heaven only to be rejected and flung back into limbo again and to the hell of their former intolerable existence in the old country. As dour and dismal as all this may seem, the play is curiously charged with a good deal of humor and wit generated by a pontificating middle-aged professor and an old woman with homey observations, two hopeful entrants to the land where "the streets are paved with gold." Each has a "sure-fire" method for gaining entrance, and each has an Achilles heel. The fainting spells of the erudite professor make him seem ridiculously deranged. And the illiterate old lady, who has a "foolproof" ploy to prove to the customs officer that she can read, seems equally unbalanced. Neither gains entry. And yet the play cannot be thought of as a spoof, because Arzoomanian's dialogue is touched with an intangible sense of innocence that attests to the playwright's compassion and humility in the presence of his characters.

These qualities were recognized by Howard Stein, Arzoomanian's playwriting teacher in the Ph.D. program at the University of Iowa (See the introduction to Arzoomanian's *Four Plays*). Elaborating on the theme of his student's sense of compassion, Stein observes that Arzoomanian never abusively mocks his characters in any of his plays. "They always had their own brand of dignity, no matter what their occupation or social status," he adds. "That was for me the first insight into the author. Arzoomanian had not only compassion for his people; he had respect."

Finally Stein notes that *Ellis Island 101* is one of the author's several dramas "through which your own population will be increased by a group of fascinating, eccentric and enriching personalities and characters. Great value exists in the environment in which they struggle for 'survival and dignity.'"

Though brief, *Ellis Island 101* scintillates like a brilliant gem. It reverberates in the senses with an alloy of emotions—constant hope contending with fear of repeated failure. It reflects the state of tension most immigrants to the United States generally must have felt, particularly those like Armenians who were forcefully transplanted and could not return to their ancient homes where genocide had been inflicted on their people.

ELLIS ISLAND 101

RAFFI ARZOOMANIAN

A Play in One Act

CHARACTERS

PETER, a middle-aged professor
ANNA, an old woman
OFFICER

PETER: This waiting . . . I wish they'd hurry up.

ANNA: Oh, they won't be long.

PETER: How would you know?

ANNA: I've been here before.

PETER: You've been—you've been at Ellis Island before!

ANNA: Yes. I was sent back, young man, sent back.

PETER: Were you ill?

ANNA: No.

PETER: Oh . . . I see.

ANNA: Do you?

PETER: To be honest, I don't, I can't think. All this in-
timidation, you go to this desk, you go to that
desk. "No, I'm not a communist, no I've never
been tubercular, no I've no wife on the continent." I'm an emotional man, I'm prone to faint.
I did on ship once, during the lifeboat drill.

ANNA: A young man like you!

PETER: With all I've been through, yes.

ANNA: Well you'd better not faint here, young man.

PETER: I'm so anxious to get on shore, you can't
imagine how anxious I am to get there. It's not
that I expect so much, I'm just tired of biding

time. My preparation on the continent took ages, the voyage took ages, it seems I've been here for ages.

ANNA: Well it won't be long. This is the last test you know.

PETER: Test?

ANNA: You see, I've been in this room before, in this very room. I know what they do here.

PETER: Do here?

ANNA: I'm as petrified as you.

PETER: Would you please be more specific? When were you here, what did they do?

ANNA: They kept me from my sons and their ten children, isn't that enough? And to think, to think there was just a mile of water between us after all these years! For thirty years I've been making my way to America like a drunked-up dog. But they sent me back, an "American" like me! My boys, they never did see me . . . such loyal boys. They later wrote me that when I was here they took a ferry that goes back and forth near here . . . hoping that I might come into view.

PETER: *(Proudly.)* That ferry you mention would be called the Staten Island Ferry! How I thrive on such details! What's more, it truly exists!

ANNA: My boys took this ferry for two days and called my name through megaphones . . . but I never heard them. They called themselves hoarse but the walls are thick here.

PETER: But what happens in this room? What will they do to us?

ANNA: Ah, they will break your heart in this room.

PETER: *(Starts wiping his forehead nervously.)* Please, specifically what—

ANNA: If you fail the test they'll draw a large "x" on you in this room. When they draw that "x" on you they will break your heart and send you back from where you came.

PETER: But they won't send me back! I've a position waiting in Boston!

ANNA: It makes no difference if you fail! They don't care!

PETER: I've an education, I'm to teach Medieval History!

ANNA: A teacher!

PETER: They need such men in the country.

ANNA: An educated man, well!

PETER: I'll be a perfect, a perfect American. I'll honor their women and abide their laws.

ANNA: I should have known by your vest!

PETER: Why do they constantly intimidate you like this! They . . . they scare you on ship, they scare you when they hoard you into this monstrous tomb of a building, and they scare you by bedding you with a bunch of snoring strangers! Madness!

ANNA: Please don't agitate yourself, there's no cause for you—

PETER: Does scaring the homeless make them better Americans!

ANNA: But you've no need to worry yourself, young man. Oh. I'm so pleased for you. I didn't know you were a teacher! And once you get over your loneliness you'll be a handsome teacher. Isn't that it . . . loneliness . . . homelessness?

PETER: I suppose so . . . yes.

ANNA: You're not alone. Some get so frightened that they pee in their pants. What-ever you do . . . don't pee in your pants . . . they'll give you an "x" for that. You promise now.

PETER: I shan't wet my pants. I'm not a child.

ANNA: And this business of fainting. They'll give you an "x" for that, too, *and* for coughing, *and* for having a rash, *and* for having a limp or backache—they've no mind to investigate symptoms, back you go . . . and they'll give you an "x" if you can't read. That's why I was sent back.

PETER: *(Suddenly relieved.)* Ah, now I understand. My, my, you had me going there. This room . . . so they're to test our literacy here—well I won't faint over that, I assure you! *(She shares his pleasure.)* Well . . . well . . . I've the feeling that it's all downhill from here. You really had me going there, mama—you don't mind my calling you that?

ANNA: Please do, professor. *(She looks on him with great admiration.)* A teacher . . . a teacher.

PETER: Mama . . . we are both from the same country, a human slaughterhouse.

ANNA: *(Thoughtfully, as to a teacher.)* Yes . . . yes

PETER: Just the thrill of a position in America. Just the notion of a natural death is so precious, so rare for our kind!

ANNA: You're a great teacher, a genius!

PETER: A natural death. I want nothing more, that's it! No more butchery, no more transiency, no more cruelty.

ANNA: Cruelty you say! Well, that Irishman's cruel, I can tell you!

PETER: Uhh . . . What Irishman would that be?

ANNA: The one that's coming in here with the papers for us to read. That's the one that tricked me.

PETER: But he can't trick you if you're able to read, mama!

ANNA: But I can't read.

PETER: You mean you couldn't read.

ANNA: No, I can't read. *(She shrugs.)* But I do like to think of myself and language as I would a competent pianist who can't read music.

PETER: But they'll send you back again, mama!

ANNA: No, not this time. He can't read our language, either, so all I need to do is a recitation. I've been rehearsing our Lord's Prayer.

PETER: But suppose he knows there's no Lord's Prayer on the paper!

ANNA: Sssh, that's not the way he catches you. The Irish fox he turns the paper sideways and then asks you to read.

PETER: The charlatan . . . sideways, can you imagine.

ANNA: Last time, when I started "reading" he gave me the "x" right here on my back. I got the same treatment as one who wets his pants.

PETER: I don't think I could take it.

ANNA: But this time—what is your name?

PETER: Peter.

ANNA: But this time, Peter, I'll not be fooled.

PETER: But how—

ANNA: You see, I've learned that the papers in this country are longer from top to bottom than from side to side. The Irishman doesn't know I was here three years ago. If he holds it sideways this time I won't be angry. I'll be kind, I'll say, "Are you trying to fool me, mister? Don't you know you're holding it sideways? Now please turn it this way so I may read it for you." Then he'll turn it so that the length would be this way *(uses her hands)* and not this way *(uses her hands again)*. I once dreamed that America would spare us such accidents. A slight shift of the paper and I would have been spared three years' longing.

PETER: But I see you're a hardy woman, you've kept yourself up!

ANNA: Anticipation, Peter, that's what keeps us all up.

(An immigration OFFICER *enters.)*

ANNA: That's him, that's the same one. You Irishman, I've got you this time. You won't keep me from America this time!

PETER: For heaven's sakes keep quiet or he'll be prejudiced against you!

ANNA: He doesn't understand what I'm saying!

PETER: But he hears you yelling, mama, now be quiet and leave this to me.

(The OFFICER *comes over and checks their tags against a sheet on his clipboard.)*

PETER: *(With a slight accent.)* I can read in American if you like, sir, or in my own language. But my ladyfriend here will do hers in Armenian.

OFFICER: All right. What's she so excited about?

PETER: She's anxious to see her sons, it's been a long time.

OFFICER: Just a moment. *(The* OFFICER *fetches some materials.)*

ANNA: What did you say to him?

PETER: Sssh. I'm setting it up. I told him about your sons. *(He winks at her.)*

ANNA: About them being on the ferry. He'll think they're crazy!

PETER: Please, please, leave it to me.

(The OFFICER *returns.)*

OFFICER: Read at least five sentences, please.

PETER: When you turn the paper rightside up I will! *(They have a nervous laugh to-*

gether.) "The growth of agriculture since 1935 has been more phenomenal than the corresponding growth in industry, said Henry K—"
OFFICER: That's good enough.

(ANNA stands and applauds.)

ANNA: Good for you, young man. God bless you for being so brilliant a young man.
PETER: *(Sheepishly.)* Thank you, mama.
ANNA: I want you to feel that I'm taking the place of your mother. She would clap too.

(The OFFICER cases ANNA and their eyes find one another. She looks back at him with apprehension and excitement.)

PETER: God be with you, mama. *(He is quite nervous.)*
OFFICER: *(To PETER.)* Don't you say anything—It's a violation, you know.
PETER: I don't need to. She reads marvelously, you watch. She's an avid reader . . . you watch. Brilliant.

(The OFFICER shows her the paper sideways and she smiles with relief. She takes her time, looking first at PETER then at the officer.)

ANNA: Are you trying to fool me, mister? Don't you know you're holding it sideways? Now please turn it this way so I may read it for you. *(She has the OFFICER turn the paper.)* Good, Now then, Our Father who art in heaven—
PETER: No, no, oh no, I, I—
ANNA: Hallowed be thy . . . hallowed be thy—

(The OFFICER pulls the paper away gently.)

PETER: Mama, mama, no, you turned the paper upside down!

(ANNA gives out a genuine but comic scream and PETER faints to the floor. As ANNA sits glassy eyed the officer marks an "x" on her abdomen, shakes his head and marks an "x" on the chest of the prone (but coming to) PETER. The OFFICER then helps PETER to his feet and sits him down. He makes an expression of condolence before leaving.)

PETER: Mama . . . mama . . . *(He recognizes what happened.)*
ANNA: You fainted . . . I told you that was a . . . violation, Peter.
PETER: Yes. *(Pause.)* Hey, come back? *(PETER jumps up and speaks towards the empty parts of the stage.)* I'm a sensitive man, that's why I faint! Only a sensitive man could average a ninety-four while starving his way to a doctorate! I

have it right here. A doctorate issued by the University of Lebanon to Peter Tehlirian—History—while I was there I mastered English, I mean American English—and I will not stand for this disgrace! Come back and at least have a talk, I'm sure we can . . . *(He exhales the rest of his air and stands nodding.)*

ANNA: Where will you go . . . to?

PETER: I . . . I don't know. Yes, I do—Paris. I know I can work there . . . until . . .

ANNA: I'm responsible, Peter. I should be dead.

PETER: Ssshhh. Where will you go?

ANNA: Oh . . . *(She feigns light-heartedness.)* Oh, I don't know . . . I can always go . . . well there are several countries where I know . . . I'll be all right. You see, I'm thinking of next time. How will I ever know when it's right side up or upside down?

PETER: Then it's Paris for you. I'll teach you how to read and you'll coach me off fainting. We'll come back.

ANNA: Yes.

PETER: How old are you, mama?

ANNA: Over seventy.

PETER: Ah.

ANNA: *(Cheerfully.)* In case you're wondering—I'll live to see the Irishman again. I'll live to die in America.

(PETER puts his arm around her.)

ANNA: I was just thinking, Peter. That something-island ferry. Does it run back and forth all the time?

PETER: From all accounts, endlessly.

ANNA: Then there's every chance that my sons are on it at this very moment with their megaphones. *(Pauses.)* Do you hear anything?

PETER: No.

ANNA: Neither do I.

PETER: Forgive me, mama, but your sons . . . they sound like a couple of idiots.

ANNA: Yes. America seems to have done them no good. No good at all.

(They look upon each other warmly as the lights fade.)

The End

WILLIAM SAROYAN

ARMENIANS

A Play in Two Acts

WILLIAM SAROYAN: DRAMATIST

One could introduce William Saroyan, in the usual way, as the prolific storyteller who established himself as a writer of unique talent and insight in the mid- and late 1930s with eight volumes of short fiction, including his landmark masterpiece "The Daring Young Man on the Flying Trapeze." But by 1939 he had begun to write in the dramatic form, gaining favorable attention for *My Heart's in the Highlands*, a play based on an earlier story. Following hard upon that success, his next play, in 1939, *The Time of Your Life* brought him the New York Drama Critics Circle Award and the Pulitzer Prize. It would be true to say, as D. S. Calonne does (in the introduction of a special Saroyan issue of *Ararat*, winter 2002) that, in terms of his fiction, Saroyan's genius allowed "his characters to speak and let the story unfold as it would, without forcing, letting one idea lead to the next in a spontaneous overflow of powerful feeling." This attribute of an apparent unstructured depiction of character in life situations became to varying degrees a hallmark of his dramatic output and in some measure put him at odds with theater critics who sought clear-cut themes that evolved out of focused plots. Subsequent full-length plays (such as *Love's Old Sweet Song*, 1940), met with lukewarm receptions and several plays that followed opened in summer stock but never reached Broadway. *The Beautiful People* (1941) had a modest reception in New York, but generally most of his plays that reached Broadway in the early 1940s were poorly received. Saroyan's dramatic works, of course, were produced in significant venues outside the New York orbit. In 1957, however, his *Cave Dellers* did receive a first-class Broadway production and noteworthy accolades.

Despite Saroyan's disenchantment with commercial show business, he believed, as we said earlier, that the writing genre best suited for capturing the attention and influencing the general public was drama. To that end he wrote innumerable plays, most unseen, unread, and unstaged. D. Kouymjian observes, for example, that in the 1960s and 1970s, Saroyan published three volumes of plays and that his play output in 1975 alone exceeded fifteen. Of these, "he submitted few for publication or performance, nor did he circulate them among close friends; instead, he carefully preserved them for their future resurrection." (*An Armenian Trilogy*, 2–3, note 47) Fortunately for us, Saroyan, in a sense, had assigned Koumyjian the task of "resurrecting" *Armenians*, *Bitlis*, and *Haratch*, which constituted his *Trilogy*. With respect to theme, the Saroyan plays are similar to those of our anthology as stated in the general introduction—genocide, identity, and transplantation. Kouymjian notes, however, that "their intensity and brilliance is not defined by action or plot, but by language and idea. Their message is universal and enduring." One is constrained to add, though, that *Armenians*, reproduced herein, without doubt or quibble, is patently a theater piece.

THE WORLD PREMIERE OF *ARMENIANS*

Armenians was produced by the Diocese of the Armenian Church of America in the Haig Kavookjian Armenian Arts Center, 630 Second Avenue in New York City on October 22, 23, 24, 29, 30, 31 and November 11, 12, 13, 14, 1974. It was directed by Ed Setrakian. The Equity Approved Showcase performances featured the following cast:

FATHER KASPARIAN	Ed Setrakian
REV. MUGGERDITCH KNADJIAN	Warren Finnerty
REV. PAPAZIAN	Luis Avalos
ALMAST	Terese Hayden
SEXTON	Nicholas Daddazio
DOCTOR ARSHAK JIVELEKIAN	Joseph Ragno
FARMER	Murray Moston
MAN FROM BITLIS	Vahagn Hovannes
MAN FROM MOUSH	Raymond Cole
MAN FROM VAN	Harold Cherry
MAN FROM HARPOOT	David Patch
VASKEN	Bob Doran
MAN FROM ERZEROUM	Rudy Bond

MAN FROM DIKRANAGERT   Sal Carollo

MAN FROM GILIGIA   Robert Coluntino

The technical staff included:

Stage Manager   Susan Gregg
Production Coordinator   Alice Eminian
Sets and Lights   John Brennan,
                                            Eric Cowley,
                                            Torkom Demirjian,
                                            and Bob Doran
Costumes   Ruth Thomason
Props   Anne Setrakian

Program Note

Prepared by the author for the premiere production.

The play called *Armenians* is about people. The time of the play is approximately yesterday, 1921. At that time the playwright was thirteen years old, and pretty much fascinated by everything that he saw in the streets and places of Fresno, California, which he visited daily in the course of his work as a newsboy—not a route carrier, that's another kind of connection with newspapers, but a seller of papers, a walker, a headline-shouter, a visitor of places, an observer of people.

Some of the playwright's observations of some of the people of Fresno are in this play, from both before 1921 and from long after, including this morning when a man outside a dentist's door said, You are not what I expected you to be.

I said, Well, I can't say I'm sorry because I don't know what you expected, or why. Do you speak Armenian?

He then said in Armenian, I expected you to be *shavlar*, or something like that, which he said was the proper Armenian word for fat.

I replied in Armenian, Oh, I thought your disappointment was the consequence of having read my books and then many years later finding me coarse and common in comparison with them. (You should have heard me in Armenian. It was really elegant.)

No, he said, from photographs in papers and from friends who know you.

And these friends of yours, I said, where are they now?

Well, he said, home, or dead. I myself am eighty-two years old and had a stroke two years ago.

How many children have you? I said, and he said, Well I married this Pennsylvania Dutch woman who is in the dentist's chair right now and we don't have any children.

Well, the man's dying, you see, and he hasn't left any fighters in the world, half Armenian and half Pennsylvania Dutch. Of course this compels regret in me because while Armenians have in America married into all races there is enough of Armenia in their kids to keep the old fight going, and so here this morning was this good man at death's door with his wife in the dentist's chair and no kids at all, and therefore no grandkids who, like as not, would be only one-quarter Armenian.

I tried not to show my astonishment and disappointment, but soon enough got back on my bike and rode off, wishing him good luck, although I can't imagine where.

This play is a little bit about that sort of thing, if in an indirect way.

In wanting ourselves continued in the fight of the world, what we really want is the continuance of the human family itself, in its broadest, deepest, most complex, most troublesome, most unaccountable, most unacceptable, most preposterous, most contradictory, and most inexhaustibly unpredictable reality.

But what for?

Why?

For the reason that only out of that awful but also magnificent *fullness* may we expect the human race to begin—*to begin*, mark you—to become the fulfillment of what has been indicated in his nature and truth for as long as there has been a chronicle of such things—chiselled in stone, painted on cave walls, put up into breathtaking architecture, murmured in lullabies, whispered and roared in symphonies, held fast and secret inside all invented shapes—ship, locomotive, airplane, phonographs, radio, television (for instance). But probably even more significantly in the *model* of all shapes, the egg, which of course eludes us entirely, having come as we ourselves have come, from the soul and heart of secrecy itself.

We certainly want everybody to continue in the fight, and that of course has got to include the Turk, may his eyes open into the privilege and helplessness which is the mark of humanity.

The play *Armenians* perhaps says, It's hopeless and we know it, but not so hopeless we don't want to find out how hopeless it is.

WILLIAM SAROYAN
FRESNO, CALIFORNIA
OCTOBER 18, 1974

ARMENIANS

WILLIAM SAROYAN

A Play in Two Acts

THE PEOPLE

FATHER KASPARIAN, priest of the Red Brick Armenian Apostolic Church

REVEREND MUGGERDITCH KNADJIAN, 48, minister of First Armenian Presbyterian Church

REVEREND PAPAZIAN, 44, minister of Pilgrim Armenian Congregational Church

ALMAST, octogenarian woman from Moush, helper to Fr. Kasparian

SEXTON, of the Red Brick Church, Markar by name

DOCTOR ARSHAK JIVELEKIAN, 58, from Boston, educated at Harvard

FARMER, 74 years old

MAN FROM BITLIS

MAN FROM MOUSH, Baghdasar Der Kaprielian by name

MAN FROM VAN

MAN FROM HARPOOT, Giragos Arpiar Der Havasarian, oriental rug seller

VASKEN, a man from Harpoot

MAN FROM ERZEROUM

MAN FROM DIKRANAGERT

MAN FROM GILIGIA

THE PLACE

The Office of the Red Brick Church (Holy Trinity Armenian Apostolic Church) on the corner of Ventura at M Street, Fresno, California.

The Armenian Patriotic Club facing the church on Ventura.

THE TIME

A morning in the Spring of 1921.

Note: The play was written in one act with twenty-one scenes in Fresno between November 10 and 30, 1971. The New York production divided it into two acts corresponding to the natural change of setting. The two-act arrangement has been retained by the editor.

ACT ONE

PAPAZIAN, KASPARIAN, KNADJIAN *in the office of the Red Brick Church on Ventura at M Street in Fresno, 1921.*

Slowly, easily, thoughtfully, with considerings of what has been said until the KEY is established and the reality is being supported by the audience.

KASPARIAN: I trust we may all stand rather than sit.
KNADJIAN: I prefer to stand, also.
PAPAZIAN: Perhaps you will not mind if I relieve the pain in my right ankle by taking this chair.
KASPARIAN: A sip of cognac is surely in order.
PAPAZIAN: No thank you, I do not drink.
KASPARIAN: And you?
KNADJIAN: On occasion.
KASPARIAN: Let this be such an occasion. My hours are long. I have been up since before daybreak.
KNADJIAN: May I propose that we drink to harmony among all of us.
KASPARIAN: Very well, harmony, then. Ah, that was good. Another?
KNADJIAN: Very good, but no more for me, thank you.
KASPARIAN: This second sip for me, and now, who will speak first?
PAPAZIAN: Let us be good Americans first, and then Armenians.
KASPARIAN: Good or bad?
PAPAZIAN: If we are good Americans, we will be good Armenians, as well.
KNADJIAN: My church has always felt close to the Mother Church.
PAPAZIAN: We are certainly all Christians. Our disputes are not religious, they are political.
KASPARIAN: Is it political to pray that Armenia will continue to be an independent nation?

PAPAZIAN: *Was* an independent nation. Perhaps you have not seen this morning's *Examiner* from San Francisco. Independent Armenia is now a part of the New Russia.

KASPARIAN: I was informed by telephone from New York last night. The Russian invaders were driven off once before.

PAPAZIAN: I don't know what to say. The suffering of the people who are there must be beyond imagining. Hunger, cold, homelessness, fear, pain, sickness, madness, despair. Isn't it enough?

KASPARIAN: There will be more—much more, I'm afraid—whether Armenia is free or part of Russia. You seem distressed.

KNADJIAN: I am. I had heard rumors of this tragic development but I hoped. . . .

PAPAZIAN: Not tragic. It may be our salvation.

KNADJIAN: How? Please tell me how?

KASPARIAN: Let us agree not to argue, at any rate. We haven't got that much time. Let us also agree that we shall be very patient about our people in the home country, and very helpful to our people right here. There is the matter of our boys and girls growing up unable to read and write Armenian. And many marry members of other nationalities. And of course many of our young people either refuse to come to this church, or even to your church, or to yours, and if they do come, they are bored, and they even tell jokes to one another during the services.

PAPAZIAN: Yes, it is true. What shall we do?

KASPARIAN: We must work on the parents. If they do not teach their children to be Armenian, we can do nothing to improve the situation.

KNADJIAN: My wife is an Englishwoman, and so my children are only half-Armenian. I must confess I have not been able to make them love Armenia.

PAPAZIAN: And that is precisely how it is with me, too.

KASPARIAN: Well, forget your own children, then, but do not forget the children of Armenia, itself. And now I must say good-day, gentlemen.

PAPAZIAN: Let me sit a little longer, and then help me up, please.

KNADJIAN: As you say. Is it really a condition, or did you make a point of sitting in his presence because of his robes and the difference between his Christianity and yours?

PAPAZIAN: His Christianity is quite all right, it's his air of authority I find a little unacceptable. He thinks we are fools.

KNADJIAN: I frequently think so, too.

PAPAZIAN: Think for yourself. I don't think I am a fool at all. The Americans respect me.

KNADJIAN: Well, of course Father Kasparian doesn't speak English, so the Americans don't know him.

PAPAZIAN: They know he doesn't speak English. He has no right not to learn to speak English.

KNADJIAN: But your ankle, is it sprained or what?

PAPAZIAN: It is nothing, but I will not do the bidding of a man who believes the strange things that that man believes.

KNADJIAN: Christianity?

PAPAZIAN: No, I'm thinking of his politics.

KNADJIAN: I rather admire his politics. He does not want Armenia to disappear from the face of the earth. He believes it is important for Armenians to maintain their identity.

PAPAZIAN: That is a decision for God to make.

KNADJIAN: He wants to help God.

PAPAZIAN: That is not necessary.

KNADJIAN: I have always believed it is the one thing that is always necessary, but never mind, will you get up now?

PAPAZIAN: A moment longer. Where did he go so abruptly?

KNADJIAN: Oh, he has chores of many kinds, both ecclesiastical and secular. I believe he is making house calls this morning.

PAPAZIAN: What in the world for?

KNADJIAN: The sexton was speaking of it to an old friend when we came in. The old friend's wife is dying, and the sexton said, He will go with you in a moment. Didn't you notice? Didn't you hear? We stood there together.

PAPAZIAN: I was deep in thought. I noticed nothing, heard nothing.

KNADJIAN: Well, then, take my hand, I'll help you up. I must return to my study.

PAPAZIAN: What do you do when you go to your study? Sleep?

KNADJIAN: Oh, no. Plenty of time to sleep, at home. I wouldn't think of sleeping when I am in my study, the place I love best in this whole world.

PAPAZIAN: Is that so? Why?

KNADJIAN: I find that I am most myself there, I am most real there, I am most deeply Armenian when I am in my study. And of course I proceed with my work.

PAPAZIAN: Church work? You prepare your next sermon?

KNADJIAN: That, too, but I prefer to *make up* my sermon as I go along. When I am in my study my work is to write.

PAPAZIAN: What do you write? Love lyrics. So many preachers are secretly very amorous—at least in the head.

KNADJIAN: No, I write history. Well, at any rate I write what I have experienced, what I remember, what I was told, what I have felt, and of course I also invent out of these things a kind of truth which I think is greater than factual truth.

PAPAZIAN: And what truth is that?

KNADJIAN: Creative truth. The truth of art. Of passion of mind and spirit. Armenian truth.

PAPAZIAN: Are you all that Armenian?

KNADJIAN: Yes, I am. And you?

PAPAZIAN: I'm not sure. Sometimes I believe I am more English, but in the end, it seems, I am no such thing. I am only Armenian.

KNADJIAN: Only? Do you think there is something better to be?

PAPAZIAN: Possibly.

KASPARIAN: Gentlemen, are you still here?

PAPAZIAN: Alas, my ankle pains me.

KASPARIAN: Shall I have somebody telephone for an ambulance?

PAPAZIAN: Oh, no no, I will be all right.

KASPARIAN: Then, shall I have the woman bring tea. I take tea now, before I go back to work.

KNADJIAN: I think a cup of tea will be just fine, and it will give me an opportunity to say that I am in deep sorrow about conditions in Armenia.

PAPAZIAN: And so am I, but we must not make them worse. The people have suffered enough. Let us be patient.

KASPARIAN: Perhaps, but not for tea. Almast, please pour for three.

KNADJIAN: And who is Almast?

KASPARIAN: A woman of the neighborhood, who helps with such things.

PAPAZIAN: Isn't the name Kurdish? Almast?

KASPARIAN: The woman is Armenian—from Moush.

PAPAZIAN: In my congregation there are no people from Moush.

KASPARIAN: They are devoted to the true church, which as you know is Armenia itself. Here's tea, then. Help yourselves to sugar and lemon. Almast, these are the pastors of the Congregational Church, and of the Presbyterian Church.

ALMAST: Do you really believe?

PAPAZIAN: Of course we do. We are Christians, just as you are.

ALMAST: That's good. Then, believe, and perhaps all will be well.

KNADJIAN: Yes, yes, in time all will be well.

ALMAST: We shall all die, but before we do perhaps all will be well.

PAPAZIAN: Thank you, thank you.

KASPARIAN: She is more than eighty years old, but still as alive as a young woman.

KNADJIAN: And she has a very strong mind.

KASPARIAN: The mind of a woman of Moush.

PAPAZIAN: Come to think of it, you yourself are from Moush, are you not?

KASPARIAN: I am.

PAPAZIAN: A villager.

KASPARIAN: Yes, and you?

PAPAZIAN: I am from Aintab, but I studied in Istanbul, one of the leading cities of the world.

KASPARIAN: I only saw it once, from the deck of a ship, but I have never been there. And you?

KNADJIAN: I am from Marsovan.

KASPARIAN: I passed through Marsovan. My friends, the church in our country was the nation itself until the arrival of the missionaries. I do not know why you two became students at the missionary schools, but I am sure your reasons were sensible. They were the best schools with the best teachers, and in addition to everything else you studied and learned English.

PAPAZIAN: Also French, and a little German.

KASPARIAN: I read and write and speak only Armenian, as you know. I met all of the missionaries in Moush as a boy and I found them strangely unacceptable. They were Christian but they were not Armenian, that was what made the difference. And you are Christian, but you have each of you lost a little of that part of yourselves which was entirely Armenian.

PAPAZIAN: We are men of the world. The Christian world, of course.

KASPARIAN: That is true. I have heard about the sermons you have given in the English language, which have been heard by many Americans.

KNADJIAN: Since we are in dispersion it is desirable and necessary for us to become members of the society in which we find ourselves.

KASPARIAN: No doubt, but do you forget Armenia instantly? Can't you wait just a little? Give us a little time?

KNADJIAN: We need at least twenty years.

PAPAZIAN: At the very least ten.

KASPARIAN: No, gentlemen, we need a hundred years, at least.

PAPAZIAN: Let me thank you for asking us to come and visit, and also for this excellent tea. What kind is it?

KASPARIAN: I wanted to see you both, I wanted to have you see me, I wanted to exchange a few words with you, I wanted to find out if there is anything that we may expect from either of you.

PAPAZIAN: And the tea?

KASPARIAN: It is tea from the store. Lipton's. Ten cents. But Almast adds cloves and cinnamon and other things.

KNADJIAN: And I thank you for having me come to visit. As for the matter of what we may expect from one another, that is indeed something we are eager to learn—all of us, all our lives, but I wonder, do we ever learn, do we ever really find out?

PAPAZIAN: I expect from you a continuation of your traditional ecclesiastical procedures, in accordance with your training and the expectations of your congregation. Perhaps you will accept that volunteered statement, and then perhaps you will tell me what you expect of me.

KASPARIAN: Yes, that is only fair, but the expectation I am thinking of is not quite so superficial. Of course I shall do my work as I have been trained to do it, and you shall do yours as you have been trained, but there are other areas of expectation that I am concerned about.

KNADJIAN: What may we expect of one another not as men of God, if I may put it that way, but as men of the world, of the human race, of the nation, of the family?

KASPARIAN: Yes, that is coming nearer to the expectation I am thinking of.

PAPAZIAN: As a man I believe I may be counted on to take a neutral stand in all matters of politics.

KASPARIAN: Well, that is certainly a clear statement, but do you really believe it is possible for any man, let alone a man who gives guidance and instruction to hundreds of other men, to be neutral. Is there such a thing as neutrality?

PAPAZIAN: I believe there is. For instance, I am aware that you do not cherish the arrival of the Russians into the life of the new Armenian nation. I believe you have a perfect right to that feeling. Isn't that neutrality?

KASPARIAN: I don't know, but whatever neutrality is, it is not very useful to anybody, and time is running out, if we do not do useful things whenever it is possible or necessary to do them, we shall soon be totally departed from the human scene, and forgotten, or remembered only for having disappeared. Armenians are too vital to be permitted to throw themselves away in neutrality, comfort, well-being, satisfaction, and so on and so forth.

KNADJIAN: I believe I understand what you are saying. Please tell me what you would like to expect from both of us, or each of us, one at a time. What can I do for Armenia? We are nine thousand miles away from Armenia, and the Russians are *there*, what can I do at the First Armenian Presbyterian Church of Fresno, at Santa Clara and J Street?

KASPARIAN: Yes, you have every right to ask me, to ask yourself, to ask him that question. You can do precisely what you are obliged to do in the conduct of your duties, but you can add to all of that the powerful belief that Armenia, although occupied by the Russians, *is* Armenian, not Russian, and that the Armenian people will become more and more Armenian with time passing and more experience and wisdom of the world coming to them, and that furthermore Armenians in dispersion all over the world, but especially here in California, in Fresno, will continue to be Armenians, they will not become so foolishly American that being also Armenian will even be an embarrassment to them, and something to forget as quickly as possible, by marrying foreigners and bringing up children who neither know nor care that they are Armenians.

PAPAZIAN: I can't understand your excitement. It makes you say things that I'm not sure make sense.

KNADJIAN: I'm sure you do understand, for I do, and we both have children who are not interested in being Armenians.

SEXTON: Father, have you forgotten? They're waiting.

KASPARIAN: Ah, thank you, Markar. The funeral, is that correct?

SEXTON: No, Father. This is a baptism.

KASPARIAN: A boy or a girl?

SEXTON: Two boys, twins.

KASPARIAN: We don't often have twins.

SEXTON: The father is Irish, it's the mother who is Armenian.

KASPARIAN: And the father wants his sons baptised in the Armenian church?

SEXTON: He insists on it.

KASPARIAN: Who is this man?

SEXTON: The name is Michael Higgins. He will be able to say a few words to you in the Armenian language.

KASPARIAN: That is very interesting, I must say. And the mother, who is she?

SEXTON: Alice Bashbanian.

KASPARIAN: Bashban. Alice Bashbanian. And what are the names of the boys? Michael? Patrick? Something like that?

SEXTON: No, Father. Aram. Dikran.

KASPARIAN: Amazing. Aram Higgins. Dikran Higgins. It has a strange ring to it. Gentlemen, please keep your places, enjoy the tea, if you want anything, I will send Almast. Do not go. Wait for my return.

KNADJIAN: May I be present at the baptism?

KASPARIAN: Of course. I'm sure you know the ritual.

KNADJIAN: Yes, and I use it now and then.

PAPAZIAN: Please forgive me if I remain seated. My ankle.

KASPARIAN: Rest easy. Oh, Almast, please ask Reverend Papazian to have more tea and cakes.

ALMAST: Please let me fill your cup, and please have another cake.

PAPAZIAN: Thank you, and how long have you been serving the good Father?

ALMAST: Oh, just these few years. I have nobody now, these few years.

PAPAZIAN: Something happened? A loss?

ALMAST: Yes, several losses.

PAPAZIAN: If it is not too painful, perhaps you won't mind telling me about them.

ALMAST: They have all died. They were all killed.

PAPAZIAN: During these past few years? Who was it? Where did it happen?

ALMAST: Well, it was all of them. I am alone, except for the good Father, and the other people who come to the church.

PAPAZIAN: Being alone is sometimes a good thing, but it is also a very bad thing. I hope you have become at home within yourself, alone.

ALMAST: No, that has not happened. It is now six years since I lost them all, but I have not become at home within myself.

PAPAZIAN: You have God.

ALMAST: Yes, He is here in the church, always.

PAPAZIAN: And you have Jesus.

ALMAST: Well, I don't know about Jesus. I know we say we have Jesus, but I don't know. I know we have God, but I don't know Jesus, I really have no experience of Jesus.

PAPAZIAN: We are Christians, of course you have Jesus.

ALMAST: Yes, sir, if you say so.

PAPAZIAN: Our whole nation has Jesus.

ALMAST: Our nation is lost, and I lost all of my family in our loss of the nation. I do not blame Jesus, but I don't know if He has ever helped us.

PAPAZIAN: What you say is very strange for an Armenian. It was for Jesus that so many of us died.

ALMAST: But *we* did not, you and I, did we? Perhaps we don't care for Jesus very much.

PAPAZIAN: You are a very strange woman, I must say.

ALMAST: The good Father does not think so. We have talked about this many times, and he has never said that I am very strange.

KASPARIAN: Well now how is your foot?

PAPAZIAN: Better, thank you, Father, but it is not my foot, it is my ankle.

KNADJIAN: You should have seen the twins. One is blonde with blue eyes, the other is black haired with dark eyes—but they are brothers.

PAPAZIAN: I had a very interesting chat with your housekeeper, Father.

KASPARIAN: Will you have a drop? I need a drop.

PAPAZIAN: No, Father, thank you very much. I do not drink.

KASPARIAN: It might do your foot good.

PAPAZIAN: But they say alcoholic beverages are the very *cause* of gout.

KASPARIAN: Your gout is caused by something else, perhaps a drop will cure it—at least for a moment.

PAPAZIAN: The point is, I don't believe Almast is a Christian.

KASPARIAN: She is a woman, and a good woman.

PAPAZIAN: But this is a Christian church.

KASPARIAN: And Almast is a very important part of this church.

PAPAZIAN: But she doesn't believe in Jesus.

KNADJIAN: Take a sip of this fine *rakhi*, it will do you good.

PAPAZIAN: I do not believe in the use of alcoholic beverages under any circumstances.

KNADJIAN: Take a sip *without* believing.

PAPAZIAN: That is not possible for me. Is it possible for you?

KNADJIAN: Yes, I accept certain things without knowing very much about them.

PAPAZIAN: Such as? Are you speaking in riddles, parables, and proverbs?

KNADJIAN: Oh, no. But I don't know very much about anything, and yet I *have* everything that I have in this kind of ignorance and faith.

PAPAZIAN: I like to know what I have and what I don't have, and why.

KASPARIAN: I am renewed.

PAPAZIAN: By the alcohol? Is that what you are saying?

KASPARIAN: By the variety that is in as few as three or four people. The inexhaustible variety of the human race. Of the Armenians. Of one family of Armenians. And perhaps by the inexhaustible variety in only one Armenian.

PAPAZIAN: Which Armenian is that?

KASPARIAN: Any Armenian. Yourself, for instance.

PAPAZIAN: I am consistent, and uncontradictory, there is no variety in me.

KASPARIAN: Perhaps, or is it that you don't know about yourself, your consistency, your contradictions, and your variety.

PAPAZIAN: I am a steadfast Christian. But that is an established fact. The whole world knows that. I share the pulpits of many churches in this city. I am written about in both of the daily newspapers.

KASPARIAN: I have heard. What do you *say* in your sermons?

PAPAZIAN: Well, of course that depends on the topic, doesn't it? On Mother's Day I speak of mothers. On Father's Day I speak of fathers. I tell the world to be like Jesus.

KASPARIAN: Yes, that is a good thing to tell anybody. Again, I must tear myself away from such good company and such good talk. Almast is here to remind me of my next chore.

ALMAST: This is an emergency. Akob Dudu's dying. She wants you to give her the last rites. Her granddaughter has come to fetch you. The little girl will take you to their house. It isn't far.

KASPARIAN: Very well, and thank you, gentlemen. Please come again and let us continue our discussions.

KNADJIAN: Thank you, Father, but I hesitate to intrude and take up your valuable time.

KASPARIAN: No, no, come any time you like, if I'm not here, I will be soon enough. And you, be sure you come here any time you like. I enjoy our talks.

PAPAZIAN: I don't seem to make any impression on you, however. You don't seem to mind at all if somebody who works in your church is not even a Christian.

KASPARIAN: I mind, but I mind other things, too. Good day, gentlemen.

KNADJIAN: Then, let me help you to your feet, and back to your church.

PAPAZIAN: Do you have a carriage, to take me?

KNADJIAN: No, but I can support you as we walk. It's only four blocks. In the old country we ran four miles as if it were nothing.

PAPAZIAN: This is not the old country, and we are no longer boys, we are men, and old men at that.

KNADJIAN: I do not consider myself an old man. But up, now, lean on me, up, what's the matter with your ankle?

PAPAZIAN: Both of my ankles have gone bad. First one and then the other. I don't know what it is. I am forty-four years old, is that your age, also?

KNADJIAN: I see, I see. I am even older than you, I am forty-eight, and I do not consider myself an old man, at all, I consider myself nearer to boyhood than to senility. Why should your ankles go bad?

PAPAZIAN: I wish I knew. I really wish I knew.

KNADJIAN: And your doctor, what does he say? You have gone to a doctor, I presume. A man of your character does not neglect bad ankles. An Armenian doctor, because when a man is in pain he likes to speak the family language.

PAPAZIAN: Yes, yes, your understanding is quite good. I went first to the Americans—to three different doctors, the most famous ones—and then I went to the old Armenian.

KNADJIAN: Jivvy?

PAPAZIAN: Do you call him Jivvy?

KNADJIAN: Jivelekian is an old friend, and we have always spoken to one another as if we were still boys in the old country. He calls me Mugo, for Muggerditch of course. Jivvy is not only a good doctor he is a good man. And what did he prescribe to relieve the pain?

PAPAZIAN: He didn't prescribe anything. Ah, well, how shall I put it. He told me to pray. Imagine the impertinence of such a suggestion. Praying is my profession, medicine is his. I went to him for medical help, he turns around and tells me to get ecclesiastical help. He tells me to pray.

KNADJIAN: Jivvy's very wise.

PAPAZIAN: Well, of course I did not let him know I was annoyed. After all, I consider myself a man of some refinement.

KNADJIAN: Speak of the devil. Dr. Jivelekian, what are you doing *here*?

JIVELEKIAN: Gentlemen, gentlemen. The priest sent for me. It seems somebody is dying. Where is the priest?

PAPAZIAN: He's gone to the dying woman's bedside. Look here, Dr. Jivelekian, my ankles are making a terrible fool of me. Surely there are pills I can take to restore the ankles to their proper strength.

JIVELEKIAN: Aspirin. I suggest aspirin to everybody, for everything. Are you taking aspirin?

PAPAZIAN: No, Doctor. Aspirin is for headaches. It is my ankles that hurt.

JIVELEKIAN: Take two aspirin every time you remember that your ankles hurt. Before you know it they won't hurt any more. Your feet and your ankles and your legs, and for that matter your whole body seems to be quite sound. A couple of aspirin now and then is all you really need. Who is dying?

PAPAZIAN: An old woman. An old woman.

JIVELEKIAN: Well, I must get to her. Who is she? Where is she?

KNADJIAN: Akob Dudu. Do you know where she lives?

JIVELEKIAN: Yes, of course, I've been there many times.

PAPAZIAN: Poor woman.

KNADJIAN: Why are you sitting down, Dr. Jivelekian?

JIVELEKIAN: I can't help her.

KNADJIAN: What is her illness?

JIVELEKIAN: I don't know. The same as the good Reverend's ankle trouble. Who knows?

KNADJIAN: Let us go across the street to the Patriotic Club and have a small coffee apiece. Here, hold onto me, you'll be all right.

PAPAZIAN: Thank you, thank you, friendship is a fine thing.

JIVELEKIAN: And a game of cards, too. Agreed, Mugo?

KNADJIAN: Agreed, Jivvy.

ACT TWO

The Armenian Patriotic Club on Ventura Street opposite the Red Brick Church.

KNADJIAN: Dr. Jivelekian, are you sure we should be sitting here in the Patriotic Club sipping coffee?

JIVELEKIAN: Of course I'm sure. Why do you ask?

KNADJIAN: I find that I have great anxiety about the old woman, Akob Dudu. Perhaps you and I, who have good ankles, ought to get up from this table immediately and hurry to her house, where the good Father is, and do what we can for the old lady.

JIVELEKIAN: Forget it. I have been to Akob Dudu's house a dozen times so far this year. She is just fine.

PAPAZIAN: But you said you couldn't help her. How can she be just fine?

JIVELEKIAN: She's eighty-eight years old. Little things go wrong with her all the time. My visits improve the day for her, a little, I suppose. The last time I was there, day before yesterday, she was bored, that's all.

PAPAZIAN: Doctor, I hesitate to say this, but it seems to me that now more than ever, you of all people, should go to the old woman and keep her company. I would go except for my ankles, but my being with her couldn't mean anything much, considering Father Kasparian is there, and he will attend to the needs of her immortal soul, but you are needed, for you attend to the needs of her body. It is your duty to go to the old woman.

JIVELEKIAN: I suppose it is in a way, but I am afraid I am not going to do my duty today. I'm going to sit here and enjoy this coffee and then a game of cards—will you play, Reverend Papazian?

PAPAZIAN: Cards? Oh, no, no, no, no, no, no. Look at all of these unfortunate men in this Patriotic Club, all of them past fifty, all of them able-bodied, and all of them idle. Idleness is very dangerous. It leads to trouble. They should be out in the world doing good works.

KNADJIAN: I believe they *were* out in the world and they have done their good works for the year, now it is time to rest. The season's over, the crops are harvested, the year's rewards have been received, the interest on the bank loans have been made, clothes have been bought for the children, so they can look well at school, and so these good farmers are enjoying a well-earned rest.

PAPAZIAN: Farmers? They are not all farmers, only one or two are farmers, the rest are loafers, that's what they are. Useless men. They produce nothing.

KNADJIAN: There isn't one man in this place who hasn't produced children.

JIVELEKIAN: And I have brought into the world about half of those children. All healthy, too, I might say. Let the boys have their innocent fun.

PAPAZIAN: But is it innocent? Is idleness ever innocent?

JIVELEKIAN: They are not idle. They are busy concentrating on the card games, or the backgammon games, or the reading of the coffee grounds in their cups, or the news from Armenia. Well, what is it now?

KNADJIAN: For the second time in a year the Russians have taken over Armenia.

JIVELEKIAN: Is that so? And if it is so, and there is nothing we can do about it, what shall we do?

PAPAZIAN: Nothing. That is the wisest course in such political matters. Let time make some sense out of the wrongs and rights.

JIVELEKIAN: Yes, there is something to that. Be patient and something will happen.

KNADJIAN: In the meantime, are we entitled to forget that members of the Armenian government have been placed in jail and some of them have been shot, and others will be jailed and shot? That is the question.

PAPAZIAN: How can we help them? Did we do anything to have them jailed or shot?

KNADJIAN: No, I only mean, this is something to think about, at least.

JIVELEKIAN: If you want to know the truth, any time I can't sleep I find that I am thinking about our *intellectuals* jailed and shot. I don't like it.

PAPAZIAN: Of course not. What do you see in your coffee grounds?

JIVELEKIAN: Mountains and meadows and rivers—Armenia. It makes me angry.

KNADJIAN: Well, shuffle the cards and let's have a game, shall we?

JIVELEKIAN: We shall, we shall indeed.

FARMER: Dr. Jivelekian, excuse me.

JIVELEKIAN: Yes, what is it?

FARMER: Can I speak to you a moment?

JIVELEKIAN: Yes, go right ahead, just speak.

FARMER: My back hurts.

JIVELEKIAN: What have you done in the way of work to make it hurt?

FARMER: Well, of course I've been loading heavy boxes of raisins onto wagons for taking to the packing house.

JIVELEKIAN: How heavy?

FARMER: Well, the small boxes are eighty pounds, but the big boxes are two hundred, and two men lift the big boxes.

JIVELEKIAN: Rest your back, it will be all right.

FARMER: It hurts.

JIVELEKIAN: I'm here for a little recreation, in the form of a card game. If you want to go into the matter more extensively, go to my office at two o'clock this afternoon.

FARMER: Your office? If I go to your office, you will charge me a dollar, we are countrymen, how can you be so mercenary?

JIVELEKIAN: Go to my office, and I promise, I will charge you nothing. I want to finish this game of *scambile*.

FARMER: But if I go to your office I will have to leave the backgammon tournament, and I'm winning.

JIVELEKIAN: Well what do you want me to do? I'm perfectly willing to be as patriotic as possible. Your back hurts. You've been lifting heavy boxes, so of course it hurts. I've told you, rest your back. You are not satisfied with that. What will make you happy, sir?

FARMER: I'm seventy-four years old. I thought you would want to study my back.

JIVELEKIAN: Very well. Turn around. There you are. Your back is very strong. You've strained the muscles a little from doing heavy work, but if you avoid such work, your back will be just fine again very soon. I'm fifty-eight years old.

FARMER: Suppose I get into a hot tub tonight before bedtime? Will that help?

JIVELEKIAN: Yes, it will.

FARMER: And what are we going to do about the news from Armenia?

JIVELEKIAN: Is your back all right, now?

FARMER: The Russians have taken the country again.

JIVELEKIAN: I've heard. I'm thinking about it. I don't know what we can do. I would certainly like to finish this game of *scambile*.

FARMER: Our intellectuals, they say, poets, and professors, they are in jail, and some of them have been shot. Shall we raise money?

JIVELEKIAN: Yes, I think raising money would be a very good idea.

FARMER: How much money?

JIVELEKIAN: Well, twenty-eight thousand dollars.

FARMER: What shall we do with money?

JIVELEKIAN: Send it to Armenia, of course.

FARMER: So the Russians will eat it? Oh, no, thank you very much Dr. Jivelekian, we have done foolish things in the past, and we will do foolish things in the future, but we are not going to send our twenty-eight thousand dollars to the Russian invaders.

JIVELEKIAN: Send the money to the Armenians in jail.

FARMER: You must be very innocent of the world, Doctor. The Russians wouldn't let the Armenians in jail have a pomegranate apiece, let alone money.

JIVELEKIAN: Is your back all right?

FARMER: It seems a little improved.

JIVELEKIAN: Go and talk to somebody over there about these matters, and be sure to argue with him.

FARMER: Argue? Why?

JIVELEKIAN: It will make your back feel better. It is amazing how any Armenian feels that he is entitled to intrude on any other Armenian simply because each of them is Armenian.

KNADJIAN: It's not amazing at all. We are a small people, and we have been in geographical, political, cultural, economic, and religious trouble for a long time. We need one another, every last one of us.

JIVELEKIAN: Are you saying I should not have asked the farmer to go away? Is that it; if so I will call the farmer back.

KNADJIAN: No, my friend, I am not saying any such thing, but I am saying that it is perfectly reasonable for any Armenian to make demands on any other Armenian solely because they are Armenians. If we can't bother one another as long as we are on this earth, can we do so in heaven? I am a Presbyterian preacher, and I do not recall that being free to bother another Armenian is one of the promises of the Christian heaven.

JIVELEKIAN: Of course it isn't. Besides, I did suffer the fool—oh, please forgive me, I must not be so crude, so rude, so unkind, the man is not a fool, he is a farmer, but in any case I did suffer him, I listened to him, I gave him the best advice I was able to give, there is no need for every Presbyterian preacher who comes along to nag at me that I am neither a good Armenian nor a good Christian. Now, if the truth is told I am in fact not much of a Christian, I don't really think it is anywhere near as good a religion as one or two of the others, and while I am not prepared to remark that there really is nothing special about being an Armenian, I also cannot say that that fact alone permits any of us to believe we are entitled to anything anybody else is not entitled to.

KNADJIAN: Do you know what you are talking about?

JIVELEKIAN: Of course not. The farmer took my mind from the peace I came here for, and then your Presbyterian reproach annoyed me so deeply, because you know we are friends, that I have forgotten really how to think, so you tell me what are we talking about?

KNADJIAN: He wanted to know what we are to do about the situation in Armenia.

JIVELEKIAN: I see, and what did we tell him. I, as a doctor, and you, as a preacher. What were we able to manage between us as a message of wisdom or comfort for the farmer. Did I say perhaps the most sensible thing for you to do, sir, is to attend to your vineyard, prune your vines, water them, harvest your grapes, eat them, give away some, and the rest sell to the packing houses or the wineries. Did I say that?

KNADJIAN: You did not.

JIVELEKIAN: Should I have said it?

KNADJIAN: Perhaps, if you might manage to say it without being sarcastic.

JIVELEKIAN: I am not sarcastic, I was not sarcastic, I hate sarcasm, I hate sarcastic people, the people of Bitlis are sarcastic people, I hate the people of Bitlis, they are always pointing out the pretenses and pomposities of other people, I am afraid of the people of Bitlis, I know they will see through me and laugh at my silly eccentricities, my little vanities, my pride, or whatever else in me that is flawed and unworthy—the people of Bitlis will see it and say something sarcastic about it. God deliver me from the people of Bitlis.

BITLIS: Excuse me, I couldn't help overhearing a little of what you were saying. Do I understand you are looking for somebody from Bitlis to perhaps give you valuable guidance in a matter of business. I am from Bitlis.

JIVELEKIAN: How do you do, how do you do?

BITLIS: How can I be of help to you, sir.

JIVELEKIAN: I am a doctor, and I get these pains at the back of my head.

BITLIS: Very simple, doctor. When you go home tonight put your feet in a tub of hot water and at the same time drink four glasses of hot lemonade. The pain will go.

JIVELEKIAN: Thank you.

BITLIS: Don't mention it.

MOUSH: Why are you sitting here playing cards when Armenia is bleeding from its terrible wounds?

KNADJIAN: Well, we are having a short rest before returning to our sorrow about Armenia. And who are you, sir?

MOUSH: Surely you can tell from my speech that I am a man from Moush.

KNADJIAN: Yes, that's true. And your profession is . . . watchmaking?

MOUSH: There has never been a watchmaker from Moush.

JIVELEKIAN: Furthermore, we are not playing cards, although we sat here in the *expectation* of doing so, but who can play cards when people from Bitlis and Moush come up and ask questions?

MOUSH: The interruption of your card game costs you no blood.

JIVELEKIAN: I thank God for that. Have we your permission to play?

MOUSH: There is always time to play. You are grown men. This man is a preacher. A Protestant of course, but still some sort of a Christian and some sort of an Armenian. I don't know what you are.

JIVELEKIAN: I am a doctor.

MOUSH: Of philosophy or something like that?

JIVELEKIAN: A medical doctor.

MOUSH: A medical doctor in this place of patriotic idleness, instead of in his office, healing the sick and comforting the hale?

JIVELEKIAN: This is in fact my lunch hour. I must also have a moment of diversion, the same as everybody else.

MOUSH: I do not have a moment of diversion. I have never had a moment of diversion. I stand guard over the soul of Armenia at all times.

JIVELEKIAN: I really would like to play this hand of *scambile* with the good Protestant preacher here.

MOUSH: Which doctor *are* you doctor? By name?

JIVELEKIAN: Jivelekian, from Boston, Harvard Medical School.

MOUSH: I've heard of you.

JIVELEKIAN: And may I ask which man of Moush are you?

MOUSH: I am Baghdasar.

JIVELEKIAN: Baghdasar of Moush, is that right?

MOUSH: That is right.

JIVELEKIAN: Have you a family name?

MOUSH: Der Kaprielian. Baghdasar Der Kaprielian.

JIVELEKIAN: That's very impressive, very impressive indeed. And what is your profession, sir? What do you do for a living?

MOUSH: Well, in season I add corks to wine bottles.

JIVELEKIAN: You add corks to wine bottles.

MOUSH: For Krikor Arakelian.

JIVELEKIAN: How long is the season?

MOUSH: A week. A solid week. The sorrow and darkness. . . . Have you ever put corks into the mouths of wine bottles, Doctor?

JIVELEKIAN: No, I haven't.

MOUSH: Stick to your own work, then. Who will ever know, who will ever guess what I have been through in order to earn the money for bread?

KNADJIAN: You are quite right, no man knows another's suffering.

MOUSH: But a week of corks and bottle-mouths is not the same as being in jail in Armenia.

KNADJIAN: That's quite true, there is a difference.

MOUSH: So what are we going to do about it? Our brothers are in jail.

JIVELEKIAN: We certainly can't do anything from here, so perhaps you will permit us to continue our game, after all.

MOUSH: If you insist on being irresponsible and insensitive, then by all means go ahead, but do not expect me to think of you as an Armenian.

JIVELEKIAN: But I am an Armenian.

MOUSH: Only in word, not in act. God help us one and all if *you* are to be our salvation.

JIVELEKIAN: Ah, well, let me put it this way. I do my best. I do my best.

MOUSH: Your best is not good enough.

JIVELEKIAN: All right, Reverend Knadjian, what shall we do? Shall we sit here and chat with our countrymen, shall we sit here and play cards, or shall we sit here and sip coffee?

KNADJIAN: Well, Dr. Jivelekian, I see no reason why we shouldn't do all three. We certainly have *already* done them in any case, haven't we?

JIVELEKIAN: We have not played cards.

KNADJIAN: Ah, well, perhaps we can forget cards.

VAN: I understand you gentlemen have been discussing the realities of very recent Armenian history. What is your position?

JIVELEKIAN: You take this one, Reverend Knadjian.

VAN: Oh, you are a man of the church, are you? From your clothes it is not perfectly clear, although your face does have the earnestness of a man who believes in prayer. Can praying help recent Armenian history, Reverend?

KNADJIAN: Yes, I think we are all pretty much in agreement about that, since we are Christian, but I would say that praying must be supplemented by goods and action.

VAN: I see. Goods and action. What goods? What action?

KNADJIAN: Well, first of course we pray, and then we consider what our countrymen need—money, medicine, food, clothing, shelter, but most of all the moral support of a powerful nation which can force the oppressor to cease and desist, and to leave our country and return to his own.

VAN: And who would that nation be, may I ask?

KNADJIAN: Well, our neighbors are the Persians, the Syrians, the Turks, the Greeks, and the Russians. But of course the Russians have invaded our country, and they are the biggest and most powerful of our neighbors. Of the others none is powerful enough to force the Russians away, and so we must think of a powerful nation which is not a neighbor.

VAN: England?

KNADJIAN: England could do the job if England would be willing to do it.

VAN: Italy?

KNADJIAN: No, Italy is not powerful enough. And for that matter neither is France. The truth is only England in Europe can do it, and in the rest of the world only America can do it.

VAN: Then, we must ask America to help us.

KNADJIAN: We have done so—officially, and with proper intelligence, but America has refused.

VAN: So now what do we do?

KNADJIAN: Well, unless we are willing to believe that perhaps the Russians will *not* be oppressors of our people, we must think about trying to drive the Russians out of Armenia. And that means that we must raise money and buy goods and pay to ship them to Armenia, and we must hire experts of all kinds, and pay them to do their work.

VAN: We don't have money like that.

KNADJIAN: Yes, the problem is a difficult and complicated one.

VAN: Well, now, about these Russians in Armenia, what are they doing?

KNADJIAN: Their propaganda claims that they are rescuing Armenia from its enemies, within and without, and they are bringing hospitals, schools, industry, agriculture, security and peace to the Armenian people.

VAN: Do you believe that?

KNADJIAN: I suppose not, but at the same time if we can't throw the Russians out, we are almost *obliged* to believe it, aren't we, or at any rate to believe some of it. We don't have any choice. We have fought many losing battles. We really ought not to fight any more.

VAN: I don't know, I don't know. I am from Van, and we have lost so many souls.

KNADJIAN: Yes, we are all in sorrow.

BITLIS: What is it now, you two? Have you made another man unhappy?

JIVELEKIAN: I don't think so, but if we have, it has not been intentional.

BITLIS: It doesn't matter about that part of it, you shouldn't say things to good Armenians and make them unhappy. That man over there from Moush, he is in tears.

JIVELEKIAN: What is he in tears *about*?

BITLIS: Armenia, of course. When, when, when is Armenia going to be permitted to be free?

KNADJIAN: Well, we are all concerned about that. We are all asking God that question.

BITLIS: Since God has not answered the question, let us ask somebody else.

MOUSH: What is your suggestion? Who shall we ask?

BITLIS: Woodrow Wilson.

KNADJIAN: Well, of course we might ask our friend Woodrow Wilson, but I am afraid he is dead.

MOUSH: Woodrow Wilson is dead? Are you sure?

KNADJIAN: Yes, he died quite some time ago. Of a broken heart, they say.

JIVELEKIAN: As well as a good variety of other things. The fact is he had a stroke.

BITLIS: Heartbreak, heartbreak killed our only friend in the world, the father of Armenia Restored, Mr. Woodrow Wilson. Oh, this is a sad day.

MOUSH: Doom, doom, doom. Is that to be forever the lot of Armenians?

VAN: Never. Don't say that. We have been stopped here and there and now and then, but in the end let us not forget that we have always moved on. Shame on you men of Moush and Bitlis, giving up to despair. We of Van believe in Armenia, we believe in Armenians.

MOUSH: Do you believe in Russians? They have occupied our country.

VAN: Yes, I believe in Russians.

MOUSH: Do not say that, sir. You will force me to the knife.

VAN: Look here, if it's Russians who have taken the chair of government in Armenia, hadn't we better watch and wait before we begin to stick knives into one another. Where all this is happening is very far from here. I understand it is eight thousand miles from the Patriotic Club on Ventura Avenue in Fresno, California to the seat of government in Erevan, Armenia.

MOUSH: Nine thousand, and the Russians are sitting in that seat. I want them out.

VAN: Drop them a line, tell them you can't sleep for the sorrow in your heart, or tell them that if they don't get out, you will write a second letter.

MOUSH: It is stupid to argue with a man from Van. Let me say to my neighbor from Bitlis, we must not let our beloved cities fall away from Armenia.

JIVELEKIAN: They have already fallen away, they are not even a part of that Armenia which is now governed by the Russians. Bitlis and Moush are part of Turkey, gentlemen.

MOUSH: I beg of you, don't say that

JIVELEKIAN: I'm sorry, it's true.

MOUSH: How did it, how did it *ever*, please tell me sir how did it happen, how did it happen?

JIVELEKIAN: Woodrow Wilson drew a map of the true and real Armenia, but neither he nor anybody else saw to it that the Armenians became the lords of their own country, and the map grew smaller and smaller until it was almost nothing but Erevan and two or three vineyards around it—not even as much land as we have in Fresno *county*.

MOUSH: Is this true?

JIVELEKIAN: Yes, it is, I am sorry, yes, it is.

MOUSH: *Vy*, alas, glorious Armenia, alas majestic Moush, gone, gone, torn away from one another. I refuse to speak.

JIVELEKIAN: This is a place of rest, why is everybody here so restless?

BITLIS: Perhaps you will answer your own question, but if you can't do that, isn't it because we are all of us here in mourning for Mother Armenia? Isn't it because we are at the funeral of our beloved nation?

KNADJIAN: Yes, we are all very much concerned about the second invasion of the Russians.

MOUSH: We drove them out the first time, and it did seem that now at last we would be a free and independent nation, but no, the Russians came back, and they are now sitting in Erevan: Why? Why does God give us so little reason to thank Him? You are a man of the church, although a Protestant, tell us why?

KNADJIAN: Well, of course I am not any more pleased about the unhappy situation in Armenia than you are. We are all of us very unhappy about having the invaders back a second time, but I wonder if we have a right to take the attitude that it is God who has brought them back a second time.

BITLIS: Did God bring them in the first time?

KNADJIAN: Well, I'm not sure we can believe *that*, either.

JIVELEKIAN: If we are going to drag God into this, hadn't we better begin at the beginning? Did God create the earth, or did the earth happen as the consequence of some other order of event, entirely? That is, not a creation, at all.

BITLIS: How can that be? What are you saying?

KNADJIAN: Yes, even these unschooled men are astonished at such talk. It is heresy.

JIVELEKIAN: It is meant to be *only* science. If you are going to forget your schooling, I am not going to forget mine, these good men deserve the latest information that is available to the human race.

MOUSH: What are you talking about? Are you being professors with peasants, is that it? Talk our language.

JIVELEKIAN: I am asking how can we blame God for bringing the Russians to Armenia the first time and then the second time, when first of all we are not sure God did any such thing, and in the second place we don't even know if God brought the human race itself to the earth — in the first place.

MOUSH: Of course God did it. God did it all, and that's the end of the matter, it's what we believe, and we don't have any reason, therefore, not to believe it.

JIVELEKIAN: Well, there is *that*, of course, but it isn't scientific.

BITLIS: What is scientific, if you don't mind? Perhaps it will help us to understand why God has betrayed us twice — recently. A thousand times, twice, in times gone by. And we are Christians. So what is scientific?

JIVELEKIAN: I can't speak for all who respect science, but I think I may say that science is simply the study of the truth about everything. You find out in science, whereas in religion you believe, you agree to believe, and you pay no attention to new discoveries in the realm of truth.

BITLIS: Are you saying that what we believe, what we have believed for so long is untrue? Are you an Armenian, or something else?

KNADJIAN: Let me intercede here for the Doctor. He is indeed a Christian, a good man, a believer in God, a lover of humanity, and a true Armenian, but he is also a doctor of medicine, he saves human lives by medicine and surgery, and he knows that if he had not learned medicine, he would not have been able to save lives.

MOUSH: Let him save the life of Armenia—if he knows so much.

JIVELEKIAN: I will certainly do my best to help save the life of Armenia, just as you will do your best, as each of us will. That is both science and religion—and perhaps even art.

MOUSH: I don't understand.

KNADJIAN: Gentlemen, boys, men of Van, Moush, and Bitlis, patriotic Armenians one and all, let me suggest that we bear in mind that we are at a disadvantage at this moment insofar as speaking intelligently with one another is concerned, for we are unhappy about our beloved Armenia. In other words, let us make a point of not fighting one another.

BITLIS: Who's fighting? Our brothers in Armenia have been fighting, and many of them have been killed and injured, while we have been living like kings in Fresno, California.

MOUSH: We have been living, but not like kings. A man dying in Armenia is living like a king. A man living like a king in Fresno is actually dying like a dog. Is this a life? Is this living?

VAN: Well, we are here, in any case, and we were not forced to come here. Of course this is a life, it is a good life. Of course this is living.

MOUSH: This is dying, this is not living at all. Our brothers are living, even the ones who are dead. And I'll tell you why, too. They are home, they are in Armenia, they are in the land under the sun of our noble race, but where are we—we are somewhere else, far away.

JIVELEKIAN: I would like to suggest that it is a very good thing that we are in fact here. This is a great place to be.

MOUSH: How can you say that. Is Fresno Moush? It is not. Is it Bitlis? It is not. Is it Van? It is not.

JIVELEKIAN: Of course not. It is Fresno, though. It is where so many of us have made ourselves at home, doing our work as we know how to do it, buying and cultivating vineyards, learning and practicing professions, opening stores, practicing crafts. Gentlemen, we are here. We are not in Armenia.

VAN: Please don't remind me of that.

JIVELEKIAN: Don't you like it here?

VAN: It is not what I expected.

JIVELEKIAN: Well, we are all of us always disappointed when we go to a place about which we have heard many many beautiful stories. What did you expect?

VAN: I expected a much better life than this life.

JIVELEKIAN: Well, that may be a personal matter. Perhaps you must think about it a little longer. You look very well for a man of fifty or more. You wear good clothes. What is it that you don't like?

VAN: The water. It's not as good as the water of Van. The greens are not as green, either. Parsley, onions, bell peppers, cucumbers, they are all greener and better in Van.

JIVELEKIAN: Those are serious failings, no doubt about it, but I find it hard to believe that you do not like the water of Fresno. It is the best water I have ever drunk.

VAN: You have never quenched your thirst on the water of Van?

JIVELEKIAN: Alas, no.

VAN: The water of Van is water. This is also water, but it is not the water of Van, it does not give life to the soul, it gives life only to the body. Armenians are people with soul. And the soul must have air, light, and water.

JIVELEKIAN: It seems to me that we are forgetting to be grateful, which is a very foolish thing. Gentlemen, we are lucky, we are very lucky to be in Fresno, to have our families here, and it is wrong not to remember this.

BITLIS: I remember it. I am very happy to be here, but that doesn't mean I don't also remember Bitlis—we were up, up, high up, far, far below we saw the river of Bitlis racing through the deep valley to the heart of Bitlis itself. I can't forget that, can I, just because we are here?

JIVELEKIAN: No, that's quite true, but you are here, so enjoy it.

MOUSH: Do we have to?

KNADJIAN: Ah, here, you, are, sir. Please sit down. Take my chair. I'll get another.

PAPAZIAN: No, no, I shall stay only a moment, I simply must go to a doctor about my ankles. I only want to say, countrymen, each of you, let us thank God that Armenia is still there, and that we are still here, and that we owe it all to the grace and goodness of God.

MOUSH: What did he say, this Protestant? Countrymen, something and something.

VAN: Be careful, this is Reverend Papazian. He has given sermons in American churches in the English language.

MOUSH: I know who he is. He thinks the Americans are the real people, and he tries to be like them, and to think like them, because he thinks Armenians are too backward and too loud and too unreasonable and too angry about everything, and of course he means me, he means you, and he means that man from Bitlis, he doesn't mean himself when he thinks about Armenians, he means us, he thinks Armenia would be just fine if *we* had been killed instead of the people who were killed, but we *were* killed because we are the same kind as the people who were killed, and that's why we are always thrashing around from the pains we knew before we died, and that's why we always want to know before we die that our dying helped, that our terrible dying helped Armenia remain Armenia, what does a pompous little Protestant preacher know about Armenia, and Armenians, this little black-bearded man is no Armenian, he is not American, he is a member of no nationality because he thinks he and God are comrades who go about spreading benedictions everywhere. Well, sir, little sire, just forget the bargain sanctity and spread some guns and bread to Armenians, that's all.

PAPAZIAN: The man is obviously insane, but I forgive him.

MOUSH: Yes, well, I don't forgive you. Who asked you to come here and insult the tragic Armenian soul?

KNADJIAN: That's enough, sir, that's enough, whatever it is that moves you to anger and sorrow, do not take it out on a perfectly innocent preacher of the gospel. He is a good man, he works hard, he helps everybody he can, please do not imagine you must believe he is your enemy. You Van, you Bitlis, please take your friend away. Get him a small coffee, sit down together, think, think before you speak, think twice before you shout, think three times before you go mad. Tell the waiter to bring the bill to me, I'll pay for it.

BITLIS: Oh, you are most generous, sir. Three coffees, five cents each, fifteen cents. You have just saved Armenia, no doubt about it. How can we ever thank you? Shall we build a monument to you, and to your little black-bearded brother, and put it in the Court House Park of Fresno? Why do Protestant preachers feel that the people are all fools?

JIVELEKIAN: Gentlemen, gentlemen, I can only speak for myself, a practicing physician and surgeon, and I must say that my heart is sick with sorrow, not only because of recent developments in Armenia, of the second return of the Russians to the seat of government, but because of recent developments right here, among us. Can't we understand that this sort of annoyance and belittlement of one another is terribly destructive, that it will soon enough destroy us? That we will become a people without a culture, and must therefore perish forever?

MOUSH: We shall *not* perish. Armenia shall not perish. Armenians shall not perish. Doctors and preachers may perish, and let them perish, that is no affair of ours, but we shall not, we shall never agree to perish, the more appealing the world makes perishing the more we shall refuse to perish. We are Armenians, and even though we are eight or nine thousand miles away from where we were born, we are still in Armenia, we are still there, and this very place, this patriotic coffee house, is Armenia. Preachers and doctors can go to hell. The people lie in their Armenian graves, or stand in their homes, or sit and stand in this place, and refuse to be polite about indestructible Armenia.

KNADJIAN: Dr. Jivelekian I'm afraid it is useless to remain in this unhappy atmosphere, and so let me put down these cards and say goodbye, I must go.

JIVELEKIAN: But the game hasn't even *started*, Reverend Knadjian. Surely you don't expect me to waste the opportunity to test your mettle at cards. I've paid the dime for the deck of cards, for one hour. I shuffled, you cut, I dealt, and now suddenly you stand and say you must leave this unhappy atmosphere, you must go. What about my dime?

KNADJIAN: I love the game, and I would gladly test your mettle in the playing of the game, but we sat down at a time of great unhappiness in the people who come here every day. And of course when they see a man of the Church with a man of Medicine, it is understandable that they want to talk, but when they do talk, they argue, they ask impossible questions, it wears out a man's soul just trying to know what they mean. Sir, if you don't mind what do you mean?

MOUSH: I mean exactly what I said, exactly what I have always said, exactly what every Armenian with any salt and vinegar in his veins would say. We are here. We are Armenians. Whether we are from Van, Moush, Bitlis, Harpoot, Dikranagert, Trabizond, Erzeroum, Malatia, or wherever, we are here, and we are Armenians. And Van is there, and Moush is there, and Bitlis is there, and all of the other Armenian cities are there, and our dead are there, and perhaps a few of our living are still there, God help them one and all, surrounded by enemies and danger, famine and homelessness, but let us just remember this, that whoever they are which are still there, in the cities of the real Armenia, not the Russian Armenia, *they* are the nation, and the nation shall not end, it is the will of God, it is the will of the World, it is the will of History and Truth, it is the will of Art that Armenia shall not end, Armenia shall endure, that is what I mean, sir, that is exactly what I mean, what do *you* mean?

BITLIS: I am dumbfounded. Where the devil did you ever learn to talk that way? Was that *you*?

MOUSH: It *was* me. It is me. But it is really Armenia, it is Moush, it is Shah-Mouradian, the singer of the song of our country.

KNADJIAN: I knew him. I admired him. I was his friend.

JIVELEKIAN: All the more reason to sit down and pick up your cards and start the game.

KNADJIAN: At a time like this? How can you be so insensitive. This good man has been talking with the soul and voice of Armenia itself, and all you want is for me to sit down and play cards? Doctor, are you sure you aren't sick yourself?

JIVELEKIAN: No, no, I'm in perfect health.

KNADJIAN: Then, please be good enough to be moved by this good man and the amazing voice with which he says the amazing words of truth about Armenia.

JIVELEKIAN: I was moved by the words, I am moved by the voice, do you think I am less an Armenian than yourself, or less than anybody else, anywhere? But there comes a time when even the most profoundly passionate Armenian wants to forget it for a moment and play a game of cards. That moment has come. Sit down, pick up your cards, let the game start. Am I right?

MOUSH: Yes, I think a pleasant game of cards is sometimes a good thing.

JIVELEKIAN: There. He said so himself. The very man who said Armenia, Armenia.

KNADJIAN: Well, as long as you've paid the dime, very well, but remember I do not really believe in cards.

JIVELEKIAN: That's all right. A lot of people who go to church don't really believe in Jesus, either.

KNADJIAN: A lot of people who go to hell don't believe in heaven either.

MOUSH: No, no, don't play the ace, play the eight. Have you no sense at all of the appropriate?

HARPOOT: I am from Harpoot. There are more people from Harpoot in Fresno than from any other city in Armenia. I could not help noticing the commotion around this card table from far across this smoke-filled room, and of course many of the words that were spoken here carried across the room, so that I know you have been talking about matters of great concern. Well, I stood there and watched and listened, and suddenly it seemed to me I had better come here and protest. Let us be practical, gentlemen. Let us be reasonable. Let us be men of the world. Do you think you can talk about Armenia and leave out Harpoot? It is impossible. But you have talked and you have talked but not once has anybody mentioned Harpoot. What are we, orphans or something?

MOUSH: What do you want, a medal?

HARPOOT: Never mind a sarcastic medal, all I want is a straight answer to a simple question. Is Harpoot a part of the sorrow of Armenia, or not?

BITLIS: Why should you ask that question? What is the real purpose in asking such a question? Why do you wish to ridicule us?

HARPOOT: Me? Ridicule? I'm scared to death, almost, to open my mouth, for fear one or another of you, from Van, Moush, or Bitlis, will tell me to go back to my stupid rug business. Well, it is true that I am in the rug business, and that many of the people of Harpoot are in the rug business, it is an honorable business, and there is great beauty and art in many of the rugs that are in my shop.

VAN: Ah, please, please, sir, whoever you are, hasn't the Armenian name suffered enough because of the rug sellers? Why did you even mention that you sell rugs? Can you expect us to be sympathetic with a man whose sole purpose in life is to make a big fat profit from some perfectly ignorant and unsuspecting American who wants to believe he has become successful and prosperous. I hate rug sellers. I have always hated them.

HARPOOT: There, you see, everybody hates me. What right have you got to hate me for trying to make a living and to live in a nice home and to send my children to college? The rug merchant is a man of importance in all of the great cities of the world.

MOUSH: Perhaps he is, but it is not quite clear whether he belongs to the Armenian nation or to the Money nation.

HARPOOT: *What* nation? Money, did you say? What nation is the Money nation? Why are you ganging up on a man from Harpoot? I came here to let you know that my sorrow about the return of the Russians to Armenia is as great as your sorrow. The people of Harpoot will not be outdone in a matter of sorrow. Why are you trying to belittle a man from Harpoot?

VASKEN: Harpoot? I'm from Harpoot? What's wrong with Harpoot?

HARPOOT: These men of Van, Moush, Bitlis, and these professional men of Fresno seem to think that the people of Harpoot don't count when it comes to sorrow for Armenia, and they also seem to think that if a man sells rugs he cannot be considered an Armenian, even, he is a member of another nationality, the Money nationality, and I consider that a terrible slander.

VASKEN: Who's a rug merchant?

HARPOOT: It happens, countryman, that I am. Here's my card. Giragos Arpiar Der Havasarian at your service. Oriental Rugs. 2228 Mariposa Street. Rare rugs for sale. Also cleaning and repairing.

VASKEN: I see. I've passed your store many times. You do indeed have good merchandise. Have you ever sold a rug to an Armenian?

HARPOOT: Only to members of my family. The others of course avoid my place. When will the Armenians learn to buy from Armenian merchants.

BITLIS: Just as soon as Armenian merchants stop cheating, that's when.

HARPOOT: Look who's talking. A man from Bitlis. Well, you must surely know from personal experience what you are talking about.

KNADJIAN: Gentlemen, let us try to speak to one another with respect and a certain amount of charity, in the name of our Lord Christ Jesus.

MOUSH: You keep Him out of this. He's done enough damage to the Armenian nation. Keep Him in the backroom at the Red Brick Church, and let Him out only on big holy days.

ERZEROUM: In a family there are many children. Each child has a character of his own. One may be swift in nature, another may be slow. A third may be melancholic, a fourth may be entirely blithe. And so on and so forth. It would be foolish if we imagined that in our family all of the children are alike. Let us not be surprised by any of our children. There is nothing wrong in a man who sells rugs for a living.

KNADJIAN: Yes, that was nicely put. Are you perhaps a Presbyterian preacher?

ERZEROUM: No, but I don't consider it a poor profession. I am a farmer.

JIVELEKIAN: You don't speak like a farmer.

ERZEROUM: Nobody speaks like a farmer or a rug merchant or anything else of that kind. Every man is who he is before he is what he does for a living. I have watched this corner of this room for a good hour or more and it seems to me that somebody must soon inform us that we do not have to be the only nation in the world, the only nation of all time, which is composed solely of saints, heroes, giants of soul and intellect, marvels of productivity, paragons of virtue. Gentlemen, we belong to the human race, the same as everybody else.

MOUSH: Of course we belong to the human race, but let us please remember that we belong to the Armenian branch of it, and some of us to the Moush branch of the Armenian branch of it, and these things make a difference.

ERZEROUM: A small difference, that's true, but only a small difference.

BITLIS: All well and good, but the cause of our sorrow is Armenia itself, where Armenia is, so it is not necessary to notice that we are a nation of many kinds of people with many kinds of character. I have certainly seen Armenians who might be the descendants of soldiers invading our country from Manchuria, Siberia, Mongolia, China—we do not know about such things. Blue eyes and red hair I have also seen—from invaders who came from England, France, Germany, Sweden. What do we know. We are Armenians. We are from Bitlis or from Van or Moush or somewhere else. Our sorrow is the consequence of a fear that perhaps now after all this time, after centuries, Armenia may be coming to an end—the Russians in the seat of Government in Armenia where Armenia is, and the rest of us faraway learning new languages and living among new peoples and forgetting how to read and write our own language, changing our names, marrying outsiders, letting it go, letting it all go. That is what is making it sorrowful.

VAN: I am from Van, my wife is from Van, my children although born here are children of Van, we shall never stop being children of Van, and Armenians.

JIVELEKIAN: I wonder—please do not take this emotionally—I wonder if it is possible for even a man like yourself to remain in Armenia while he and his family live in another place, in America, in California, in Fresno, in the Armenian Quarter of Fresno, is it possible, is it actually possible that he can in fact go on as if he were still in the family home in Van, in Armenia?

VAN: I say it is possible. Furthermore, I say it is necessary. Unless we are to vanish from the face of the earth, swallowed up by the rest of the human race, it is necessary.

MOUSH: My children not only speak Armenian, they go to Armenian school at the Red Brick Church, they read Armenian, they sing classical Armenian in the choir at the church every Sunday and every Holy Day. We are Armenians and we shall continue to be Armenians as long as . . . as long as . . . as long as what shall I say? As long as we . . . what is the word I want?

ERZEROUM: There is no word. We are Armenians while we are Armenians. After that we are not Armenians. But do not despair, there is no way for any of us not to be members of the human race, and in the end isn't that what we are really concerned about? Each of us to be his own special kind of member of the human race? Aren't all of the nations of the world made up of Armenians, as a matter of fact? And are not Armenians made up of all of the other nationalities? We are sorry not for Armenia but for the human race.

DIKRANAGERT: Look here, Armenians. We do not need to use up all of our time and energy feeling sorry about Armenia. There is such a thing as feeling sorry and then feeling something else, and a little later feeling something else, and after a little while feeling something else, and little by little feeling almost hopeful, almost happy. It is possible, Armenians, and it might just be sensible. What do you say we stop feeling sorry? Look, we are here, we are none of us wounded, we are all of us quite healthy, let us enjoy our good fortune.

MOUSH: What about our brothers in Armenia? What shall they enjoy?

DIKRANAGERT: They will enjoy whatever they can, of course. Perhaps they will enjoy nothing more than another morning. What did we enjoy when each of us was in trouble, as of course each of us has been, as we would have had to be even had we not been Armenians, had we been in fact anybody else, anybody at all, fortunate or unfortunate, trouble is the lot of the human race, not the Armenian nation—although lately we have had a good deal more than our share—but what's the good of thinking only of that? Why not move along to a fresh start, a new attitude, a useful program?

VAN: And just who are you, sir?

DIKRANAGERT: Nobody, nobody, of course. But it is not wise for grown men to let themselves sink into deep and useless melancholy. Can we help our brothers in Armenia? Apparently we can't. Well then hadn't we better see about helping ourselves and one another and our children, and our friends, and our neighbors, and if it comes to that our enemies, why shouldn't we help even our worst enemies, wouldn't that surprise them and make them think about the whole foolishness of hating somebody or being afraid of somebody? I mean, I am from Dikranagert, but I have been gone from there many years, and my six children were all born here, and we are all of us very fortunate and in good health, is it not permissible for us to be grateful for our good luck, and to be no longer in mourning for our brothers in Armenia? We have all of us lost members of the immediate family, but mourning them forever isn't at all sensible, it does nobody any good at all, and it does make us look just a little silly. We have got to stop being in mourning somewhere, sometime. Isn't this the proper place and the proper time?

BITLIS: We can of course stop mourning and we can of course be grateful for our good luck, but we can't forget, that's all. We just can't forget. A man's father dies, a man doesn't forget his father, ever. He remembers him, he remembers all that he knows about his father, he remembers for the rest of his life. A man's brother disappears, a man can't stop wanting to know what happened to his brother. He can't stop thinking about his brother. Of course it is unwise to mourn the dead forever. The living have a right to our deepest concern, but there is always something of the soul left over for the dead.

KNADJIAN: Gentlemen, may I volunteer this small thought? At the very least let us just agree among ourselves far from Armenia that we have not forgotten, we will not forget, we shall always remember our family, dead and alive, and in the meantime we shall see to it that we ourselves, each of us, works and lives a decent life, and takes care of his people and is kindly towards all others, and then—yes, I agree with the man from Dikranagert, and then, each of us laughs and sings and in this manner worships God and the Great Mysteries.

JIVELEKIAN: I had hoped to play out a hand of cards, but it seems to me that the fates will not permit it. Well, then, let me say this to you good Armenians: countrymen, I am a doctor, my office is in the Rowell Building, my name, Arshak Jivelekian is in the phone book, if you take sick, or if a member of your family takes sick, telephone me from the store or wherever you phone from, and I will come to your house and do my best to relieve your pain and restore your health.

MOUSH: Again we have failed. We cannot even talk together about the same thing. Our minds wander. Well, all the same, I say long live Armenia.

KASPARIAN: What's going on, gentlemen? A messenger came running to tell me there is a crisis here? What crisis is it?

PAPAZIAN: I have been sitting here and listening and all I can say is that there is indeed a crisis here. We cannot speak to one another in a meaningful way, every one of us is a leader, a general of the army, a king, a president, the greatest thinker of all time, and so on and so forth. This is the curse of the Armenian race. We are a nation of great men. We do not have a population. We do not have people. I have sat here in absolute sorrow, disbelief, despair, pain, and a kind of strange pride—thank God we are who we are and what we are. After all, there has got to be a reason why we are all equally great. We are finished, I suppose, but who knows, who knows, perhaps all of the others are finished, and *we* are not.

MOUSH: Who asked you? What right have you got to give a Protestant sermon here in the Patriotic Club? I've seen you, I've seen you, I know who you are, and there is one thing I can tell you. You want to be an American, that's all. So be an American. But don't tell me all about myself and all about my family and all about my heart and mind.

PAPAZIAN: I said nice things. I certainly tried to say nice things.

MOUSH: Keep your nice things to yourself, please. You are nobody, you said so yourself, while the rest of us are national heroes.

VAN: It is not necessary to be rude at a time like this. Let us at least permit these three men of the church to speak to one another in peace.

BITLIS: Peace? But there is no peace. The Russians sit in the chair of government in Armenia. Is that peace? If this is the end, we have the right to know it, and to gather ourselves together in dispersion, in memory of what we were and what we had and what is now forever lost. Excuse me, Father, but I went to the school of the missionaries in Bitlis—it was the only way any of us there could get a little education.

KASPARIAN: It is desirable to acquire knowledge. The missionaries did not convert anybody to Christianity, they only took some of the Christians away from the national church and put them into their church.

VAN: The international church, perhaps? Isn't it the aspiration of all civilized people to become citizens of the world rather than merely citizens of one country? I must confess that I am strongly tempted to aspire, now, to such citizenship. Now, that it does appear as if our long day is coming to a close.

KASPARIAN: Yes, we may find that Armenia will soon be a memory for most of us, and that we shall be happy to share the life and culture of the place and people where we now live, but I do not believe any of us, believers or unbelievers, can give up hope, short of the grave. I do not believe anyone here is prepared to really believe that Armenia is finished. Let every Armenian in the world be a leader who leads nobody anywhere. Let the land of Armenia be divided among its neighbors. Let foreigners sit in the chair of government. Still, I do not believe any of us is willing or able to believe that Armenia is finished, that it is a thing of the past.

DIKRANAGERT: Is it necessary for Armenia to be Armenia now and forever?

KASPARIAN: No, of course not. But it is also not necessary for the human race to be the human race now and forever. We know nothing. We do nothing. It is all known and done without our knowledge or participation. I must return to my small daily chores. Will you let me help you to the street?

PAPAZIAN: Yes, yes, by all means, let us all return to our small daily chores. I am ashamed of my foolish disability at a time when I should be vigorous and swift.

KNADJIAN: I must go, also. Goodbye, gentlemen. Have faith, have conversations, have arguments, have fun, this may be a better beginning than we know, and a better ending than any ending heretofore.

MOUSH: Heretofore? Ah, well, I did not go to the missionary schools.

BITLIS: Long live the human spirit!

VAN: Long live the Armenian spirit!

GILIGIA: Just a minute. Let me put in my two cents worth. I am from Giligia.

The End

NISHAN PARLAKIAN

GRANDMA, PRAY FOR ME

In 1990, through a generous grant from the Armenian Literary Society, New York, a publication of the play by Griffon House Publications was made possible.

Dedicated to the memory of my grandmother, Makroohi Parlakian, whose old ways became my new ways, whose art of life became my life in art.

THE BIRTH AND GROWTH OF
GRANDMA, PRAY FOR ME

I was a young veteran of World War II in the mid-1940s. I had been drafted while studying electrical engineering at New York's City College and upon returning home transferred to Syracuse University to study English and drama. My parents may have thought it impractical, but though I might "starve," I did it my way.

To the extent possible, the courses I took were in acting, stage design, and American dramatic literature under Sawyer Falk (head of the National Theater Conference). I began acting for the first time and before graduating starred in William Saroyan's *The Beautiful People.*

A critical point in my education occurred in an advanced writing course. After modest approval of my stories and poems, Professor K. D. Wylie, returning my story "Makroohi," about my grandmother, asked me to read it before the class. I did and my voice began to quaver with emotion. The class responded with abundant applause. It did not completely dawn on me that ethnic writing might be the right path for me, and inspired by American playwrights such as Eugene O'Neill, I began writing short plays, one of which was produced at Syracuse. In 1948 in New York at Columbia University, I continued my study of theater and took playwriting under the noted John Gassner. By 1949, Drama Lab, a group consisting of graduate students in theater, produced my anti-Nazi play *Their Hills Are Scarred.*

But the adulation for "Makroohi" remained with me, and I began to write this play about her. Additional motivation no doubt came from my directing Armenian plays at the Eastern Diocese of the Armenian Church. I was moving from story to drama. I expanded the dramatis personae to include my whole family in the character orchestration. From time to time, I took opportunities to write dramas on varied subjects and translated five plays from the Armenian. Several, in both categories, were produced and published at the Diocese, in colleges, and in off-Broadway venues. But I kept coming back to *Grandma*.

As much as drama can be true to life, *Grandma* is true. Makroohi did read her large print Armenian Bible every day and went to the Armenian Church every Sunday. She brought back *mas*, the bread blessed by the priest, so we could all have a "sense" of religious participation. She used her "worry beads" as prayer beads, audibly whispering prayers. My father (the play's Deacon) was familiarly called in Turkish "*Hajibeg Ami*" (the uncle who had gone to Mecca) not because he had gone to that holy city, but for the fact that he had a spiritual nature, being a poet and a philosopher as well as a phenomenally expert jeweler. Like the Deacon of the play, he rose at four in the morning to write in the kitchen for three hours while smoking and drinking Armenian coffee. After a cold-water bath he walked to work at his nearby jewelry shop. He wished he had more time for poetry, the true work of his life. My mother came to him as a "mail order" bride from an orphanage in Aleppo where she had gone after a 1915 genocidal trek through the Syrian desert of Der ez-Zor. My father extolled her virtues in his poems. She was a "Diamond," most precious of all jewels, and she was so named in the play. While she truly appreciated his love poetry, she may have expected more from the "American" way of life. But she loved him and learned the Armenian way of life—the cooking, baking, and intricate needlework—from the examples set by Makroohi. The play's Agate, living in the apartment above Deacon, came into dramatic being from a stray statement I heard about an Armenian woman in the family's homeland city having been promised to my father before the genocide haphazardly drove them hither and yon. The story made for an interesting complication in the play. As it happened, the Armenian woman neighbor above us had a daughter who could have been the model for the play's Pearl. The doctors of our piece, like the Armenian doctors of old, made house visits. One seemed oddly comedic (as are the play's doctors), especially when he offered treatment for hair loss at a time when no medically approved treatments for the anomaly were available. But they assiduously served the community in emergencies well before the coming of trained paramedics.

By the time *Grandma* went into production in 1988, I had eaten all the varied foods loved by all Armenians: *basterma, soojook, sarma, madzoon, paghatch, choreg, shakarishee, dolma, tass kebabee,* and of course *shish kebab,* which I claim I make better than anyone else in the world. And I say, as Mickey the character standing for me says at the end of the play, they'll never make a frozen version of it.

NISHAN PARLAKIAN

GRANDMA, PRAY FOR ME: THE PREMIERE

The Classic Theatre—Executive Director Nicholas J. Stathis and Artistic Director Maurice Edwards—and The Armenian General Benevolent Union presented the world premiere of *Grandma, Pray for Me,* by Nishan Parlakian, as "A New Play About An Armenian Family in America," on February 19, 1988, at The Shakespeare Center, New York City. Later that year it received the first International Arts Award of Columbus: Countdown 1992.

Cast and Crew of the Premiere Production

MICKEY	Joseph Forbrich
GRANDMA	Eileen Prince Burns*
DIAMOND	Elizabeth Bove*
PEARL	Terri Galvin*
AGATE	Janet Aspinwall*
DEACON	Krikor Satamian
VIRGIL	Alan Dolderer
DR. CYCLOPS	Warren Kliewer*
DR. ACHILLES	Larry Swansen*
DOCTOR	Jeff Robins
ATTENDANTS	Alan Dolderer
	James Whelan
Sets	Daniel Proett
Costumes	Natalie Walker
Lighting	Bernadette Englert
Sound	George Jacobs
Production Stage Manager	James Whelan

*Appearing through the courtesy of Actor's Equity Association.

GRANDMA, PRAY FOR ME

NISHAN PARLAKIAN

THE CHARACTERS

MICKEY
GRANDMA
DIAMOND
PEARL
AGATE
DEACON
VIRGIL
DR. CYCLOPS
DR. ACHILLES
DOCTOR
ATTENDANTS

TIME

The Prologue and Epilogue are in the present. *The main action in both acts 1 and 2 are* in the past.

SETTING

The main action of the play takes place in the past in a ground floor living room and outside yard of a two-story house, a little world apart from the world. In the yard are hedges, flowers, and a small fence. A wooden stairway leads to the unseen apartment above. In the living room there are a doorway leading to the kitchen and an archway through which other rooms may be reached. The period furniture is well-worn.

Doilies decorate the soft chairs and the sofa. The prologue and epilogue take place in the present in a neutral part of the stage.

PROLOGUE (THE PRESENT)

MICKEY, *as an older man, is lighted in a neutral part of the stage. He wears a raincoat and hat. As he approaches the audience, appropriate elements of scenery and characters become illuminated as though a memory of his past takes on life again.*

MICKEY: Every now and then I drive off the highway before leaving the city for my home in the suburbs. A kind of unconscious impulse takes over and I always end up here—at the beginning. I walk down this street—it's all changed now. New people. Abandoned houses. Years ago I lived here on this street. In this house. There's nobody here now. But I remember when it throbbed with life. It was a different kind of time. Laundry hung on back yard lines, push cart vendors lined the curbs, doctors actually made house calls. I was born here out of a need—how shall I put it—it was a need for the decimated Armenian people to live on after the holocaust of 1915. God tossed them to the far corners of the earth. My people came to America. Early on, hard working men like my father—Deacon as he was familiarly called—had little time for writing poetry. *(Illuminate* DEACON.*)* Somehow he made time between midnight and dawn to express his deepest thoughts. Mom worked hard too, marketing, cooking, cleaning. *(Illuminate* DIAMOND.*)* And so did Agate the widow in the apartment above us living on a small pension. *(Illuminate* AGATE.*)* Her daughter Pearl became a typist right after graduating high school. *(Illuminate* PEARL.*)* And I finally buckled down too, even though I had poetic inclinations like my father. The same faith that pulled Armenians through the centuries guided our family through those prayerful days of my youth. Prayer— Grandma convinced us that prayer had more power than medicine. I see her there framed in the window fingering her beads and reading her Bible. *(Illuminate* GRANDMA.*)* On a sunny morning, I would call to her—"Grandma, come out into the sun!"

Blackout

ACT ONE

When the lights come up, we are in the past. MICKEY *as a young man (raincoat and hat discarded), moves into the scene. It is a morning many years ago. The sun shines brightly. In the yard,* MICKEY *looks into the sky and stretches.* GRANDMA *sits in the darker living room knitting.*

MICKEY: Grandma, come out into the sun!

GRANDMA: Let me finish my work.

MICKEY: Come out. You need the sun.

GRANDMA: Without it there is no life.

MICKEY: Everybody knows that.

GRANDMA: Only when you ask them.

MICKEY: How can you get well without the sun?

GRANDMA: My time for getting well is gone.

MICKEY: I'll open your folding chair for you.

GRANDMA: I used to sit in the sun for hours with you. In that chair. Your father brought it when he saw one day I was old. I used to wheel your carriage to the sun to make you strong. And I sat in that chair. But that chair is good for the young, hard for the old.

MICKEY: You're not old, grandma.

GRANDMA: These white hairs mean I know something. I know I am old. The old know such things.

MICKEY: What things do they know?

GRANDMA: At the door of death they know all of life.

MICKEY: Then you can't know much.

GRANDMA: I know that every day is a day to live.

MICKEY: Everybody knows that.

GRANDMA: Not until you ask them. Do you know it? Do you know it today?

MICKEY: Today I thought I'd think.

GRANDMA: And yesterday?

MICKEY: I thought.

GRANDMA: And tomorrow?

MICKEY: I need more time. Everything is disconnected and sad.

GRANDMA: Keep sad thinking for night.

MICKEY: Don't you see, grandma. I've got to think things through, I've got to find my place in the sun.

GRANDMA: You'll find it in the moon.

MICKEY: But today is different. I feel it. Today something is going to happen. Today I'm going to find my way.

GRANDMA: Today is a beacon day. It tells you once again that you are alive.

MICKEY: I know I'm alive.

GRANDMA: Not many people do.

MICKEY: Everybody knows they're alive.

GRANDMA: Only when you ask them. Only then. In the old country, in Armenia, called Turkey, I was born—who knows what day. But as I grew older, I learned I needed a birthday. A day to celebrate life. Give this birthday of yours to life. It helps you remember to live for all your days.

MICKEY: What are you trying to tell me, grandma?

GRANDMA: Life is a gold coin for every breath.

MICKEY: I know that, grandma.

GRANDMA: Not many people do. And by the time they learn, it is too late.

MICKEY: Oh grandma, do you really know me? My feelings, my thoughts, I'm not like other men.

GRANDMA: All grass is green.

MICKEY: What are you trying to tell me, grandma?

GRANDMA: You are a seed which has not taken root. Our life is not stone which stands for centuries. Flesh goes fast.

MICKEY: Wait!

GRANDMA: I wait and I pray. Whatever you have done, I have prayed. But you confuse the angels.

MICKEY: Where have I gone wrong?

GRANDMA: My boy, we have come to this earth to go to death in pain. Adam gave it to us. Not many people know that.

MICKEY: Everybody knows that.

GRANDMA: Ask them and see. I read it in the Bible in the warmer season when more light comes through the window. My father used to tell me not to fear around this time of year that the days were getting short. He used to say a lighter season would come again. If it comes again for me, I will read again and I will pray for you. But if it does not come, I cannot pray.

MICKEY: Grandma, pray for me.

GRANDMA: Winter is coming. I want you to buy a coat. *(She puts her hand under the cushion of her chair and pulls out a piece of folded newspaper. She hands it to* MICKEY.*)* Open it. *(He does and holds up a gold bead necklace.)* It is gold. Buy your coat with it.

MICKEY: I can't take it.

GRANDMA: Take it from your grandfather. He gave it to me when we were married. We were not rich, but we were not poor. You should have seen our house. It was not on the top of the hill and not on the bottom. It was in the middle. I wore those beads of gold to the cathedral. I was a golden girl and had other things of gold. My husband gave them all to me. He would have given me more, but they killed him when he was young.

MICKEY: I'll use it when I need it.

GRANDMA: I will put it on the bottom of my chest again. When I die, Mickey, you will find other things there I want you to have. There are the pictures of my daughter and her two little sons. They were killed in the genocide. The children would have been married now. There would have been the children of children.

MICKEY: I'll have children, someday.

GRANDMA: Buy the coat first. Earn the money for your marriage.

MICKEY: If I wanted to get married, I'd get married. You don't need money to get married.

GRANDMA: Yes, that is what they tell me. People borrow to live. The systems change. In my time I went with a good dowry to my husband. Find a girl with a good dowry.

MICKEY: Wait. Wait a little longer.

GRANDMA: I am a dried grape. I am but today's guest.

MICKEY: Stay for tomorrow.

GRANDMA: I am tomorrow's stranger.

MICKEY: Never to me.

GRANDMA: A spinning comes in my head when I go from room to room. It will bring me down some day. Last year I could dry your mother's dishes. This year a dizziness comes over me. And my eyes. I am almost blind. And my feet . . . they can hardly carry me. There are only small things left for me to do. I can still pray over my beads. I pray for you.

MICKEY: What are you trying to say?

GRANDMA: Is the upstairs one in your eye?

MICKEY: I don't know.

GRANDMA: Does she favor you?

MICKEY: I don't know.

GRANDMA: I've seen you talking to her.

MICKEY: But not about getting married.

GRANDMA: I have heard that you showed her around the town.

MICKEY: We took a walk. This isn't the old country. People fall in love before they get married.

GRANDMA: The systems change. When my husband was killed I knew I loved him. I never walked with him before we were married. He had seen me drawing water from the village well.

MICKEY: That's what I mean. He was like a stranger.

GRANDMA: He was a neighbor and a countryman. In those days that is all an eligible man had to be.

MICKEY: You wouldn't want me to marry the upstairs one, would you? You said her mother was evil eyeing me.

GRANDMA: But I know all about the mother. Marry her daughter and she will bless you.

MICKEY: I haven't asked her to go out again.

GRANDMA: I know. I know. You have no coat and you are ashamed.

(DIAMOND, MICKEY's *mother, enters.*)

MICKEY: The question is, grandma: Will I be happy if I marry her?

DIAMOND: Who are you marrying?

MICKEY: No one.

DIAMOND: Who is "her"?

MICKEY: Pearl, upstairs.

DIAMOND: You wouldn't want to marry her.

GRANDMA: You might.

DIAMOND: She's not good enough for you.

GRANDMA: She is old with the old and young with the young.

DIAMOND: She isn't your type.

GRANDMA: She has a sweet face and obedient manners.

DIAMOND: There are better faces and manners.

GRANDMA: For birds with brighter plumes.

MICKEY: Talk to her, ma.

DIAMOND: I can't talk to your grandmother sometimes.

MICKEY: Talk to her, grandma.

GRANDMA: Diamond, I am going to talk to you.

DIAMOND: I'm not talking to you these days.

GRANDMA: My ear is so old I have not missed you.

DIAMOND: I'll talk to you if you'll listen.

GRANDMA: My ear is brittle, Diamond, but it can bend to you a little.

DIAMOND: Let my boy alone. Let him enjoy his one life.

GRANDMA: Let him.

DIAMOND: But you don't. You want him to marry Pearl.

GRANDMA: He has walked with her in town. Everybody has seen him.

DIAMOND: So they walked. He must walk with many to find the one. Because we didn't do what he must do, we have not gone forward.

GRANDMA: Where would we have gone?

DIAMOND: Where are we? Still in these walls, only with more years.

GRANDMA: And my son's years. His son's years. And yes, Diamond . . . your years too.

DIAMOND: You had no right to my years.

GRANDMA: I'm sorry I took them. But God knows there is a reason. I know, I know I have bruised your heart for all these years. I wish time could flow back for you and for me smooth out this curled flesh. But your years were good to me and I grew to love you.

DIAMOND: Oh, mama, mama, I came to you an orphan. I came to you hungry for love. And I married *you*, not your son. And you took those young years. I hated you for taking them caring for you. But now your wrinkled face is familiar to me like one washing hand is to another. And I love you. I hate you and I love you.

GRANDMA: Soon, soon I will be gone from your eyes and only love will remain in your heart for me.

DIAMOND: Don't go, old woman. But let me run my house at least. My sin has brought me you, but let my son be.

GRANDMA: He is where he has always been.

DIAMOND: There is time for him to see the world.

GRANDMA: Let him take to his hands and feet. You are not with him forever.

DIAMOND: I will prepare my son.

GRANDMA: And who will prepare for his son?

DIAMOND: He will learn.

GRANDMA: His eyes are closed. He has no place to turn.

DIAMOND: You're starting things all over again!

MICKEY: Don't argue. Listen to me. Listen, mama, listen, grandma. *(They turn to him.)* I've been offered a job. I mean it. It's with Best Way Foods, a frozen shish kebab outfit. It could have a great future. I'd be a kind of billing clerk in the stock room.

DIAMOND: You don't have to take it.

GRANDMA: Take it, today.

MICKEY: Not today, grandma.

GRANDMA: Then there is no job.

MICKEY: There is. There is. All I have to do is make a phone call.

GRANDMA: Then call. Call.

DIAMOND: Mickey, we need bread.

MICKEY: Right away, ma. *(He goes to the door.)* I need money.

DIAMOND: *(Hands MICKEY a bill).* Buy some canned goods, sugar, and eggs, too. *(MICKEY goes out.)* Come have breakfast.

GRANDMA: I have had mine. The coffee is made. The honey and olives are on the table.

DIAMOND: Thank you, mama.

GRANDMA: Diamond.

DIAMOND: Yes.

GRANDMA: Today is Mickey's birthday.

DIAMOND: Do you want me to get a present for him?

GRANDMA: *(Displays her knitting.).* No, I am almost finished with this.

DIAMOND: That's good, mama. It has a pretty design. *(She turns to leave.)*

GRANDMA: Diamond.

DIAMOND: Yes, mama.

GRANDMA: Deacon never had a birthday. As you know, all I remember is that he was born in April one week after Easter. It was in a year there was a flood. The waters washed the houses away. But our house remained because we were not near the water. We were not too high on a slope, but enough. You should have seen the sight. Even the heavy bread ovens went. And with them the hot breads, too. You can see it was April because the rains came and swelled the Kizil Irmak, the red river that ran through Sivas.

DIAMOND: I know, mama. The floods came and then the fire, the genocide and the slaughter of millions of us Armenians. The faces of my mother and father are faint memories. I was so young.

GRANDMA: I know, Diamond.

DIAMOND: Knit, mama. Knit your twine glove, your *toufa*, for Mickey's birthday. He will scrub his back with it and it will comfort him.

GRANDMA: I knit. But the light of my eye fails.

DIAMOND: Then stop, mama. Stop and think of more stories to tell.

(DIAMOND *goes out.* GRANDMA *begins to knit.* PEARL, *the girl who lives above comes down the stairs and looks in through the window of the living room.*)

PEARL: Hello, grandma.

GRANDMA: Hello, young girl. Are you going to work so early?

PEARL: It's not really that early.

GRANDMA: Ah yes, autumn mornings seem early.

PEARL: What are you knitting?

GRANDMA: This is for Mickey's birthday.

PEARL: *(grimacing).* Is it today?

GRANDMA: Yes, today. Ah, why that face? What is it?

PEARL: I was thinking I don't get paid until tomorrow.

GRANDMA: Give him this. *(She extends the wash glove.)*

PEARL: Would it be right?

GRANDMA: How old are you?

PEARL: Almost eighteen.

GRANDMA: You are not young, anymore.

PEARL: Oh, I know. I know.

GRANDMA: I had a child at your age. It takes a marriage to make a girl blossom.

PEARL: Did he love you?

GRANDMA: My husband? I had hair like yours once. It was not so light. But it was lighter than any other girl's around. They called me golden girl. I used to come from the public baths with my cheeks red from the steaming waters. I used to wear a fine cloth lined with beads of gold around my head. They used to whisper in the streets: Here comes the golden girl. My husband gave me the head cloth. I obeyed him. I took care of his grandfather. He was so old I had to lead him around by the hand. I lit his pipe with a magnifying glass held to the sun. And I bore the sons of the son of the son of that man. I took their generations unto myself. By all this, I mean to say I know my husband loved me.

PEARL: Did my father love my mother?

GRANDMA: You see, my girl, he died too soon. I know what your mother is like. She was like a second daughter to me. Now she lets her tub overflow. Our ceiling was dripping yesterday.

PEARL: She's been angry these last few days.

GRANDMA: When she thinks of your father she becomes angry with me.

PEARL: She talks with her head turned away and her eyes on me.

GRANDMA: That is one of the ways of the eye. Something disturbs her my girl. She married an unhealthy man. She soured when he died.

PEARL: Grandma, she'll never let me get married.

GRANDMA: There is nothing to be afraid of. You will not grow sour or stale. Your mother has not thrown her head in here in days. I know she was well yesterday. Her line of clothes was long. How is she today?

AGATE *(off)*: Pearl!

GRANDMA: She sounds well.

PEARL: How does she know I'm here?

GRANDMA: That Agate. Her nose takes smells. And her ears take sounds. The devil can do those things.

PEARL: She always makes me go to work early to impress the boss. Goodbye, Grandma.

AGATE *(Catches* PEARL *about to leave)*: Ah, ha. So you aren't gone yet.

PEARL: It was so early. I decided to talk to grandma awhile.

AGATE: She's no relation of yours. She is not your grandmother. What were you whispering about?

GRANDMA: We were whispering like all natural things do. What do trees do in a breeze, Agate? What do they whisper about? They whisper.

AGATE: Go to work. You must never be late.

GRANDMA: She is a responsible girl. She knows the time.

AGATE: My daughter won't be like your lazy grandson who gets up at noon.

PEARL: Mama.

AGATE: Am I to hear something from you?

PEARL: Talk nice.

AGATE: Your father is dead. We need the money you earn. Go to work. *(*PEARL *goes off, holding back her tears.)* Are you trying to turn my daughter's mind?

GRANDMA: Surely, not me, Agate.

AGATE: Don't try it, mama.

GRANDMA: Her mind is hers.

AGATE: Her mind is mine. I didn't know your grandson was courting my daughter in secret.

GRANDMA: Who knows secrets?

AGATE: It was those summer months, and those dresses with the open armpits and the low fronts. I wish winter would come quickly.

GRANDMA: It comes quickly enough for some of us.

AGATE: That's good. They won't be able to sit in the parks . . . or go to the roof. You don't know I suppose. They were coming down from the roof two weeks ago.

GRANDMA: The stars are closer there.

AGATE: It's dark and lonely there, too. You can't get my daughter the way you got your Diamond.

GRANDMA: Mickey is a good boy. His face is comely.

AGATE: They are not for each other.

GRANDMA: Why, Agate?

AGATE: The why is mine. *(Points to her heart.)* In here.

GRANDMA: You are sour, Agate. Every year at this anniversary time of your husband's death you become sour.

AGATE: Then I become sour. It's my right.

GRANDMA: But there's no need to trouble us all like this every year. Your husband is dead. My husband died when I was younger than you.

AGATE *(Points to the archway in the apartment)*: My husband could have been living now.

GRANDMA: That story is old, Agate. Too old to bring up.

AGATE: I can never forget it, mama. It's not in the mind. *(Points to her heart in that classical way again.)* It is here.

GRANDMA: And that is why I have had you over me all these years. Are you a curse Agate that every Monday we must get the water from your wash? Are you a curse that we must listen to your stampings and bangings?

AGATE: That could be, mama. You promised Deacon to me and you took back your promise.

GRANDMA: It was just a way of talking.

AGATE: Over here it would have been a way of talking. But over there it was not a way of talking. Didn't I used to carry your water for you from the village well. I used to sit by the well in the middle of the square over there, and wait for you to come every day. And didn't you used to say: My son is yours my little Agate.

GRANDMA: Then the Turks killed my husband, my daughter and my other sons and their children. I came here with only that one son. You were late in coming here, my dear. I never knew if you would come or even if you were alive. He became of age and even more and married. I tell you this story, it could be, for the last time. Hear it well and forgive and forget.

AGATE: Only death will make me forgive and forget.

GRANDMA: Death will. Ah. Ah.

DEACON *(enters)*: Good morning, mama. Who are you talking to?

GRANDMA: Agate.

DEACON *(Goes to the window and bends over to talk to AGATE)*: Oh, hello, hello, Agate. How are you?

AGATE: Oh, well. How are you, Deacon?

DEACON: Not too well now that you ask.

AGATE: You look well.

DEACON: Do I?

AGATE: Your color is good.

DEACON: Come in then a while. It's hard to see you bending like this.

AGATE: I have work upstairs.

DEACON: Come in for my sake for a little while only.

AGATE: All right, Deacon. *(She goes to the door.)*

GRANDMA: Tell her about the ceiling.

DEACON: That's woman's business. *(AGATE enters.)* Sit down. Sit down. That looks like a new dress.

GRANDMA: It has been on her line for a year.

DEACON: Your eyes are turning on you, mama. That looks like a new dress.

AGATE: You just haven't noticed it before, Deacon.

DEACON: Perhaps.

AGATE: I like your tie.

DEACON: That's my taste.

AGATE: Yes, I like it.

DEACON: Diamond doesn't like it. It's a fitting tie to work in on a day like this.

AGATE: You don't usually go to work this early.

DEACON: There are a few orders I have to fill.

AGATE: How is work?

DEACON: Slow for us especially who are in our autumn years.

AGATE: You aren't old yet, Deacon.

GRANDMA: If we get old should not our sons, Agate?

DEACON: That's true too, mama.

AGATE: Your son should be working at your side.

DEACON: I think he should. Yes. And I brought him in. He liked it even less than I do. He quit in one week. What about your daughter? What does she do these days?

AGATE: She works.

DEACON: I see her sometimes in the morning. She is a good-looking girl.

AGATE: Your son is a good-looking boy.

DEACON: But alas, he doesn't work.

AGATE: Maybe he will soon.

DEACON: If he did he could take my burden from me and marry your daughter, too.

AGATE: I don't know, Deacon.

DEACON: You hurt me, Agate. After all we meant to each other. I thought some day our children could get married to each other.

AGATE: Oh, Deacon!

DEACON: Oh, Agate!

AGATE: Oh, Deacon!

DEACON: Agate, Agate, I would be a contented man if something went right. And I had thought our children marrying was the right way.

AGATE: Oh, Deacon, it could be.

DEACON: Do you think so, Agate?

AGATE: Mama says his looks are comely.

GRANDMA (to DEACON): I have always said he looks like you. (DIAMOND enters unobserved.)

AGATE: And you look comely, Deacon.

DEACON: Yes, you always said it.

AGATE: Even when I was young and used to carry mama's water.

DIAMOND: He is not so comely in his underwear.

DEACON: Good morning, Diamond. Agate says she likes this tie.

DIAMOND: She is thinking of twenty-five years ago. Yellow would have looked good on you then. Your breakfast is ready.

DEACON: Excuse me all. I must, as they say, fuel up my body. *(DEACON and DIAMOND exit to the kitchen.)*

AGATE: Do you think your grandson will go to work with his father?

GRANDMA: If the wind blows that way.

AGATE: You ought to talk to him about it.

GRANDMA: Why, Agate?

AGATE: For his good.

GRANDMA: For his good, eh Agate. Well, I am not certain, Agate. His mother tells me not to talk to her son.

AGATE: You have a right to. You have cleaned his diapers.

GRANDMA: Your advice could make a little trouble.

AGATE: What's a little trouble for friends?

GRANDMA: Your talk is warmer than it was.

AGATE: It's no warmer or colder.

GRANDMA: Agate, why do you say you do not like me when you do?

(DIAMOND enters.)

AGATE: I don't dislike you mama, or any of you.

DIAMOND: Then why do you stomp on your floors.

AGATE: Your ear takes such sounds.

DIAMOND: Not as much as yours. You know who is in our house from upstairs.

AGATE: You make such noise. Your voices come through my windows and even wake me in the night.

DIAMOND: You pay attention. You even know what we eat.

AGATE: I can smell the cooking.

DIAMOND: You sit on the landing steps.

AGATE: I don't have to.

GRANDMA: This Agate. This Agate, Diamond. She does not have to.

DIAMOND: You two are too friendly, today.

GRANDMA: Our days are too short to be unfriendly.

DIAMOND *(to GRANDMA)*: Only yesterday you were complaining about the water.

AGATE: My tub is small.

DIAMOND: Do you wash your clothes on the floor?

GRANDMA: Daughters, let your hearts be cool.

DIAMOND: Is she a daughter, now?

AGATE: I didn't ask to come in. There won't be the day I'll come again.

GRANDMA: Come again, Agate.

AGATE: My heart has turned to stone.

GRANDMA: That is so hard.

AGATE: You will have to make your fires hot to melt this heart. *(AGATE exits and goes upstairs.)*

DIAMOND: Why give face to that woman?

GRANDMA: She has her good days.

DIAMOND: She is after my son.

GRANDMA: She has her dreams.

MICKEY *(Enters with a bag of groceries, places it on the table and offers the change to his mother)*: Can I keep the silver?

DIAMOND: Take the dollar.

MICKEY: I'm keeping a record of everything I owe you.

GRANDMA: Write your debts on ice.

DEACON *(Enters from the kitchen)*: I am here.

GRANDMA: I greet you with the sun.

DIAMOND: Did you finish your breakfast?

DEACON: Yes. Yes. I ate the eggs.

DIAMOND: And one slice of toast.

DEACON: Two slices.

DIAMOND: How many times must I tell you. You'll get fat.

DEACON: You have no interest in my shape. So what difference is there?

DIAMOND: You're the one who wants to look young.

DEACON *(Hand on belly)*: I have decided this can't be helped. If our age doesn't give us wrinkles it gives us other things. *(He walks to the door and stops. He seems like a diver afraid to dive from a high board.)* I am going to work. I am going to work! I am going to work!!

DIAMOND: So go. You go every morning.

DEACON: Well, say something to me.

DIAMOND: What can I say?

DEACON: Say . . . come home safe.

DIAMOND: Come home safe.

DEACON: All right.

GRANDMA: Goodbye, son.

DEACON: Goodbye, mama, I am going to work. One of you say you love me.

GRANDMA: I love you, son.

DEACON: I know you do, mama. You have always loved me. Love me forever. Son, say you love me.

MICKEY: Pa.

DEACON: All right.

DIAMOND: Goodbye.

DEACON: I am going to work!

DIAMOND: Deacon!

DEACON: Oh world, I am going to work. Once again I am going to work and I am almost sixty. I would not go, but I go. And I am smiling and crying. *(Goes to the door.)* I understand oh world how you feed me and hurt me. *(Puts his hand out the door.)* Look at my fist; it is in the sun. This fist is hot. It is another heart. My outside heart. I need it to boil my blood and push it around. I am not well on shady days and in the winter. My heart is then gone and I become frail. Son, be my sun.

MICKEY: What pa?

DEACON: Be my sun in wintertime and take my hand. Warm it and push my blood around.

MICKEY: Sure pa.

DEACON: But you can't, son.

MICKEY: I will, pa.

DEACON: You will take my hand in wintertime? I am alone, son. I am alone. I work for you and you and you. I am almost sixty and I am going to work. I am only one hand. Have mercy on me. Soon winter will be here.

MICKEY: I'll help you.

DIAMOND: He's in one of his moods. He thinks he's declaiming his poetry again. Go have breakfast, Mickey.

MICKEY (Goes to his father): Pa, here I am.

DEACON: Don't touch me. It's all right. I am a man. Oh what a man. Stay away from me. I am alone, but I am not alone. I have my thoughts. I have such visions. If I could stay home today and put them down on paper what would Tolstoy's or Goethe's thoughts be compared to mine. Ah, ah it is good to be alone and not to be alone.

DIAMOND: You should have been a monk.

DEACON: I should have been a lot of things. Now I have your thoughts in my thoughts. And all your thoughts are so many small thoughts. They weigh mine down, create imbalance, and now mine cannot fly, fly high up to the sky. Ah, ah, where did your lives intermingle with mine and your thoughts . . .

DIAMOND (protectively): Go eat, Mickey.

DEACON: Body, blood, and sweat. Eat, eat.

DIAMOND: Deacon! Leave him alone he is only a boy.

DEACON: Are you a boy, my son?

MICKEY: I wish I knew, pa.

DEACON: If you are, I am a young man. When you were a boy I used to rub your head.

MICKEY: I know, pa.

DEACON: My father did that to me. When I was small. Oh, father, father, why did you leave me? My father was a God! Mama, tell them about papa.

GRANDMA: My husband was a good man.

DEACON: You see son. He was great. Go eat. Goodbye.

(DEACON *exits.* DIAMOND *follows him,* MICKEY *enters the kitchen.* DIAMOND *and* DEACON *pause in the yard.*)

DIAMOND: Deacon.

DEACON: What?

DIAMOND: You won't forget.

DEACON: Forget?

DIAMOND: It will soon be cold.

DEACON: I know.

DIAMOND: And smile today.

DEACON: I smile a little every day.

DIAMOND: Not often enough.

DEACON: I used to smile. Oh, oh, you should have seen me when I used to. Barefoot, I would run to the hills and I would sit under a cool summer sky . . . for it was cool on the hills in the summer. I would smile at the sky and then my eyes would fill with tears.

DIAMOND: Smile like that again.

DEACON: No more. No more.

DIAMOND: No more for me, only for Agate.

DEACON: Her I knew when I was twenty-five and she was twelve. I was promised to her.

DIAMOND (with mock fervor): And now you're mine, all mine.

DEACON: Are you jealous, my Diamond?

DIAMOND: Of losing your flashing eyes and black hair? No Deacon, just smile.

DEACON: You don't understand. You never understood. You took my smile away.

DIAMOND: *I* understand. *She* would not have.

DEACON: No. Not at all. She is hope; you reality. That's all. Women, women take the philosophical smile of men away. That smile which is the soul.

DIAMOND: Then Deacon you stole your own soul away.

DEACON: You took my loneliness from me. I used to commune with things and thoughts.

DIAMOND: Then you should have stayed with those thoughts and things and not come near me.

DEACON: I was not so young, but you were my first beloved.

DIAMOND: I knew less than you.

DEACON: Please, my Diamond. My jewel, I love you. I love you after all these things. This is an autumn love. But be satisfied that I love you. The first folly was passion. Forgive me and yourself and take this autumn love.

DIAMOND: I was lost in this country. And then we married. And I was still lost. There was no romance. Not even a little like the romance of a movie story or a soap opera.

DEACON: And no romance of my thoughts. The romance of looking up to the sky and smiling in pure happiness and crying in pure joy.

DIAMOND: All right, Deacon. It is done. We are done. We are in the mold and the wax is cold. He is here and he is our son. And you must learn that.

DEACON: He is our son. And today is the day he was born. We will be ready for him tonight. Take care of my mother.

DIAMOND: She is my necklace.

(DEACON *exits and* DIAMOND *enters the house.*)

GRANDMA: Diamond.

DIAMOND: What is it, mama?

GRANDMA: Take care of my son.

DIAMOND: He is my yoke.

GRANDMA: He is just tired.

DIAMOND: So are we all. We need a change.

GRANDMA: It will come.

DIAMOND: When?

GRANDMA: The Lord knows, soon. (DIAMOND *begins to go.*) Diamond. (DIAMOND *stops and turns.*) Forgive me for speaking to your son. But I could not help it. He has not had my milk. But I too have cleaned him.

DIAMOND: Old woman, you are too old to ask for forgiveness. Your age is wisdom. When I am worn a little more, I too may speak like you. Yet there is that red coal of adventure glowing in me, but long since gone from you. I see only the highest and greatest things for my son. Things that most of us have in our dreams, only. (MICKEY *enters.*) Did you eat?

MICKEY: I'm not hungry.

DIAMOND: Breakfast is an important meal.

MICKEY: The taste of his sweat is in it.

DIAMOND: What's the matter, Mickey?

GRANDMA: Come to me.

DIAMOND: Mama, what is this? What is he talking about? Mama, it is like Deacon when he was a boy.

GRANDMA: Diamond, there is nothing to fear. I am praying. (*She bows her head to pray.*)

DIAMOND: Mama, he needs less pressure, more rest.

GRANDMA: Diamond, go to your kitchen.

(DIAMOND *exits in tears.* GRANDMA *begins to pray with her beads.*)

MICKEY: Are you praying for me?

GRANDMA: I am, son of my son.

MICKEY: What are you praying for?

GRANDMA: Peace of mind.

MICKEY: And heart.

GRANDMA: And soul.

(*There is a moment of deep silence. Church bells sound softly and the room is illuminated by light that comes from stained glass windows.*)

MICKEY: Are you still praying, grandma?

GRANDMA: The peace of God and the fellowship of the Holy Ghost remain with you always.

MICKEY: Your voice is the sounding of church bells. And in your eyes is the brilliant light of stained glass. How can I express it? *(He kneels beside her.)* Shouldn't there be thunder, grandma?

GRANDMA: It will come.

MICKEY: Will I see the lightning?

GRANDMA: I pray the heavens will open and you will see the light.

(There is thunder and lightning. This continues for a while during which time MICKEY *makes a phone call.)*

MICKEY: I am going to work, grandma. Pray for me. *(He pauses at the door.)* I am smiling and crying. I am going to work. Somebody say something.

GRANDMA: *Der Voghormia.* Lord have mercy.

(End of Act 1)

ACT TWO

The same scene in the late afternoon. The sun still shines but weakly. VIRGIL, *a small delivery boy, is ringing the door bell.* GRANDMA *goes to the window.*

GRANDMA: What is it?

VIRGIL: I've a delivery to make.

GRANDMA: Come here, boy.

VIRGIL: The name is Virgil, ma'am. *(He crosses to the window.)* Are you the old woman of this house?

GRANDMA: There are none older, here.

VIRGIL: I've seen older than you.

GRANDMA: Oh, where?

VIRGIL: Not live ones.

GRANDMA: That is comforting to know. What have you brought?

VIRGIL: This is for you. It's from your grandson. He bought it on credit at lunchtime. *(He gives* GRANDMA *a package. She opens it and takes out a chrome-handled cane.)*

GRANDMA: It has a silver handle.

VIRGIL: It's chrome. But the wood is sturdy. Here, let me show you how to use it. *(He takes the cane. Leaning against the walls and furniture as she goes,* GRANDMA *steps into the yard.* VIRGIL *demonstrates with the cane. After describing two circles, he goes back to* GRANDMA.*)* You take it from there. *(He gives* GRANDMA *the cane.)*

GRANDMA: I have no money. Take these two prayer beads from my string.

VIRGIL: I don't believe in those things. Don't spoil your string. *(He stops before going off.)* But say a prayer for me . . . in case.

GRANDMA: Son, what will you become when you grow up?

VIRGIL: I'm thirty-three, now.

GRANDMA: Then, I'll pray that you grow taller . . . in spirit.

(He leaves. Falteringly, GRANDMA walks around with the cane, fingering her beads all the while. AGATE appears on the outside stairway. She descends cautiously and with an air of expectancy. GRANDMA enters the house. AGATE comes to the window. GRANDMA fingers her beads rapidly.)

AGATE: Hello, mama.

GRANDMA: So you have thrown your head in, again.

(GRANDMA hides the cane from AGATE's view.)

AGATE: What are you doing, mama?

GRANDMA: Praying, Agate.

AGATE: Your beads move too quickly for prayer.

GRANDMA *(sniffing)*: I am giving three beads to a prayer. What are you cooking that smells so much.

AGATE: I'm boiling fat. I need some newspapers to put around the stove.

GRANDMA: You did not boil fat last week, but you borrowed newspapers then, too.

AGATE: Sometimes I put them on the floor after I mop.

GRANDMA: Do you still collect newspapers to sell?

AGATE: Not since my husband died. He was a reading man, you know.

GRANDMA *(pointing)*: Take those then. *(AGATE takes the newspapers, looking at GRANDMA all the while.)* What is it, Agate?

AGATE: Why do you ask?

GRANDMA: What are you looking at, Agate?

AGATE: I don't know yet, mama.

GRANDMA: I think you think I have something back here, Agate.

AGATE: How does that wind blow into your head?

GRANDMA: You have your newspapers, but you do not go.

AGATE: I'm being friendly, mama.

GRANDMA: Your ear has taken sounds again, Agate.

AGATE: Well yes, I thought I heard the doorbell pushed and then voices.

GRANDMA: You heard the right things, Agate. *(She shows AGATE the cane.)* This cane came for me. *(AGATE touches the chrome handle.)*

AGATE: This looks like silver. It must be expensive.

GRANDMA: My grandson sent it. He went to work today; you might know.

AGATE: But he hasn't been paid yet has he?

GRANDMA: Everything can be bought with dreams, today.

AGATE: Soon he'll be able to fix a house of his own.

GRANDMA: In time, Agate.

AGATE: He is a man, mama.

GRANDMA: No more than Pearl is a woman.

AGATE: She could have had children years ago.

GRANDMA: Yes. She is getting on in years.

AGATE: In this country she is just the right age for marriage.

GRANDMA: Are you making me understand something, Agate?

AGATE: Do my words walk with you?

GRANDMA: They are like oil seeping in under the closed door. The door is open, Agate.

(Dr. CYCLOPS, *a man in his forties, has appeared carrying an eye chart. He rings the bell.*)   :

GRANDMA *(Goes to the window)*: Hello.

CYCLOPS: Is there an old woman in this house?

GRANDMA: I am an old woman.

CYCLOPS: I am Dr. Cyclops.

GRANDMA: Do you want to see me?

CYCLOPS: I do see you. May I come in?

GRANDMA: Come in, doctor.

CYCLOPS *(He enters the apartment)*: This place radiates. It has an answer to a question.

GRANDMA: Ah, what is the answer?

CYCLOPS: Ha, what is the question?

GRANDMA: Why have you come?

CYCLOPS: Your grandson came to me during his lunch hour. He asked me to visit you . . . without a fee, until he gets paid.

GRANDMA: You can go if you want.

CYCLOPS: Old woman, I understand that you can barely see. I am here to make you see clearly. May I begin my examination?

GRANDMA: You may. But I think only heaven's light can restore my vision.

(CYCLOPS *seems puzzled. He adjusts the eye chart in* AGATE's *arms.*)

CYCLOPS *(to* AGATE*)*: You dazzle my good eye. *(To* GRANDMA.*)* What do you see here?

GRANDMA: Faint marks.

CYCLOPS: Old woman, do you know that these marks which you see have said all the great things about life? Often in translation. Not to see this letter E is not to see the greatest thoughts ever written. The great philosopher Plato used this letter. Think of the title of his greatest work — *The Republic.* In that title the E and only the E is used more than once. Theee Reeeepublic. Old woman, I implore you to see this letter E. Old woman, I ask you again: What do you see here?

GRANDMA: Clouds in the shape of a flower. A white rose.

CYCLOPS: This chart tests sight not vision! *(To* AGATE.*)* She frightens me. What is your name?

AGATE: They call me Agate, for my eyes.

CYCLOPS: Ah yes, Agate eyes. Drink to me only with thine eyes. *(Sings)* "Drink to me only with thine eyes and I will pledge with mine."

AGATE: You have a strange look.

CYCLOPS: Oh yes. You see, one eye is glass.

AGATE: Which one?

CYCLOPS: I forget. You . . . do your eyes always tear so?

AGATE: Yes.

CYCLOPS: Ah, that's a wonderful problem. It challenges the scientific inquirer in me. Would you like to come to my office? Professionally, of course.

AGATE: I'm not sure I can make the time.

CYCLOPS: You see, I have hours in the morning. I have a passionate interest in you. That is, in your eyes in the interest of science. And in the interest of science there would be, ah, no charge.

AGATE: Then I'll come.

*(*CYCLOPS *gives* AGATE *his business card. A very dapper Dr.* ACHILLES *enters wearing a pinstripe suit and a hombourg. He carries a case. He rings the doorbell.* GRANDMA *goes to the window.)*

GRANDMA: Yes.

ACHILLES: Is there an old woman in this house?

GRANDMA: I am an old woman. Can I help you?

ACHILLES: May I come in?

GRANDMA: Come. Come in.

ACHILLES *(enters)*: I'm Doctor Achilles.

GRANDMA: Ah, yes. My grandson sent you.

ACHILLES: Yes, you see . . .

GRANDMA: At lunch time . . .

ACHILLES: Yes. How . . .

GRANDMA: He did not pay.

ACHILLES: Oh, but he will. I know he will because he argued with me and I agreed to charge half my fee.

GRANDMA: Half your help is enough. All your help could not make me walk firmly again.

ACHILLES: Tell me, old woman. . . . Why can't you walk?

GRANDMA: I have little need of it,

ACHILLES: We must create a need.

GRANDMA: I have given away my wares.

ACHILLES: Sit down; take off your shoes. These hands will massage faith into your feet.

GRANDMA: My life is in Greater Hands.

ACHILLES: You musn't talk like that. You must imagine how successful I am at my office. Imagine that you enter a reception room thickly carpeted, decorated in exquisite taste. And there . . . there on the wall, are my college diplomas—in Latin—to give you confidence in me.

CYCLOPS: Mine are in Latin too. I've a medical degree from Syracuse. The eye is my specialty. I take it yours is the foot.

ACHILLES: Theater Arts.

CYCLOPS: Sir?

ACHILLES: M.F.A. Carnegie Tech.

CYCLOPS: Sir, I don't quite understand.

ACHILLES: I've studied life in the theater and the theater in life.

CYCLOPS: Sir, you're a quack.

ACHILLES: Quack, sir?

CYCLOPS: Quack.

ACHILLES: Quack?

CYCLOPS: Quack. Quack.

ACHILLES: How dare you, sir? Why I have done more to keep people vertical than any of you medicine men.

CYCLOPS: You presume, sir.

ACHILLES: I tell you, sir, I get results. I don't need carpets, decor, or diplomas. I know life. (*He turns to* GRANDMA *with hands outstretched in a dramatic pose.*) Old woman, are you listening to me?

GRANDMA: I am a browned fallen leaf.

ACHILLES: Listen!

GRANDMA: I listen.

ACHILLES (*His voice takes on a mystical note. Imitations of other voices seem to emanate from him as he gesticulates like a stage hypnotist.*): Grandmother, listen to me.

GRANDMA: Yes, Mickey.

(DIAMOND *enters, turns on a soap opera and then watches the proceedings with mild interest,*)

ACHILLES: Mother-in-law, listen to me.

GRANDMA: Yes, Diamond.

ACHILLES: Mother, listen to me.

GRANDMA: Yes, Deacon.

ACHILLES: Wife, listen to me.

GRANDMA: Yes, husband.

ACHILLES: Daughter, listen to me.

GRANDMA: Yes, your holiness.

ACHILLES: Girl, listen to me.

GRANDMA: Yes, papa.

ACHILLES: Child, listen to me.

GRANDMA: Yes, mother.

ACHILLES (*clucking to a baby*): Come here little one. (*He stretches his arms out.*) Come to me. Come, come to my arms. Come little one. Walk. (*Suddenly the dialogue of the soap opera, underscored with organ music, booms out. The mood of the hypnotic proceedings is shattered.*) No! (*in a frustrated rage*) No! No!

CYCLOPS: You're mad.

AGATE: Stop it. You'll frighten the old woman.

DIAMOND: What's going on here?

ACHILLES (*Turns off the soap opera angrily*): You! Do you know what you did?

DIAMOND: Who are you?

ACHILLES: No! Who are you?

DIAMOND: I'm the woman of this house.

ACHILLES: And she?

DIAMOND: She is the old woman.

ACHILLES: Ah, Ah. Old woman, the selfish world intrudes. You will have to endure your pain.

DIAMOND: We all do.

ACHILLES (*sensually, sympathetically*): And, what is your pain? Is it the foot?

DIAMOND: No, the heart.

ACHILLES: Ah, I know the heart, too. Is it, perhaps, a kind of heartburn?

DIAMOND: No, more like a burned heart.

ACHILLES: Ah, I see. For that you need an appointment at the office. Here is my card.

DIAMOND: Thank you, doctor. Why don't you continue with the old woman?

ACHILLES: The mood is ruined.

DIAMOND: She walks anyway, doctor. Not well, but she walks.

ACHILLES: Were you fooling me, old woman?

GRANDMA (*coming out of her trance*): You took me back again to old places and lands for the last time.

ACHILLES: You were fooling me.

GRANDMA: When I had to walk, I walked. There was Diamond to teach how to cook. There were the church festivals to bake cakes for. There were the home breads with their sweet, sweet smells. Those were the days of walking.

AGATE: Oh, I remember those days, mama. What smells. Glory to your hands, mama. And glory to your feet.

GRANDMA: They were dancing feet, once. When I first came to this country they asked me to dance. And I danced for the joy of being in a new home free from hunger and fear. I danced when this hair still had streaks of gold in it. Oh, what memories. And now where are the memories. There are shadows of memories.

(Suddenly GRANDMA *becomes rigid. Her eyes close tightly.)*

CYCLOPS: What is it old woman?
GRANDMA: It is a dizziness.
DIAMOND: Mama, come lie down.
GRANDMA: These are the signs of age, Diamond. This used to happen when I dried the dishes you washed. And now it happens when I sit.
AGATE: Go lie down, mama.
GRANDMA: This is my grandson's day. I have not read my Bible. This haze. This haze, doctor.
CYCLOPS: Read no more, old woman.
DIAMOND: I'll read to you, mama.
GRANDMA: These beads need a new string or they will lose their use.
DIAMOND: Count your beads in bed, mama.

(All but AGATE *and* ACHILLES *enter the other room.* ACHILLES *points his foot at the eye chart.)*

AGATE: Are you going to kick it?
ACHILLES: I'm reading it.
AGATE: Wouldn't it be easier with your shoe off?
ACHILLES *(Hurt pride)*: Please! *(With effort.)* The first letter is E.
AGATE: You peeked.
ACHILLES: Try *your* foot at it.
AGATE: My feet are tired.
ACHILLES: Oh? Sit down. Sit down. Let's have a look. *(*AGATE *sits.* ACHILLES *kneels, takes off her slipper and holds her foot tenderly.)* Hmm.

*(*AGATE *notices* DEACON *entering the yard and looking at the window.* ACHILLES *tickles her foot.)*

AGATE *(giggles)*: Gently, doctor.
ACHILLES *(He fondles her foot as* CYCLOPS *enters.)*: This is an exquisite foot. The arch is so high. Obviously unburdened. The foot of a single woman.
AGATE: A widow.
ACHILLES: Ah.
AGATE: But I have problems.
ACHILLES: Of course. And I can take care of them. Come to my office. I have hours in the evening. *(He gives her his card.)*

CYCLOPS (*Desperately tries to win her away from* ACHILLES): Agate eyes.

AGATE: He says I have a wonderfully high arch.

CYCLOPS: He's a fraud.

ACHILLES: I know the remedy for this woman's problem.

CYCLOPS: You can't trust him. Besides, you promised to visit me.

AGATE: Your hours are in the morning. His are at night.

CYCLOPS: Ah, I have always lacked a depth of vision.

AGATE: I am coming to you first.

CYCLOPS: Those who love with eyes never win on earth.

ACHILLES: I must go. There is no more to be done here.

AGATE: Oh, gentlemen, how do you find the old woman?

(They move into the yard.)

CYCLOPS: The light of her eye is dimming.

ACHILLES: Her foundation is crumbling. *(Exits.)*

CYCLOPS: Remember me. (CYCLOPS *falls to his knees and passionately kisses* AGATE'*s hand. He dashes off.*) Remember me.

AGATE (*Calls after him*): I shall.

DEACON (*Comes forward as* AGATE *places her foot on the first step, on her way upstairs*): Ah. Ah.

AGATE: Ah, you're home early.

DEACON (*Puts down his package*): Ah.

AGATE: What is it, Deacon?

(DIAMOND enters from the bedroom, crosses to the window and listens to the voices in the yard.)

DEACON: My dream of you is shattered, Agate. I had always seen you as that innocent child looking at me with love.

AGATE: I've been married, Deacon.

DEACON: What I never saw. . . . Forgive me, Agate. I forget that you are no different from the world.

AGATE: And you, Deacon. Who were you promised to when you married?

DEACON: I remember, Agate.

AGATE: I need a man just as you need a woman.

DEACON: I know, Agate.

AGATE: Don't be jealous, Deacon.

DEACON: I'm not, Agate.

AGATE: At least I remained in the same building with you for over twenty years. How many times I lied to my husband that we could not afford to move. I did it to be near you . . . your spirit, Deacon.

DEACON: Go then, Agate. Go to some one else's house. I have been a spiritual bigamist too long.

AGATE: I bequeath my daughter to you, Deacon.

DEACON: To my son who is me. Oh, but Agate he is not me. He is far from me. And today I said to myself I will say he is me. I will come home early and make a rite of it. I will bring him this cake and this gift. But I don't feel the rite. I do not feel it deep inside of me. Deep inside where I used to feel things the times I thought my deepest thoughts.

AGATE: He's nearer to you than you think, Deacon. He's just like you. He went to work, today.

DEACON: He went to work today? My son went to work?

AGATE: So many good things have happened from his going.

DEACON: I'm happy. I guess it was just a matter of time.

AGATE: I always said that boy was going to be something. I never knew what, but I knew he was going to be something. He sent your mother a silver cane. And he sent those two fine doctors that you saw.

DEACON (indicating the package): He'll need this new coat now that he's working.

AGATE: Are you happy, Deacon?

DEACON: I am happy.

AGATE: Will you let me be happy, now, with my freedom?

DEACON: We are divorced, Agate.

AGATE: Thank you, Deacon.

DEACON: Why think of what life could have been like when this one is a success. You ought to be happy with one of those fine doctors.

AGATE: One of them needs me.

DEACON: Go to him, then.

AGATE: Give me to him with a kiss.

DEACON (comes close to her): With this kiss, I thee give. (They kiss tenderly.) It is hard . . . to give you away with a kiss. (DIAMOND turns on the radio in an agitated manner.) But it is so ennobling. Farewell. Let's look to our children.

AGATE: Farewell, Deacon.

(AGATE exits up the stairs. DIAMOND stalks into the kitchen. The soap opera comes on loudly. DEACON enters the house and shouts above the sound. He puts his package in a corner and the box on the table.)

DEACON: I am home. I am home. I am home! Oh, Universe, I am home. Oh world, I am home. Oh family, I am home. Some one come out and kiss me a welcome. Some one come out and say hello to me! (There is a moment of silence. DIAMOND enters and looks sullenly at DEACON.) You have come to say hello. (There is silence again. DEACON extends his arms and laughs.) Then you have come to kiss me welcome.

DIAMOND (Turns off the soap opera): Haven't you had enough kissing today.

DEACON (*realizing*): Oh, Diamond, don't take offence. Agate and I were saying farewell.

DIAMOND: Maybe I should say farewell. Then you could go to that man eater.

DEACON: There is no need to say that.

DIAMOND: I saw her with those men.

DEACON: She's serious about one of them.

DIAMOND: I could have been serious with one of them too.

DEACON: Stop it, Diamond. Stop it! You frighten me.

DIAMOND: You're lucky that I find my romance in those soap operas only. Be glad that that is the only thing you have to be jealous of. Some day, Deacon, some day it may be different.

DEACON: What do you want of me?

DIAMOND: Be a husband, Deacon.

DEACON: It is fall . . . the autumn of our lives.

DIAMOND: And there is a chill. Put your old arm around me. I feel alone. If my son should go tomorrow, there would be nothing. And there must be something . . . some warmth . . . some romance.

DEACON: There is romance for us, now. Mickey is taking hold. He's gone to work.

DIAMOND: And you're going to give that romance away to her girl. Then where is our romance, Deacon. Then there is none, Deacon. Then I warn you, Deacon. I don't know what kind of woman I shall become when he is gone.

DEACON: Diamond, precious Diamond, stop frightening me. (*Indicates the box on the table.*) Let's not talk like this. Let's prepare these things for our son.

DIAMOND: All right, Deacon. We'll prepare for our son. We eat lean, today. I'll cut some dried beef. Your mother is inside lying down.

(DIAMOND *exits.* DEACON *reflects a little, cheers up, and goes to the entrance of the bedroom on tip toes.*)

DEACON (*singing*): Mama . . . Mama . . . Mama . . . Mama. (*He enters the bedroom. His voice comes from off stage.*) This is your son. This is your son. It's too dark in here.

GRANDMA (*off*): I'll sit outside.

(DEACON *and* GRANDMA *come out. He holds his mother as he leads her to a chair shuffling in a small dance step and humming as he goes along.*)

DEACON: Let's go. Let's go. That's right. Let's go. Sit here. Sit here. (*He helps her to a chair and then looks at her with admiration.*)

GRANDMA: How were things at work?

DEACON: I'm tired, mama.

GRANDMA: That is your age, my son. I grow old. Should not you?

DEACON: This is no time to grow old, mama. We still like to eat.

GRANDMA: One day lean . . . one day rich. One day bread and cheese . . . one day bread.

DEACON: That was over there, mama. Over here we need vitamins.

GRANDMA: We will have those some day, too.

DEACON: Are you well, mama?

GRANDMA: Well enough.

DEACON: Are you happy, mama?

GRANDMA: Happy enough. We have two working men in this house, now.

DEACON: Isn't that good. I'm glad I bought this cake. We have real cause to celebrate. *(He opens the box on the table and extracts a layer cake. He places a box of candles next to it.)* Put the candles on the cake, mama. We'll have a party after supper. *(GRANDMA starts putting candles on the cake while DEACON dances and sings.)* Under the apple tree. / Under the apple tree / I loved my love, / Under the apple tree. *(He looks at the cake.)* That's a nice way to put candles in. I'm going to eat now.

(DEACON exits into the kitchen. GRANDMA continues putting candles on the cake. PEARL enters the yard and crosses to the window.)

PEARL: Grandma, are you there?

GRANDMA: Come in, Pearl.

PEARL *(enters)*: It's a beautiful cake.

GRANDMA: It is for Mickey's birthday. You put the rest of the candles in.

PEARL *(Does so)*: I wish I could see the candles lit.

GRANDMA: If not this year, the next. Be reserved.

PEARL: Will he come to me?

GRANDMA: He has gone to work, so he will.

PEARL: But how can you be sure?

GRANDMA: Work and love go together.

PEARL: I'm worried about mama.

GRANDMA: No need to worry anymore. She knows he is working.

PEARL: But he doesn't have to work for me. I'm strong. I work for mama now. I could work for him. And then he would find his way. And I would be happy . . . happier than I've ever been since papa died.

GRANDMA: Do not appear anxious.

PEARL: I'm not. I don't look anxious, do I? Do I?

GRANDMA: And never go to him until he calls.

PEARL: I never will.

GRANDMA: Remember that. Will you now?

PEARL: I will. I will. Good night, grandma.

(PEARL enters the yard and then exits upstairs. GRANDMA adjusts the candles. MICKEY enters looking very sad and somewhat nervous.)

GRANDMA: Mickey?

MICKEY: It's me, grandma.

GRANDMA: Are you home already?

MICKEY: I am.

GRANDMA: Your face is so long.

MICKEY: I'm tired, grandma.

GRANDMA: So was your father.

MICKEY (*anxiously*): Is he home so soon? (*Sees the cake.*) What's this?

GRANDMA: He bought it for your birthday.

MICKEY: It's nice that he remembered.

GRANDMA: He's eating. Go eat with him.

MICKEY: I'm not hungry.

GRANDMA: You're shivering. Go sit in the sun.

MICKEY (*Looks at the waning sun*): The sun, grandma, is almost gone. The light you see is not the laugh of the sun, but the smile. It is the sad smile from which the melancholy moon warms itself.

GRANDMA: Was your work hard?

MICKEY: No, grandma.

GRANDMA: The cane came. It's beautiful.

MICKEY: The handle is only chrome.

GRANDMA: It's the best metal for a short life.

MICKEY: It's not paid for yet.

GRANDMA: You may be able to return it if I have no use for it. Your doctors came, too.

MICKEY: I picked them because they seemed so full of hope.

GRANDMA: One of them fell in love with Agate. We will not fear her evil eye any more. Her daughter is ours.

MICKEY: I don't know what we're going to do with her.

GRANDMA: Your father favors her.

MICKEY: I've got to talk to him.

GRANDMA: Mickey, I want you to have my beads.

MICKEY (*fearfully*): No!

GRANDMA: The beads went slowly in my fingers today. It was as if they were saying to me: old woman, you have prayed enough.

MICKEY (*Dashes to the window and holds on to the frame as he looks out*): No! Keep using them, Grandma. I don't know how to pray.

GRANDMA: What are you doing, Mickey?

MICKEY: I'm looking for a sign.

GRANDMA: Out there?

MICKEY: In the sky.

GRANDMA: Don't look out. Look in, my boy.

MICKEY (*Rushes to her, kneels beside her and begins to cry*): Grandma.

GRANDMA: Don't cry, Mickey.

MICKEY: I left my job. I let you down. I let papa down.

GRANDMA: Put these beads in your pocket. (She puts her prayer beads in his pocket.) Go wash your face. (MICKEY exits to the bedroom. DEACON enters from the kitchen feeling his paunch as he walks along.) Are you content, my son?

DEACON: When the belly is full, it makes me sleepy and content with life, mama.

GRANDMA: Your son is home.

DEACON: He's home in good time. It must be a good job. Did he see the cake? (He calls into the kitchen.) Diamond, bring some matches. (To GRANDMA.) Wait until he sees the surprise I bought him.

DIAMOND (off): Don't light the candles now!

DEACON: Mickey is home.

DIAMOND (Enters calling loudly): Mickey! Come join us!

GRANDMA: He seemed tired, Diamond.

(MICKEY enters wiping his face with a towel.)

DIAMOND: Are you tired, Mickey?

MICKEY: I'm okay.

DIAMOND: Did you see the cake?

MICKEY (mumbling absently): It's nice, mama, very nice.

DIAMOND: What's the matter?

DEACON: Nothing. Nothing is the matter. It's just his first day at work and he's tired. Give me the matches. You'll have a piece of cake, Mickey. We have a lot to celebrate tonight.

MICKEY: Pa.

DEACON: Yes, Mickey. (He continues to light the candles.)

MICKEY: Pa.

DEACON: Talk, Mickey, talk while I light the candles.

MICKEY: Pa, it's about my job.

DEACON (Goes to the light switch and turns it off; the scene continues in candlelight): Out with the lights. You don't like work I know. Human beings are like wild horses. They must be broken for work. You don't know what it is to bend your neck during the daylight hours. You must learn.

MICKEY: No, pa.

DEACON: No what?

MICKEY: Pa, I left my job.

DEACON: Again? In half a day?

MICKEY: In four hours, pa.

DEACON: But why? Why?!

DIAMOND: Deacon, let the boy alone.

DEACON: Let him talk. Let him talk to me. Why?

MICKEY: I don't know. I mean. Well, it was the clips and the pins.

DEACON: Don't talk nonsense with me.

MICKEY: I was in a stock room and there were papers that came in. You understand, pa? These papers that came in looked the same. All of them. Thousands of them. They came in with pins on them. And I . . . I sent them out to someone else with clips on them. The clips went out and the pins came in. And in three hours I had a pile of pins and no clips. A pile that wasn't a pyramid, or a parthenon, or a cathedral. Only pins. Thousands of them . . . sharp and one inch long. And I asked myself, why? Why, I asked, should the clips go out and the pins come in?

DEACON: The meaning is like the falling of mountains to time and filling of seas with mountains. Meaning? There is as much meaning as that!

MICKEY: But pa, somehow I ended up in a stock room and something deep down bothered me.

DEACON: Indolence bothered you! Indolence!

MICKEY: No, no, pa. I was thinking . . . thinking hard.

DEACON: You will learn not to think, some day. I used to think. Mama, tell him what a thinker I was. Over there. What did our greatest national thinker say about me, mama?

GRANDMA: He said you were a thinker.

DEACON: You hear that. I was a philosopher and poet, that's what I was. And I looked for meanings. Oh, oh! I remember my golden days. You hear me? I used to run to the tops of hills, barefoot, and look at the sky. I used to stand panting with blood beating in my temples and a cool breeze brushing my face. And with each beat I was aware!! Bump!! Bump! Bump! Aware, do you hear, that there was something I had to know. And I looked hard into the sky until my eyes filled with tears. I was a chosen one who would see an answer or a sign. Ha. Ha. Ha. Ha. Ha. *(Crying.)* I am laughing and I am crying, do you hear. I asked myself in my mind: Who is the Creator?!! For what do we work in His eyes?!! Yes! Yes! Who is He?!

MICKEY: Tell me.

DEACON: Ah, to tell you . . . to tell you that, . . . what things I thought about Him!

MICKEY: Give me the answer.

DEACON: Never mind. I won't tell you. I forgot those things about Him. And when I forgot those things I forgot Him. Because in this world . . . when your father is dead . . . and you are small and hungry . . . you must forget to be good. And yet believe me I am not bad.

MICKEY: What are you, pa?

DEACON: What I am is a believer, a thinker . . . I am a great man. No . . . no, what am I talking about? I am not those things. Rather I was those things. But I have to earn a living, now. You see, what I'm trying to say is I am and I am not those things.

MICKEY: You mean, we come to go. We live to die?

DEACON: Ah! Ah! Ah!!! It is. It is. It is a devil of a thing . . . waiting for death to come . . . in his own sweet time.

DIAMOND: Deacon, no more talk. Let's cut the cake.

DEACON: There is no taste in such things, now.

DIAMOND: The candles are half burnt.

DEACON: Let them burn . . . burn away and leave us in the dark.

DIAMOND: Don't talk that way in front of the boy.

DEACON (raging at her): You. You. What do you know what I'm talking about. I am telling him things about life on earth. (To MICKEY.) You hear me son?!! Do you hear me when I talk to you?!! Do you hear me when as a father, as your unwilling father, I say to you: Go back! Go back to your job! I say to you: Go back! Go back!! GO BACK!!!

MICKEY (shouting back): All right, go back! But how?!! How do you go back?!!!

DEACON: You walk!!! You walk in. That's all!!!

MICKEY: My soul cries no!!!

DEACON: Don't think for one moment you have one!

MICKEY: I'm looking for a sign!

DEACON: The immortal soul of man is not!

MICKEY: How can I go back without one?!

DEACON: How do I go back without mine? Yes, how do I walk into my work without my immortal soul? Yes, how dare I? I am a man of almost sixty. . . . How dare I not have an immortal soul. I walk into work because I have a family. I have had the weight of life on me from childhood. And then a wife. And then a family. I gave up my immortal soul for these things.

MICKEY: Don't talk like that in front of grandma.

DEACON: Would she had never borne me. You're a man. Now I'll tell you. The immortal soul of man goes with one great wrong. I lost mine with my only woman!

DIAMOND: Deacon!

DEACON: All right. All right. I haven't said a thing, Diamond. Have I said anything, son? Son, have I?

MICKEY (crying): You never said a thing, pa.

DEACON: Son, the immortal soul of man goes with one great wrong.

(GRANDMA stiffens, closes her eyes, and then remains motionless. There is a moment of silence as the birthday cake candles flicker in the dark.)

MICKEY: Then, what is there in all of this?

DEACON: There is love. I love you, son.

MICKEY (Goes to his father): Love, pa. Can you wait while I'm searching? (They embrace impulsively.)

DEACON: My life is yours. Diamond, give him his gift.

DIAMOND *(She brings the package to* MICKEY*.)*: From your father and me.

MICKEY *(Opens the package and takes out the coat)*: You shouldn't have gone to such expense. *(He puts it on.)* It's warm.

DIAMOND: It'll keep the winter from your back.

MICKEY: Thanks. Thanks. Grandma, look at my coat! *(He crosses to her.)* She's asleep. Grandma, what's the matter? Ma. Pa. She doesn't answer. Her eyes are blinking. She's moving her mouth but she can't talk. Grandma, speak to me!

DEACON: Mama. Mama, what is it?

DIAMOND: It's a stroke. She's had a stroke. Mickey, call the hospital. Rub her hands, Deacon. *(She dashes out and calls up the stairs.)* Agate! Agate! Agate! Agate!

DEACON: Mama. Mama. Talk, talk.

*(*MICKEY *goes to the phone and calls the hospital.)*

AGATE *(off)*: What is it?

DIAMOND: Come down. Something has happened to mama.

AGATE *(Comes down the steps and enters)*: What is it?

DIAMOND *(Embraces* AGATE*)*: Oh, Agate. She's dying, I think.

AGATE *(Holds her tightly)*: Don't cry. Don't cry. *(She calls up the stairs.)* Pearl. Pearl. Pearl come down. *(She turns away from the stairs.)* Never mind her. Let me see mama. *(She approaches* GRANDMA*.)*

DIAMOND: Do something, Agate.

AGATE: Mama. Mama. This is your Agate. Will you talk to me? Get hot towels and cold towels. We'll put them on her head in turns. Rub her feet, Diamond. Keep rubbing her hands, Deacon.

DIAMOND: Mickey, heat water, chop ice.

*(*MICKEY *exits into kitchen.)*

DEACON: Mama . . . mama. I'm sorry for what I said. You've been a good mother to me all these years. I love you mama. You know I love you. I said what I said because I was tired. Mama you know I love you. Look, Diamond . . . Agate . . . look she understands me. She forgives me.

AGATE: She forgives you, Deacon. You can see that she is smiling.

DEACON: Oh, mama. My dear mama, thank you. Thank you. Here's a kiss for you. Don't be like this. Was this the way you were to be? Sing to me like you used to sing. Touch my head. Bless me like you used to and pray for me.

AGATE: Her eyes bless you, Deacon.

DEACON: Thank you, mama. I love your silver hair. I loved it when it was gold and fell on my face when I was small. Look, this strand falls on me. There, I put it back.

AGATE: Rub her hands, Deacon.

DIAMOND: Is it serious, Agate?

AGATE: I have seen these things before.

DIAMOND: Is it bad?

AGATE: It is good, too.

MICKEY (*Enters with the towels*): Here're the towels. The ambulance is on its way.

AGATE: It will come.

(*They continue to aid* GRANDMA. *There is a distant wail of a siren that becomes progressively louder.*)

MICKEY: There it is. (*He dashes out as the sound of the siren gets louder. There is the sound of brakes as the ambulance comes to a halt off right.* DOCTOR *enters with a bag. Two* ATTENDANTS *remain in the yard.*)

DOCTOR: This the house?

MICKEY: It's my grandmother. Make her well, Doc.

DOCTOR: We'll see. (*He enters the house, followed by* MICKEY. *There are general greetings.* DOCTOR *opens his kit, adjusts his stethoscope and examines* GRANDMA.) Uh huh. (*He leaves* GRANDMA's *side and comes to the others.*) Looks like a stroke. Her left side is paralyzed.

DEACON: She doesn't talk.

DOCTOR: The speech area of the brain is probably damaged. Her heart is fibrillating badly.

DEACON: Doctor, I'm her son. What does this mean?

DOCTOR: Well, she's old.

DEACON: But Doctor, this is my mother.

DOCTOR: That's what makes it difficult every time.

MICKEY: (*Approaches* DOCTOR *and his father.*) What are you saying, doc?

DOCTOR: Easy, son, easy.

DEACON: Oh, Diamond, Diamond.

DIAMOND: I'm here, Deacon.

DEACON: Hold my hand, Diamond.

DIAMOND: I am, Deacon.

DEACON: What are we going to do?

DIAMOND: We'll live.

DOCTOR: I want to get her to the hospital. (*He goes to the door and calls the* ATTENDANTS.) Boys, no stretcher. We'll take her in the chair. (*The men enter and take up* GRANDMA *in the chair and exit.* DOCTOR *addresses the older people.*) You people can come along if you like. (*To* MICKEY.) I don't think you'd better come, son.

MICKEY: Pa.

DEACON: Stay here, son.

MICKEY (*Hugs his father*): Pa.

DEACON: This is my job to be with my mother. Your time of sorrow will come.

(DIAMOND *and* AGATE *exit while* DEACON *lingers a moment with his son.* DEACON *then follows the women.* MICKEY *tries to follow, but the doctor blocks his way.*)

DOCTOR: Take it easy, son. This comes to everyone. Calm down.

MICKEY: I'm sorry, doc. You don't know what it is. . . . You see too much of sickness and death.

DOCTOR: I had a mother once.

MICKEY: I'm sorry, doc.

DOCTOR: That's all right. So long. (*He is going off, then stops and turns.*) Oh, by the way. Have you heard about the war?

(*The announcement seems to make little impression on* MICKEY. DOCTOR *exits. The motor starts offstage and the siren begins to wail.* MICKEY *takes the beads from his pocket and begins praying.*)

MICKEY: *Der Voghormia.* Lord have mercy.

(*The sound of the siren recedes and fades out. At that instant a musical note of the same sad frequency sounds.* MICKEY *reacts to the change in sound. He straightens and listens intently. The last candle on the cake goes out and only smoke rises from it like the smoke from a censer. As* MICKEY *turns into the yard,* PEARL *comes to the head of the stairs and then comes half way down. They clasp hands.*)

MICKEY: Have you heard about the war?

PEARL: What war?

MICKEY: Let's go to the corner newsstand and find out.

Blackout

EPILOGUE (IN THE PRESENT)

(*The lights come up on the older* MICKEY *with raincoat and hat.*)

MICKEY: Best Way Foods was understanding and gave me back my job. I worked till I was drafted for military service. I fought in Europe. I was lucky. No purple hearts. Not even a scratch. I came back here after the war and married Pearl. She worked while I went to college on the G.I. Bill. Somehow it was in the stars—I went to work for Best Way again. In quick time I rose to Vice President of the frozen food division. As you know frozen foods took off after the war. But frozen shish kebab?—Never. It was—as I said—a different kind of time . . . A prayerful pause between one holocaust and another. *(He takes a final look into the apartment and then salutes the audience goodbye, finger to brow.)* It's always that way: You end at the beginning.

Fade out

End of play

BARBARA BEJOIAN

DANCE MAMA, DANCE

A Play in Two Acts

THE PLAYWRIGHT

Barbara Bejoian is a 1984 graduate of Brown University's playwriting M.F.A. program. She is the recipient of the 1983 Brown University Creative Writing Award and the 1997 Brown University Presidential Fellowship. Commissioned by the artistic director, George Houston Bass, Bejoian became the first Caucasian woman to write and produce three Armenian American plays for Brown University's Rites and Reason Company. The third production, *Dance Mama, Dance*, in 1989, was under a Rockefeller Grant. A 1995 Fulbright Scholar, a 1994 Critics Choice Award Winner at the Edinburgh Festival Fringe, Bejoian has also been awarded ten National Endowment for the Arts Artist-in-Residencies for playwriting, the Rhode Island Feminist Theater Premier Award, and the Massachusetts Artist Foundation Finalist Award. Bejoian's ten plays have appeared in Boston, Providence, New York, Fort Lauderdale, London, Edinburgh, and Erevan. She received her education from Brown University, the British Broadcasting Company, Radcliffe College, and Wheaton College. Bejoian has been faculty and guest lecturer on playwriting at Brown University, Rhode Island School of Design, Rhode Island College, American University in Armenia, Erevan State University, Vanadzor Teaching College, and New York University. She is best known for her Armenian plays, *Dance Mama, Dance, Eagles Without Wings, Horses Without Legs*, and her piece on Virginia

Woolf, entitled *A Play of One's Own.* Currently she is faculty at New York University's Gallatin School of Individualized Study and completing her new play, *Al-Khatun*, focusing on the life of Gertrude Bell, the first woman to graduate from Oxford University, who became the first female British Central Intelligence Agent at the turn of the twentieth century. Bejoian grew up in Watertown, Massachusetts, and lives in Providence, Rhode Island, with her husband, Newell Thomas, and their sons, Casey and Ian.

GROWTH AND MATURATION OF
DANCE MAMA, DANCE

George Houston Bass commissioned *Dance Mama, Dance* partly because he was fascinated with Armenian culture and history. He felt that Armenian stories had a great place in his African-American Theater due to the centuries of struggle endured by the Armenian people. He was further interested in the vast divisions of the Armenians regarding their religious and social politics, the communication between the diaspora and the Armenians who remained in Armenia, and the embracing nature of Armenian literature, music, art, and food. Barbara J. Merguerian, director of publications for the National Association of Armenian Centers, was engaged as the scholar overseeing the truthful and factual nature of the script, and Bass directed the production himself. The Tashnag and Ramgavar (active vs. moderate) political controversy—concerning the freeing of Armenia from Soviet domination—became a key element in the play's action because of its very real nature in Watertown, Massachusetts, during the twentieth century. That schism, which divided the community, has all but healed today, due to peaceful steps made toward reconciliation by apparently partisan churches and to respectful communication between Armenian Americans. The play is focused on the women's voice in Armenian life and Armenians' hope of sustaining pride for both their men and women in America and globally.

Because *Dance Mama, Dance* covers so much pertaining to Armenian life and living in the past hundred years, it is of considerable interest to see what George H. Bass, the director, has said about the Rites and Reason Method, which helped Barbara Bejoian bring her play to total fruition. In the play's program, Bass observed that RRM is "an ongoing community dialogue that allows people to actively participate in the creative process of making new plays about their own realities." An important part of this evolutionary process is what he calls "Folkthought Sessions" with scholars, theatre artists, and members of the community. He notes that *Dance Mama, Dance*

> was first produced by Rites and Reason in 1984 as part of the Research-to-Performance project, "Women in Transition." As part of the continuing development of the performance work, members of the Armenian com-

munity were invited to join Rites and Reason staff and friends in a public reading of the rehearsal script in the week preceding rehearsals for the current [1989] production. A *Folkthought Session* followed the reading and information gathered from the discussion was used by Barbara Bejoian to rewrite the script during the first weeks of rehearsal. Scholars from Soviet Armenia, Cambridge, Massachusetts, and Providence, as well as persons from Beirut, Lebanon, Watertown, Massachusetts, and the Providence Armenian community made it possible for Rites and Reason staff to make effective use of its Research-to-Performance method in its development of Bejoian's original script. The collaboration between theatre artist, Armenian scholars and members of the Armenian community has resulted in a stronger and clearer voicing of the experiences of Armenian American women. Bejoian's revised text more broadly reflects the shared experiences and perceptions of Armenian people from their own point of view than was the case in the 1984 production. The 1989 production of *Dance Mama, Dance* well demonstrates the usefulness of Rites and Reason's method for theatre production in a multi-cultural, multi-racial and pluralistic society.

Dance Mama, Dance was produced in 1989 under the auspices of Brown University's Rites and Reason Theatre, George Houston Bass, artistic director.
Directed by George Houston Bass

Assistant Director	Gilbert McCauley
Stage Manager	Samuel Moses
Technical Coordinator	Jack Feivou
Set Designer	Charles McClennahan
Costume Designer	Mirjana Mladinov
Lighting Designer	Jean Shorrock
Sound Designer	Barry Fishman

The Cast of Actors in the 1989 Premiere

LUCENE	Lowry Marshall
LUCENE (BRIDE)	Julia S. Martin
LUCENE (CHILD)	Liz Simon
VIOLET, Lucene's Mother	Bernice Bronson
ELENA, Lucene's best friend,	Katie Broomfield
MRS. AROOTSIAN, Lucene's favorite Armenian School teacher	Michelle Bach
ANNE (Ani), Lucene's Daughter	Jennifer Harmon
TAWKOHEE, Lucene's Mother's best friend	Rosalind Clark

NISHAN, Der Hayr of Lucene's parents' Church   Jim Prest
ARLENE, Der Hayr's Daughter   Sarah Clossey
VARTAN, Der Hayr's Son   Christopher Browning
TAWVEET, Lucene's Father, and the voice of
    Krikor, Lucene's Husband   Jan Koerbelin
THE GREAT COUNCIL OF ANCESTRAL MOTHERS   Michelle Bach,
                                 Bernice Bronson,
                                 Maritza Mezdurian

Additional characters (doubled by listed cast members wherever possible):
ARMENIAN DEACONS, ARMENIAN PRIEST, two YOUNG ARMENIAN GIRLS (LUCENE and ELENA as children), ARMENIAN MEN and WOMEN.

The playwright noted in the 1989 program that transliteration from the Armenian is a problem. She followed Dr. Barbara Merguerian in using a modified Library of Congress system within the play. That notwithstanding, there are many variant dialects of Armenian that can make pronouncing them phonetically, by means of the English alphabet, still problematical for the listener.

DANCE MAMA, DANCE

BARBARA BEJOIAN

The cast of characters corresponds to the list given for the premiere production.

PROLOGUE

A voice over of VIOLET AREVIAN *is heard.* THE GREAT COUNCIL OF ANCESTRAL MOTHERS *are listening.*

VIOLET AREVIAN: The final years of another age have come and gone. The old ways have fallen and lie in ruins of confusion. Only the pain of recollection is left. Men, women and children must sort through the ruins of tradition to gather whatever can be saved and used to move onward.

I, Violet Arevian, a Mother blessed with only one child, have recently departed from the living. I have asked The Great Council of Ancestral Mothers, immortal keepers of fortune and fate, to call forth from the ruins of confusion, the life memories of my daughter, Lucene, and help her to see the good of life . . . Help her move beyond the grip of old fears. And so, the Ancestral Mothers have come to a place called Watertown to review my daughter's fate and the lot of humanity about her.

ANCESTRAL MOTHERS (1): *(In low voices)* Lucene Arevian Kinsor. *(This is repeated over and over again)*

ANCESTRAL MOTHERS (2): *(In high voices and joining the low voices)* Lucene Arevian Kinsor.

ANCESTRAL MOTHERS (3): *(In medium voices, joining "all" voices)* Lucene . . .
Lucene . . . Lucene

VIOLET AREVIAN: As was the case many times before and many times after the great
flood when Noah and Moses and "the woman at the well" were challenged to
make a choice that marked the fortune of what was to come, Lucene's moment of judgement is here.

Lucene, The Woman . . . Lucene, The Girl . . . Lucene, The Bride . . . will
stand life's test for a troubled woman—divided in thought . . . A troubled people—divided in custom. The sifting and sorting of Lucene's life memories will
tell us if, a person and a people, so divided against itself can reclaim a sense of
wholeness and walk onward, away from the ruins of the past to an illumined
future.

End of prologue.

ACT ONE

Scene One

The stage is dark. A spot comes up on LUCENE. *Haunting Armenian music from a single instrument is heard.*

LUCENE: There is a concentration camp of the mind
In which women have been forced to dwell
And my Father was the first man to lead me there.
It is an ancient camp
Where women have been taught
To wear veil upon veil
That hides their loveliness.
It is an ancient camp
Of silent voices
Where duty still demands
That all women surrender
Their personhood to wifery.
And even here on the modern streets
Of this new and different land,
The habits fashioned in those
Ancient days, from those too—too
Ancient ways still hold fast,

Denying my beauty, denying my strength,
Denying my power to flee.
I remain in the concentration camp of the mind
That my Father showed me
As the only good and rightful place
A good woman, a good wife, a good mother
Can be or ever want to be.
My Father was always known to be
A very truthful man.
Perhaps—
My father lied to me.

Lights come up on the Armenian Church. Armenian Church music is playing.
LUCENE *enters the church. She is wearing a shawl that was once worn by her Mother*
VIOLET, *who has died recently.*

[All Armenian translations or explanations will be put in these brackets. They are not part of the spoken script.]

ARMENIAN DEACONS: (*Chanting in brash and rough toned voices*) Sourp Asdvadz, sourp yev huzor, Soorp yev anmah, vor hariaree merelots, voghormia mez! [*Holy God, holy and strong, holy and immortal, who rose from the dead, have mercy on us*]

LUCENE *is jolted by the chant. She begins to hear other sounds as she continues on into the church.*

ARMENIAN PRIEST: (*Chanting in a calm, but forceful voice*) Put the Holy Oils on the child!! Anon Hor, Yev vort toe, Yev hokoone, Surpo, Amen . . . [*In the name of the Father, the Son and the Holy Spirit, Amen.*]

TWO YOUNG ARMENIAN GIRLS: Ipe, Pen, Kim, Ta, Yech, Zah . . . [*Beginning of the Armenian alphabet*]

LUCENE'S MOTHER VIOLET: (*With a slight Armenian accent*) I'm you're Mother, that's who!! . . . Of course you're pretty . . . of course you're smart . . . you're an Armenian girl!!

ARMENIAN DEACONS: (*Speaking with brash and rough toned voices*) Havadamk ee mee Asdvatz, ee ariun amenagal, haroutuin yergni yev yergri . . . !! [*We believe in one God the Father almighty, maker of heaven and earth.*]

LUCENE *is haunted by all of the sounds she is hearing. She pulls out a five dollar bill and puts it in a gold plate lined with maroon velvet by a stack of white candles. While looking all around, petrified, she takes a candle, places it in the candle stand and lights it with a match in memory of her deceased Mother.*

ARMENIAN PRIEST: *(Chanting loudly)* Burn the candle for the Mother who is dead!!!!

ARMENIAN MEN AND WOMEN: *(A loud whisper)* Gearagnoryah tebrotz, Hie-gagon tebrozt, Americawn tebrozt!! *[Sunday School, Armenian School, American School.]*

TWO ARMENIAN GIRLS: *(Sounds of them marching in place can be heard)* Im Hera-vor hirerreneek . . . im paravorr Mirerreneek . . . *[My Fatherland . . . My Motherland . . . The beginning of an old Armenian marching song to let the Turkish people know that they cannot break the Armenian spirit.]*

TAWKOOHEE: She married a Tashnag . . . *[Pro-active political party]*

ARMENIAN WOMAN: She married a Tashnag . . .

ARMENIAN MAN: She married a Tashnag . . .

TAWKOOHEE: You make for "amot" *["shame"]* . . . You are Armenian voman with Armenian duties!!

ARMENIAN MEN AND WOMEN: *(A loud whisper)* Amot . . . Amot . . . Amot . . . *[Shame . . . shame . . . shame . . .]*

LUCENE'S MOTHER: Don't listen to the them!! They don't mean what they say!!

LUCENE *is incredibly frightened. She runs to a pew, kneels and begins to pray.*

LUCENE: *(Angry and lashing out)* They do mean what they say!! (Making the sign of the cross) Oh God, help me . . . keep the voices away!! Oh God!! Anon nor, yev vort toe, yev ho koone, surpo Amen . . . Hiyr mer vor hergins yes, soorp yeghitze anoon koh, yeghitze . . . *[In the name of the Father, the Son and the Holy Spirit, Amen. Our Father who art in Heaven, hallowed be thy name, Thy . . .]*

LUCENE *continues to say the Lord's Prayer trying to ignore her tormentors, but she cannot.*

FIRST YOUNG GIRL: Krisdos ee metch mez haidnetzav . . . *[First line of the Armenian "Kiss Of Peace" it means, Christ was made manifest amidst us.]*

SECOND YOUNG GIRL: Orhnial eh haidnootiunn Kristosi! *[Second line and final line of the "Kiss Of Peace" it means: Blessed is the manisfestation of Christ.]*

ARMENIAN DEACONS: An Armenian girl is her Father's daughter until she is her Husband's wife!!

ARMENIAN WOMEN: Eat the pomegranate, it will bring you children.

ARMENIAN PRIEST: (Chanting) Mgurdootuin yev artaranal, surpel ee meghatz . . . *[To be baptised and justified, to be cleansed from sins . . .]*

ARMENIAN WOMEN: Ani . . . Ani . . . Ani . . .

ARMENIAN PRIEST: *(Chanting)* Put the Holy Oil on the child!

TAWKOOHEE: Mekh eh . . . mekh eh . . . *[It's a sin . . . it's a sin]*

ARMENIAN WOMAN: Mekh eh . . .

ARMENIAN MAN: Mekh eh . . .

LUCENE: *(Calling out to all in the Church)* Leave me alone!! Let me bury my Mother in peace!! God . . . please?!

ARMENIAN MEN AND WOMEN: *(A loud whisper)* Mireega merav . . . Hireega merav . . . *[The Mother is dead . . . The Father is dead.]*

ARMENIAN MEN AND WOMEN: Oor eh Krikora? Oor eh Krikora? Mekh eh . . . mekh eh . . . *[Where is Krikor? Where is Krikor? It's a sin.]*

TAWKOOHEE: You got duty!!

ARMENIAN WOMAN: You got responsibility!!

ARMENIAN PRIEST: Take the maws . . . Take the maws . . . Take the maws . . . *[Maws is the blessed Thin Bread given to Armenians to eat after Sunday Church services.]*

LUCENE'S MOTHER: Eat the maws . . . *(Almost crying)* Lucene, eat the maws . . .

LUCENE: *(Crying from the pressure of the voices)* NO MAMA!! NO!

FATHER NISHAN enters, but LUCENE does not see him. She bows her head and folds her hands trying to pray the voices away.

TAWKOOHEE: Shame . . .

ARMENIAN WOMAN: She changed her name . . .

ARMENIAN MEN: She changed her name . . .

TAWKOOHEE: You changed your Armenian last name . . . inch-choo . . . inch-choo? *[Why . . . why?]*

ARMENIAN DEACONS: *(Chanting in brash and rough voices)* Soorp Asdvatz, soorp yev huzor, soorp yev anmah . . . !! *[Holy God, holy and strong, holy and immortal]*

LUCENE: *(Calling out)* Stop it!!

TWO ARMENIAN GIRLS: *(Singing and Marching)* Im Hairavorr hirerreneek . . . im paravorr Mirerreneek . . . *[As before . . . My fatherland, my beautiful motherland]*

LUCENE: *(Calling out)* Go away!!

ARMENIAN DEACONS: Soorp Asdvatz, soorp yev huzor, soorp yev anmah, vor hariar merelots, vogh ormia dmez . . . Soorp Asdvatz—*[Holy god, holy and strong, holy and immortal, who rose from the dead, have mercy on us.]*

LUCENE: *(Frantic)* Stop!! Leave me alone!! *(Running out of the church haunted and dropping her shawl)* Oh God!!

LUCENE exits. NISHAN looks on. Armenian Church music is playing. A red ball rolls by. The GIRLS run off the stage. NISHAN's eyes follow them. He picks up the shawl and looks towards where LUCENE exited.

Blackout

LUCENE *runs to her house, afraid of what has just happened at the church.*

LUCENE *is looking frantically for her* MOTHER's *old fashion music box. She finds it, winds it and opens it to listen to the music. Inside the box are items that her* MOTHER *wore or used: A gold mesh evening bag, a necklace with gold beads from Armenia, a handkerchief, spare buttons, tiny bottles of perfume, pins, earrings, the glasses that she used when she read or sewed, old photographs, an Armenian cross and a small leather prayer book.*

LUCENE: *(Catching her breath)* Oh God, I can't stay here! Mama, I'm sorry. I can't stay here in this house. I can't go back to that church. I can't breath here . . . I can't think here. Mama, I've got to go home.

Blackout.

Lights come up. Sounds of the past are heard, the ARMENIAN WOMEN *enter.*

ARMENIAN WOMAN #1: Poor Lucene . . . got big trouble.

ARMENIAN WOMAN #2: She married that man!!

ARMENIAN WOMAN #3: That man name Krikor!!

ARMENIAN WOMAN #1: Did you hear?

ARMENIAN WOMAN #2: He's a Tashnag!!

ARMENIAN WOMAN #3: *(Gasping)* OH!! Amot!! *[Shame]*

ARMENIAN WOMAN #2: *(Gasping)* Amot!! *[Shame]*

ARMENIAN WOMAN #1: He left her for the C.I.A.!

ARMENIAN WOMAN #2: No!! He left her for the F.B.I.!

ARMENIAN WOMAN #3: I heard that he vas vanted by the KGB . . .

ARMENIAN WOMAN #1: Voch!! Voch!! *[No!! No!!]*

ARMENIAN WOMAN #3: I heard that he vas "big shot" in the A.S.A.L.A.l [the Armenian Secret Liberation Army]

ARMENIAN WOMAN #1: No one knows where he is . . .

ARMENIAN WOMAN #3: No von knows vhere he's gone . . .

ARMENIAN WOMAN #1: And LUCENE is pregnant.

ARMENIAN WOMAN #3: She's pregnant with a Tashnag baby . . .

ARMENIAN WOMAN #2: And where is Krikor?

ARMENIAN WOMAN #1: Der Hayr Nishan marry them.

ARMENIAN WOMAN #3: I bet he sorry now!

ARMENIAN WOMAN #2: Krikor's a Tashnag . . . they're all crazy!!

ARMENIAN WOMAN #3: She should have married a Ramgarvar. She should have stayed with her own kind. *[Moderate Party.]*

ARMENIAN WOMAN #1: Oh, but Krikor is so good looking!! That kind of man gonna be "anybody's kind"!

The ARMENIAN WOMEN *laugh thinking of Krikor's physical attraction.*

Blackout.

End of scene one.

ACT ONE

Scene Two

VIOLET AREVIAN's *home in Watertown.* LUCENE *is packing to leave Watertown. She is haunted by sounds of her deceased Father,* TAWVEET, *who enters singing an Armenian folksong.* VIOLET *joins him.* THE ARMENIAN GIRLS, LUCENE (CHILD) *and* ELENA (CHILD) *enter and dance in an Armenian manner to* TAWVEET's *song, which is about an Armenian Apple Tree. All characters are happy in* LUCENE's *memory, but it is only a memory.*

LUCENE: *(Calling her daughter)* Anne? Anne!

ANNE *enters.*

TAWVEET, VIOLET *and* THE ARMENIAN GIRLS (LUCENE *and* ELENA) *exit.* LUCENE *continues to pack and call for* ANNE.

LUCENE: Come on Anne, get going! We're leaving today and—
ANNE: *(Interrupting and completely surprised)* What?! We can't leave today!! Armenian tradition says that we're supposed to mourn Grandma's death for forty days!
LUCENE: We can mourn in New Hampshire. Don't just stand there!! Get going!
ANNE: Why? What happened when I was gone?
LUCENE: And you being gone is another thing. Where were you? We had work to do in this house.
ANNE: I was with Arlene and Vartan Manian. (Thinking of VARTAN) He is one "tall, dark and handsome man!!"
LUCENE: *(Angry)* He's Armenian and the son of a Priest!!
ANNE: I know and he knows so much about being Armenian. Mama, don't look so angry.
LUCENE: What were you doing with them?

ANNE *does not answer.*

LUCENE: Anne!

ANNE: I can't tell you.

LUCENE *gives* ANNE *a hard look.*

ANNE: It would ruin the surprise I'm planning for you!!

LUCENE: I don't need anymore surprises in Watertown. This place is jinxed with disaster!!

ANNE: For you maybe, but not for me . . . I love it here!! Everything's Armenian!!

LUCENE: *Armenian?!* You can't love something that you know nothing about?! Good God! You're talking like a fool! Why do you think we left twenty-two years ago?! There was no place here for us to belong. I was a widow!! You were the daughter of a Tashnag and a Ramgarvar and those were people who weren't supposed to mix! And so we didn't mix!! We left! And I've spent years protecting you from all that ignorance and hate. We became American. I sent you to the best American schools and gave you a good American life . . . And I refuse to let you throw it away on some Armenian nonsense!!

ANNE: *What?!* You taught me how to think for myself! I know what I want and I know what I love about this place . . . Don't you feel Grandma and Grandpa here? Don't you see yourself here as a child?! I do!!

LUCENE: You don't know what you're talking about. Armenians are a backward people—a "busy-body-lot." When your Father died, I took you away from all of it!!

ANNE: A backward people?! A busy-body-lot?! You and I are Armenians!!

LUCENE: You and I are Americans!! Now, get up those stairs and finish what I've asked you to do! We're leaving today!

ANNE: I'm not going anywhere. I want to stay!

LUCENE: Anne!! Don't make this difficult!!

ANNE: Mama!! Don't you make this difficult. I'm not leaving this house.

LUCENE: Don't you take that tone with me!! You don't know who these people are. I'm only trying to protect you!!

ANNE: *From who?!*

The red ball bounces onto the stage. THE ARMENIAN GIRLS *run onto the stage, catch the red ball and sit. Lights dim on* ANNE *and* LUCENE. LUCENE (THE WOMAN) *sees the children and watches them, remembering her childhood in the house.*

LUCENE (CHILD): I love my house and I'm never going to leave it!!

ELENA (CHILD): Never?

LUCENE (CHILD): Never!!

ELENA (CHILD): I'm going to leave my house when I grow up!! I'm going to sail around the world in a pirate ship and look for buried treasures, if I don't get married!! Don't you want to look for buried treasures with me Lucene?

LUCENE (CHILD): No. I just want to stay home with my Mother and my Father. I want to stay at home, cook, tell stories like my Mother and dance.

ELENA (CHILD): Like a Russian ballerina?!

LUCENE (CHILD): *No!*

ELENA (CHILD): I would!!

LUCENE (CHILD): Like an Armenian girl on the highest mountain . . . Mount Ararat!! Where Noah landed!

ELENA (CHILD): Mount Ararat?! You could never climb that mountain!! It's too far away!! It's too big!! How could you dance on that mountain Lucene!!

LUCENE (CHILD): How could you sail around the world in a pirate boat Elena?!

ELENA (CHILD): But Mount Ararat is in Armenia!! We're in America!!

LUCENE (CHILD): My Mother taught me how to dance on the mountain! *(Running to the stairs)* This is my Mount Ararat!! I can climb these stairs and dance like a beautiful Armenian girl holding a red pomegranate on the highest mountain!!

Armenian dance music is heard. LUCENE (CHILD) *runs up the stairs of the living room with the red ball in her hand and begins to dance in an Armenian manner.* ELENA (CHILD) *looks on with amazement and applauds her friend.*

LUCENE (CHILD): See, I told you!! I can dance like an Armenian girl!! I can dance like an Armenian girl on the top of Mount Ararat!!

Giggling, the two children run up the stairs and exit.

ANNE *is looking at her "Watertown Box."* LUCENE *watches as the children exit and tries to busy herself by packing "odds and ends" into a cardboard box.*

ANNE: You don't understand. If we leave I'll miss out on everything.

LUCENE: Everything?! We won't miss out on anything!

ANNE: But we haven't found Grandma's box!!

LUCENE: Will you forget those foolish boxes!!

ANNE: Forget them?! You promised! My Father made those boxes!! They're the only things of him we have!! I found Grandpa's *(She gets up to get the box and brings it to* LUCENE*)* and I know we'll find Grandma's if we keep looking!

LUCENE: *(Angry)* Where did you get that?

ANNE: I found it last night, when you were sleeping. It was in Grandpa's bureau.

LUCENE: I asked you to let me go through those things. Give it to me, now.

ANNE: I haven't opened it yet. I was keeping it for us to go through together. *(Opening the box.* LUCENE *sits down next to* ANNE*)* Look at the stuff in here!! Here's his pipe and some old tobacco . . . some cigars . . . some maps . . . some hard candies, God, they look old!! Do you remember how he use to always offer me candy and you'd say no?! He'd wait until you left the room and give me the candy anyway!!

LUCENE: That was my Father. A real stubborn Armenian man who always got his way. What else is in there?

LUCENE *takes the box into her lap and start to sort through the things in the box.*

LUCENE: *(Pulling out a document)* Oh my God!

ANNE: What? What's that?!

LUCENE: Dad's Citizenship papers!!

ANNE: I forgot Grandpa was American. He was always talking about going back to the old country and showing me his maps. He wanted to fish in Lake Sevan again and walk home with his catch.

LUCENE: Mama and Dad took their citizenship oath together. It was a warm and beautiful day . . . I was eight and dressed in my new Shirley Temple sailor dress with red, white and blue stripes. Mama and Dad wanted me to look "just right" when they became American Citizens. My Father held me and I watched his mouth go up and down as he said those American words he had worked so hard to remember. We went to Durgin Park for dinner that day—

ANNE: *(Interrupting)* Durgin Park?!

LUCENE: Yes, Durgin Park. My Father said that we had to eat there, because the greatest American of all had eaten there, George Washington!

ANNE: (Looking at her) Mom . . . this is the reason I don't want us to leave here.

LUCENE: What?!

ANNE: Look at us!! Look at me! We're happy. You're telling me stories. I want to hear more! This never happens to us in New Hampshire. It only happens in this house.

LUCENE: We could have been anywhere.

ANNE: But we weren't. We were here—in the house that you grew up in. And your stories are important to me. I don't want to leave!!

LUCENE *begins to reminisce.*

Lights come up on another part of the stage. LUCENE (BRIDE) *enters holding her baby and talking with her Mother,* VIOLET.

LUCENE (BRIDE): I don't want to leave, but I have to—

VIOLET: Don't listen to the vomen . . . they don't mean vhat they say—

LUCENE (BRIDE): They do and before Ani grows up to understand, I want to leave.

VIOLET: But Krikor's gone . . . who's gonna take care of you and the baby?

LUCENE (BRIDE): I won't be that far . . . I'll go to New Hampshire. I'll get a job. You can come and visit me.

VIOLET: Your Father never going to let you go. Vhat Krikor going to say vhen he come back?

LUCENE (BRIDE): Dad and Krikor have nothing to say about this. I make my own decisions now.

VIOLET: But there's no Armenian church in New Hampshire . . . how you and Ani gonna go to church?!

LUCENE (BRIDE): We're not.

VIOLET: *(Putting her hand over her mouth in shock)* Asdvatz-im!! *[Oh my God]* Vhat are you talkin' 'bout? Inch choo?! *[Why?]* Vhat do you mean?!

LUCENE (BRIDE): Just what I said. Mama, it doesn't work for me anymore. Being in the Armenian Church . . . being with Armenians . . . it's not fun anymore . . . I'm not happy. *(She's crying)*

VIOLET: *(Holding her and the baby)* Mee lawr achchigus . . . Mee lawr . . . *[Don't cry girl, don't cry.]* You're hurt, but the pain is goin' to go avay—Krikor's goin' to send letter or something . . . I know this . . . you vait—you vait here, vith your Father and me and ve goin' to take care of you and your Ani . . . I promise you . . . *(Rocking back and forth)* you stay—you go back to college. Ve gonna get you bigger degree—I gonna talk to your Father! . . . You stay, achchig *[Girl]* . . . Ve gonna make everything okay . . . This is America—ve don't have any trouble here that ve can't handle. Come on, ve gonna eat the maws *[a holy bread]* from church today . . . *(They take the maws out of the small bag. VIOLET breaks a small piece in two. Both women place it on the top of their left hand and eat it with their tongue. LUCENE (BRIDE) is secure with her Mother by her side.)*

Blackout.

Lights come up on ANNE and LUCENE. ANNE is holding VIOLET's music box. She opens it and it begins to play. She and LUCENE look at each other and the hint of smiles, warmth and love for each other appear while the music box plays.

Blackout.

Lights come up on TAWKOOHEE and NISHAN in the Manian kitchen. TAWKOOHEE is kneading her third and last choreg dough. The other two large balls have been placed in the large old fashioned bowls and the red and white checkered cloth is over each bowl. One empty bowl and checkered cloth remains, waiting to be used.

NISHAN: *(Holding LUCENE's deceased Mother's shawl)* I don't want my family involved!!

TAWKOOHEE: You're makin' big mistake!!

NISHAN: Let them have their forty days of mourning. It's none of our business.

TAWKOOHEE: I gonna make it my business!! Violet vas good voman . . . my best friend and now her daughter makin' disgrace in her town. Everybody keeps goin' to the house to try and see Lucene and say how sorry they are and to bring her good food, but she doesn't answer the door, she doesn't open the door . . . she doesn't even peek out of the vindows to see who's at the door!! No!! I gonna make this my business!

NISHAN: Just take the shawl to the house and leave it on the doorstep!

TAWKOOHEE: I gonna take the shawl . . . I'm gonna get my key and I gonna let myself in!! *And* you gonna bless me some maws—*[Holy Bread]* . . . Lucene gonna put the holy bread on the top her hand and eat it. Then everything goin' to be fine.

NISHAN: Tawkoohee!! You can't make everything that happens in this town your business!! Leave the woman alone. She left Watertown a long time ago. You can't change history . . . you can't always have things your own way!! Lucene is her own woman. She'll find her own way.

TAWKOOHEE: She not gonna find anything, but big headache. She make one lie after another.

NISHAN: What are you talking about?

TAWKOOHEE: Ani!!

NISHAN: Ani?! You mean Anne?

TAWKOOHEE: Ani!! Your memory short or something?! You baptise that baby! I know!! I vas there! I remember!! Her name is Ani!!

NISHAN: So what?! This is America . . . lots of Armenian families give their children American names . . . it's not a crime.

TAWKOOHEE: It's big crime when Ani has to live a lie because of her Mother's lies.

NISHAN: Just make your *choreg* and take that shawl over to the house before the end of today. I want to be done with this.

NISHAN *starts to leave.*

TAWKOOHEE: Nishan, you vait right there!! You can't be done vith this! Or I gonna blame you for everything bad that happen!

NISHAN: What are you talking about?!

TAWKOOHEE: Vhen Violet begged you to help Lucene find Krikor you did nothing . . . I know this . . . and in Violet's heart she know this too. Oh yes, "you bigshot priest" you made believe you looked for Krikor . . . you put on good show for Lucene . . . everybody else believe you tried your best, but I know you.

NISHAN: I did all I could do!

TAWKOOHEE: *(Completely frustrated by his answer)* Off-Ba-Bum!! *[A phrase used during a frustrating moment. It's like "Oh Brother!" or "For Pete's Sake!" or "Oh Give Me a Break!"]*

TAWKOOHEE *puts the dough in bowl to rise and making the sign of the cross on the bowl.*

NISHAN: Leave the past in the past!!

TAWKOOHEE: Anoun hor, yev vortvo, yev hokvoyn surpah, amen. *[In the name of the Father, the Son and the Holy Spirit, Amen.]*

TAWKOOHEE *places the red and white cloth over the large bowl and then places it next to the other bowls on the table.*

TAWKOOHEE: I know you, Nishan!! There has always been something funny in this. There has alvays been something I cannot figure out. Vhy you marry that girl to that man? You and Tawveet let Krikor run avay . . . you never go after him?! Vhy you let innocent girl go back to Armenia to look for her husband all alone?

NISHAN: We tried to stop her.

TAWKOOHEE: Vhy didn't you go vith her? Vhy did her Father let her go all alone?

NISHAN: He couldn't stop her from marrying Krikor, how could he stop her from going to Armenia?

TAWKOOHEE: Vhy did you let Krikor leave?

NISHAN: Krikor Kinsorian doesn't take orders. He gives them.

TAWKOOHEE: Who is this Krikor Kinsorian? Vhat you know about Krikor that you're not telling me?!

NISHAN: This is man's business. You make your *choreg* and stay out of it.

TAWKOOHEE: Ani vas "man's business"! Krikor let her down vith "man's business"! And then you let her down and vhen you let her down, the church let her down. All that girl's hope vas gone. I don't like vhat Lucene has become, but I'm not goin' to keep quiet vith Ani involved!

NISHAN: Ani's been raised like an "odar"! *[A non-Armenian]*

TAWKOOHEE: *(Shocked by what he has just said)* Odar?! Odar?!?! You call von hundred percent Armenian girl *Odar*?! Amot *[For shame] (Looking up and calling to her deceased husband)* You hear that Hagop?! *(To* NISHAN*)* Amot!!

NISHAN: *(Waving his hands into the air)* Asdvatz-Im!!! *[My God]*

TAWKOOHEE: You better pray to God. I gonna be up there soon and I gonna tell everything!

NISHAN: You don't know what you're talking about. There was a cold war going on. My hands were tied. Krikor was involved in things no one could talk about.

TAWKOOHEE: Vhat kind of things?

NISHAN: He was a freedom fighter. There was a price on his head, that's all you need to know.

TAWKOOHEE: Vhat price?

NISHAN *remains silent.*

TAWKOOHEE: Vhat price Nishan?

NISHAN: *(Standing firm)* Leave it alone, Tawkoohee! It's not a woman's affair!

TAWKOOHEE *is confused and disgusted with* NISHAN*'s attitude.* NISHAN *stands firm in silence and then exits.*

TAWKOOHEE *goes to her work table and in an angry manner kneads the final ball of* choreg *dough.*

TAWKOOHEE: *(Throwing down the* choreg *dough to knead it)* Everybody tellin' me "Mind my own business!" . . . Nishan says "Keep your nose out of it!!" Arlene says "Vhat are you gonna do Auntie . . . it's spilt milk?!" . . . and I tell her and everybody else that I gonna do something . . . I gonna say something!! *(Looking up and talking to Hagop)* But Husband—Hagop . . . *(She throws the dough)* . . . Vhat am I goin' to do?! *(Calling out frustrated)* Nishan . . . Nishan . . . he's just my baby brother and he keeps saying, "This is America . . . not the old country vhere everybody's business is everybody's business!!" *But* Hagop, I say this is Vatertown . . . *(She throws the dough)* . . . My Armenia!! And as long as I'm livin' here I'm goin' to mix the old country vays with the new country vays. I know in America I don't have to take orders from everybody all the time!! *(Looking up)* Even you use to say "Speak up Tawkoohee . . . you re-member, Hagop?! *(She throws the dough)* I got my own brain!! I read Ameri-can newspaper and I know about American Vomen's Lib and I read Armenian history and I know about the old country's vomen who voted in political elec-tion even before American vomen had the right to stand up and vote and so I gonna tell everybody right now that—I got my own brain and I got seventy-two years visdom to speak vhat's in my brain and I gonna speak it today!! And no-body gonna tell me to be quiet!! Nobody gonna tell me pearanna coatseh!! *[Keep quite!!]* *(She throws the dough)* And nobody gonna eat my *choreg* if they gonna give me trouble!!

Lights fadeout.

TAWKOOHEE *exits.*

Laughter is heard.

Lights come up on the Manian grape arbor. ANNE, VARTAN *and* ARLENE *are picking grapes and eating them as they fill their baskets.*

ANNE: Stop it Arlene!! He can't be that bad!!
ARLENE: I swear his Mother still dresses him!! Did you see him at the coffee hour in the corner eating one *choreg* after another with his pants pulled up to here!!
VARTAN: *(Trying to explain)* Aram's had "a crush" on Arlene since high school, but he's never had the guts to ask her out.
ANNE: That's sweet!

ARLENE: It's pathetic!! He's a thirty-four year old man! On Sunday, he started chasing me around the table trying to make me taste his *choreg*!! I mean this man is pathetic!!

VARTAN: *(Defending Aram to ANNE)* He's good guy, he's just a little old fashioned.

ARLENE: *(Enraged)* Old fashion?!?! Smelly mothball paisley ties, old fashion creased pants—his Mother irons them every Sunday morning! And hair has been lacquered with "wild root" white cream everyday of his life since I can remember!! Sometimes the wild root is even hanging off of his ear lobes when he comes to church!! Agh!!

VARTAN: Dad says what Aram needs is a good woman like Arlene. After that Aram has endless possibilities!!

ARLENE: I can promise Dad—that it's not going to be me walking down any aisle with Aram and his pants up to here!!

ARLENE *imitates Aram's walk with his pants pulled up high above his waist.* ANNE *cannot stop laughing.*

ANNE: Stop it!!

VARTAN: *(To ARLENE)* Hey, just leave the man alone.

ARLENE: Well, Anne wants a crash course on Watertown and no crash course would be complete without "Aram Stories"!!

ANNE: I've missed so much growing up in New Hampshire . . . I would have given anything to grow up in Watertown!

ARLENE: *(Rolling her eyes)* Oh, please . . .

ANNE: I'm serious!! Mama's done everything she could to keep anything Armenian away from me.

VARTAN: *(In disbelief)* Everything?

ANNE: Practically . . . There was one time I watched her dance with my Grandmother . . . Grandma was humming some Armenian song . . . Mama got up . . . threw her shoes off and started dancing . . . her hands, her feet, her whole body was smiling. She picked me up and held me so tight!! I will never forget that moment.

Armenian music is heard.

VARTAN: I'll bet you dance beautifully too.

VARTAN *pulls out his hankerchief and begins to dance with* ANNE. ARLENE *starts humming and dances too.*

ANNE: No! Stop! I can't!

VARTAN: *(Dancing)* Relax . . .

ARLENE: It's fun! Anybody can do it!

ARLENE *pulls* ANNE *into the dance until they twirl and dance so fast that all three fall down and into the grass. The music stops.*

VARTAN: What else do you want to know about Armenians? I give better crash courses than my sister!!

ARLENE: But she asked me Vartan, not you!! And besides, she's my guest—

ANNE: Tell me about Tashnags and Ramgarvars!

ARLENE and VARTAN: *(Laughing and in shock)* Why?!

ARLENE: Ask about *paklava* . . . ask about *choreg* . . . ask about the Armenian Genocide . . . ask about—

VARTAN: *(Interrupting)* How wonderful Armenian men are!!

ARLENE: Oh!! Spare me!!

ANNE: Come on you guys!! I'm serious!! My Father was a Tashnag and my Mother was a Ramgarvar and—

VARTAN: *(Interrupting)* "Is" a Ramgarvar!! Once a "Ramgarvar," always a "Ramgarvar"!!

ARLENE: *(Disgusted by VARTAN's comment)* Shut up Vartan!! (To ANNE) There's no difference between a Tashnag and a Ramgarvar!! They're both brash, stubborn and acutely stupid!

VARTAN: *Bullshit*!! We have separate churches . . . Separate clubs!! We're different people with different politics!!

ARLENE: And the same Armenian Blood!!

ANNE: *(Overwhelmed by their argument)* Wait a minute you guys, this is over my head. I think I'll just stick to my "Watertown Box".

ARLENE and VARTAN: Your what?!

ANNE: My "Watertown Box." My treasure chest for my Armenian treasures. Like my Grandmother's bastech recipe.

ARLENE: *(To VARTAN)* That's why she's here. We're going to make it together.

ANNE: It's a surprise for Mama. She loves it. It'll bring back good memories for her. I use to watch my Grandmother make sheets of *bastech*. I'll never forget the smell of the purple grapes boiling and the clean white sheets she'd spread the mixture on to dry and shake powdered sugar over.

ARLENE *and* VARTAN *begin to dream with her forgetting their previous argument.*

VARTAN: . . . And the first taste when it hardened—

ARLENE: . . . And the strips pulled right off the white sheets—

ANNE: Mmmm . . . It would melt in your mouth . . .

ARLENE and VARTAN: *(Imagining a piece of* bastech *in their mouth)* Mmmmm . . .

ARLENE *and* VARTAN *are charmed by their new friend.*

ARLENE: *(Putting out her hand)* Recipe—please!

ANNE *hands* ARLENE *the recipe out of her Watertown Box.*

ARLENE: *(Reading the recipe with* ANNE *looking on)* Separate the grapes, wash and boil—*(Remembering)* Oh Vartan!! I didn't tell you! I received my letter from the Saint Nersess Seminary today and I start in September!

VARTAN: Dad isn't going to like that!

ARLENE: *(To* VARTAN*)* Why shouldn't I have the right to be an Armenian Priest? I'm a woman!! Women brought Christianity to Armenia!!

VARTAN: How could Aram marry a Priest?!

ARLENE: Why do you have be so stubborn Vartan?

VARTAN: I'm not stubborn, and you can't change centuries of tradition!!

ANNE: Why not?

ANNE *and* ARLENE *are separating the grapes.* VARTAN *is looking at* ANNE's *Watertown Box.*

VARTAN: Because it's not right!!

ARLENE: It's not right?! It's not right?!! You're going to be a doctor—something you've always wanted to be. I got stuck being a high school English teacher. I want to be a priest!

VARTAN: You can teach at the Sunday School!! You're on the Parish Council in the church!! You're important to the church! What more do you want? Why do you always have to try and be different?

ARLENE: It's not being different!! It's being a human being!! I'm a person with just as much importance as you in this world!!

ANNE: Stop fighting!! Both of you!! Calm down!! We're making *bastech*!! We should be having fun!

ARLENE: Oh Anne, forget it!! He and every other Armenian man are a hopeless cause!! Women are their father's daughter until they're their husband's wife . . . there's no clout in having a daughter!! There's no honor in being a woman, unless of course you can be the bearer of sons!! An Armenian man wants sons and that's a tradition that's been "held for centuries"!!

VARTAN: That's a lie!!

ANNE: I can't believe that. My Grandfather loved me and if my Father were alive he'd love me too.

ARLENE: If you had had a brother or a male cousin, you would have seen what I'm talking about!! Men are the pampered sex in the Armenian household!! And I'm sick of it!!

VARTAN: Go out with me tomorrow night Anne and I'll show you that Armenian men are romantic, strong spirited, intelligent and true leaders!!

ANNE *blushes.* ARLENE *rolls her eyes and is all fired up.*

ARLENE: *So are Armenian women!!* (*Separating the grapes furiously*) *And* we've had to be the backbone to everyone of you!!

VARTAN: (*To* ARLENE) Not bad for someone who came from a rib . . . (*To* ANNE) Will you go out with me?!

ANNE *does not get a chance to answer him.*

ARLENE *is furious.*

ARLENE: A *rib*?! A *rib*?!?! Was it a *rib* who helped you pass your chemistry tests?!?!

ANNE: (*Happily to* VARTAN) Yes, (*Totally frustrated with* ARLENE *and* VARTAN) but stop fighting! I came here to get away from fighting. Why is it that Armenians are always fighting about something?! My Mother's probably home fighting with herself!!

ARLENE: That's Watertown!!

VARTAN: No, it's not!!

ARLENE: It's Armenians around the world!! And what do you expect?! Everything's divided!! We can't agree on anything!

ANNE: Alright, alright, *alright*! God! You're sounding like my Mother. I don't need to hear any of this. I just want to enjoy being Armenian.

VARTAN: (*To* ARLENE) Now, there is a very smart Armenian woman!! (*To* ANNE) Eight o'clock?!

ARLENE *rolls her eyes at* VARTAN. ANNE*'s frustrated, but happy that* VARTAN *asked her out.* VARTAN *is simply full of himself.* ARLENE *exits with the bowl of grapes ready to be washed and* ANNE *and* VARTAN *follow in a flirtatious manner.*

Fade out.

End of scene two.

ACT ONE

Scene Three

Lights come up in the church. Armenian church music is heard. NISHAN *is on stage, and praying at the altar.* ARMENIAN WOMEN *enter.*

NISHAN: Door inztee imas-doo-tuin . . . Give me wisdom!

ARMENIAN WOMAN #1: Lucene vas a good girl!

ARMENIAN WOMAN #2: Shod . . . shod aghvor buzdig achchig!! A very, very nice little girl!!

ARMENIAN WOMAN #3: Mekh eh . . . Mekh eh!! It's a sorry situation.

NISHAN: Women must stay in their "proper place."

ARMENIAN WOMAN #1: She vas the star of the Armenian School!

ARMENIAN WOMAN #2: She vas the star of the Sunday School!!

ARMENIAN WOMEN: Everybody's favorite.

NISHAN: Why do innocent children have to grow up? Door inztee imas-doo-tuin!! Give me the wisdom!!

THE TWO ARMENIAN GIRLS *enter the church.*

ELENA (CHILD): Okay Lucene, Go ahead!! Climb up onto the altar, nobody's here to catch you!!

LUCENE (CHILD): I didn't mean what I said . . . I'll get into trouble and God would never forgive me. Women aren't allowed on the altar.

ELENA (CHILD): But you're not a woman . . . you're a girl and nobody's here to catch you!

LUCENE (CHILD): Stop it Elena!! I didn't mean what I said!!

ELENA (CHILD): Yes, you did! You told me that you wanted to climb up onto the altar and see what it felt like. You told me that it would be like your Mount Ararat!

LUCENE (CHILD): *(Angry)* Be quiet Elena!! Just be quiet!!

ELENA (CHILD): You're afraid, aren't you?! You're afraid to climb up onto the altar!! *(Singing)* Lucene Arevian's a scaredy cat!! Lucene Arevian's a scaredy cat! *(Proudly)* Well, I'm not afraid . . . *(Hopping up onto the altar)* Look!! Look at me!! I'm on the Armenian Altar!! I'm on the Armenian altar and my name is Elena Gregorian!!

LUCENE (CHILD): *(Frightened out of her wits)* NO! Elena get down! I didn't mean what I said! Der Hayr will catch you!! Quick!!

ELENA (CHILD): *(Looking up)* Der Hayr and God . . . if you're going to strike me down . . . do it now!!

LUCENE (CHILD): Oh my God!! Get down!! *Get down!!*

ELENA (CHILD): See!! God hasn't done anything to me!! Come on Lucene . . . don't be afraid. Der Hayr hasn't struck me down! Come on up here, it's wonderful . . . you can see the whole church from up here . . . even the little window in the balcony steeple.

LUCENE (CHILD): *(Beginning to pray for Elena's soul. Making the sign of the cross)* Anon hor, Yev vort toe, Yev ho koone, Surpo Amen . . . *[The Father, the Son and the Holy Spirit.]*

ELENA (CHILD): Don't pray for me Lucene!! Get up here! *(She takes off her shoes)* It's great up here!! The rug is so soft!

LUCENE (CHILD): Elena!! Come down from there and put your shoes back on!!

ELENA (CHILD): No!

LUCENE (CHILD): I'm afraid.

ELENA (CHILD): But it was your idea . . . here . . . take my hand . . .

LUCENE (CHILD): No! I'm leaving Elena!! I don't like you anymore!! I'm going home. Something bad is going to happen! You don't belong on the altar . . . you're a girl!!

ELENA (CHILD): God knows that!! God knows that and he hasn't struck me dead!! He's hugging me up here. *(She begins to hug herself)* I can feel it! Come on!!

LUCENE (CHILD): *No!* I'm a girl . . . I'm a good girl!!

ELENA (CHILD): Don't be afraid!!

LUCENE (CHILD): I don't want to be afraid . . .

ELENA (CHILD): Then come up here!! It's great!! We'll see behind the altar! *(ELENA runs behind the altar)* . . . there are books, candles, candle sticks and slippers . . . Oh!! Der Hayr's got a hole in his slippers!! *(ELENA laughs)*

LUCENE (CHILD): *(Puts her hand over her mouth about the slippers and wishes she were up there)* I'm afraid . . . I'm afraid of God!!

ELENA (CHILD): Don't be . . . God is good!!

LUCENE (CHILD): *(Trying to climb up onto the altar)* Help me Elena . . .

ELENA (CHILD): You can help yourself up!! *(Watching her climb up)* There you go . . . you see. It's wonderful up here!

LUCENE (CHILD): *(Looking towards the window in the balcony steeple)* It's like being on a stage!!

ELENA (CHILD): . . . or Heaven . . . I think it feels like being in heaven!!

LUCENE (CHILD): We're up on the altar where girls aren't allowed!! We're not bad girls!!

ELENA (CHILD): God's Armenian and he loves us!! We're good girls and we're safe!!

They are secure and happy. The two children hold hands and run behind the altar and exit.

NISHAN: *(Talking to God as he enters.)* What does she want me to do?!! I promised Tawveet. I promised Krikor. I have my duty.

ARMENIAN WOMAN #1: Der Hayr gotta help Lucene.

ARMENIAN WOMAN #2: She vas baptised in this church!

ARMENIAN WOMAN #3: Such big trouble?! Violet vould never tell.

ARMENIAN WOMAN #2: Violet never even tell Tawkoohee!!

NISHAN: No one needs to know.

ARMENIAN WOMAN #3: Violet never tell anybody, but Der Hayr!!

ARMENIAN WOMEN: Now, Violet's dead.

ARMENIAN WOMAN #1: Pearanna coats-seh!! [*His mouth is shut*]

ARMENIAN WOMAN #2: His mouth is shut.

ARMENIAN WOMAN #3: And nobody gonna open a Der Hayr's mouth.

NISHAN: Krikor must stay dead.

NISHAN *bows his head in prayer. Armenian Church music is heard.* ARMENIAN WO-MEN *exit.*

Blackout.

Lights come up in the Arevian house. LUCENE *is looking for her Mother's wooden box.*

TAWKOOHEE *enters. She has let herself in with her own key.* LUCENE *does not hear her enter.*

LUCENE: *(She's going crazy looking for her Mother's wooden box)* Where is it?! Damn!! I can't find anything in this house.

TAWKOOHEE: Vhat?! Vhat you looking for? Huh?

LUCENE: *(Completely startled)* Tawkoohee?!?! Good God!! What are you doing here? Why didn't you ring the door bell?

TAWKOOHEE: Vhy ring the doorbell, vhen you never gonna answer?

LUCENE: How did you get in here?

TAWKOOHEE: I bring my own key . . . your Mother give me key for emergency.

LUCENE: Well there's no emergency, so you can go home . . . *God*, you scared me.

TAWKOOHEE: *(Breathing in the air of the house)* I smell your Mother . . . her scent is still here.

LUCENE: What do you expect? She lived here for forty years.

TAWKOOHEE: *(Looking around)* Ve vere like sisters, your Mother and me . . .

LUCENE: I know that . . . Tawkoohee what do you want?

TAWKOOHEE: You look like scared ghost Lucene!! How come?

LUCENE: What kind of game are you playing?

TAWKOOHEE: Vhat vere you looking for?

LUCENE: Nothing!! Tawkoohee, give me that key and get out of my house!!

TAWKOOHEE: Your house!! Your house!! Ha! You nothing but a big ghost in this house!! You like a dead voman here!!

LUCENE: Stop it!! You have no right to talk to me like that!! How dare you—

TAWKOOHEE: *(Interrupting)* I dare because I real Armenian voman . . . You big liar Lucene Arevian Kinsorian!! And I alvays gonna speak the truth vhen I see a liar. *(Giving her the shawl)* Here's your Mother's shawl. Der Hayr found it vhen you run out of church this morning.

LUCENE: You're crazy!! You don't know what you're talking about!!

TAWKOOHEE: I know vhat I'm talkin' 'bout!! You tell Ani lies!!

LUCENE: You don't scare me.

TAWKOOHEE: I gonna scare you into telling the truth!! You drop the I-A-N from your name and change Kinsorian to Kinsor . . . you big phony Lucene!!

LUCENE: This is America!! Not Armenia and I can do what ever I damn well please with my name!! I'm my own person!!

TAWKOOHEE: You're Armenian voman!!

LUCENE: I'm an American woman and I want you out of this house!!

TAWKOOHEE: I gonna tell you something . . . vonce you born to be an Armenian voman, you alvays gonna be an Armenian voman. You never gonna escape the bloodshed that gave you life!!

LUCENE: Don't start.

TAWKOOHEE: How the hell you think you get here?!

LUCENE: That's no concern of mine.

TAWKOOHEE: Then vhat kind of American voman are you?! Every American came here from somevhere else—pilgrim-man . . . red-faced man . . . black-man . . . vhite-man . . . china-man . . . you no different!

LUCENE: You don't have to tell me about history! I teach history!

TAWKOOHEE: Your Mother alvays spoil you!! Now you shame her memory!! Amot . . . Amot!! [Shame] Vhen Violet vas alive I promised her to keep my mouth shut, but now I gonna tell you just vhat I think of you!!

LUCENE: *Get the hell out of my house!!*

TAWKOOHEE: Maybe I never gonna leave . . . maybe I gonna move right in here and take care of things my own vay!! Yes, I gonna vait right here for Ani to come home!!

LUCENE: Anne!! Anne!! My daughter's name is Anne!!

TAWKOOHEE: You baptise her Ani! I vas there and I know vhat I'm talkin' 'bout!

LUCENE: Her name is Anne Kinsor and she won't be home tonight.

TAWKOOHEE: OH!! She gonna stay vith Arlene and Vartan, huh?!

LUCENE: What are you talking about?

TAWKOOHEE: (*Ignoring* LUCENE's *words*) Vhere's the Holy Candles? I gonna burn them for Violet. Then ve gonna sit down and eat maws. [Holy Bread] Der Hayr bless special for us.

LUCENE: I'm not eating any maws with you and I want you out of my house before Anne comes home. So leave—just leave.

TAWKOOHEE: Ani at my house right now vith my niece and nephew. I think Ani and Vartan startin' to like each other too!! Maybe ve gonna have a vedding.

LUCENE: We're leaving here. She'll never go out with him.

TAWKOOHEE: They gonna go out on a date tomorrow night. Vartan gonna ask her and your Ani's a good Armenian girl. She never gonna say no.

LUCENE: You're not telling the truth . . . Anne would never go to your house without telling me.

TAWKOOHEE: I alvays speak the truth!! You the only liar in this room Lucene. You lie about your last name!! You lie about your daughter's name. You lie about Ani's Father!! Krikor is not dead!!

LUCENE: He is.

TAWKOOHEE: He left you twenty years ago alive . . . who told you he dead.

LUCENE: Kirkor is dead in this house.

TAWKOOHEE: Vhat you think Ani gonna say when she find out that her Father's alive? She gonna call you phony.

LUCENE: She won't find out.

TAWKOOHEE: She never ask you questons about him?

LUCENE: No . . . she knows that I don't like to talk about it. She's a good girl . . .

TAWKOOHEE: You vere too.

LUCENE: Tawkoohee leave . . . just leave. It's been a long day.

TAWKOOHEE: Vhen you marry Krikor, did you love him?

LUCENE: Of course, I loved him.

TAWKOOHEE: Then you tell me vhy you make him dead vhen you love him? Huh?!

LUCENE: Because it was the only sensible thing to do! *(Reminiscing)* I met him his first day in America. He was so handsome. I went to the church dance that night. My Mother made me the most beautiful rose colored satin dress . . . I can still see her hands making the lace for the sleeves and neck . . . her smile, the glasses that she wore when she sewed . . . the music box playing as she worked. I felt so beautiful that night. The church hall was filled and it seemed like everyone was dancing.

TAWKOOHEE: I remember that night. Everyone vas dancing, even the men, it vas like big grapevine weaving in and out of the circles. Ha!

LUCENE: *(Still reminiscing)* It was Krikor who took my hand and led our line throughout the hall waving his hankerchief proudly into the air. The music was so loud. He was so tall. I had never seen this man before. He told me I danced beautifully. His eyes were intense and we stared at each other as we spoke for the first time. I couldn't take my eyes off of him. I couldn't stop listening to him. His words . . . his mind . . . his thoughts!! We didn't dance again that night, we just talked and talked and talked. Later I stayed up in my room and wrote in my journal—I wrote . . . I've met the man I'm going to marry. He was raised in Beirut, educated in France and new to America. He is the most exciting and spirited man that I have ever met.

TAWKOOHEE: I make big mistake tonight, Krikor not dead in your heart. You still love him. I see this. You know this and I know this.

LUCENE: *(Exhausted from her reminiscence)* You know nothing.

TAWKOOHEE: I know that you vorked hard to turn hurt into hate!!

LUCENE: I was a "good Armenian girl." I was a "good Armenian woman." And it got me nothing!

TAWKOOHEE: Vhat did you vant? Gold medal?!

LUCENE: Respect. I was tired of being treated like a child. Mama was the only one who really understood. I risked my life when Krikor disappeared. I went alone to look for Krikor in the motherland and all that I found were closed doors, closed mouths and closed minds. No one was willing to help me find my husband . . . Where was the Armenia that I was raised to believe in. The Armenia that my Father, Krikor and people like you told me about wasn't there! I found nothing, but the ruins of a defeated people and so I made Krikor's grave there. I placed nine stones on the banks of Lake Sevan for the nine months we spent together. I buried him and our dreams. I came back to America, took my child and moved forward!

TAWKOOHEE: You moved sidevays!! Maybe you didn't move backwards, but you never move forvard . . . you forgot who you vere and you buried yourself. You got stuck in your own pain.

LUCENE: My pain was in this town!! I wasn't going to sit in this house or in that church down the street while people like you gossiped about me!! I heard all of you . . . Poor . . . Poor Lucene, only married three months and Krikor left her . . . Mekh eh . . . Mekh eh!! Oh . . . I did move forward—I left!

TAWKOOHEE: Ve didn't say that!!

LUCENE: Oh, yes you did!! You said "I vasn't a good vife!! I vasn't a good Armenian voman and that's vhy Krikor left me!!" You all turned your backs on me!

TAWKOOHEE: Ve didn't turn our backs on you!! Ve didn't know vhat to say!! Ve didn't know how to help you!!

LUCENE: And so you old gossips talked behind my back!

TAWKOOHEE: Armenian vomen alvays gonna talk . . . But ve never gossip—ve just tell facts.

LUCENE: You didn't know how I felt! You didn't know any facts.

TAWKOOHEE: Then you tell me facts now. I'm not meddling old voman . . . I'm vo-man who cares or else I vouldn't spend my time vith you!

LUCENE: What do you want me to say?

TAWKOOHEE: I vant you to tell Ani the truth. I vant you to stop running from your-self and come home.

LUCENE *is allowing* TAWKOOHEE *to comfort her until she notices her Mother's wood-en box.*

LUCENE: *(Interrupting)* I found it!!

LUCENE *gets up to get the box.*

TAWKOOHEE: Listen to me!! I talkin' shod love *[very good]* sense to you.

LUCENE: I found it. My Mother's box.

TAWKOOHEE: So vhat!! Violet got hundred boxes!! Vhere's the Holy Candle? Ve gonna say good prayer for good luck . . .

TAWKOOHEE *looks for the candles.*

LUCENE *opens the box.*

LUCENE: Oh my God!

TAWKOOHEE: Vhat?

LUCENE: Krikor.

TAWKOOHEE: Vhat?! Vhat you talkin' 'bout?

LUCENE: Letters from Krikor. *(She takes some of them out of the box)*

TAWKOOHEE: Asdvatz-im! *[Oh my God]* I can't believe this. Vhen did he write those letters?

LUCENE: *(Can't believe what she sees)* Letters for me and Ani . . . but he didn't know about Ani . . . What is this?!

TAWKOOHEE: Are you sure it's Krikor? Vhen did he send the letters?!

LUCENE: This year . . . last year . . . the year before . . . the year before that. What's going on here?!

She holds one of the letters.

LUCENE: *(Looking at the letter)* She knew where he was . . .

TAWKOOHEE: Violet?! *(She's looking over LUCENE's shoulder at the letter and extremely confused)* Violet knew?

ANNE *enters.*

ANNE: *(Calling out)* Hello!! I'm home.

LUCENE: *(To TAWKOOHEE, who she knows is supporting her now)* She knew where he was . . .

TAWKOOHEE: *(Knowingly to herself)* . . . So this the secret Violet tell Nishan.

ANNE: Mama, I have just had the best night!! I'm sorry that I didn't tell you where I was going but—

LUCENE: *(Interrupting)* I found Grandma's box.

ANNE: Great!! But first you've got to hear about this—Mama, Vartan asked me out!

LUCENE: What?!

ANNE: Tomorrow night.

LUCENE: Tomorrow night?

ANNE: Yeah!! Vartan asked me out!!

TAWKOOHEE: *(Seriously, getting ANNE's attention)* Ani, your Mother has something important to tell you. Lucene, you tell her vhat you found in the box.

LUCENE: *(Holding the box)* Letters . . . I found letters.

ANNE: From Grandma?

LUCENE: *(Holding the box)* No. From your Father. *(Handing her a letter)* This one's for you.

LUCENE *hands* ANNE *the letter.*

ANNE: *(Confused)* What are you talking about? He didn't write this letter. He died before I was born.

TAWKOOHEE: Tell her the truth.

LUCENE: Your Father's alive.

ANNE: *(Shocked)* Alive?! *(Not believing her Mother)* No . . . he died of a heart attack in this house, before I was born. He was thirty years old. You told me. Everybody told me the story.

TAWKOOHEE: There's no story. Your Mother speakin' the truth now. Krikor not dead.

LUCENE *is motionless. She will not let go of the box. She is staring at* ANNE.

ANNE: *(To* LUCENE*)* Why . . . Why . . . Why have you lied to me all these years? Why . . . Why? *(She looks at the letter in her hand and feels left out of everything to do with being "Armenian." To* TAWKOOHEE *and* LUCENE*.)* I can't read this . . . It's in Armenian.

ANNE *exits.*

Blackout.

End of scene three.

End of act one.

ACT TWO

Scene One

1:00 A.M. the next morning. The Arevian house. LUCENE *is asleep on the couch.*

TAWKOOHEE *has left to bring her choreg dough to the Arevian house.*

LUCENE *begins to stir. She is having a nightmare. Church music is heard.*

LUCENE: *(Beginning to twist and turn while asleep)* No . . . No!! Please . . . No!!

VIOLET, MRS. AROOSTIAN, LUCENE (BRIDE), LUCENE (CHILD) *and* ELENA (CHILD) *enter.*

VIOLET: *(Whispering)* Lucene . . . Lucene . . . I vant to explain—

ELENA (CHILD): *(Holding the red ball)* Hey Lucene! Lucene!!

LUCENE (CHILD): That's not me!! Here I am Elena!! I'm right behind you!!

MRS. AROOSTIAN: *(To* VIOLET*)* Vhat do you vant to explain?

LUCENE (BRIDE): She lies!! Lucene wake up!! Wake up!!

VIOLET: Be quiet!! She's sleeping!! She's asleep!! Mekh eh . . . Mekh eh . . . *[I feel sorry . . . I feel sorry.]*

MRS. AROOSTIAN: Inchoo mekh eh?!! *[Why feel sorry?]* Armenian voman never lie!! Lucene big liar!! You can't protect her anymore!!

ELENA (CHILD): Stop bullying my best friend!! She's a good Armenian girl!! She's a good Armenian girl!!

LUCENE (CHILD): I'm a good girl!! I'm a good Armenian girl!!

LUCENE (BRIDE): Armenian?! She's American!! She's not like us!! *(Going to* LUCENE*'s body)* Let me in!! Let me in!!

VIOLET: Stop yelling!! She's my Lucene!!

LUCENE (BRIDE): I'm your Lucene!!

LUCENE (CHILD): I'm your Lucene!!

MRS. AROOSTIAN: *(Pointing to* LUCENE (CHILD)*)* There's Lucene!! Say your Ipe, Pen, Kim, Lucene!! She's my star student in Armenian School . . . My star student!!

LUCENE (CHILD): *(Proudly)* Ipe, Pen, Kim, Tah, Yech, Za, Eh, Oh, Toe—

LUCENE (BRIDE): That's me!! There I am!! I love the Ipe, Pen, Kim!! I'm an Armenian girl with two languages!!

ELENA (CHILD): *(Running to* LUCENE (CHILD)*)* You're my best friend!!

LUCENE (BRIDE): And I'm your best friend!! Krikor will be home for dinner soon, would you like to stay?

VIOLET: Maybe Krikor never comin' home again. Ve don't know vhere he is. Your Father says not even Nishan knows vhere he is.

MRS. AROOSTIAN: Vhat you do Lucene to make him go? He vas handsome man!! You makin' American trouble—heh?!

LUCENE (BRIDE): I didn't do anything wrong!! I was a good Armenian wife!! Krikor left her *(Pointing to* LUCENE*)* not me!! Let me in!! You can't keep me out forever!! You're a phony!! Let me in!!

ELENA (CHILD): Let her in Lucene!! Let her in!!

LUCENE (CHILD): She's a bad lady . . . I don't want to go in!! I don't like her anymore!!

LUCENE (BRIDE): *(To* LUCENE (CHILD)*)* Yes, you do!! Hold my hand!! *(To* LUCENE*)* Let us in!! Let us in!!

VIOLET: Spaseh! Spaseh! *[Stop! Stop!]* You are in!! You're in her heart!! Vhat more you vant?! I gonna fight you all!! Leave my Lucene alone!!

MRS. AROOSTIAN: *(To* VIOLET*)* She make her daughter Ani suffer! She take avay who she is!! She make vhite vash of good Armenian girl!!

LUCENE (CHILD): Ani has always been my favorite name!!

LUCENE (BRIDE): You—You—*You* called my Ani, Anne!!

ELENA (CHILD): Lucene Arevian's a scaredy cat!! Lucene Arevian's a scaredy cat!!

LUCENE *is haunted by the sounds of the women and continues to twist and turn on the couch.*

VIOLET: Don't listen to them!! They don't mean vhat they say!! Ve gonna light the Holy Candle!! Ve gonna close our ears!! Ve gonna eat the maws!! (VIOLET *takes out the maws and puts it on the top of her left hand and holds it out for* LUCENE) Eat the maws Lucene!! Eat the maws!!

ALL WOMEN: Eat the maws!

LUCENE: *(In the nightmare)* No!! Mama!! Why Mama? Why would you lie to me?

MRS. AROOSTIAN: Violet never lie. You vorst Armenian voman, I ever see!! You make amot!!!

ALL WOMEN: She no eat the maws . . . She no eat the maws!

LUCENE (BRIDE): I want my husband back!! I want my life back!! Give it back! In-zee doore!! *[Give it back]*

ELENA (CHILD): I don't like you Lucene!! You're bad!! You used to be good girl!! You used to play!! You used to dance!! You're bad Lucene! You used to be Armenian!!

LUCENE (CHILD): I'm good!! I'm good!! I'm good!!

LUCENE (BRIDE): You're bad!! You ran away from all of us!

MRS. AROOSTIAN: Kehsh!! Kehsh!! *[Bad.]* You're bad!! Go eat apple pie—

ELENA (CHILD): You don't eat *bastech*!! You don't eat *choreg*!! You don't eat *pakalava*!!

MRS. AROOSTIAN: Go eat your apple pie!

LUCENE: I do . . . I do . . .

ELENA (CHILD) *is on a chair impersonating Krikor on their wedding day.* LUCENE (CHILD) *is pretending to be the flower girl.* LUCENE (BRIDE) *goes over to* ELENA (CHILD).

LUCENE (BRIDE): I do!!
ELENA *(As Krikor):* I do!!

Wedding music is heard. LUCENE (BRIDE) *and* ELENA *(as Krikor) dance holding hands and laughing. Everyone is clapping and smiling. The wedding music stops.* ELENA (CHILD) *twirls back to herself.*

LUCENE (BRIDE): Krikor made me boxes!! Three boxes. Three boxes of love!
VIOLET: Three boxes of trouble. Forget those boxes!! I fix everything.
MRS. AROOSTIAN: You fix nothing nothing, but big trouble!!
LUCENE (BRIDE): Ani's going to stay with me here!! I'll teach her Armenian!! We'll go to church!! *(Calling out)* Krikor?! Krikor!! Meet our daughter!! We have a beautiful daughter and she has a beautiful name. Ani!! Ani!! Ani!!
LUCENE (CHILD): Ani!! My favorite name!!

ELENA (CHILD): The name of the old city in Mother Armenia with one thousand and one churches!!

VIOLET: Ve gonna go to church . . . ve gonna light the candles!!

MRS. AROOSTIAN: Look!! There she is!! Look!! Here she comes!! Look!! there she goes—Amot!! Amot!! And ve gonna talk all day about Lucene!! Lucene took her child and ran away from Watertown. Lucene, mekh eh . . . Lucene, don't gotta husband anymore, mekh eh . . . Lucene never gonna come home!! *Amot!!*

LUCENE (CHILD): Yes, chem sea-reh kezee!! *[I don't like you!]*

ELENA (CHILD): You lie!! You lie!!

LUCENE (BRIDE): *(To* LUCENE*)* Murderer! Murderer!

MRS. AROOSTIAN: You phony Armenian voman!! You big fake! *Yes, chem sea-reh kezee!!* [I don't like you]

VIOLET: Yes, chem sea-reh kezee!!

LUCENE: *(Turning and troubled)* Mama!! No!!

THE WOMEN *and* CHILDREN *circle* LUCENE.

ALL: Amot . . . Amot . . . Amot . . . Amot . . . Shame . . . Shame . . . Amot . . . Amot . . . Amot . . .

TAWKOOHEE *enters.* THE WOMEN *and* CHILDREN *exit circling and bowing to* TAWKOOHEE.

LUCENE *is haunted and in pain.*

LUCENE: *(Tossing and turning. Still asleep.)* No!! Amot cheh!! *[It's not a shame.]* No! Mama, why did you lie to me? No!

TAWKOOHEE *runs to her and tries to wake her up.*

TAWKOOHEE: Lucene vake up!! Tawkoohee here!! Vake up achchig. *[Girl]* Mee neghveer. *[Don't worry.]* Stop crying.

LUCENE: *(Waking up)* Oh Tawkoohee. . . I just saw her . . . I saw Mama.

TAWKOOHEE: Vhen?

LUCENE: Just now in a dream . . . a nightmare. Why? Why did she lie to me?

TAWKOOHEE: I don't know yet, but don't you vorry . . . ve goin' to find out, I promise.

LUCENE: Anne? Where's Anne?

TAWKOOHEE: She's not here.

LUCENE: We've got to find her.

TAWKOOHEE: She's okay.

LUCENE: She's not okay.

TAWKOOHEE: She's vith Vartan.

LUCENE: What?!

TAWKOOHEE: I saw them go into the church.

LUCENE: I don't want that boy to know our business.

TAWKOOHEE: Don't vorry about Vartan you only need to vorry about those letters.

LUCENE: There's a letter from Mama in the box Tawkoohee.

TAWKOOHEE: (Shocked) A letter from Violet? Vhat did it say?

LUCENE: I don't know. I didn't open it. I didn't open any of them.

TAWKOOHEE: Vhat?! Why didn't you open your Mother's letter?

LUCENE: I was afraid.

TAWKOOHEE: Your Mother loved you. I don't know vhat's in the letter, but you have to read it.

LUCENE: I know you're right, but I'm afraid. Why didn't she tell me about Krikor's letters. She was the one person I trusted all my life.

TAWKOOHEE: Then ve gonna trust her again. Ve gonna read the letter together. Now.

LUCENE *opens the letter with encouragement from* TAWKOOHEE.

LUCENE *reads the letter.*

VIOLET *enters.* LUCENE *reads the, first two lines of the letter and then* VIOLET *continues to recite the letter while* LUCENE *and* TAWKOOHEE *read the words.*

LUCENE: My Dear Lucene. I am gone now and you have found the box. When your Father died I promised him to remain silent, but I did not promise him or Nishan to keep silent after my death. The letters in the box are for you and Ani. They are from your Krikor. He has been sending the letters and the money to you since the day he left.

I did not know any of this until five years ago. Your Father swore me to secrecy before he died. He, Nishan and several other men brought Krikor to America to organize a group to fight for an independent Armenia. They had not expected you and Krikor to fall in love. The men opposed his marrying, but Krikor would not listen to them. He married you. He loved you Lucene, just as you believed he did and I believe these letters speak of his love.

Ani's Armenian treasures also came from Krikor. Your Father would put them in her "Watertown Box" each time they arrived. I know your Father loved you and Ani, but I also know the truth was not told. Tawkoohee is a woman you can trust. She knows nothing of this, but she is my friend and you can trust her to be yours. Tell Ani the truth about her Father. Make peace in your house and in your heart. You were loved by your husband. I cannot speak for your Father or Nishan or the other men . . . I can only speak for myself . . . This is America, where I am free, as a woman, to speak the truth, even though I have the courage to defie my husband only after my death. I love you Lucene and I will miss you always.

The final line is read by LUCENE *and* VIOLET. VIOLET *exits.*

TAWKOOHEE: *(Moved by the letter and angry at* NISHAN*)* Nishan not going to eat any of my *choreg* tonight!

LUCENE: *(Looking at the letter)* She defied my Father.

TAWKOOHEE: Armenian vomen are not property vithout minds.

LUCENE: It must have killed her not to tell me.

TAWKOOHEE: Ve take good and bad from our men, but this is going too far! You read your letters from Krikor. I gonna find Nishan.

TAWKOOHEE *exits.*

LUCENE *looks at her Mother's letter. She goes to the music box, winds it and listens to the music. She begins to read the letters from Krikor.*

Lights fade out.

Lights come up in the Armenian Church.

ANNE *and* VARTAN *are in the Church and sitting in a pew.*

ANNE: She lied . . . She's lied my whole life!! I feel like such a fool. What other lies has she told me?

VARTAN: You're not a fool!!

ANNE: I believed her story. She told me my Father was dead!! He has a grave!

VARTAN: But she didn't know where he was!!

ANNE: Everyone knew my Father was alive, but me.

VARTAN: I didn't know. Anne, don't make it ugly . . . your Father's letter is beautiful. Your Mother—

ANNE: *(Interrupting)* My Mother and Father made it ugly . . . My Father left—My Mother lied—It doesn't get much uglier. We were never a family.

VARTAN: You can't think like that. People's lives are crazy and I don't know why or how they can get so mixed up, but they do and instead of complaining you should be thinking of what's really happening tonight. Your Father's alive. You have a beautiful letter from a Father who loves you and your Mother. He says that! It's in writing!!

ANNE: Then why did he leave? Why was his life a secret from me? I don't believe that he was off fighting to create an independent Armenia.

VARTAN: I believe it.

ANNE: What man would leave a woman he loved and a new born child to fight for a worthless cause?!

VARTAN: A man who believed his cause wasn't worthless. A man who was so committed to the will of his ancestors that he couldn't come back . . . I don't know . . . I don't have the answers, but I know that Armenians are a passionate and good people and that they'd never do anything to hurt their children consciously.

ANNE: Armenians!! *Armenians*!! I'm such a stranger to them and they are strangers to me!! I don't know who they are?! Who are they? How am I to know?

VARTAN: We're complicated—

ANNE: *(Interrupting)* You're all crazy—

VARTAN: *(Interrupting)* We're all wonderful!

ANNE: None of this is wonderful. I'm so angry. I'm hurt and it feels horrible.

VARTAN: Your Mother's probably feeling the same way.

ANNE: I know, but I can't worry about her. I'm like an "odar." *[A non-Armenian]* I'm an Armenian who can't even make *choreg* or spell it!

VARTAN: *(Interrupting)* At least you can say it.

ANNE: But I'm an outsider!! I can't even read a letter from a man who claims to be my Father.

VARTAN: Plenty of Armenians can't read Armenian!! What's the big deal?

ANNE: Tawkoohee!! Tawkoohee says that "A true Armenian speaks the language of the Motherland's!" I know I'm not a true Armenian. I can't even read the Armenian alphabet!

VARTAN: Bareh Mayreeg, Bareh. *[Dance Mama, Dance]*

ANNE: *(Surprised by what he just said)* What?

VARTAN: Bareh Mayreeg, Bareh. Dance Mama, Dance!! The words that you embroidered on the sampler in your "Watertown Box" . . . you can speak Armenian . . . you embroidered Armenian words on cloth when you were eight years old!

ANNE: *(Remembering the happy memory)* Those were my first Armenian words.

VARTAN: See!?!

ANNE: *(Feeling badly for herself)* See what?! Dance Mama, Dance?! Three words? Three words that my Grandmother taught me to say like a parrot?

VARTAN: No, not like a parrot . . . Three Armenian words to build on!! You can learn to speak the language. You can one day read your Father's letter for yourself . . . You can do anything that you want, but you can't stay angry at a situation you had no part in creating!!

ANNE: I didn't even know that you had noticed my sampler.

VARTAN: It was beautiful!! The box was wonderful!! I've never known anyone who created a "Watertown Box" . . . who created anything—just to keep Armenians with them always.

ANNE: The box was Grandma's idea. I hated leaving her after every visit. The box was a way of keeping Grandma and Grandpa with me. Everything in it is an Armenian treasure from them.

VARTAN: It is a brilliant idea and it is the perfect place to keep your sampler. *(He begins to dance and flirt with* ANNE.*)* Bareh Mayreeg, Bareh—Come on Ani . . . dance!

ANNE: Stop that! We're in a church! And it was my Mother dancing, not me!

VARTAN: I know the story—

ANNE: Not all of it! I drew a picture with black crayon on a cotton cloth like the one we used for bastech. Grandma cut the picture into a square and wrote Bareh Mayreeg, Bareh . . . *(Reminiscing)* "See Ani," she said, "These letters are Armenian and they mean Dance Mama, Dance! You liked your Mama dancing and now she will dance always for you on this cloth like she did for her Father when she was a little girl. Here, she said, give me the needle and I will show you how to put the colored threads into the cloth."

VARTAN: And the colors are still beautiful . . . you have got to frame that cloth.

ANNE: Oh come on, it's not that good . . .

VARTAN takes her hand and pulls her towards him.

VARTAN: It is. *(He kisses her and then holds her)* Ani . . . I need to get you home.

ANNE: Ani?!

VARTAN: You want to be Armenian . . . you want to feel Armenian . . . We'll start by calling you Ani. Okay?

ANNE: Okay.

VARTAN: Come on then, Ani.

ANNE: No. I can't go home tonight.

VARTAN: Then you'll come home with me. You can sleep in our Arlene's room. You've got to get some sleep.

ANNE: Are you sure it will be okay with Arlene?

VARTAN: Yes, but tomorrow morning you head home to face your Mother. Deal?

ANNE: Deal. I'll call her from your house.

VARTAN: And remember, a good Armenian daughter "must always" forgive her Father and Mother . . .

ANNE: What?!

VARTAN: Trust me, I was raised in this church . . . I was raised in this town . . . and I've never known an Armenian yet, who never forgave a brother, a sister, a Mother or a Father . . . let's go.

VARTAN offers ANNE his hand. ANNE takes his hand happily.

Blackout.

Lights come up in the Manian kitchen.

ARLENE: She's a grown woman. She's seventy-two years old.

NISHAN: She should be home and in bed. It's one thirty in the morning!! And where's your brother?!

ARLENE: Asleep!!

NISHAN: He's not upstairs!!

ARLENE: Well, then he's at the library?! I don't know?! How should I know?! Who cares?! Auntie and Vartan can take care of themselves.

NISHAN: What's wrong with this family?!

ARLENE: Nothing? We're all fine. What's wrong with you?!

NISHAN: Tawkoohee and Vartan should be home. Here. In this house.

ARLENE: Vartan's probably researching something and Tawkoohee's old enough to do what she wants.

NISHAN: She went back to the Arevian house with my choreg!!

ARLENE: What?!

NISHAN: She came home and then went back to be with Lucene and took the *choreg* with her that she said she was making for me!!

ARLENE: Why?!

NISHAN: It doesn't matter why!! She should be home, minding her own business!!

ARLENE: I'm not getting in the middle of this. I'm going back to bed. I was asleep and I woke up because I heard you down here bumping around. I thought you needed me, but you just want someone to yell at!!

NISHAN: I want order in this house!! I don't want everyone acting crazy!! Ignoring me!!

ARLENE: Then just let us be the adults that we are! Stop trying to run our lives!

NISHAN: I'm the head of this household!! I know what's right for all of you!!

ARLENE: No you don't!!

NISHAN: Your Mother would be ashamed to hear you talk like that!! I'm your Father!

ARLENE: Mom never tried to run my life!! She taught me to think for myself.

NISHAN: You have responsibilities to me and to this family.

ARLENE: (Interrupting) And to myself!! Dad, you can't run my life. And you may as well know right now that I received my letter today.

NISHAN: What letter?!

ARLENE: You see, you don't ever want to listen to what you don't want to hear. I told you four months ago and again last week that I applied to the Saint Nersess Seminary in New York! Well, today I got my letter and I made it. I've been admitted for the fall term.

NISHAN: What? No! I won't allow it!! I won't pay a penny.

ARLENE: I have my own money and I'm going!!

NISHAN: I won't approve!

ARLENE: I don't expect you to approve, but Auntie Tawkoohee approves, she helped me apply and she's going to help me pay for my books if my savings run out.

NISHAN: Tawkoohee? Tawkoohee?!?! Why wasn't I told!! She's made a lot of trouble today!!

ARLENE: You were told!

NISHAN: I never saw your application!! You didn't discuss it with me.

ARLENE: You wouldn't find the time!

NISHAN: This is what I'm talking about!! I'm not informed in my own house!! I won't have it!! I will have order in my house!! You're not going to any seminary!! You're going to stay here and marry Aram!!

ARLENE: *Aram*!?! I've never even had a date with Aram!! This isn't the old country and I'm not about to sign my life away on an arranged marriage!!

NISHAN: He's got a good job, he's got a good Mother, his Father was a good Armenian man! He's Armenian!! What more do you want?!

ARLENE: A grown man!!

NISHAN: He's thirty-four!!

ARLENE: Dream about that wedding all by yourself. I want to get married, I really do and I will get married someday, but not to someone who's afraid to be a man.

NISHAN: Is that why you're going to the seminary—to find a husband?!

ARLENE: No!! *(Totally frustrated)* Agh!! I'm going because I have something to say!! I want the right to speak to Armenian people with my own voice. Armenian women have taken the back seat to you men far too long. We're Armenia— Mother Armenia! We're the very reason why Armenians have survived until now. We're the very reason Armenians became Christians in 301 A.D. The first Christian Nation in the world. You're my Father and I love you, but I'm sick of catering to you and every other man in this community. I have my own voice. I have my own life. I have pride in being Armenian and I'm leaving here in September to become an Armenian Priest!!

NISHAN: That's what you think!

ARLENE: By the First Five Armenian Women Saints . . . I know!

NISHAN *puts his head in his hands.*

ARLENE *stands strong.*

TAWKOOHEE *enters.*

NISHAN: *(Looking up and making fun of* TAWKOOHEE*)* AAAhhhh! You came home!

ARLENE: *(Noticing* TAWKOOHEE*'s anger)* Auntie, what's wrong?

TAWKOOHEE: *(Looking at* NISHAN*)* How many years you and I go back, huh?! How many times somevon lie to us on our vay to America and ve swear ve alvays goin' to tell the truth? Huh?

ARLENE: Auntie, what happened?

NISHAN: *(Not caring)* I'm going to bed.

TAWKOOHEE: That's right . . . go to bed, but vhen you close your eyes you gonna have nightmares! You knew vhere Krikor vas!

NISHAN: I told you to leave it alone.

TAWKOOHEE: Vhat you think, you God? You talk about visdom . . . you pray for visdom . . . vhere vas your visdom when you and Tawveet keep Krikor's letters and money from Lucene?!

ARLENE: (Shocked by the accusation) What?!

NISHAN: Who told you that?

TAWKOOHEE: Violet.

NISHAN: (Shocked by what he's heard) Violet?!

TAWKOOHEE: Violet. She left a letter for Lucene explaining everything. Lucene found the letter today. The truth alvays going to come out, no matter how many people try and cover up the lies. I'm ashamed of you. Vhat kind of Der Hayr [Priest] are you?

NISHAN: The kind that wants Armenia to stand on its own again.

TAWKOOHEE: At whose expense?

NISHAN: Lucene got in the way. We didn't plan for Krikor to fall in love with her, but he did. Violet was wrong to write that letter.

TAWKOOHEE: She vas her Mother. You had no right to keep Krikor's letters from Lucene and Ani. And you had no right to make Violet keep a promise against her daughter.

NISHAN: It was always too dangerous.

TAWKOOHEE: For who?

NISHAN: For all of them! Krikor works in the underground! A life that we can't even imagine. He and his men move from house to house, from country to country. Armenian men from all around the world send him money for the cause.

ARLENE: (Not believing what she's hearing) The cause?! How could you fall for that line? Armenia will never be free!

TAWKOOHEE: (Trying to understand NISHAN) He vanted Armenia back—

NISHAN: (To TAWKOOHEE and ARLENE) Is that so hard to understand?

VARTAN and ANNE enter.

VARTAN: What's everybody doing up?

TAWKOOHEE acting like nothing is going on.

TAWKOOHEE: (Smiling) Ve just talkin'. Ani, it's late—You goin' to go home tonight?

VARTAN: (Explaining for ANNE) Actually, she thought she'd spend the night here with Arlene.

ARLENE: Sure—No problem!

ANNE: Thanks.

NISHAN: *(To* ANNE*)* What about your Mother?

ANNE: *(Embarrassed)* We're sort of having a misunderstanding and—

TAWKOOHEE: *(Interrupting* ANNE *to help her)* You don't need to explain, Ani—This house alvays open to you! I'll tell your Mother you're here . . . Don't you worry.

ANNE: Thank you.

TAWKOOHEE: Arlene, you take Ani upstairs and give her clean nightgown and towels. It's late. Everybody goin' to go to bed. Tomorrow there's going to be *choreg* baking for everyvon!

ARLENE: *(To* ANNE*)* Come on.

VARTAN: *(With his arm around* ANNE*)* You'll be fine here.

ANNE, ARLENE, *and* VARTAN *exit.*

NISHAN: *(Watching* VARTAN *and* ANNE *exit)* Is that what I think it is?

TAWKOOHEE: Vhat's happened to you? Vhat's wrong vith you? All our life I think I know you, but I know nothing! I have to go call Lucene and tell her that Ani is here.

NISHAN: *(Feeling a little guilty)* The situation was out of my hands.

TAWKOOHEE: *(Exhausted by* NISHAN's *attitude)* God only gonna ask you to answer for yourself Nishan . . . But remember, I gonna be there too.

NISHAN: *(Somewhat angry)* Understand . . . this *was* and *is* man's business!

TAWKOOHEE: There vas a young bride, who now is a grown voman, who trusted you and her Father and you mean to tell me that you let her down because of "man's business"?

NISHAN: Don't twist it, Tawkoohee.

TAWKOOHEE: Do you. remember the animal hole our mother hid us in the day she died?

NISHAN: Of course I do—

TAWKOOHEE: *(Interrupting)* It vas damp and cold and the earth around us vas so soft that I thought if the Turks didn't get us that Mount Ararat vould . . . that ve vould sink into the earth and no von vould ever find us again.

NISHAN: Tawkoohee, we're safe! That was a long time ago. We survived.

TAWKOOHEE: To vhat Nishan? To "Man's Business"?! I vas older than you. I remember the village square, the people, the mountain side . . . I vas eight . . . you vere five. I carried you vhen our parents vere killed. Vas that "Man's Business"? It vas a voman, me, your sister who found food for you. I fed you first vhen both our stomachs growled. I held you vhen you cried for our parents. I vorked to send you to seminary. As long as about family business. Men don't need to keep secrets from the vomen. Ve don't need to talk about "Ramagarvars and Tashnags"!! Ve don't need to divide. Ve need to come together.

NISHAN: *(Trying to explain)* Tawkoohee . . . the genocide took our manhood from us . . . what good are we men to our women, if we can't even get back our country?

TAWKOOHEE: *(Exhausted and angered by his deduction)* This is not about some political cause. This is about the lives of real people.

NISHAN: Aren't we men real people too?

TAWKOOHEE *feels* NISHAN'S *pain, but also the pain of* LUCENE *and* ANNE.

Blackout.

End of scene one.

ACT TWO

Scene Two

The next morning. THE ARMENIAN WOMEN *enter.*

ARMENIAN WOMAN #1: I see Lucene's house from my bedroom and all night long
  her lights vere on!

ARMENIAN WOMAN #2: Her lights vere on and Tawkoohee vas going in and out of
  the house — I saw this vith my own eyes!

ARMENIAN WOMAN #3: And her daughter vent into the church vith Vartan after
  midnight!

ARMENIAN WOMEN #1 AND #2: *(Putting their hands to their mouths)* Oohh!!

ARMENIAN WOMAN #3: Vhat kind of trouble going on in that house?

ARMENIAN WOMAN #1: Maybe Tawkoohee and Lucene havin' big fight?!

ARMENIAN WOMAN #2: Maybe Tawkoohee helpin' Lucene fix her Mother's things.

ARMENIAN WOMAN #3: Maybe they plannin' big dinner for Violet's friends! Oooh!
  Ve goin' to be invited to a memorial dinner!

ARMENIAN WOMAN #1: *(Excited)* They gonna serve shish kebab! That vas Violet's
  favorite.

ARMENIAN WOMAN #2: Vith pilaf and green bean and tomato!

ARMENIAN WOMAN #3: And paklava! Lots of paklava! Violet made the best *paklava*
  I ever tasted!

ARMENIAN WOMEN: *(Thinking of the meal)* Mmmmmm . . .

ARMENIAN WOMAN #2: Are you sure there's goin' to be a party?!

ARMENIAN WOMAN #1: Vhy else Lucene's light goin' to be on all night? She's plannin' party for Violet's memory, I feel this . . . I know this!

ARMENIAN WOMAN #3: Come on then . . . Ve goin' to go shopping to buy present
  to take. Ve goin' to buy hard candy — they last long time! Come on.

THE ARMENIAN WOMEN *exit.*

Blackout.

Lights come up in the Manian kitchen. TAWKOOHEE *is shaping the last of her choreg dough. There is choreg baking in the oven and choreg on the counter or table baked and cooling. She is twisting the choreg into buns, brushing the tops with egg and sprinking sesame seeds on the tops before baking the choreg that has been placed on the cookie sheets.*

ANNE *enters in her nightgown and robe.*

TAWKOOHEE: Ani?! Vhat are you doing up? You should be sleeping . . . it's early.

ANNE: I smelled the *choreg* baking.

TAWKOOHEE: Oh, I understand then—It smells good vhen *choreg* is baking first thing in the morning . . . huh? (TAWKOOHEE *is taking baked* choreg *off the baking pan*)

ANNE: Yes.

TAWKOOHEE: Did you sleep well?

ANNE: No. I kept dreaming about Mama lying to me.

TAWKOOHEE: She didn't mean to lie to you.

ANNE: We've always been so close, but I can't seem to forgive what she's done.

TAWKOOHEE: So, vhat are you goin' to do?

ANNE: I don't know.

TAWKOOHEE: (*Putting a hot* choreg *in a napkin and pouring a glass of orange juice*) You goin' to sit right down vith me and eat my *choreg*. Here.

ANNE: (*Breaking off a taste with her fingers*) Mmmmmm . . . it's so good. Thanks.

TAWKOOHEE: Ani? Do you love your Mother?

ANNE: Yes, but—

TAWKOOHEE: (*Interrupting*) No . . . no buts! You said "yes."

ANNE: You were there Tawkoohee! You saw what happened.

TAWKOOHEE: She had her reasons.

ANNE: But I feel like an idiot. She hates Armenians. And she must have hated my Father to kill him!

TAWKOOHEE: No! She didn't kill him—she buried him, there's a difference and don't talk about "hate." That vord never goin' to be useful to anyvon!

ANNE: Tawkoohee, I know you mean well, but even you can't fix this.

TAWKOOHEE: You know, vhen Vartan's Father and I vere little, I almost lost my faith in God and mankind, but somehow, somevay I held on—

ANNE: You're talking about the genocide, aren't you?

TAWKOOHEE: Yes, I talkin' about the genocide. That vas bad time vhen in my heart I believed that no von vas capable of fixin' anything in Armenia and makin' it right again . . .

ANNE: But it's not right again—Armenia doesn't exist anymore.

TAWKOOHEE: Oh Ani . . . you're wrong! Ve survived! Armenia is here *(She puts her hand to her heart)*, in our hearts.

ANNE: I really don't know anything about being Armenian.

TAWKOOHEE: Then Tawkoohee going to fix that! I'm goin' to tell you a true story and I promise you, vhen I finish, you gonna know something about being Armenian! You see, there vas the mountain . . . Mount Ararat . . . but there vas no von to save my Mother or my Father . . . My brother, Nishan vas five years old vhen they kill our Father . . . our Father had been hunting on Ararat and ve heard a rush of horses come to the house. My Mother told us not to look outside because she feared that they vere not the horses of our countrymen. Ve listened as they passed the house and shook vhen they threw something on our porch. Ve didn't move for at least five minutes and then my Mother got up and vent outside. Nishan and I just sat there afraid. It vas dark and the moon vas small. I vanted my Father to valk in. Oor ess, highreeg? *[Where are you, Father?]* Myreeg? *[Mother?]* Oor ess, highreeg? *[Where are you, Father?]* Nishan started to cry. I took his hand to search for my Mother. She vas crying vithout sounds, bendin' herself backvards and forvards and hugging this dark red thing. My Father and his Father before him had hiked and hunted Ararat everyday of their lives. They vere the finest woodsmen in the territory. The Turks had killed my Father that night and axed off his legs to throw them at his family. Our Mother held both legs, unable to move until morning vhen her sister had to pull them forcibly from her arms. Three veeks later, hiding throughout the mountainside vhere ever ve could find a hole or cave, the Turks found my Mother. It vasn't enough that ve had lost our Father . . . they vanted his voman too. Not only to kill, but to have their vay with her . . . you know vhat I'm talkin' 'bout?

ANNE: *(ANNE nods her head)* Yes.

TAWKOOHEE: Seven men tracked us for days, but my Mother vas a smart voman and strong. She knew vhere to hide, vhere to find food . . . vhere to sleep. Up and down the mountain ve marched praying to God for protection and help. *(Reminiscing and shouting)* Vazeh!! Vazeh!! *Vazeh! [Run!! Run!! Run!]* The Turks vere close. Nishan and I vere put in animal holes with dirt and grass to cover our faces . . . Nishan told me that ve vere okay, because ve vere under the ground like our Father, I told him that people aren't suppose to be buried alive and that ve vere alive and Highreeg *[Father]* vas dead. Vith a blackened face he just stared at me and I began to wonder if the hole ve stood in vould be our grave . . . Dagrun chooneem . . . Achchig chooneem . . . Inch gooess? Inch gooess?! *[I don't have a son! I don't have a daughter! What do you want? What do you want?]* She began to pray . . . Hayr mer vor . . . *[The beginning of the Lord's Prayer in Armenian]* I vatched the rape from vhere I hid. Each man except for von, who vas crying and hiding his tears for her, mounted my Mother. Four men held her down. Von on each leg and von on each arm. She must have had a heart attack, because I heard her cry for my Father very softly and then I heard nothing. They inspected her body laughing, lifting her breasts, spreading her legs . . . touching her long black braids. With his saber a Turk cut her hair for a prize. He vas cheered on and my Mother laid in the mountain dirt vith her head shorn and the Turk putting her braids into his leather satchel. They looked around for us, but ve made ourselves smaller than ever before. I did not let Nishan see any of the rape, as I vas on top of him and both taller and older. They left and ve did not move for fear they vould come back.

ANNE: But how did you and Der Hayr escape?

TAWKOOHEE: The man who cried the tears during the murder of my Mother came back. It vas dark and he had a torch which provide much light. He looked for Nishan and me and vhen he stood over my Mother's body he told her he vas sorry for her and my Father's death. He found us and told us to come out of the hole. Get into the sack, he said to us. I want to bury my Mother, I said. I want to bury her vith my Father!! He looked very sick and sorry. He vas a Turk, but he vanted to help us. He put my Mother over his back and ve held onto his clothes as ve walked to vhere my Father vas buried. He dug the hole, lifted the cover on my Father's box and placed my Mother's body on top of my Father's body. It smells, I cried. She does not smell vhat ve do, nor does he . . . they are together, it vill be alright. He put us in the sack and carried us down the mountain to his home. His wife vas a good voman and fed us and put us to bed. In the morning, ve vere fed breakfast and put into a sack again and taken to the Black Sea. Ve vere put on a boat with other Armenian children sailing to Vestern Europe.

ANNE: I'm surprised a Turk helped you.

TAWKOOHEE: He vas a good man vith many bad men. For every nationality there alvays gonna be good and bad men and vomen. Some you can trust and some you can't. Ve have to remember our ancestors and the memory of the homeland, but nothing ever gonna be von sided. You gotta look at each person—individually—before you make judgement. You gotta stick up for vhat you believe in! Ve can't hate everyvon, even if they hate you . . . because vhat are ve going to do if everyvon hates this person or that person? Huh? Ve never goin' to move forvard! Ve never goin' to learn to forgive and trust God! You understand vhat I'm talkin' 'bout?

ANNE: The Genocide was so horrible. We lost so much.

TAWKOOHEE: This vas holocaust of human spirit! Ve lost so much more than blood and nobody noticed, but somehow . . . somevay . . . ve still go on! Ve're strong peoples and nothin' ever goin' to keep us down . . . ve goin' to live and re-live every day on this earth and vhen ve die ve never goin' to stop breathin' life into our children!!

ANNE: You want me to forgive Mama, don't you?

TAWKOOHEE: Of course!! You see? You already learning something about bein' Armenian! You're smart girl, I know this! Nothing in life ever goin' to be perfect—you need to talk vith your Mother and listen to vhat she says . . .

ANNE: But I trusted her and—

TAWKOOHEE: *(Interrupting)* And you goin' to trust her again! Come on, you gonna need your strength—ve goin' to eat another *choreg*. Armenian food alvays goin' to give you strength!

ANNE *smiles and they both eat another choreg.*

Blackout.

Lights come up on LUCENE *reading a letter from Krikor. She has not stopped reading the letters all night.*

LUCENE: *(Reading one of Krikor's letter)* . . . I received news that you have given birth to a girl. The name Ani is a beautiful choice. Ani Elena Kinsorian will do great things one day. Perhaps she will grow up to walk on the land of an independent Armenia and dance as beautifully as you did the night we met. Enclosed are gifts for Ani and money for you. I will write again. Enough now to know that you and our daughter are safe. You are in my thoughts and heart always. With love, Krikor. September 25, 1969. *(She puts the letter back into it's envelope)* 1969. Krikor her name is Anne now, not Ani and our life is here in America, not in a dream filled Armenia. *(*LUCENE *winds her Mother's music box and listens)*

ANNE *enters holding a rolled cloth with bastech on it and a basket of choreg.*

ANNE: *Bastech* and *choreg.*

LUCENE: Anne! *(*LUCENE *goes to hug* ANNE. ANNE *does not return the hug completely)* I was so worried about you.

ANNE: Tawkoohee thought you might need something to eat. She made this *choreg* this morning and I made the *bastech.*

LUCENE: You made the *bastech?*

ANNE: Yeah . . . Arlene and I made it. The recipe is Grandma's.

LUCENE: *Bastech's* my favorite. *(Realizing)* This was the surprise.

ANNE: Yeah, right. So much for surprises. You were right, this place really is jinxed.

LUCENE: No—Not for you—

ANNE: For both of us.

LUCENE: Anne, I'm so sorry that I didn't tell you.

ANNE: I feel so betrayed—

LUCENE: I made decisions for us. Your Father left me before we even knew that I was pregnant. I'm not sure he would have left if he had known, but he didn't know and he has a cause to fight for, one that he had committed himself to, long before he met me.

ANNE: But you were married—you're not a widow—you're not divorced—you're still married to a man that you haven't talked to in twenty years!! Why didn't you fight for him? Why didn't you go look for him and tell him about me?

LUCENE: I did fight and I did go look for him.

ANNE: When?!

LUCENE: You were too young to remember. Grandma helped me to go to Armenia to search for him.

ANNE: *(Remembering)* When I was eight.

LUCENE: Yes. I was hopeful and happy and—

ANNE: *(Interrupting)* Dancing!! You were dancing.

LUCENE: What?!

ANNE: I was brought here for a vacation. You were going away. Far away you told me, but you'd be back. You were so happy—Don't you remember? Grandma was humming some Armenian folksong and you kicked off your shoes and—

LUCENE: *(Interrupting)* Started dancing! *(Smiling)* Yes—I remember—

ANNE: *(Getting her sampler and taking it to her Mother)* Do you remember this?

LUCENE: Where did you get this? How did you manage to save it?

ANNE: It was you dancing Mama, you were happy.

LUCENE: I was dancing when I met your Father—and it's him that we need to talk about—Anne, he didn't forget us.

ANNE: I don't know him—I don't know this side of you, who could care about a man who left us.

LUCENE: There are parts of us that our children can never know. I didn't know that Mama knew about the letters. She wrote me this. *(Handing her Violet's letter)* I found it after you left.

ANNE: What? Grandma knew?

LUCENE: It's all in the letter.

ANNE: *(Reading the letter)* Grandpa?

LUCENE: It's crazy and it's complicated and I'm not sure what to think right now, I've never regretted telling you that Krikor was dead—I stood by my decision, but now that I know that others knew the truth, well—

ANNE: *(Interrupting)* You're talking about Grandpa and Der Hayr Nishan—

LUCENE: Yes. You know, when I was a little girl being Armenian was an honor—I didn't call myself Armenian, I simply was. For snacks, Elena and I were given dried chick peas to eat, instead of potato chips—We had rice pilaf on Thanksgiving, instead of mashed potatoes—We breathed Armenian air in our American houses. When your Father left it killed me and I killed everything Armenian in me, because I couldn't find him. Elena had died, Krikor was gone, the gossip, the church, everything became overwhelming—there was no place for me here. I could hear my own voice. There were only the sounds of men chanting in the church that I grew up in—in the church that I had loved as a child.

ANNE: And so you gave up.

LUCENE: No. We left.

ANNE: But then I didn't get to feel the pride in being an Armenian. You made the decision that there was no honor because of your anger. How can things change in the Armenian culture if all of their women get up and leave?! You could have stopped the gossip—you could have found my Father—we could have stayed here and you could have made changes in front of me within our culture. You had no right to run away.

LUCENE: Maybe not, but I don't know that. I only know that here is a box with letters from my husband and your Father. *(Handing her the letters)* Here, these are yours.

ANNE: *(Looking at the letters)* But I can't read these.

LUCENE: We'll read them together.

ANNE: Here? In this house?

LUCENE: Yes. If you want to . . .

ANNE: I want to stay the full forty days of mourning. I want to go into the church that you grew up in and light a holy candle.

LUCENE: Alright, "Ani," we'll stay.

They embrace.

Lights begin to dim. A spot comes up on LUCENE. *She begins to recite the opening poem.* ANNE *exits.* LUCENE *moves to center stage.*

LUCENE: There is a concentration camp of the mind
    In which women have been forced to dwell
    And my Father was the first man to lead me there
    It is an ancient camp
    Where women have been taught
    To wear veil upon veil
    That hides their loveliness
    It is an ancient camp
    Of silent voices
    Where duty still demands
    That all women surrender
    Their personhood to wifery
    And even here on the modern streets
    Of this new and different land,
    The habits fashioned in those
    Ancient days, from those too—too
    Ancient ways still hold fast

Denying my beauty, denying my strength,
Denying my power to flee
The concentration camp of the mind
That my Father showed to me
As the only good and rightful place
A good woman, a good wife, a good mother
Can be or ever want to be.
My Father was always known to be
A very truthful man
And yet—
My Father lied to me.

Music is heard. LUCENE *exits.*

End of play.

LESLIE AYVAZIAN

NINE ARMENIANS

To my family: Sam and Ivan Anderson;
Dr. Fred and Gloria Ayvazian,
Andrea and Gina Ayvazian;
and grandparents;
Dr. Haig and Shorhig Ayvazian and
Rev. A. A. and Marie Bedikian,
with love.

THE PLAY AND THE PLAYWRIGHT

Nine Armenians has had many productions in notable theaters throughout the country, including New York's Manhattan Theatre Club, Los Angeles's Mark Taper Forum, Colorado's Denver Centre Theatre, Chicago's Apple Tree Theatre, and Rhode Island's Trinity Repertory Theater. Its various directors in these and other venues have heaped superlatives on the work—in particular for how the playwright gives insights into the Armenian way of life and Armenian history and yet broadens her theme to a universal level that appeals to people of all ethnicity. Small wonder, then, that the play won the John Gassner Outer Critics Award for best new play, the Susan Smith Blackburn International Play Award (second place), the Roger L. Stevens Award from the Kennedy Center, the Anahid Literary Award from Columbia University, a grant from the New Jersey Council of the Arts, and was selected for the anthology of *Best Plays by Women* in 1996.

Ayvazian has written several other plays of distinction, including *Singer's Boy* which opened at San Francisco's Geary Theater starring Olympia Dukakis. One-act plays such as *Practice, Plan Day, Deaf Day, Twenty Four Years, Hi There,* and *Mr. Machine* were produced in the New York City's Marathon Festival at the Ensemble Studio Theatre and published by the Dramatists Play Service.

Ayvazian's considerable experience as an actress no doubt has been of help in creating characters in her plays. She has appeared on Broadway in *Lost in Yonkers* and at the Manhattan Theatre Club in Terence McNally's *Lips Together, Teeth Apart* and *Jenny Keep Talking*, a one-woman show. Many have seen her playing several roles on television's *Law and Order*. In particular, the recurring role as Judge Valdera on *Special Victims Unit* has come to the attention of TV audiences.

Nine Armenians received its premiere at the Intiman Theatre Company (Warner Shook, artistic director; Laura Penn, managing director) in Seattle, Washington, on 16 August 1995. It was directed by Christopher Ashley, with set design by Loy Arcenas, costume design by Gabriel Berry, lighting design by Donald Holder, sound design by Steven M. Klein. The original music was written and performed by George Mgrdichian; the dance consultant was Christina Pashaian; the dramaturg was Robert Menna; and the stage manager was Renee Roub.

Nine Armenians was produced by the Manhattan Theatre Club (Lynne Meadow, artistic director; Barry Grove, managing director) in New York City in November 1996. It was directed by Lynne Meadow; the set design was by Santo Loquasto; the costume design was by Tom Broecker; the lighting design was by Kenneth Posner; the sound design was by Aural Fixation; the original music was written and performed by George Mgrdichian; the choreography was by Michele Assaf; and the production stage manager was Diane DeVita. The cast (with character names finalized) was as follows:

ARMINE/Mom	Linda Emond
JOHN/Dad	Michael Countryman
POP/Vartan, elderly MAN	Ed Setrakian
NON/Marie	Kathleen Chalfant
Virginia/GINYA	Ellen Muth
RAFFI	Cameron Boyd
AUNT LOUISE	Sophie Hayden
UNCLE GARO	Richard Council
ANI	Sevanne Martin

THE GENESIS OF *NINE ARMENIANS*

When I was in third grade, living in Leonia, New Jersey, and attending public school, I used to walk to my Grandparent's house for lunch. While my classmates sat in the school cafeteria eating sloppy joes and tuna melts, I was in my Grandmother's kitchen eating *Tass Kebob* (lamb stew), *beoregg* (cheese pies) and *annoushourg* (pudding). Every day, before lunch, it was my job to call my Grandfather down from his attic study. And every day, he came down the stairs, dressed in a suit, carrying letters in his hands. Letters he wrote to Armenians living all over the world. Or sometimes he was carrying pages from the sermon he would deliver that Sunday or articles for any number of Armenian publications, several of which he had established himself. Papa would sit at the table, stir honey into his coffee and talk to me.

I don't know how often he told me the story of the massacres. Perhaps only a few times. But he wore his history like his suit, even on the hottest summer days. I knew his family had been killed by the Turks in 1915. They were forced to walk into the desert until they dropped dead of starvation. The same was true for both sets of my Grandparents. They lost their families. And the peculiar truth was, no one here seemed to know. My friends didn't know who the Armenians were or where they came from. It was obvious the food we ate, the music we listened to, our language, was different. But the dark fact that our history was a secret, was possibly the single greatest characteristic of our uniqueness.

My sisters and I went to American schools in American towns and played on teams in American sports. We lived in the suburbs. We had no Armenian friends. My Grandfather, the minister of the Armenian Evangelical Church in New York City for forty-five years, passed away at the age of ninety-five. And my Grandmother, a concert singer and a scholar, died seven years ago at ninety-four. I inherited their house. My husband, my baby son, and I moved from New York City back to Leonia. I walked through the house, the attic, the basement. I opened trunks and ran my hands over tapestries, laces, a wedding trousseau, historic photographs, and scores of books on Armenian history.

At the same time, my sister, Andrea, went to Armenia. She organized a peace misssion with thirty participants to travel to Russia. Yerevan, the capital of Armenia, was a scheduled stop. While there, she and her group were invited to a village in the mountains. When they arrived, the entire village had gathered in the ancient local church. They burst through the doors and greeted her with white doves, tambourines, dancing, singing, and food gathered from their meager gardens. She and all thirty members of her group were welcomed and celebrated for one afternoon in a village in Armenia. They received her this way because she was Armenian. Andrea says, at the end of the day, as the bus traveled three hours back down the winding mountain roads to the city of Yerevan, no one spoke.

This story and the move into my Grandparents' house, inspired me to begin this play. I went up the stairs to my Grandfather's study, sat next to his Armenian typewriter, and wrote the first draft of Nine Armenians. The story begins in a driveway. The first words of the play are "Bye Bye!" It then takes the family twenty-five minutes to get in the car. Three generations run in and out of the house, the car, and the back yard with its big tree, carrying pans of food, blowing kisses, yelling, giving hugs, shouting: "Goodbye until next Tuesday!" Through the course of six teen scenes, the idealistic college daughter journeys to Armenia to witness its destitute conditions. Her experience there and its impact on the family bring us back to the driveway, reunited and changed.

Nine Armenians is my contribution to piercing the silence around Armenian History. The Armenians have felt as though they didn't count. The massacres in 1915 were unrecognized in the eyes of the world. To this day, the Armenians are struggling to survive. These nine in this family have been counted. Thank you.

LESLIE AYVAZIAN
OCTOBER 2003

NINE ARMENIANS

LESLIE AYVAZIAN

CHARACTERS

NON (Marie) — The grandmother
POP (Vartan) — The grandfather
ARMINE — Their daughter, the mother
JOHN — Her husband, the father
ANI — Their oldest daughter, 21 years old
VIRGINIA (GINYA) — Middle child, 15 years old
RAFFI — Youngest child, 11 years old
AUNT LOUISE — John's sister
UNCLE GARO — Her husband
ARMENIAN MAN — Played by the actor who plays
    POP

All nine characters wear coats in every scene: fall coats, winter coats, and spring coats, except sweaters in summer.

TIME AND PLACE

The time is 1992.

The place is an American suburb (probably in New Jersey) and Yerevan, Armenia.

Armenian music is played on Armenian instruments.

A simple set. Needs to include: an offstage tree with branches visible onstage. A bush. A doorway. A car.

SCENE 1

A driveway.

A car is parked in the driveway.

There is a suggestion of a house: steps or a door, etc.

A rhododendron bush is downstage.

A tree is offstage. We see a branch.

Armenian music plays.

Lights come up as members of the immediate family (all except ANI) are coming together to say good-bye. They are wearing their coats and carrying pans of food wrapped in aluminum foil.

JOHN: Good-bye!
ARMINE: Bye, bye, Pop!
NON: Manock parov! *[Good-bye!]*
ARMINE: Bye, bye, ma!
NON: You have the food?
JOHN, GINYA, and ARMINE: It's here!
NON: All right.
RAFFI: It's spilling!
NON: You need a rubber band!
ARMINE: No, no.
GINYA: Good-bye, Non!
RAFFI: Good-bye, Papa!
NON and POP: Good-bye, dear!
JOHN: Good-bye, good-bye everyone! *(They all hug and kiss each other.)* Come on,
    Armine. let's go! *(They break apart.)*
ARMINE: See you Tuesday, Ma!
NON: Bye, bye.
ARMINE: Come on, Raffi.
NON: *(She squeezes RAFFI's cheeks.)* Bachigs! *[Kisses!]*
JOHN, ARMINE, RAFFI, and GINYA: Bachigs! Bachigs! Bachigs!
NON and POP: Bachigs! Bachigs! Bachigs!
POP: I must go inside.
ARMINE: Bye, Pop.
POP: Marie!
NON: What?

POP: I'm going inside.

NON: Yes, Vartan, go. Armine!

ARMINE: What, Ma?

POP: Come in, Marie. That's enough.

NON: Yes, yes. I'm coming. I.O. *[Yes.]*

ARMINE: What, Ma?

NON: *(To* ARMINE.*)* Call when you get home.

ARMINE: Of course.

POP: Good-bye, Annushigus. *[Dear one.]*

ARMINE: Bye, Pop. (POP *exits.)*

JOHN: Come on, dear!

ARMINE: Ma, good-bye. Go inside!

JOHN: Give regards to Sarkis . . .

ARMINE and JOHN: . . . and Va Va.

NON: Ya. Ok.

ARMINE: Ma, go!

NON: Ya. Ya. (NON *exits.)*

ARMINE: Where's Raffi? Raffi! Come on! Time to go!

RAFFI: Ok, Mom. (RAFFI *doesn't move.)*

GINYA: Look at this bird!

RAFFI: Mom, can I take my coat off?

ARMINE: No, no, dear.

JOHN: *Everybody in the car! Let's go!*

ARMINE: Let me get a rubber band! (NON *enters carrying a rubber band.)*

NON: Here's a rubber band! Why not take the tass kebob? *[lamb stew]* (JOHN *goes in house.)*

ARMINE: Ma, there's no room.

GINYA: Nonnie, look at this bird!

NON: Yavroom *[Darling]*, you can hold the tass kebob. Put it on the floor under your feet.

GINYA: *Between* my feet, Non. It's *between* my feet.

NON: What is, darling?

ARMINE: Raffi! Ok! Come on! Let's go!

GINYA: No! Look at the bird.

ARMINE: Where's Pop?

NON: Inside. What bird?

GINYA: Right there!

ARMINE and NON. Where?

GINYA: By the branch there. At the end. See? (JOHN *enters carrying a big pot of food.)*

JOHN: *Ok! Everybody in the car!*

ARMINE: What's that?

JOHN: I took the tass kebob.

NON: *Afarehim!* *[Excellent!]*

ARMINE: *Raffi!*

RAFFI: Ok, Mom. (RAFFI *doesn't move.*)

ARMINE: Where's Pop?

NON: In the bathroom.

ARMINE: I want to say good-bye.

JOHN: *Armine! You said good-bye!*

GINYA: Dad, don't start the car.

JOHN: Why not?

GINYA: Come look at this bird.

NON: A cutie-pie!

JOHN: It's time to go!

GINYA: *(Pointing to bird.)* Look, Dad!

ARMINE: (ARMINE *enters, carrying tray of baklava.*) I think Pop is locked in the bathroom.

JOHN: Oh, Jesus.

NON: Vy vy vy! *[My, my, my!]* Ah see inch chay? *[What is it?]* Vartan! (NON *goes into house.*)

JOHN: Oh, Jesus!

ARMINE: You talk to him, dear.

JOHN: Tell your mother. . . . Tell your mother to take the goddamn locks off the doors! (JOHN *goes into house.* ARMINE *follows, still carrying tray of food.* RAFFI *stays by the bush and takes out small pad and pen and draws.* GINYA *watches bird. From the house, we hear:*) Vartan! Vartan! It's John!

POP: John!

JOHN: I'm here. You're locked in the bathroom!

POP: John! I'm locked in the bathroom!

JOHN: It's ok, Pop.

POP: What do I do?

JOHN: Put your hand on the lock.

POP: Help me! (*Ginya goes into house.* RAFFI *takes off his coat and ties it around his waist.*)

ARMINE: Put your hand on the lock, Pop.

POP: Help me!

JOHN: It's ok, Pop.

GINYA: Hi, Pop! It's Virginia!

POP: Ginya! I'm locked in here.

GINYA: It's ok, Pop.

POP: What do I do?

ARMINE: Just relax, Pop.

JOHN: Turn the knob toward the window. Toward the window!

POP: Which?

ARMINE: The window!

GINYA: The window, Pop.

JOHN: Not the tub!

NON: Not the tub, Vartan!

POP: Marie! Are you there?

NON: I'm here, Vartan.

JOHN: Turn in the other direction from the tub!

POP: Which one?

ALL: *(Including* RAFFI.*)* Not the tub!

JOHN: Pop! Listen to where I'm knocking on the door. Listen, Pop!

POP: Ok! *(Knocking sound.)*

JOHN: Turn toward the sound, Vartan! *(Knocking continues.)*

POP: Ok.

JOHN: That's it, Pop!

ALL: Yaaaaaaaaaaaaaaaaaaaaay!

NON: Afarehim! *[Excellent!]*

ARMINE: All right now. (GINYA *enters. She goes to tree.)*

GINYA: Bird's still there.

RAFFI: Where?

GINYA: See that white thing? (ARMINE *enters still with tray of food.)*

ARMINE: *Manock parov, Ma. [Good-bye.] Be careful, Papa.* Come on, kids. Raffi, put your coat on.

RAFFI: Why?

ARMINE: It's better. (NON *enters with another tray of food.)*

NON: Don't forget the kata. *[rolls]* (JOHN *following* NON.*)*

JOHN: Marie, we have no room for any more food.

NON: On the trunk!

GINYA: *In* the trunk, Non. It's *in* the trunk.

NON: What is, darling?

JOHN: *Come on, kids!*

ARMINE: Come on, kids. What are you doing?

RAFFI: Look at this bird.

NON: Aman. Shad Annushig! *[So sweet!]*

ARMINE: That white bird?

RAFFI: In the leaves.

JOHN: What bird?

GINYA: That's not a white bird. It's a little brown bird holding a Kleenex

JOHN: A brown bird?

ARMINE: A Kleenex?

GINYA: It might be a paper towel.

ARMINE: Maybe he's taking it to his kitchen! *(Laughs.* POP *enters. All are looking at the bird.)*

POP: What is it? What are you looking at?

ARMINE: It's a bird, Pop!

JOHN: What's in his beak?

NON, ARMINE, AND GINYA: Toilet paper. Kleenex. Paper towel.

POP: What?

RAFFI: He's stepping on it!

JOHN: I think it's a napkin.

POP: What, Marie? What is it? Ah see inch chay? *[What is it?]*

NON: Ice Turchuna *Kleenex* oonee! *[The little bird has a Kleenex.]*

POP: Turchuna Kleenex? *Boh! (Laughs.)*

RAFFI: He keeps stepping on it.

ARMINE: I bet he's taking it to that nest under the eaves.

RAFFI: I feel sorry for the bird.

NON: Yavroom, it's good! He's doing his work!

GINYA: He's bringing home a big white Kleenex for his family!

POP: Good for him! *(They all watch the bird fly over their heads.)*

ALL: Ohhhhhhhhhhhhhhhhhhh!

ARMINE: He's under the eaves!

GINYA: *Oh no! It ripped!*

RAFFI: *It ripped?*

ARMINE: No, no, it's all right! Now he has a more manageable piece in his mouth.

RAFFI: Why is he just standing there?

JOHN: He's waiting for us to leave!

POP: Ok! Let's go!

JOHN: That's right! Let's go! *(They come together again, and hug, and kiss good-bye. They break apart when* POP *says:)*

POP: Good-bye!

RAFFI AND ARMINE: Bye, Pop! *(*RAFFI *goes to bush and sits.)*

ARMINE: Bye, Ma. Don't forget, on Tuesday, we go to the podiatrist.

NON: Ya.

JOHN: Oh! Marie, did you sew my buttons?

NON: Aman, of course. I'll get.

JOHN: I'll get.

NON: I'll get. *(*NON *and* JOHN *go in the house.)*

POP: They went inside! Ginya!

GINYA: Yes, Pop?

POP: When do you have your commencement?

GINYA: In three years, Pop.

POP: Ah. Are you successful, Ginya? Do you succeed?

GINYA: In life?

POP: Boh! *(Laughs.)* Life! *(*GINYA *laughs too.)* Ahhh. *(Smiling.)* What's so funny?

GINYA: Life?

POP: Boh! *(Laughs again.)* Ya.

ARMINE: Pop, are you ok?

POP: Ya.

ARMINE: Do you want to go in the house?

POP: No dear. I'm enjoying my visit.

ARMINE: Ok.

POP: Yavroom *[dearest]*, what is your favorite pastime?

GINYA: I'm a pretty good athlete, Pop.

POP: Sports?

GINYA: Yea.

POP: *(Remembering.)* You run!

GINYA: Yea!

POP: And you write!

GINYA: Ani writes. I run. Raffi is the boy.

POP: Ya, of course. You run, Annushig *[sweetie or darling or my love]*! Who taught you?

GINYA: My gym teacher.

POP: Bravo!

GINYA: Yea.

POP: Do they teach the history, Ginya, also, in the school?

GINYA: No, Pop.

POP: Shall I come to your school? Shall I speak?

GINYA: I don't know, Pop.

ARMINE: John! Where are you?

RAFFI: He's in the house!

POP: Raffi! There you are!

RAFFI: Hi, Pop.

POP: Hi. Are you content, Raffi, with your bush?

RAFFI: Sure, Pop.

POP: Afarehim! *[Excellent!]*

ARMINE: Raffi? What's going on?

RAFFI: Nothing, Ma.

POP: Ginya! We were speaking.

GINYA: Yes, Pop?

POP: Do you know? It is happening again.

GINYA: What is, Pop?

POP: The Armenians are starving. Do they tell you this, Ginya? Do you know? What is your age?

GINYA: Fifteen.

ARMINE: Ginya, where's your father?

GINYA: In the house. I'm fifteen, Pop.

POP: Armenia, Ginya, has one railroad. It goes through the country to the north. Do you know which country?

ARMINE: *John! Come on!*

GINYA: Turkey?

POP: Turkey? No. Georgia, Ginya, has the railroad that brings the supplies from the sea towns to Armenia.

ARMINE: Where's Raffi?

POP: It is stopped. It is dismantled. The country is starving.

GINYA: He's by the bush, Ma.

POP: Aman . . . We are dying.

GINYA: Yes, Pop.

ARMINE: Ginya! Get your father!

POP: Where's Ani?

GINYA: She'll be home soon. (GINYA *goes into house.*)

POP: What do you draw, Raffi, in your pictures?

RAFFI: Um. Aliens.

POP: Aliens?

RAFFI: Yea. (*Gives* POP *picture.*)

POP: So this is what they look like!

RAFFI: Yea!

POP: I see. Raffi, do you ever draw a landscape?

RAFFI: You mean a picture of some land?

POP: Ya, some land. Perhaps also with a mountain?

RAFFI: Well, not usually.

POP: Perhaps, Mt. Ararat, Raffi. The mountain in Armenia where . . .

RAFFI AND POP: Noah's Ark landed.

POP: Boh! (*Laughs.*) Ya. Aman.

RAFFI: I'll draw it, Pop.

POP: Bravo!

ARMINE: John!

(JOHN *enters.* NON *follows carrying pressed pants on a hanger.* GINYA *follows* NON. *They cross to the car.*)

JOHN: I'm here!

POP: Marie! Where is Ani?

NON: Ginya, tell Pop.

GINYA: She's in Nevada. The desert.

POP: Why didn't she come today? Marie, shouldn't she come today?

RAFFI: She can't, Pop. She's in jail.

POP: She was arrested?

ARMINE: She's all right. She's in jail with two nuns.

POP: Why?

ARMINE: They prayed on the test site.

POP: Marie, what is it?

NON: Aneen Nevada Ah nuclear bombs see head-day. *[Ani is in Nevada with nuclear bombs.]*

POP: Aman, Marie!

NON: She's all right, Vartan.

ARMINE: Ma! Did you sew John's pants?

NON: I did. I gave.

JOHN: I have. They're here.

ARMINE: Ok.

JOHN: Let's go!

POP: Marie, should we write a letter? Should we write a letter to the jail?

NON: Armine, talk to Pop.

ARMINE: Pop, she'll be home soon.

POP: I'll write.

ARMINE: Ok, Pop.

POP: Marie, I'll write.

NON: All right, dear.

JOHN: Ok! I'm counting!

NON: Counting what, dear?

JOHN: Minutes!

NON: Aman! The grape leaves!

ARMINE: We don't have time, Ma.

NON: Ginya, you go pick some grape leaves in the back for your mother. Vartan, you help her.

POP: Did you give Ani the book, Marie?

NON: What book, dear?

POP: My book.

NON: She has them, Vartan. She has them.

POP: My last book, Marie!

GINYA: Papa, let's go.

NON: All right, dear, I'll give it.

POP: Marie, she should be here.

NON: I know, dear.

GINYA: Pop, let's pick the grape leaves.

POP: We are landlocked. We have no port.

NON: Vartan, what are you saying?

POP: The conditions, Marie. The conditions!

NON: Yes, dear. It's true. Are you tired?

POP: I am not.

NON: Ok. . . . Go on, Vartan.

POP: Marie, one minute! Just one minute!

NON: Yes, dear. What is it?

POP: Where is my photograph? Have I asked you this, Marie? The photo, with my father. At the church. In the frame. Where is it?

NON: The wire has broken, Vartan, It is being repaired.

POP: Ok! . . . Marie . . .

NON: Yes, dear?

POP: We must make a gift to Ani, when she returns. She should have that photograph. The photo and the book.

NON: All right, Vartan. We'll give them to her.

POP: Make sure.

NON: Yes, dear, of course.

POP: All right.

GINYA: Come on, Pop.

POP: You don't go outside after dark, do you Ginya?

GINYA: No, Pop.

(POP *and* GINYA *exit.* ARMINE *heads for house.*)

JOHN: *Armine! Where are you going?*

ARMINE: Bathroom!

JOHN: Let's go, Raffi!

NON: John, Louise is having heart pains.

JOHN: I know, Marie.

NON: Yavroom *[dearest]*, she's your sister.

JOHN: Don't ask me, Marie.

NON: She wants you to listen to her chest

JOHN: I have listened to her chest, Marie. *Let's go, Armine!*

NON: She's not sleeping well, dear.

JOHN: That's not new, Marie. (ARMINE *enters.*)

ARMINE: Is your sister coming?

NON: She wants him to listen to her chest. (RAFFI *has walked up and joined
them.*)

ARMINE: What do you need, dear?

RAFFI: Nothing.

ARMINE: Ok. We'll go in a minute. Get in the car. (RAFFI *gets in car.* GINYA *enters
with aluminum foiled package.*)

JOHN: Armine!

GINYA: Papa gave me the rest of the baklava.

NON: Where are the grape leaves?

ARMINE: John, please, Louise is having pain.

JOHN: I don't have my stethoscope! Do you think I have my stethoscope?

NON: Armine, never mind, dear. You're right, John. You go. Raffi! (RAFFI *sticks his
head out car window.*)

RAFFI: What?

NON: (*Surprised.*) Ah! You're hiding, Annushig *[sweetie]*! Good-bye, darling!

GINYA: Non, Pop didn't want me to pick the grape leaves.

NON: Ya. Ok.

ARMINE: The sink! Oh, John, the sink!

JOHN: Jesus, Armine, Jesus.

(He storms into the house. ARMINE *and* NON *follow.)*

ARMINE: He never tells me why he's upset.

(Beat. GINYA *and* RAFFI *get out of car.)*

RAFFI: What sink?

GINYA: Who knows. (GINYA *crosses to bush, takes a piece of toilet paper out of her pocket. She tears paper into little pieces, making a little pile.)*

RAFFI: When we get home, I want to show you what I found.

GINYA: Ok.

RAFFI: But don't talk about it, ok?

GINYA: Ok.

RAFFI: Don't tell me things about it. Don't *tell* me things.

GINYA: Ok. Shut-up.

*(NON *enters carrying her light weight porch chair. She sits.)*

NON: What do you study, darling, in your school?

GINYA: The regular stuff.

NON: Anything about the Armenians, darling?

GINYA: Not yet, Non. I'll tell you when.

NON: Ok. That's perfect.

GINYA: Non, Papa didn't let me go through the gate to pick the grape leaves.

NON: Ya.

RAFFI: He thinks you'll get your thumb shot off, right, Non? Like his sister?

GINYA: Was it his sister, Non?

NON: It was his sister. First they shot her hand when she put it on the fence gate. Then they shot her in the back.

RAFFI: Oh.

GINYA: Non, will you move this to the windowsill, if it rains?

NON: Your little pile? Ya.

*(JOHN *bursts out of house.* ARMINE *following.)*

JOHN: I can't fix sinks! Call someone who fixes sinks! Call Ernie Breed! He fixes sinks!

ARMINE: Ma, I'll call Ernie Breed.

JOHN: I can't fix sinks.

LOUISE: *(Offstage.) John! (Aunt* LOUISE *runs on. Her husband,* GARO, *follows. Both in coats.) John! Pleurisy! Irregular pulse, John!*

JOHN: That's not pleurisy, Louise.

LOUISE: I have the symptoms, John.

GARO: *(To* GINYA.) Hello, dear.

GINYA: Hello, Uncle Garo.

JOHN: Pleurisy is an inflammation of the lining of the lung, Louise. You don't have that.

LOUISE: I think I do, John.

JOHN: No, you don't, Louise. Go home.

LOUISE: Just listen to my lungs.

JOHN: You couldn't have run here, Louise, in fifteen minutes. You couldn't have run at all.

LOUISE: I need a shunt.

GARO: She thinks she needs a shunt.

JOHN: She doesn't need a shunt. Her brain is fine. Her heart is fine. Her lungs are fine.

LOUISE: My hands are swelling. My rings are tight.

JOHN: I'm going in the house.

LOUISE: *John! (Exiting.)*

GARO: *(To* ARMINE.) How are you dear?

ARMINE: Busy.

LOUISE: He never listens to my heart.

GARO: *(To* GINYA.) How's my favorite dancing partner?

LOUISE: Garo, don't cha-cha!

GARO: Have you been practicing?

GINYA: Not really.

RAFFI: *Hi!*

LOUISE AND GARO: *Hello, Yavroom! [Darling!]*

GARO: Raffi, come watch. We're going to practice. (GARO *sings cha-cha music.* GARO *and* GINYA *dance.)*

ARMINE: *(To* LOUISE.) Hello, dear.

LOUISE: Where's Ani?

NON: Nebraska. Arrested on the grave site.

ARMINE: The *test* site!

NON: *Test* site! Aman *[an expletive: good gracious].*

LOUISE: I thought she was coming today. Didn't she say she would be here? Didn't she say she would come for Sunday meal?

ARMINE: She was delayed.

LOUISE: Vy Vy Vy. *[My, my, my.]*

RAFFI: Mom, can I leave my coat in the car?

ARMINE: No, no dear. You need it.

LOUISE: Vartan has been waiting for Ani, you know, Armine.

ARMINE: Louise, for Pete's sake, I know, what should I do?

LOUISE: Tell her, there is disappointment! Tell her, Armine!

ARMINE: No no no. . . . (JOHN *yells from house.*)

JOHN: *Where's the annoushabourg? [Pudding?]*

ARMINE: She'll be home soon.

NON: Garo, how are you?

ARMINE: *It's in the fridge,* John!

GARO: Fine, Marie.

JOHN: *I looked in the fridge! Don't tell me the fridge!*

LOUISE: Oh, my heart.

NON: *(To* ARMINE.*)* Maybe it's in the car.

ARMINE: No, Ma. *John! Look on the counter.*

GARO: Hey! Look at that bird!

LOUISE: What bird?

NON: On the *little* counter, Armine.

GARO: It's got a white thing!

LOUISE: Where is it?

ARMINE: *Look on the little counter!*

GARO: What is that?

LOUISE: That bird? *(JOHN enters.)*

JOHN: Pop is dead.

GARO: What?

NON: That's a nap, dear. He's napping.

JOHN: No, Marie. *(Armenian music plays. Lights shift and come up on:)*

SCENE 2

A church. The family sits, in their coats. JOHN *is at the pulpit.*

JOHN: . . . and many of us were baptized by him, married by him, as he stood at this pulpit, in this church.

I think of this and I think of the church he built in one night in Casaria.

The church he built with his father, in one night, from sundown to sunrise, because the Turkish laws forbid the construction of a Christian house of worship.

So, they built through the night: an altar, twelve benches, three and one half walls. Then the sun rose. And they stopped building.

But the people came.

Even through the winters, people came.

And he preached to them.

Remarkable. *(Beat.)*

I have a picture. *(Beat.)*

I'll show you. *(Bows his head.)*

Asht-vatz-hogeen Los Ah Vor reh. *[May God illuminate his soul.]* *(Beat.)*

Ani. *(JOHN steps down.)*

ANI *(Ani goes to the pulpit carrying a piece of paper.)*: My Grandfather.

Papa.

My Papa.

The Minister from Armenia. Told stories.

When I was young enough to sit on my Papa's knee, I would lean my head against his vest, and he would say: "Which, Ani, my Annushig, which story?"

And together, we would choose:

The: Noah's-Ark-Landing-on-Mt.-Ararat-Story,

Or:

The Margaret-Mead-and-her-Armenian-Son-in-Law-Story!

Or:

The Mesrop-the-Great-Who-Invented-the-Armenian-Alphabet-in-400-A.D.-which-I-could-never-figure-out-when-that-was-Story.

Or:

The-Good-Turk-in-Istanbul-Story.

The Good Turk who sat on the porch with his chair and his gun. And when the Turkish soldiers came with their orders to: "Kill All the Armenians!"

The Good Turk said: "These people are my neighbors. I love them."

And the soldiers moved on.

Papa told stories. Papa wrote sermons. Papa wrote letters.

Non told me that during World War Two, Papa wrote to every Armenian soldier. Every one. More than once.

Our Papa.

Who babysat on Sunday evenings and polished the copper bottoms of the pots and pans while we watched the television. And before bed, he would sit with us on the front steps, stirring honey into his coffee, clinking, clinking.

Papa.

The Minister from Armenia.

Our Papa, who wrote fifteen books on Armenian history, on his Armenian typewriter, which I now have in my room.

Papa tried to tell us about the history. The massacres.

But we resisted.

So he waited.

He waited to tell his American grandchildren in American schools, playing on teams in American sports. I knew he was waiting and I didn't want to hear.

My friends didn't know about the Armenians.

Pam Hansen didn't know that my grandfather's family was forced to walk across a desert without food or water, until they dropped dead.

My American friends who became more important to me than school. Or grades.

Or Papa.

And now, again the Armenians are starving.

And no one knows.

I want to go to Armenia.

I have to go.

I want to witness.

For Papa.

I am going to Armenia.

RAFFI: Wow!

LOUISE AND GARO: Shhhhhhhhhh!

JOHN: She can't do that.

ARMINE: John!

NON: Shhhhhhhhh! *(Lights shift. Armenian music, "Yerevan," plays.)*

SCENE 3

NON's *bedroom.*

Music plays throughout.

As "Yerevan" is being played, NON *walks into her "bedroom."*

ANI *picks up her backpack and follows.*

As the song continues, NON *gives* ANI *several items. Each item is given with the intention of preparing* ANI *for her journey.*

First, she gives ANI *a babushka, which she puts on* ANI's *head. Then* NON *gives* ANI *Papa's book.* NON *opens it to the first page. Together, they silently read the inscription. Then* ANI *puts the book in her backpack.*

Then NON *gives* ANI *a beautiful Persian urn.* ANI *carefully puts the urn in her backpack.*

The last thing NON *gives* ANI *is the shawl she is wearing.* ANI *folds it and places it on top of the urn in her backpack.*

Next NON *takes* ANI's *head in her hands, kisses the top of her head, looks at her and then turns away from her.*

ANI *stands a moment in silence.*

Then ANI *exits, carrying her backpack.*

Lights shift. We hear the sound of planes.

SCENE 4

An airport waiting room. Entire family is gathered with exception of NON. *They sit in their coats.* ANI *is wearing her backpack. She has removed her babushka. They are waiting.*

LOUISE: Ani, do you know about your Great Great Uncle Mugerditch?
ANI: Uh-huh.
RAFFI: Great Uncle who?
LOUISE: Mugerditch!
RAFFI: Mugerditch?
LOUISE: Yes! He was knighted by the Sultan in 1790!
RAFFI: What's a Sultan?
LOUISE: A Sultan is a pasha, a monarch.
GARO: A king.
RAFFI: Oh.
LOUISE: Ya. A fat king.
JOHN: They weren't all fat.
LOUISE: Usually, ya, they were all fat.
GINYA: A fat king knighted our Great Great Uncle Muger—who?
LOUISE AND GARO: Mugerditch!
LOUISE: I can tell you this story! Somehow, in his village, your Great Great Uncle
    Mugerditch invented a precious thing! Something he knew the Sultan would
    want for his armies, and perhaps for himself also, this precious thing would be
    desirable!
RAFFI: What was it?
LOUISE: I will tell you. This is the suspense! Sit down.
RAFFI: Ok.
GARO: Go on, dear.
LOUISE: Ya. So, he traveled with a caravan, all the way from his village in the
    mountains to Constantinople. He traveled by horseback, with his precious in-
    vention here, in his breast pocket.
GINYA: What was it?
JOHN: Tell them what it was, Louise.
LOUISE: I'm telling! So. The caravan was attacked! More than once. Their horses
    were stolen! Their goods were stolen!

GARO: Everything was stolen!

LOUISE: Everything was stolen! But your Great Great Uncle Mugerditch was wily! And he arrived safely in Constantinople!

RAFFI: Then what?

GARO: He finds an acquaintance who can introduce him to the Sultan!

GINYA: How did he do that?

LOUISE: Through a friend.

GINYA: A friend of the Sultan's was a friend of an acquaintance that our Great Great Uncle Mugerditch knew?

LOUISE: Yes, he was.

GARO: Distant! A distant friend. You should say, Louise. It was distant. Go on, dear.

JOHN: Go on, Louise!

LOUISE: *I'm going*! So he, your Great Great Uncle Mugerditch, has an audience with the Sultan! And he walks in, wearing his zavalla [*pathetic*] suit. Nothing in his hands. He bows.

GARO: A deep bow.

LOUISE: A deep bow. Then carefully, he removes from his pocket, his precious invention, which had weathered the journey in perfect condition. And with two fingers, he holds it up to the Sultan, so that he could see. What do you think?

GINYA AND RAFFI: What?

LOUISE: Basterma!

GINYA AND RAFFI: What?

LOUISE: Basterma!

JOHN: Beef jerky.

LOUISE: Ya.

GINYA: He was knighted for discovering beef jerky?

LOUISE: Yes, he was!

ARMINE: The plane's so late. My goodness.

RAFFI: What is beef jerky?

LOUISE, JOHN, AND GARO: Dried meat!

RAFFI: Puke.

ANI: I thought he carried it in his cummerbund.

JOHN: That's correct.

LOUISE: It was the breast pocket.

ARMINE: Never mind.

GARO: It was the cummerbund, because it had the taste of sweat.

LOUISE: That doesn't disqualify the breast pocket, Garo. You know that doesn't disqualify the breast pocket!

JOHN: You distort your facts! You consistently distort and misconstrue your facts. You misconstrue! You never listen!

LOUISE: You always say I misconstrue, John! When you took me to the pool and left me there and I almost drowned, you said I misconstrued!

JOHN: I can't fight with you.

GARO: Don't fight with her.

JOHN: No one can fight with her.

GARO: Don't fight.

JOHN: She's blameless. She's without blame!

LOUISE: Why should I be to blame? Never mind! Aman! Your daughter's leaving for Yerevan! Why? No one knows!

JOHN: It was the cummerbund! He carried the basterma in his *maroon* cummerbund! Not in his breast pocket! Nor in his more favored *magenta*-colored cummerbund, because the *magenta* would attract attention from looters! So, the basterma was tucked in the *maroon* cummerbund. And the *magenta*, which he brought in preparation for his audience with the sultan, was carefully folded and carried in his *breast pocket*! That's the story! The basterma was carried in the *cummerbund*!

LOUISE: Never mind.

JOHN: Ani! Why are you going to Yerevan? For Pete's sake! It is blockaded! There is no fuel! You are alone!

ANI: I'm not, Dad. I'm with a group bringing supplies.

JOHN: Where? Where is the group bringing supplies?

ANI: Dad! I meet their plane in Chicago!

ARMINE: We've been through this, John. She meets their plane in Chicago.

JOHN: How many? How many in this group?

ARMINE, ANI, AND GINYA: Twenty-two.

GARO: Twenty-two?

LOUISE: Ya.

JOHN: Why did I agree to this? I forget why I agreed to this.

ARMINE: You agreed.

GINYA: Cher went

GARO: Cher who?

LOUISE: Cher Cher!

GARO: Cher Cher?

JOHN: Cher no last name Cher!

ARMINE: It was Sarkisian, dear.

JOHN: *Ok! Cher! Cher Sarkisian! Cher Sarkisian went to Armenia! It's pathetic!*

ANI: *Dad*.

JOHN: Witness! Witness, you said! I want to witness for Papa! This witness notion! Kar khan eh geen! *[Turkish swear word.]* Cher wants to witness! Her publicist wants Cher to witness!

ANI: *Dad!*

JOHN: Our parents escaped! And you want to witness! *Es shag! [Turkish swear word.]*

ARMINE: John!

JOHN: My Father! *My Father, the only doctor of his village . . .*

ARMINE: *John!*

JOHN: *Was forced to serve in the Turkish army . . .*

JOHN AND ANI: *With no shoes!!!*

JOHN: *That's right!*

ANI: I know!

RAFFI: Why didn't he wear shoes?

JOHN: *He was forced, every day . . . every day, he was forced to administer care to the Turkish soldiers, who would return to camp, after a day . . .*

ARMINE: *John!!!*

JOHN: *Of killing Armenians!* (To RAFFI.) So he couldn't run away.

RAFFI: Oh.

GINYA: Oh.

RAFFI: Did he have a horse?

JOHN: Armenia is dangerous, Ani. It's uncomfortable.

GARO: (To RAFFI.) He didn't have a horse.

ARMINE: She's used to that, John. She's been to jail, John.

JOHN: *Jail! Aman! For what? Three days? She sang songs with nuns! She slept in a heated room! She ate cooked food! Armenia is cold! The people there want to come here!*

ARMINE: Shut-up, dear.

LOUISE: Good for you, Armine!

GARO: Shut-up, dear.

JOHN: *Bravo, Garo! Does she do it? When you ask her to shut-up, Garo? Does she?*

GARO: Never mind.

LOUISE: Aman.

RAFFI: I liked your story, Aunt Louise.

LOUISE: Thank you, Annushig! *[dear]*

ANI: You agreed, Dad. You can change your mind and take back the money that I am borrowing, if you want. But I'll go eventually, Dad.

JOHN: Ani, you don't even speak Armenian! You think you understand it, Ani, but you don't. You think you speak Armenian, Ani, but you don't. You don't speak Armenian! You don't understand Armenian!

ANI: I know I don't! I know I don't know how to speak Armenian! How was I supposed to learn it? I could never hear it! The only time you spoke Armenian in the house was when you and Mom told secrets. *You whisper in Armenian! You yell in English! And you curse in Turkish!*

ARMINE: You're yelling in the airport, dear.

ANI: *Yes, Mom, I'm yelling in the airport! We're all yelling in the airport! We all yell everywhere! We are yellers! We yell! And what are we yelling about? Cummerbunds and basterma!!*

ARMINE: Sit down, dear.

ANI: *(Sits down, then stands up.)* Dad!

JOHN: *We don't all yell!* Your Mother doesn't yell.

ARMINE: Sometimes I do, John.

JOHN: When, Armine?

ARMINE: In the evening, John.

JOHN: No dear. You don't yell, dear. In fact, you get quieter.

GINYA: There's no room for her to yell.

JOHN: What?

ARMINE: Never mind! Aman.

LOUISE: Ginya's right!

ARMINE: Shhhhhh, Louise!

JOHN: What were we talking about?

ANI: *Me!* We were talking about *me!*

ARMINE: Yes, we were. You speak, Ani.

ANI: Dad! My friends, Dad, my friends don't even know where Armenia is. They think . . .

JOHN: Ani . . .

ARMINE: Please let her speak, John.

ANI: You have taught me, Dad. Papa taught me. 1915!

JOHN: Yes.

ANI: Over one million Armenians were killed.

JOHN: That's right.

ANI: And to this day, the history books make no mention—not one word of the genocide!

JOHN: And to this day, Ani, Armenia has no allies! It is unprotected.

ANI: Because no one has witnessed!

JOHN: Aman.

ANI: I have to go to Armenia, Dad. I have to go so I can see things and write things. And then send the things I write to newspapers. I want to yell things in newspapers! I want to yell things in newspapers!

LOUISE: What is she saying, Garo?

GARO: She wants to yell things, dear.

GINYA: She did it in Nevada!

JOHN: What?

ARMINE: Yes, John!

GINYA: Remember? Remember that story?

ARMINE: In the newspaper!

GINYA: *Yea!*

ARMINE: They got attention! In Nevada!

RAFFI: *Yea!*

ARMINE: It was important, John.

RAFFI AND GINYA: *Yea!*

JOHN: Aman.

GARO: *Bravo, Ani!*

LOUISE: What, Garo?

GARO: I am moved.

JOHN: Garo! You are moved! I am worried!

GARO: I understand, of course.

JOHN: For Pete's sake!

GARO: Of course. Of course

ANI: Dad . . . Please.

JOHN: Ani. Do you understand . . . we . . . I . . . am frightened.

GARO: Now, it's said.

ANI: I know, Dad. Your family escaped. And you'll never go back. But I can go, Dad. I am ready! . . . Mom? . . . Mom?

ARMINE: She can go, dear. We cannot. But she . . . believes she can.

ANI: I know I can! Look at me!

JOHN: What will you do there?

ARMINE: She will help.

JOHN: How, Armine?

ARMINE: In her way, John.

JOHN: Aman . . .

ANI: Dad.

JOHN: *(Takes candles from his coat pocket.)* You'll need candles, Ani. You must take some candles. Here.

ANI: Thank you.

JOHN: Keep them for yourself.

LOUISE: Armine, did you give her food to eat on the plane?

ARMINE: Of course.

GINYA: Basterma?

ARMINE: No, no. Too much garlic.

GARO: *(Handing* ANI *a small box.)* Here, Ani. I made this. A gift. It's nothing. A small thing. *(She opens box, it's a ring. She puts it on.)*

ANI: Thank you, Uncle Garo.

GARO: Good-bye, dear.

LOUISE: I brought you some cheese boeregg [*turnovers*], darling.

RAFFI: I got you some Blow Pops, Ani.

GARO: When you come back, Ani, we'll *yell* our heads off! *(He starts to dance.)* Bravo! Bravo! Louise. Caro! Aman! *(Flight announcement.)*

GINYA: It's time to go, Ani. Here, I bought you a pen.

ANI: It's pretty. Thanks, Gin.

GINYA: Bye, Ani. Bye, bye.

ARMINE: Kehzee guh serum, Ani . . . [*I love you.*]

ANI: Mom . . .

ARMINE: I know, darling.

LOUISE: Bachigs, Yavroom. *[Kisses, dear.]* (LOUISE *crosses to* ANI *and* ARMINE. *Hugs. Then* GARO, RAFFI *and* GINYA *join hug.)*

GARO: Good-bye, Ani. *(Hug breaks up.* ANI *looks at her father. She goes to him. They hug. Then* ANI *begins to leave.)*

LOUISE: *Take the boeregg!* (ANI *stops. Louise hands her the little shopping bag containing boeregg.)*

ANI: Raffi!

RAFFI: Yea?

ANI: Thanks! *(Holds up the blow pops.)*

RAFFI: Cool.

ANI: Bye bye. *(They all raise their hands to wave a still wave. Lights shift.)*

SCENE 5

The cemetery. NON, GINYA, *and* RAFFI. RAFFI *is poking the dirt with a stick. He has his coat tied around his waist.*

RAFFI: What do they do when they've run out of room?

NON: For what, dear?

RAFFI: To bury people.

NON: Oh. Well . . . let's see . . .

GINYA: Don't ask questions like that.

RAFFI: Why not?

NON: It's all right, dear. Raffi, I'll think about your question.

RAFFI: It's Ok, Non.

GINYA: Do you have another stick?

RAFFI: Yup. *(Tosses her one.)* Don't forget to give it back.

GINYA: Ok. Thanks. Put your coat on.

RAFFI: No. Why?

NON: It's better.

RAFFI: It is?

NON: Ya. *(Puts his coat on.)*

RAFFI: Non, did you tell Papa, Ani's in Yerevan?

NON: Not yet.

RAFFI: Oh! *(Covers his mouth.)* Sorry.

NON: It's all right, dear. He knows.

GINYA: Duh.

NON: Shh shh.

RAFFI: Yea, Ginya, be quiet!

NON: You know what?

GINYA AND RAFFI: What?

NON: I think soon there will be babies in the nest in our tree!

GINYA: The all white nest?

NON: Ya.

RAFFI: Awesome!

NON: It's browner now. Beege.

RAFFI: What?

NON: Beege.

GINYA: Beige, Non. It's beige.

NON: What is, dear?

GINYA: The nest.

NON: Ya. Ok.

RAFFI: Oh, brother.

GINYA: Raffi!!

NON: Shhhhhh.

GINYA: Do you talk to Papa, Non?

NON: Yes, but not out loud.

RAFFI: In what language?

NON: Armenian. Some Turkish.

GINYA: I don't like to think about Papa here, Non. I mean, here. *(Points to grave.)*

NON: Our Papa, darling, what shall I say . . . his spirit is everywhere.

GINYA: Yea. But his body is in the ground. (RAFFI *stops poking the dirt.*)

RAFFI: Can we go now, Non?

NON: Soon, Raffi. Do you want some pistachios?

RAFFI: No, thanks. Isn't it time to go?

NON: In a minute. I think first, I must tell you my secret.

GINYA: A secret?

RAFFI: In English?

NON: Of course!

GINYA: Wow!

NON: Wow, ya! Your first big secret! An event!

RAFFI AND GINYA: Yea.

NON: Are you ready?

RAFFI AND GINYA: Yea.

NON: Do you want some figs?

RAFFI AND GINYA: No thanks.

NON: Ok. My darlings . . . I had Papa put in ashes.

GINYA: *Cremated?*

RAFFI: *What? What is it?*

NON: Cremated! Ya. He is not in this grave. His body is ashes.

RAFFI: Ashes?

NON: Ya. And the ashes are with Ani.

GINYA: With Ani?

NON: In her packback!

GINYA: *Back*pack!

NON: Ya.

RAFFI: *Awesome!*

GINYA: Why?

NON: She is taking them back to his church in Casaria, to be buried with his father.

RAFFI: And his mother.

GINYA: No, his mother was lost, right, Non?

NON: Ya. She was lost. His father built, with Papa he built, the three walled church in Casaria. So, Papa, I think, by now, he is there.

GINYA: Is the coffin in the ground here empty?

NON: No, no.

RAFFI: What's in it?

NON: Birch logs.

RAFFI: Birch logs?

NON: Ya. To make it heavy.

RAFFI: From birch trees?

NON: Ya. Papa liked birch trees.

GINYA: So, there are logs in the coffin, and Papa's in Armenia?

RAFFI: Yea. But he's dead.

NON: Ya. Too bad.

RAFFI AND GINYA: Ya.

NON: Better dead than never! Right? Is that it?

GINYA: Not really.

NON: Never mind.

GINYA: You did all this, Non?

NON: Ya.

RAFFI: *Wow!*

NON: I deserve Ph.D.! It was difficult! Until a miracle! What do you think? The father-in-law of the funeral director. He was Armenian! *Dichran Papazian!* Aman! They call him Digger!

GINYA: Digger?

RAFFI: Gross.

NON: Digger, darling! He helped me!

RAFFI: I'm hungry. Can I have some kata? *[Rolls]*

NON: Of course, Annushig, it is for you! Here, darling. And for the birds, I brought baklava.

GINYA: Baklava? (*She takes out aluminum foil package and sprinkles pieces of baklava on the grave.*)

NON: Ya. I think Papa's grave is a good place for the birds to have a party! Here, now they can live, how you say, high hog?

GINYA: Ya. High hog.

RAFFI: This is our secret, Non?

NON: Papa? Ya!

GINYA: No one knows?

RAFFI: Digger knows.

NON: Just a little. Mostly, you, you, me. And Ani.

GINYA: Cool.

NON: Auksome.

RAFFI: Yea! (ARMINE *enters.*)

ARMINE: Come on. Let's go. It's time to go. *(To Papa's grave.)* I love you, my Father. Kehzee guh serrem. *[I love you.] (To them.)* Come on. Louise is in the hospital having tests. Dad's coming home early. Garo is missing. And we got a letter from Ani. Let's go. Say good-bye to Papa. (ARMINE *exits.* NON, GINYA, AND RAFFI *face out and yell:)*

NON, GINYA, AND RAFFI: Good-bye Papa! *(Lights dim.)*

SCENE 6

We hear the distant sound of thunder. A storm. NON *sits at a table in her kitchen. She wears a shawl.* ARMINE *enters carrying candles. The lights in the room flicker and go out.*

NON: Vy Vy Vy. *[My, my, my.]*

(They light more candles.)

(ARMINE takes a letter from her pocket.)

ARMINE: From Ani.

NON: I.O. *[Yes.]*

ANI: *(Enters on opposite side of stage. She is wearing a babushka and shawl, carrying a candle. During this scene,* ANI *is recalling the letter. She is in her hotel room. She has her journal, a pen, a hand mirror, and* NON's *shawl. Through the course of the scene, she walks around the small room, she looks out the window. She tries to dance. She remembers the song and sings.)* Ok.

ARMINE AND ANI: Parev. *[Hello.]*

ARMINE: *(Reading.)* I'm here!

ANI: I'm fine.

ARMINE: Don't worry! I hope this letter makes its way to you.

ANI: There's so much to say.

ARMINE: Everyone here sounds like you, Nonnie. And the whole city smells like your house! I have seen Mt. Ararat!

ANI *(Looking out window.)*: Mt. Ararat is beautiful. It's so easy to imagine the Ark on top! Also, from my window in the hotel, I can see the fountain in Central Square. It is enormous. But it has no water!

ARMINE: It has no water. There is no water, Mom.

NON: Go on, dear.

ARMINE: *(Continuing.)* There is so little fuel.

ANI: We only have three hours of power a day.

ARMINE: Sometimes, at two o'clock in the morning, all the lights will go on and everyone will get up and cook, bathe, clean, and read, until the system is exhausted. And then everyone goes back to bed.

ANI: There is so little fuel. All the trees have been cut down and burned for firewood. The ancient poplars that lined the roads are gone.

NON: Aman.

ARMINE: There are no trees, and no tree stumps.

ANI: There are no wooden doors or window sills left in the city

ARMINE: And no wooden desks in the schools. But the children continue to attend school. They go for half the day, for half the year. When it's not too cold. . . . Tune garta asee, Myrig. *[You read this, Mother.]*

NON: I.O., *[Yes]* of course. *(Reads.)* I must tell you what happened to us! Guess what! The owner of this hotel is the mayor of a small village in the mountains.

ANI: He's been very kind to me.

ARMINE: Who is he?

NON: Don't worry. *(Continues reading.)* He invited me and all the members of our group to visit his village. So we traveled in a rusty van, three hours up the mountain roads, to his little town.

ANI: The first thing he showed us was the village farm.

NON AND ANI: Sandy little rows of eggplants and onions, tomatoes and okra.

NON: The Mayor (his name is Zaven) was so proud! He told us: "We made everything here! The hinges. The faucets. Even the peeps!"

ANI: He meant pipes!

NON: Peeps! Aman.

ARMINE: Go on, Mother.

NON: As we toured the farm, it became obvious to all of us that we hadn't seen a single other person. The town was empty. But we didn't ask and the Mayor made no mention.

ARMINE: Read faster, Myrig.

ANI: Then we all went to the village church.

NON: The ancient village church. As soon as we arrived, the church doors burst open and the entire town came out, dancing, singing, and playing tambourines! *(Armenian music plays. ANI begins to dance as though she is learning. She continues to dance through the following section.)* The last to come was a Priest, dressed entirely in white robes. His hands were crossed in front of his chest and in each hand he was holding a white dove. He walked directly to me, bowed in greeting and then released the doves to the sky. They flew together like synchronized swimmers and perched on the church steeple. Then again, the tambourines played, the women danced and they led us into the church. (ANI's *hands move like the flight of birds.* NON *raises her arm, still seat-ed, she dances.*)

ARMINE: Mother. Continue.

NON: Ah. (ANI *and* NON *lower their arms at the same time.*) Once we were inside the church, we sat on the stone floors and were served a feast of the tiniest por-tions. All vegetables from the sandy, little garden. Then the children, two small children, stood in costume, and sang to us. As they sang, another child translated from the Armenian to English. (ANI *begins to sing the first verse of* "Yerevan." *She sings as* NON *reads the translation.*)

Yerevan.

The great dream of our little land.

Cherished for centuries.

Centuries old

But youthful still.

The Beauty of Stone.

(NON *hums the last few lines; or sings the second section of song. In either case,* NON *sings the last word* "Yerevan.")

ARMINE: Mother, please.

NON: As we drove home, winding down the mountain roads, it grew dark and we were silent. They knew Papa.

ANI: They knew Papa.

NON AND ANI: So they did this for me.

NON: Aman.

ANI: So often, I think I see Papa's face. I hear his voice.

ARMINE: Mother.

NON: Most of the group is leaving tomorrow.

ANI: I've decided to stay.

NON: I'm going to stay.

ARMINE: What?

NON: I want to write something.

ANI: I want to go to people's homes.

NON: And to the libraries, the churches, the orphanages and record the conditions. The conditions.

ANI: Don't worry.

NON: Don't worry. I have my candles, my Blow Pops, and my pen!

ANI: Love you.

NON: Love you. Bachigs, Ani. (ANI *begins to untie her babushka.*) P.S.

NON AND ANI: I found a thin pair of scissors in my room. (ANI *picks up a hand mir-ror.* ARMINE *takes letter from* NON.

ARMINE: Ancient sewing scissors. (ANI *looks at herself in mirror, she removes her babushka, her hair is gone.*) I'm thinking of cutting my hair. . . . Good night.

ANI: Good night. (*Sound of thunder.* LOUISE *enters wearing a raincoat, carrying a pan of food.*)

LOUISE: Oh my God, this storm! The bazaar was canceled! The church basement looked wonderful before the lights went out! All that food, sitting on tables, in absolute darkness! I brought you some sarma [*stuffed grape leaves*]. It needs lemon. VaVa is thinner, Sarkis is fatter, they send love. Rosine has a boyfriend!

NON: Armenian?

LOUISE: No. Odar! [*A non-Armenian!*]

NON: Aman. (*Sound of thunder.*)

LOUISE: Ah! This storm! It gives me palpitations.

NON: You want some coffee?

LOUISE: Garo is lost again.

ARMINE: My daughter . . . My daughter cut off all her hair.

LOUISE: Ah!

NON: Perhaps!

ARMINE: I know it. (*Music. Lights shift.*)

SCENE 7

Lights come up to reveal GARO *sitting on the curb in his coat. We hear* LOUISE *call: "Garo!" Then* LOUISE *crosses out of kitchen, wearing a coat. She is carrying kata [a roll], wrapped in a napkin.*

LOUISE: Garo! (*She walks to him.*) Do you want some kata?

GARO: I.O. [*Yes.*] (*He takes the kata and eats. She stands behind him.*)

LOUISE: What are you looking at?

GARO: Nothing.

LOUISE: How are you?

GARO: Fine.

LOUISE: Shall we go inside?

GARO: I.O. [*Yes.*] (*He stays.*)

LOUISE: Garo?

GARO: I'll stay here.

LOUISE: No, dear.

GARO: This is pleasant.

LOUISE: This is the curb, dear. Are you a dog? Garo, are you a dog?

GARO: I am not.

LOUISE: That's correct. Come inside.

GARO: Do you know the gift I gave to Ani. Louise, do you know?

LOUISE: For good luck.

GARO: Ya. Good luck. For safe journey.

LOUISE: It was very good.

GARO: It was a small thing. Nothing.

LOUISE: She will be all right, Garo. She is wily.

GARO: Wily. Your Uncle . . .

LOUISE: . . . was wily. Ya.

GARO: I am not.

LOUISE: You are Garo. Garo on the curb.

GARO: That is me.

LOUISE: Are you all right? Are you cold?

GARO: I'm all right.

LOUISE: All right. Come inside.

GARO: All right. *(She starts to exit.)*

LOUISE: Garo, we will listen to the music. Come inside!

GARO: Ok.

(She exits. He stays. She turns up the music. Cha-cha music. GARO stands. He considers the house. Then he chooses to go for a walk. RAFFI enters on Rollerblades. They acknowledge each other. GARO exits.)

SCENE 8

RAFFI on Rollerblades is listening to a Walkman. We hear contemporary music. He is Rollerblade dancing. He's a pro.

GINYA enters. Also on Rollerblades. It's her first day. She stumble-skates across the stage to Raffi and plows into him.

GINYA: *Raffi!*

RAFFI: Hey! (GINYA *holds onto* RAFFI *and skates around behind him. They skate, then* RAFFI *turns off his Walkman and the music stops.)*

GINYA: Sorry. I'm sorry.

RAFFI: What are you doing?

GINYA: Raffi, come on. Just show me how to stop.

RAFFI: Use the brake!

GINYA: *What brake?*

RAFFI: Let go of me and I'll show you the brake!

GINYA: Promise?

RAFFI: Yea!

GINYA: Ok. *(She lets go. She keeps skating. She can't stop.)*

RAFFI: Hey! Those are Ani's skates, Ginya.

GINYA: She said I could use them.

RAFFI: She did not.

GINYA: Just show me where the brake is.

RAFFI: Duh.

GINYA: *Raffi!*

RAFFI: *This is the brake!*

GINYA: *What do you do with it?*

RAFFI: You have to drag it. It slows you down.

GINYA: How do you *stop?*

RAFFI: You jump up and pivot turn! *(He does it.)*

GINYA: That was good!

RAFFI: *(Lets go.)* All right, See ya. *(He skates away.)*

GINYA: *Wait, Raffi, wait!*

RAFFI: *What do you want, my whole life?*

GINYA: I want you to teach me to stop. *(He takes her hands and guides her.)*

RAFFI: Press down on the right foot. The *right* foot. Slide it. *(She slides it.)* That's good. Ok! *(RAFFI turns GINYA around and pushes her Down. On push.)* You're outta here!

GINYA: *Ahhhhhhhhhhhh!*

RAFFI: *Brake! Brake! (She brakes.) Ok!*

GINYA: Was that good?

RAFFI: Well . . . You stopped.

GINYA: Yea. Thanks.

RAFFI: Sure. *(They practice.)*

GINYA: Did you pick something to send to Ani?

RAFFI: No, and don't tell me anything.

GINYA: I bought her a new journal. You can send it.

RAFFI: Ginya, when's Ani coming home?

GINYA: Who knows.

RAFFI: Does Dad know?

GINYA: I don't know if he knows. Nobody speaks in English anymore.

RAFFI: I'll say. We live on *Planet Armenia!*

GINYA: Don't yell! *(RAFFI skates in a circle and yells:)*

RAFFI: *Planet Armenia!! (Beat.)*

GINYA: *Planet Armenia!!! (Beat. They both chuckle.)* Ok, I'm gonna go home. I'm going home.

RAFFI: See ya. *(Raffi skate dances again.)*

GINYA: *(Skates and brakes.)* You coming?

RAFFI: Nope.

GINYA: *(Skating off.) Raffi, come home before dark!*

(RAFFI turns on Walkman and skate dances. Beat. He skates off in GINYA's direction. Lights shift.)

SCENE 9

Evening. A hospital room. GARO *is in the bed.* LOUISE — *in her coat — and* JOHN — *in lab coat — are on either side of* GARO.

LOUISE: Do you think it's the diet? Too much fat?

JOHN: No.

LOUISE: He eats so much fat, John. And he stopped moving. Except for those walks to Pal Park. Oh my God, those walks! His knees were swollen. John, his knees were swollen.

JOHN: It's his circulation, Louise.

LOUISE: His circulation and his nutrition, John.

JOHN: Louise, I'm not his doctor. This isn't my ward. I'm due at a conference. I stopped in to say hello. I didn't know you were here.

LOUISE: Where else would I be?

JOHN: I thought you'd left.

LOUISE: No. I'm here. Stop hating me.

JOHN: Garo, can you hear me? Squeeze my hand.

LOUISE: He can't hear you.

JOHN: Louise, please, I'm speaking to Garo.

LOUISE: He can't hear you, John. Why don't you speak to me?

JOHN: Garo, I've spoken to your doctors.

LOUISE: John! Me! Here I am! Talk to me!

JOHN: *(To* LOUISE.*)* They're going to run some tests. Non-invasive. He'll be comfortable. Don't worry.

LOUISE: Thank you.

JOHN: You're welcome. I'll stop in tomorrow, Garo.

LOUISE: John, listen to me.

JOHN: I have to go, Louise.

LOUISE: I need you to listen to my heart.

JOHN: Louise, if you're having pain, go see a doctor.

LOUISE: I'm seeing a doctor! I'm seeing a doctor right in front of me, with his stethoscope in his pocket, John! I'm seeing a doctor who is my brother, standing right in front of me.

JOHN: I'm not your doctor, Louise.

LOUISE: Just sixty seconds, John.

JOHN: I'm late for the conference.

LOUISE: Half a minute!

JOHN: You're in a hospital, Louise! Ask a nurse!

LOUISE: *John!*

JOHN: Ask some unsuspecting nurse, Louise. Ask a nurse!

LOUISE: John, you never listen to my heart.

JOHN: That's not so, Louise. I have listened to your heart. I have listened to your lungs. I have read your X rays. You are fine! You're a horse, Louise. A horse!

LOUISE: I'm not a horse, John.

JOHN: I'm sorry, Louise. I'm late.

LOUISE: You're miserable, John. You're miserable. You're a miserable man.

JOHN: That's true, Louise. (JOHN *exits.*)

(*Beat.* LOUISE *takes* GARO's *hand. She starts to sing cha-cha. She makes his hand dance a cha-cha. Then she takes his arm and dances the cha-cha. She stops. She feels the weight of his slack arm. She puts his hand on her cheek.*)

LOUISE: Garo. Let's go home, darling. (*She sits on the bed, facing him, wraps his arm around her, as she puts her head on his chest. She holds his arm around her.*) Let's go home. (*Lights shift.*)

SCENE 10

The cemetery. Garo's grave is next to Papa's.

LOUISE: Who would have thought?

ARMINE: I know.

LOUISE: Do you think I killed him?

ARMINE: *Shhhhhhhhhh*, Louise, ridiculous, don't say that.

LOUISE: With my craziness? With my craziness, did I kill him? Did he hate me?

ARMINE: Louise, Garo loved you. He showed you he loved you. Look at your hands! Look at all those rings on your hands. Think of all those anniversary presents! His pride and joy! You were his pride and joy! (LOUISE *looks at her hands.*)

LOUISE: He was a jeweler!

ARMINE: And he made all those rings just for you! They are unique.

LOUISE: Armine! Tell me the truth! Did I ignore him? Was I a terrible companion? What was it? What happened?

ARMINE: Shhhhhhhhhhhhhhhhhhhhhhh.

LOUISE: My heart. My heart is breaking.

ARMINE: He needed you.

LOUISE: No.

ARMINE: You know what, Louise, he had fun with you.

LOUISE: Fun?

ARMINE: Ya.

LOUISE: Huh. Garo. Was he fun?

ARMINE: He was a good dancer.

LOUISE: Ya.

ARMINE: And a good listener.

LOUISE: Ya. Why is there so much bird shit on Papa's grave?

ARMINE: Mother feeds the birds.

LOUISE: Oh. That's nice. I think he was running away. I think he died running away. What do you think, tell me.

ARMINE: I think he was going for a walk. He liked the blue sky.

LOUISE: Armine, Aman. Don't say that!

ARMINE: I'm sorry.

LOUISE: The sky? The sky? For Pete's sake! Through the windows, Armine, he can see the sky! He doesn't have to walk to another town!

ARMINE: Perhaps he was . . . I don't know.

LOUISE: Tentative. Did you feel he was tentative?

ARMINE: Ya.

LOUISE: When we married, I thought, no matter, I'll back him up.

ARMINE: And you did.

LOUISE: I never did! I kept him tentative, Armine. I kept him that way, I'm sure of it.

ARMINE: Why do you say that?

LOUISE: I know it.

ARMINE: Do you want to say you're sorry?

LOUISE: We find ways, Armine, at all costs, we find ways to . . . what is the word. . . . Like a pet! . . . What is it? . . . *House-broken*! . . . That's it! . . . We find ways to housebreak our husbands, Armine!

ARMINE: Why?

LOUISE: *Why?* . . . So that . . . *Why?* . . . So that. . . . They will keep their eye on us!

ARMINE: Vy Vy Vy. *[My, My, My.]*

LOUISE: They will watch! They will stay! They will stand guard, Armine!

ARMINE: I.O. *[Yes.]* We have our reasons.

LOUISE: Oh, God . . . What do you say, Armine? What do you have to say, Armine?

ARMINE: About you?

LOUISE: Ya.

ARMINE: You'll be all right, dear. (ARMINE *puts her arm around* LOUISE *and rocks her. She rocks her more aggressively as the scene goes on.*)

LOUISE: What else?

ARMINE: That's all.

LOUISE: And Ani? How is she?

ARMINE: She's there.

LOUISE: I know she's there! Why do you say that? It's so upsetting!

ARMINE: *Shhhhhh, Louise, shhhhhhhhhhh.*

LOUISE: And my brother? How is my brother?

ARMINE: The same.

LOUISE: The same! The same! He's going to have a *heart attack!*

ARMINE: *Shhhhh, Louise, shhhhh.* Be quiet!

LOUISE: What?

ARMINE: Don't talk.

LOUISE: Oh, my heart!

ARMINE: Ya, ya . . .

LOUISE: Who would have thought, Armine. Tell me! Who would have thought?

ARMINE: No one. Don't think. *Shhhhhhhhhhhhh . . .*

LOUISE: *Stop it, Armine! Stop it!* (LOUISE *punches* ARMINE *in the arm.* ARMINE *punches* LOUISE *back. Then* ARMINE *stands up, they look at each other. Then* ARMINE *gently pats the spot where she hit* LOUISE *and exits.* LOUISE *sits alone. Cries. Then* JOHN *enters.*)

JOHN: It's time. Come on. Let's go. It's time.

LOUISE: John . . .

JOHN: Ya. Come. Shhhhhh. (JOHN *helps* LOUISE *up. They exit with his arm around her, her head on his shoulder. Lights shift.*)

SCENE 11

ANI *is in her hotel room in Armenia. She is wearing her babuska. The other half of the stage is Non's front lawn. Ani is holding the book from Non. She opens it and reads:*

ANI: "To my granddaughter, Ani, our sweet, Crusader:
    Whenever you open this book, my dear, take a moment to read or pray. Think of those of us who love you and take heart. . . . Your devoted, Papa."

(ANI *puts down book and picks up letter. Lights up on other half of stage.* RAFFI *skates on. He practices backward circles.* ARMINE *is planting pachysandra. She wears a little cap.* ANI *is reading letter.*)

    Ani. Ani . . .

(RAFFI *stops skating.*)

ARMINE: Ani.
    I have realized.

(RAFFI *skates again.*)

ANI: I can no longer . . .

ARMINE: I can no longer imagine you there.

RAFFI: Do you still have candles?

ANI: Do you have food?

ARMINE: Are you warm enough?

ANI: Do you write?

RAFFI: What do you do there?

ARMINE AND ANI: Life here is the same.

RAFFI: Ginya is wearing your skates.

ARMINE: Raffi—he is fine—

ANI: Always with his secrets.

ARMINE: Dad and I are planting pachysandra. Spring is coming.

ANI: It is warm.

ARMINE: We miss you.

ANI: Love, Mom.

ARMINE: Love.

ANI: Mom.

RAFFI: Mom?

ARMINE: What?

RAFFI: Nothing. (RAFFI *skates off.*)

ANI: P.S. Write to us, Ani. Write. (JOHN *enters.*)

JOHN: Do you have Ani's postcard?

ARMINE: Next year, John, I'd like to plant more grass on Mom's lawn.

JOHN: She likes pachysandra. Do you have Ani's postcard?

ARMINE: It's in my pocket. Grass is nice, John.

JOHN: You don't have to mow pachysandra. Can we read it now, Armine?

ARMINE: I don't mind mowing, John.

JOHN: Armine . . .

ARMINE: I mowed the lawn of the postman's house that summer in Hudson, New York. Remember that house we rented, John? When I was pregnant with Ani? Remember?

JOHN: Ya.

ARMINE: I mowed.

JOHN: I remember the backyard of the postman's house.

ARMINE: Ya.

JOHN: The postman!

ARMINE: Ya.

JOHN: Who was insane. Buried everyone's mail in his backyard.

ARMINE: Not everyone's mail, John.

JOHN: *Most* of the mail.

ARMINE: The junk. The junk mail!

JOHN: *No mail should be in a backyard!*

ARMINE: Never mind.

JOHN: Let me read Ani's postcard, Armine.

ARMINE: In all this time, John, one letter. Two cards.

JOHN: Yes, dear.

ARMINE: This postcard, John, is very short. Not many words.

JOHN: Let me read it, Armine. Then you can put it back in your pocket.

ARMINE: John. Remember the bird in the chimney?

JOHN: Aman!

ARMINE: When I was pregnant with Ani. The bird. The thunderstorm. Remember, John? It escaped. John?

JOHN: Yes. The bird in the chimney. The bat in the bedroom!

ARMINE: The bat! You shooed the bat!

JOHN: I shooed the bat with your tambourine!

ARMINE: Ya. My tambourine. *(She waves her hand like a tambourine.)* John!

JOHN: Armine. *(He extends his hand for postcard.* NON *yells from house.)*

NON: *Armine! Did you get the sponges?*

ARMINE: *Under the sink, Ma!*

NON: *Under the sink?*

ARMINE: *It's easier than in the cupboard. (Beat.)*

NON: Ok. (ARMINE *takes out comb. She combs the top of her head.)*

JOHN: She'll put them back in the cupboard.

ARMINE: I know.

JOHN: And continue to stand on the stool to get them.

ARMINE: Ya.

JOHN: Armine, my dear . . .

ARMINE: Ya.

JOHN: You are combing your hat.

ARMINE: Aman, John, inch khentz pannay. *[How silly.]*

JOHN: It's all right. If you give me the postcard, I will look. I will give it back.

ARMINE: No.

NON: *(Offstage.) Time for lunch!*

ARMINE: Ah! Lunch time!

JOHN: Yes, I heard. (NON *enters carrying a plate of sandwiches.)*

NON: Here. Time to eat! I made my specialty.

JOHN: *(Taking one.)* Thank you, Marie.

ARMINE: What is this, Ma?

NON: *(Returning to house.) Tuna!* (NON *exits.* ARMINE *holds her sandwich.)*

JOHN: Boh! *(Laughs.)*

ARMINE: Don't laugh, John.

JOHN: Aman. *(He eats.)*

ARMINE: John, your chewing.

JOHN: What?

ARMINE: It is very loud.

JOHN: It is how I chew.

ARMINE: No. You can chew more softly, John. Chew more softly.

JOHN: Armine, this is not your concern. My chewing is not your concern.

ARMINE: I think it is John.

JOHN: Eat! You. Eat! Armine. That is the concern of the moment.

ARMINE: Ya. I am happy to eat. *(She doesn't eat.)*

(NON enters with her porch chair. She sits behind ARMINE.)

NON: I made placemats. Do we know anyone who needs a present?

ARMINE: Lucy and Hagop.

NON: What is it?

ARMINE: Anniversary.

NON: Ok . . . Any babies?

ARMINE: What?

NON: Do you have friends, Armine, with any babies?

ARMINE: No, Ma.

NON: Too bad. I made some mittens.

ARMINE: What color?

NON: Green.

ARMINE: Green?

NON: Ya.

ARMINE: Dark green?

NON: No, no.

ARMINE: Spring green?

NON: No.

ARMINE: What then?

NON: Like leaves, Armine.

ARMINE: Like that leaf there, that green?

NON: Which?

ARMINE: There?

NON: No.

ARMINE: There?

NON: No.

ARMINE: There? There?

NON: Where?

ARMINE: There.

NON: There? *(ARMINE looks at NON. NON looks at ARMINE. They end up staring in each other's faces.)* I don't see it.

ARMINE: Ah.

JOHN: Aman.

NON: Have you read Ani's postcard? Have you read Ani's postcard?

ARMINE: In a minute! Let me eat, Ma, for Pete's sake. Just wait!

NON: Of course. We will wait, Armine. We will all wait *(All three eat. ARMINE takes one bite.)*

ARMINE: All right. *(She takes postcard out of her pocket.)* John. *(JOHN takes postcard.)*

JOHN AND ANI: *(Together)* Parev!

JOHN: It is unbearably cold.

ANI: There is no fuel.

JOHN: Some families are living in cargo containers. Metal boxes. No windows. No air. So hot in summer.

ANI: So cold now.

JOHN: Those who can, are leaving. So many Armenians are leaving!

ANI: What will happen?

JOHN: What will happen? Love, Ani. *(Beat.)*

ARMINE: Ma. (ARMINE *puts her head in* NON's *lap. She cries.*)

NON: John, it's time. It's time now.

JOHN: I know, Marie.

NON: For Ani. It's enough now.

JOHN: Yes. I'll get her home.

NON: You can do this, John?

JOHN: I think so. I.O. *[Yes.]*

NON: Let me help you.

JOHN: I can manage, Marie.

NON: Let me help you, John.

JOHN: I can manage!

ARMINE: Let her help! For Pete's sake. Let Mother help! Let her help, John!

NON: Shhhhhhh.

JOHN: Of course.

NON: Shhhhhh.

JOHN: I apologize, Marie.

NON: It's all right, dear.

JOHN: Aman.

NON: It's all right. *(Lights shift.)*

SCENE 12

Moonlight. ANI *is still in her hotel room. She has one candle burning. She is holding a letter. She reads aloud.*

ANI: " . . . These are your instructions, Ani. Enclosed, find your ticket." *(She looks and finds ticket. Then picks up letter again.)* "And two additional things I must tell you, dear . . ."

(An elderly man stands outside her door. He is cold. He knocks.)

Hello? Parev? *[Hello?]*

MAN: *(The actor who plays* POP *also plays this man.)* Hello? American? *(He knocks again.)*

ANI: Yes? I.O.? *[Yes]* Yes?

MAN: Help. Please. *(He knocks.)*

ANI: What do you need?

MAN: Shad kagh tsahtz em. *[I am hungry.]*

ANI: What? *Ah see inch chay? [What is it?]*

MAN: *Shad kagh tsahtz em. [I am hungry.]*

ANI: Um. *Inch goozess?* [What?]

MAN: *Please. Shad shad kagh tsahtz em!* [I am very hungry!]

ANI: Shad. Shad *kaghts . . . ? Oh!* Hungry? . . . Oh, I have nothing!

MAN: *(He knocks.) Bahdarma hahts. [Piece of bread.]*

ANI: What? What?

MAN: *Gurnass inzee ocknell! [Can you help me!]*

ANI: *Gurnass . . . Gurnass . . . Inch goozess?* [What?]

MAN: *(Knocking loudly.) Gernass inzee ocknell! [Can you help me!]*

ANI: *Please. Speak. More. Slowly.*

MAN: *Mursoom mem! [I'm cold!] (Knocking.)*

ANI: *I'm sorry. I can't . . . Oh.*

MAN: *Hello please.*

ANI: *Yes. I'm sorry. I'm sorry. I'm. Sorry. I'm sorry.*

MAN: *Shad mursoom mem! [Very cold!]*

ANI: *I don't understand you. (Silence. The man turns to walk away. Then returns. And again, loud knocking.)*

MAN: *Ockneh eenz! Ockneh eenz! [Help! Help!] Gernass inzee ocknell!! [Can you help me!!]*

ANI: Oh God. Oh God. (ANI *looks in her room. She has nothing. Then she goes to door. Opens it. The* MAN *steps into room. She gestures: "I have nothing." She looks at him. He is cold. She takes off her coat. She offers it to him. He accepts it. He bows his head. They stand opposite each other. Each one holding the coat.)*

MAN: Shad Shad Shanor hag alem. *[Thank you so much.] (She releases the coat. He raises his head. She sees his face.)*

ANI: Oh!

MAN: Munock Parov. *[Good-bye.] (He's backing away.)*

ANI: Sir . . .

MAN: Munock Parov. *[Good-bye.] (He leaves.)*

ANI: Bye, bye. Bye, bye. (ANI *stands alone in doorway. Cold. Then she puts on Non's shawl. She crosses to table. She picks up a letter. She turns to second page. She reads:)* " . . . two additional things I must tell you, dear." *(Lights up on* JOHN *pacing in airport.)*

JOHN: Your Uncle Garo has died.

ANI: "Uncle Garo has died." (ANI *holds letter as* JOHN *continues.)*

JOHN: He suffered a heart attack. Your mother spoke at his service. She said he was a gentleman. Proud of his family. Especially you, dear.

ANI: *(Continues to read.)* "And last, Raffi asked me to enclose his picture of Mt. Ararat. Please correct it, he says, if it's wrong."

JOHN: Don't miss the plane, Ani.

ANI: "Don't miss the plane." (ANI *blows out candle. We hear the sound of planes.*)

SCENE 13

The airport waiting room.

JOHN *is waiting. Music. ("Yerevan.")*

ANI *enters. She is carrying her backpack. She is wearing the babuska. She sees her father.* JOHN *opens his arms to her. She walks to him. She rests her head against his chest. He holds her. She cries. They are joined by the rest of the family (with the exception of* NON).

Beat.

LOUISE *enters last, carrying a pan of food. She finds* ANI *in the group hug and taps her on the back.* ANI *turns and hugs* LOUISE. *Then they all exit the airport.* ARMINE *and* LOUISE *holding* ANI *between them.* GINYA, RAFFI, *and* JOHN *follow. Lights dim and come up on:*

SCENE 14

NON's *bedroom.* NON *sits, sewing Armenian lace.* ANI *stands in the doorway watching* NON. ANI *is still wearing her babushka.*

NON: What do you need, darling? (*ANI enters room.*)

ANI: I don't know. (ARMINE *enters. Stands outside room and listens.*)

NON: Are you tired?

ANI: No.

NON: You're not hungry. (ANI *shakes her head no.*) Did you watch the women sew?

ANI: Yes.

NON: In the darkness? They sewed in the darkness? (ANI *shakes her head yes.*) Embroidering their lace around scraps of cloth.

ANI: They have no hot water. They can't cook. They can't bathe their children. They are all . . . tired.

NON: And still they sew.

ANI: The daughters. The daughters sewed.

NON: Do you want to learn, Ani?

ANI: And the children. The children in the orphanages. With no one.

NON: Yes. Did you speak with them?

ANI: I couldn't.

NON: Ah.

ANI: I looked at them. I tried to draw pictures with them.

NON: Yes?

ANI: The children draw black suns, Nonnie. Always black suns in the sky.

NON: They are frightened.

ANI: Oh, God. (*Shakes her hands in despair.*)

NON: Do you want to learn to sew the lace, Ani?

ANI: I can't.

NON: Come, Ani.

ANI: All the little knots, Non. I can't stand it.

NON: We will start with the big knots.

ANI: There are no big knots.

NON: I'll show you.

ANI: It doesn't suit my hands, Non.

NON: We'll teach them.

ANI: No, Non!

NON: Come, darling.

ANI: I can't sew the lace, Non!

NON: All right.

ANI: I can't speak the language! I can't sew the lace!

NON: I know. You never learned.

ANI: You never taught me.

NON: I wanted you to ask.

ANI: I needed you to teach.

NON: Ah! Ok. What, Ani?

ANI: Non. In Yerevan. The library.

NON: Ya.

ANI: It has a room just for Papa's books.

NON: Yes. It is dedicated to him.

ANI: They have his sermons.

NON: Yes.

ANI: The people weep when they speak of him.

NON: He was a very important man. Even as a young man, he was important.

ANI: Did you love him, Non, like they do there?

NON: Ani . . .

ANI: Did you love him absolutely? Was he your first love?

NON: No, Ani.

ANI: Because I never felt you loved him absolutely.

NON: No, darling . . . He was not my first love. No one was. Until my children.

ANI: You married him, Non.

NON: Your Papa told me he would kill himself if I didn't marry him. I believed him.

ANI: Was he lonely?

NON: Yes. I'm sorry.

ANI: Were you lonely?

NON: Do you want to know? (ANI *shakes her head yes.*) Darling . . . When I was a young girl, I found a church . . . Ani, do you want to hear? (ANI *shakes her head yes.*) It was deserted, the church. And it was built into the side of a mountain! Imagine! A church built in the thirteenth century, into the side of a mountain! I went there every day. And I stood on the stone floors and I sang. I sang! And my voice went into the mountain! . . . I sang with the ancient voices in the ancient choirs, in an ancient stone church, in our ancient country. And I had joy. The greatest joy.

ANI: I can't write anything, Non.

NON: Let me tell you your heritage, Ani.

ANI: I know my heritage.

NON: Let me tell you!

ANI: Suffering! Suffering is my heritage!

NON: Yes.

ANI: Endless suffering!

NON: No!

ANI: Suffering! Hiding! Waiting!

NON: Ani! Listen!

ANI: Yearning! Silence!

NON: Ani!

ANI: Silence is my heritage!

NON: Stop it, Ani!

ANI: *Silence!*

NON: Ani, Listen to me! I'm going to tell you about your Papa's mother.

ANI: I know about Papa's mother!

NON: *You don't know!* You've been told only that she was lost. There is more. Your Papa's mother, your Great Grandmother, was taken by the Turks in a wagon and driven along the roads to be given to an officer in the Turkish Army. This officer—this man—had ordered her to be his mistress. She sat in the wagon and watched the women walk. They were walking, Ani, down the roads to the desert. They were walking to their death. Holding their children, vacant-eyed. Collapsing, bleeding, walking down the roads into the desert, where they died. And their children died. The Turks made the women walk. And the Turks stopped them to rape them. Cut them. Dismember them. And leave them to die in the roads on the way to the desert. Your Papa's mother watched the women walk. Then she ordered her carriage to stop. She got out. And she joined them. (ANI *is crying.*) She died. Your Papa lived. I married him. We came to America. We bore your mother. Our only child. She bore you. Her first child. Cry, Ani. Cry and cry and cry and then stop crying.

ANI: And what? Teach my hands?

NON: Teach your hands, I.O. [Yes.]

ANI: (*Crying.*) My hands . . . (NON *begins rubbing her own hands.*)

NON: Ani. Look.

ANI: What are you doing?

NON: Wringing. I'm wringing.

ANI: Wringing your hands?

NON: Ya. Wringing my hands. Like this, darling. Rub. . . . Squeeze. Rub . . . squeeze. *(She does it more deliberately.) Rub . . . Squeeze.*

ANI: Rub? Squeeze?

NON: Ya. *Rub . . . Squeeze.*

ANI: *Rub! . . . Squeeze!*

NON: Bravo!

ANI: *Rub! . . . Squeeze!*

NON: I.O. *[Yes.]* Now, darling. Step Two!

ANI: Step two?

NON: *Rub! Squeeze! Groan! Mmmmmmmmmmmmmmmmmmmmm!*

ANI: Rub. Squeeze. Groan. Mmmmmmmmmm.

NON: Perfect! Together!

NON AND ANI: *Rub! Squeeze! Groan! Mmmmmmmmmmmm.*

NON: *Again!*

NON AND ANI: *Rub! . . . Squeeze . . . Groan. . . .*

NON: *Into the mountain, Ani!!! Put your voice into the mountain!!!*

ANI: *Ahhhhhhhhhhhhhhhhhhhhhhhhhh!*

NON AND ANI: *Rub! . . . Squeeze! . . . Groan! Ahhhhhhhhhhhhhhhh! Rub! . . . Squeeze! . . . Groan! Ahhhhhhhhhhhhhhhh! Rub! . . . Squeeze! . . . Groan! Aaaahhhhhhhhhhhhh! (They do this until it builds to release. Beat.)*

NON: Let me see you, Ani. *(Looking at her babushka.)*

ANI: You mean . . . *(She touches her babushka.)*

NON: Ya. Let me see your head.

ANI: *(Unties and removes her babushka.)* Here it is.

NON: Ya. There it is! (NON *kisses* ANI *on the top of her head.)*

ANI: *Mom?*

ARMINE: *(From the hallway.)* Ya?

ANI: Were you listening?

ARMINE: *(Enters and stands in doorway.)* Ya.

ANI: Do you like my hair, Ma?

ARMINE: You are beautiful, Ani. Come eat. (ANI *crosses to* ARMINE.) You go, dear, to the kitchen.

(ANI *crosses out of Non's room. Now* ANI *listens in the hall.)*

NON: What is it?

ARMINE: Mother. You never taught me to wring my hands.

NON: I couldn't teach you, Armine.

ARMINE: Because I didn't ask.

NON: Because I didn't know myself.
ARMINE: When did you learn?
NON: This evening.
ARMINE: So.
NON: What do you need, dear?
ARMINE: Nothing.
NON: Ok. (*Lights shift.*)

SCENE 15

The cemetery. LOUISE *sits by Garo's grave.* ARMINE *and* ANI *enter.*

ARMINE: Ani, do you think you could manage the house?
LOUISE: I can help her.
ANI: Can I manage the house?
ARMINE: Ya.
LOUISE: I can cook, Ani. You drive and clean.
ANI: For how long?
ARMINE: One month. Next month.
ANI: You mean . . . What do you mean?
ARMINE: Will you do my job for one month?
LOUISE: Can you do her job, Ani?
ANI: You mean, cook and take care of the kids and Dad and everything?
LOUISE AND ARMINE: Ya.
ANI: Um . . .
LOUISE: I will cook for your father, Sunday meal: the boeregg, the sarma, the tass kebob. I will cook. You can help.
ANI: Ok.
LOUISE: And the podiatrist, Armine, for Marie, don't forget.
ARMINE: I'll give directions.
LOUISE: Write them down. A map!
ARMINE: Of course, Louise.
LOUISE: And put it on the wall!
ARMINE: Ya. I will, of course.
LOUISE: Do you need a suitcase?
ARMINE: No, no. I have . . .
LOUISE: A new one! With a handle!
ARMINE: Ya, Ok. I'll get . . .
LOUISE: I have one, Armine. I'll give it to you.
ARMINE: All right.
ANI: Mom? Where are you going? (ARMINE *looks at* LOUISE.)
LOUISE: She's going to Armenia.

ARMINE: I.O. *[Yes.]*
ANI: You're going to Armenia?
ARMINE: I.O. *[Yes.]* . . . I am going, Ani.
ANI: What will you do there, Mom?
ARMINE: I will sit.
ANI: Sit?
ARMINE: Ya. I will sit.
ANI: Sit?
ARMINE: Ya. I will sit with the children in the orphanages.
LOUISE: She will watch.
ARMINE: Ya. I can do that.
ANI: Yes. You can, Mom.
ARMINE: And I will send you letters, Ani.
ANI: And I will save them.
ARMINE: Ya. That's perfect.
LOUISE: Bravo! *(NON enters.)*
NON: John is waiting.
ARMINE: Ok, let's go.
NON: Aneen, keh dae? *[Ani knows?]*
LOUISE: Ya. She just told her.
NON: Ah. Ani, your mother is going to Armenia!
ANI: Yes.
LOUISE: She is able, Ani. She knows it. Because of you, dear.
ANI: Me?
NON: She waited for you, Ani. Every minute.
LOUISE: Never stopped.
ARMINE: It's true.
NON: So now, she can go!
LOUISE: Ya!
ARMINE: Ya! Look at me! *(Laughs. They all look with pride.)*
ANI: Yes, Mom! Look at you!
ARMINE: Aman.
LOUISE: Bravo!
ARMINE: Thank you, Ani.
ANI: You're welcome, Mom.
LOUISE: Who would have thought?
ANI: Does Dad know?
NON, ARMINE, AND LOUISE: Not yet.
ARMINE: Soon. I'll tell him soon. Next week.
NON: Let me tell him.
ANI: I can tell him!
LOUISE: I'll tell him!
ARMINE: I will tell him!!

LOUISE: Ok.

NON: That's best. *(Car horn.)*

JOHN: *(Offstage.) Let's go!*

ARMINE: *All right! (To* ANI.*)* Let's go, dear.

LOUISE: Marie, Papa's grave, it's all white now.

NON: Ya. Lot's of bird metzaquartz! *[poop!]*

LOUISE: Ya. Too much!

JOHN: *(Offstage.) Come on!*

LOUISE: You'll fix?

NON: I'll fix!

LOUISE: Ok!

JOHN: *(Offstage.) Come on!*

ALL: *We're coming!*

ARMINE: Let's go! *(They exit. Lights shift and come up on* GINYA *and* RAFFI.*)*

SCENE 16

The driveway. GINYA *and* RAFFI *are downstage. They are tearing little pieces of Kleenex and making a little pile.* JOHN *comes out of the house carrying a pan of food wrapped in aluminum foil. He is headed for the car.* ANI *catches up to him.*

GINYA: Raffi, those pieces are too big.

RAFFI: What? No, they're not.

GINYA: Yes! Make them smaller. Tear them smaller. Like this. (RAFFI *gives* GINYA *a "get off my back" look.).*

ANI: Want me to take that, Dad?

JOHN: Sure. Thank you. *(He hands the food to her.)*

ANI: Shall I put it in the back seat?

JOHN: *(Overlapping.)* Put it in the trunk!

ANI: Ok.

JOHN: Ok. I'll get your mother. What are you kids doing?

GINYA AND RAFFI: Nothing.

JOHN: All right. We're going. Is that for the bird?

GINYA: Yup.

JOHN: You must move your little pile, it is too exposed.

RAFFI: Where should we move it, Dad?

JOHN: The tree. To the tree. Near the tree.

GINYA AND RAFFI: Ok. *(They don't move.)*

ANI: *Dad!*

JOHN: What?

ANI: Did you like the sarma?

JOHN: It was good.

ANI: Thanks.

JOHN: Not so many raisins, perhaps, Ani.

ANI: Raisins.

JOHN: More nuts.

ANI: Nuts.

JOHN: The leaves were tender!

ANI: Mom did that.

JOHN: Ah.

ANI: Oh well.

JOHN: Ya.

ANI: Will you miss her, Dad?

JOHN: Ani.

ANI: Don't you want to go with her to Yerevan?

JOHN: She is going. She is ready.

ANI: She will help.

JOHN: Yes.

ANI: In her way.

JOHN: I must go inside. Ani, I'm going inside.

ANI: Ok, Dad.

JOHN: I will miss your mother, of course.

ANI: That's good, Dad.

JOHN: Aman, Ani. *(From inside the house we hear:)*

ARMINE: *Manock parov! [Good-bye!]*

NON: *Good-bye, dear. (Armine enters.)*

ARMINE: *See you Tuesday, Ma!*

JOHN AND ARMINE: *Shad schnora gollyem. [Thank you.] (NON enters.)*

NON: *Don't forget the tass kebob!*

JOHN: I don't think so, Marie.

GINYA: *Non! It's spilling!*

NON: *Vy vy vy. [My my my.]*

ARMINE: *I'll get a sponge.*

NON: *In the cupboard! get the stool.*

ARMINE: *I know!*

JOHN: Oh, boy. *(ARMINE and NON go into house. JOHN crosses to car. Gets in. Takes out newspaper. Reads. ANI joins GINYA and RAFFI who are still Downstage, with their little pile.)*

ANI: This is for the bird with the white nest?

RAFFI AND GINYA: Yea.

GINYA: It's browner now.

RAFFI: Beege.

GINYA: Beige! It gets dirty.

ANI: Oh. Ok.

RAFFI: Ani, did you take the ashes?

GINYA: We know.

RAFFI: Non told us.

GINYA: Did you take Papa's ashes to Casaria?

RAFFI: Did you?

ANI: No.

RAFFI AND GINYA: *No?!?*

ANI: *Shhhhhhhhhhh!*

RAFFI: What did you do with them?

ANI: I lost them.

GINYA: What?

RAFFI: She lost them!

ANI: They inspected my backpack at the airport. I couldn't explain what they were.

RAFFI: Why not?

ANI: They didn't believe me.

GINYA: Did they take them?

ANI: Yes.

GINYA: Does Non know?

ANI: This has to be our secret! You have to promise!

RAFFI AND GINYA: Ok.

ANI: For *life*! This is a *life* promise. No one can know Papa's ashes are in the airport.

RAFFI AND GINYA: Ok.

JOHN: *Let's go!*

RAFFI: Which airport?

ANI: Yerevan.

RAFFI: At least he's in Armenia.

JOHN: *Come on!*

GINYA: What do you think they do with the things they take from people?

ANI: I don't know.

RAFFI: Maybe they bury them.

ANI: Maybe they do.

GINYA: Maybe they toss them to the wind. Or to the sea!

ANI: There is no sea in Armenia. There's a lake! Maybe they toss them in the lake!

GINYA: Yea.

ANI: Yea.

JOHN: *What's going on? Why is no one in the car?* (ARMINE *enters.* NON *follows with a pot of food.*)

ARMINE: *Time to go!*

NON: *Tass kebob!*

ANI: It's time to go? (JOHN *gets out of car.*)

JOHN: You know, I remember a time, this will interest you, when I used to open the car door; get in; put the key in the ignition and start the car.

ARMINE: I remember that, dear.

JOHN: Then. I would drive. (RAFFI *exits.* GINYA *puts on Roller-blades.*)

ARMINE: Ma, it spills. The tass kebob always spills, Ma.

JOHN: Now. I open the car door . . .

GINYA: I'll hold the tass kebob, Non.

JOHN: Pick up the newspaper . . .

NON: *Bravo*, darling!

JOHN: Put it across the steering wheel . . .

ARMINE: It'll spill, Ma!

JOHN: And read, no one's listening.

NON: To what, dear? (GINYA *starts skating.*)

GINYA: *Ani!* Show Non what you learned!

JOHN: Now what?

GINYA: Show Non what you learned.

ANI: Not now.

GINYA: *Non! Look! (She points to* ANI.)

NON: Yavroom, I know, darling, wonderful, you're rollaring.

GINYA: Not me, Non! Ani!

NON: What is it, darling?

GINYA: Do it here, Ani. In Non's driveway. This is good.

NON: Ya. This is good

ANI: Oh, God.

GINYA: Come on! (GINYA *claps her hands and dances on her skates. Then* ANI *begins to dance an Armenian dance.* NON *watches, claps her hands.* ARMINE *goes into the house. Non joins* ANI. *They dance.*)

JOHN: Armine! Come on! You must see this! Armine! Betgeah asees desnes! [You've got to see this!] (ARMINE *appears on steps with her tambourine. She gives it a perfect hit and then, proudly, dances by herself. They applaud her. Then, each of the women, in turn dances some form of an Armenian dance. Ginya does something contemporary on her skates. Each one signals the next to dance. They end up together, dancing with vigor and joy.* JOHN *plays* ARMINE's *tambourine, after she hands it to him. They finish.*) Bravo! Bravo!

NON: *Afarehim, [Excellent] darling!*

ARMINE: *Good for you, Ani!*

GINYA: Where's Raffi?

ALL: *Raffi!*

ANI: *Oh my god! Raffi!*

ARMINE: *Where?*

ANI: *In the tree.*

ARMINE: *Raffi! What are you doing?*

JOHN: *Jesus oh Jesus.*

NON: *Where is he?*

ARMINE: *Raffi, why are you in the tree?* Virginia, why is Raffi in the tree?

GINYA: I don't know.

RAFFI: *I wanted to see the bird.*

GINYA: He wanted to see the bird.

RAFFI: *There are lots of white things in the nest!*

JOHN: Oh, for Pete's sake.

RAFFI: *It looks like lace, Non.*

NON: What does, dear?

ARMINE: The nest looks like lace? My goodness. It looks like lace, Mom!

NON: Armine, perhaps the bird is Armenian! *(They laugh.)* Aman!

ARMINE: *All right, darling, come down now.*

RAFFI: *I'm a little stuck.*

ARMINE: You're stuck?

JOHN: Oh Jesus.

ARMINE: *It's all right, Raffi. listen to your father.*

JOHN: *Raffi?*

RAFFI: *What?*

JOHN: *Move your right foot to the left, toward the house.*

RAFFI: *I'm stuck.*

ANI: *It's ok, Raffi.*

JOHN: *The other foot. The right foot! toward the house. Not the street.*

RAFFI: *What?*

ALL: *Not the street.*

RAFFI: *Ok.*

JOHN: *Is it looser now?*

RAFFI: *Dad?*

JOHN: *Yes?*

RAFFI: *It's not looser.*

ARMINE: Go up there, John.

JOHN: He can do it, Armine.

GINYA: I'll go up, Ma.

ARMINE: No, no darling.

JOHN: *Raffi, lift gently from the knee.*

RAFFI: *Ok*

JOHN: *The right knee.*

RAFFI: *Ok.*

JOHN: *The right knee!*

RAFFI: *Ok.*

ARMINE: *Raffi! The right knee!*

RAFFI: Oh. OK.

ARMINE: *Come down now, darling.*

JOHN: Come down now, Raffi.

RAFFI: *Ok, Dad.*

NON: Be careful!

ARMINE: You're ok?

RAFFI: *I'm ok!*

GINYA: *Hurry up!*

RAFFI: *Ok!*

ARMINE: *Slow down!*

RAFFI: *Ok!*

JOHN: *For pete's sake!*

RAFFI: *Ok!*

ARMINE: All right, now!

RAFFI: I'm here!

ALL: *Yaaaaaaaaaaay!*

JOHN: All right, come on.

GINYA: Nice going.

RAFFI: Shut-up.

GINYA: Duh!

RAFFI: Duh-yourself!

GINYA: Duh-face!

JOHN: Ok! Everybody in the car!

RAFFI: Mom, can I take my coat off in the car?

ARMINE: All right, dear.

RAFFI: *Awesome!*

ANI: Non, I have something to tell you.

ARMINE: Come on, Raffi. Get in. *(Everyone starts getting in the car except* ANI.*)*

ANI: *(Whispers.)* Non . . .

NON: I know, dear.

ANI: You know?

NON: Ya. The airport.

ANI: I'm sorry.

NON: It's all right, Yavroom.

JOHN: *Ani, say good-bye.*

ANI: Ok, Dad. *(To* NON.*)* How did you find out?

NON: My Uncle Herrant, you remember?

ANI: Uncle Herrant . . . You sat by the Sea of . . .

NON: Marmara!

ANI: He drank his coffee, you ate your baklava.

NON: Correct!

ANI: Uncle Herrant! He's dead, right?

NON: Ya. His son is Zaven.

ANI: Zaven?

NON: The Mayor!

ANI: The Mayor! Zaven! *Aman!*

NON: Ya.

JOHN: *This is it!*

ANI: Non! Maybe Mom could get Papa's ashes! ”

NON: No, darling. They are lost.

ARMINE: Come on, Ani!

ANI: Bye, Non.

NON: Yavroom. *[Sweet one.]* (*Hugs, kisses.* ANI *gets in car. All yell out the windows to* NON.)

ALL: *Byyyyyyyyyyyyyeeeeeeeeeeeeeeee!* (LOUISE *runs on carrying food.*)

LOUISE: *Hiiiiiiiiiiiiiiiiiiii!* (*She waves.*) *I just wanted to be here for the good-bye!* (*Everyone waves and yells.*)

ALL: *Good byeeeeeeeeeeeeeeeeeeeee!*

LOUISE: *Hugs! Hugs!* (*Everyone's door—except* JOHN's—*open. They all get out and form a clump around* LOUISE. *And again, from the clump we hear:*)

ARMINE: *Good-bye, dear.*

LOUISE: *I brought you some baklava!*

NON: *Manock parov! [Good-bye!]*

LOUISE: *Take the baklava!*

ARMINE: *We have boeregg.*

JOHN: *Get in the car!*

LOUISE: *Ani, I brought you a ring!*

ARMINE: *Go inside, Ma!*

NON: *You need a rubber band.*

GINYA: *It's spilling!*

NON: *What is, Darling?*

JOHN: *Armine!*

ARMINE: *Let's go.* (ARMINE, RAFFI, GINYA, *and* ANI *cross to the car and get in. As they cross:*)

LOUISE: *Call when you get home!*

NON: *See you Tuesday!*

ARMINE: *Ok.*

NON: (*Blows a kiss.*) *Bachigs! [Kisses!]*

LOUISE: Ya! Bachigs, bachigs, bachigs! [Kisses, Kisses, Kisses!]

ALL IN THE CAR: (*From the car.*) *Bachigs, bachigs, bachigs! [Kisses, Kisses, Kisses!]*

JOHN: Let's go! (*They slam the doors. Lights out. Music.*)

The End

HERAND MARKARIAN

MIRRORS

A Play in Eight Scenes

To my mother
Noonoofar Markarian
a survivor of the Armenian Genocide of 1915

Acknowledgment: I wish to express my deepest appreciation and love to my daughter Yeraz, for suggesting the
writing of this play, to my son Gahmk for his valuable
comments, and to my wife Janet, who meticulously re-
viewed the writing of *Mirrors* from its inception to the
current finished version.

THE PLAYWRIGHT

Herand Markarian was born in Basra, Iraq, in 1938 and emigrated to the United States in 1962. He holds B.S., M.S., and Ph.D. degrees in chemistry, and an M.S. in management of technology. He studied directing and playwriting at The Circle in the Square, New York University, and The Schreiber Studio in New York City. But before this formal theatrical training, he had already *appeared* in Armenian theater at the age of eighteen in his birthplace, in 1956, debuting subsequently as a director at the age of twenty.

Markarian has authored some two dozen plays in Armenian and one in English. Founder of New York's Hamazkayin Theater Group in 1967, he staged thirty-six productions, four multimedia cultural programs, and the works of thirteen Armenian poets and writers, and acted in forty roles, including Johannes Lepsius in the feature film *Assignment Berlin*. His plays have been performed in Armenia, Canada, England, Greece, Lebanon, Syria, and the United States.

The author has received the following awards: the Saint Mesrob medal for cultural accomplishments bestowed by His Holiness Catholicos Karekin II of the Holy See of Cilicia, 1987; the Gold Medal, conferred by the Regional Executive Committees of Hamazkayin, United States and Canada, 1980; the Gold Medal, presented by the New York Chapter of Hamazkayin, 1987; Best Playwright, by the Writers'

Union of Armenia of which he became a member in 1992; and the Gold Medal from Armenia's Ministry of Culture, 2002.

THE PLAY

Yeraz Markarian, Markarian's daughter, first directed the original short version of *Mirrors*, written in English at her behest, on 9 December 1993, at the Minor Latham Playhouse, Barnard College, New York City. A second version was staged by Arminé Minassian at Queens College in 1994. The Theater Company of Hamazkayin Armenian Educational and Cultural Society of New York presented the professional world premiere of the current version of *Mirrors*, off-Broadway, on 22 October 1995 at the Phil Bosakowski Theater.

The Cast of the World Premiere Production

OLD TENY	Anahid
YOUNG TENY	Yeraz Markarian
MRS. DAVIS (NURSE)	Talene Amadooni
DR. BROWN	Joe Corey
DR. WILLIAMS	Sy Young
MOTHER	Norik Checkosky
MARY	Lara Milian
GARO	Richard Callahan
GENDARME	Aram Deirmenjian
MEDICAL PERSONNEL	Production crew

Production Credits

Director	Herand M. Markarian
Musical arrangement	Narek Boudaghian
Makeup	Arminé Minassian
Set Design	Herand M. Markarian
Costumes	Gary & Susan Lind-Sinanian
Sound	Rita Gragossian
Sound System	Sevan Loughran
Stage Manager	Janet Markarian
Set Construction	Alan Gragossian
Art Work	Bedig Kahwejian
Publicity	Sonia Bezdikian
Production Manager	Hovhannes Bezdikian

"The SELF, without it we are empty souls"

Mirrors is a psychological drama about three individuals embroiled in the exhaustive search to find their elusive selves. It is a voyage into the intricacies and the convolutions of the "Self."

The "Self," an abstract term, refers to a person's individuality, identity or personality. It is the melding or merging of the conscious, unconscious, intellectual and emotional elements of human existence, Descartes's "I am."

We (our "selves") are in a constant state of dynamic change. We differ in our acceptance of the realities we are forced to face. We each react to and adapt to events and interactions with people differently. We evolve during arguments, when listening to music, or reading a book—all of these interactions trigger something unique within us that resonates and causes us to re-form ourselves over and over again.

Psychologists and psychiatrists have made it their lifelong task to understand the concept of the "self," to explain the characteristic of individuality which defines each unique "self," and to guide those "selves" which have diverted from the ubiquitous "norm." This endless search for our elusive selves, however, often leaves us with additional and much more complex questions. The onerous search for the "self" can be an agonizing experience, whereas finding our true "selves" is a feeling as tranquil as a placid sea.

Mirrors is a study of the reflectivity within the "self" and between "selves." It is a sampling of the vast experiences of suffering within the human race. The play focuses on three individuals who have come together, unaware of one another's history. The characters each have elements of their selves reflected in another person: Dr. Williams sees the reflection of his youth and keen determination in Dr. Brown. Young Teny discovers that the passion and excitement of young love are reflected by her beloved, Garo. Garo sees a more somber reflection in Young Teny, however, namely his concerns over her safety as well as that of his own family in the midst of an omniscient enemy. Teny's mother witnesses her own youth being reenacted in front of her very eyes, in her daughter. The Nurse, Mrs. Davis, has found peace in her hard work with the person she most admires, Dr. Brown.

The characters in this play are common, everyday people, each with a unique experience. When we first meet her in the hospital, Old Teny appears to be an ordinary woman who has experienced a psychological breakdown. We soon learn of her tormented soul and her bravery living throughout the Genocide; her story of survival, self-sufficiency, torment, and strength. This relentless woman breaks down only when the single missing fragment of her life, her brother, returns to her reality.

Dr. Brown is in search of a past that does not exist. He is an enigma undefined by research texts on psychological traumas. His total immersion in his search for his past resembles the desperation of an escape artist hanging from a burning rope, constantly fighting against time to complete his Self. Mary exemplifies the purity that is marred by unfortunate events. She is in a fixed state of amnesia, and with a fragile sensitivity searches for an outlet, a completeness, which Old Teny helps trigger into being. And thus the characters mirror one another in different dimensions throughout the play.

The set design given in the text reflects this interconnection of the characters. Directors and set designers, however, are not bound by the design described here.

Mirrors was written for my daughter, Yeraz, as part of her senior thesis in theater at Barnard College, New York City. She had suggested that I base the play on the experiences of her grandmother (my mother), whose stories of the Armenian Genocide she had heard as a child. I took her advice and expanded it to include the agony of my late father, my wife's father, and all those whom I had known in my childhood and whose manifold stories still haunt my conscience.

Although I have dedicated this play to my mother, who at the age of ninety-five still shivers from her childhood memories, in essence this play is dedicated to all people of all races and creeds who have suffered precious losses in their lives.

HERAND M. MARKARIAN

MIRRORS

A Play in Eight Scenes

HERAND M. MARKARIAN

THE CHARACTERS

MEDICAL PERSONNEL, Any number of people
OLD TENY, A lady in her sixties with a slight limp
YOUNG TENY, A young woman in her teens
MRS. DAVIS, A nurse, in her thirties
DR. JIM BROWN, Senior psychiatrist, in his forties
DR. JOE WILLIAMS, Psychiatry department chair-
     man, in his sixties
MARY, A patient in the hospital in her twenties
GARO, *"Fedayee"*—a freedom fighter in his twenties
TENY'S MOTHER, A woman in her thirties
GENDARME, A man in his twenties

SETTINGS

*The stage has no curtain. The background scenes—a
hospital room, flashbacks, and fields are created by
employing several identical triangular columns with
three panels. Each panel is six feet high and two feet
wide. There are wheels under the columns to aid in
rotating them.*

The three panels are:

*Side 1—Mirrors of different shapes and sizes on a
black background used for flashback scenes.*
Side 2— A light gray texture, used for hospital scenes.
*Side 3—A light blue background used for field
scenes.*

MUSIC

The song "Delé Yaman" is an authentic old Armenian song. It is intertwined with OLD TENY's *world. Variations on the theme can be used. The whole song is heard only once.*

The musical notes of "Delé Yaman" and the Armenian transliteration of the song are given at the end of the text along with a loose translation.

LIGHTING

Three distinct colors are used to recreate OLD TENY's *early life in her village: blue representing the vibrant sky; violet reminiscent of her joy in the presence of flowers; and amber reflecting the wheat fields where she spent her youth.*

PLACE

A room in a New York psychiatric hospital. A wheelchair center stage. A table and a chair next to it, left. A nurse's desk, cabinet, and chair, stage right.

TIME

The mid-nineties

SCENE ONE

(The stage has no curtain. Downstage: The columns are placed in a semicircular manner. The mirrored sides face the audience blocking the set. In the darkness, ambulance sirens are heard followed by loud pounding heartbeats. There is strobe lighting throughout this scene.)

*(*MEDICAL PERSONNEL *enter in white coats. They move the panels upstage by rotating them to the gray sides (hospital wall). Their voices are heard during this action. Afterwards they exit sporadically.)*

MALE AND FEMALE VOICES: —She's unconscious.
    —Take her in.
    —Did she have an attack?
    —I don't know.

—Oxygen!

—Pulse?

—Heart rate 42. Hardly any pulse.

—Dry off her sweat.

—I.V., now!

—I can't find a vein. Seems collapsed.

—She is going to die on us.

—What's her name?

—I don't know.

—More oxygen!

—O.K.!

—She's breathing.

—Pulse?

—It's coming back!

—I have the I.V.!

—She seems to be calming down.

—Pulse is normal.

—Thank God, she's going to make it.

—Thank God.

(Fade to scene two.)

SCENE TWO

(Afternoon. A room in a psychiatric hospital. The pounding of the heartbeat from scene one continues. A violet light bathes the background. An amber spot falls on OLD TENY. *The music of "Delé Yaman" begins as the heartbeats subside.)*

*(*OLD TENY *in a wheelchair, wearing a simple home dress, staring ahead with a blank expression.* YOUNG TENY *under amber lighting, enters stage left, she is wearing a long white dress, crosses downstage in a dreamlike walk and exits stage right.* OLD TENY *does not look at her.)*

(The music fades out.)

MRS. DAVIS: *(In nurse's uniform, with a stethoscope around her neck, enters in an upbeat mood carrying a plastic shopping bag.)* Good afternoon, Ms. Ross. How are you today? How did you sleep last night? Your belongings are in this bag. I'll put them right by your bed, O.K.?

*(*OLD TENY *is silent.)*

MRS. DAVIS: (*Gets a thermometer and blood pressure equipment from her desk and approaches* OLD TENY.) I'll be taking your temperature and checking your blood pressure, all right? Please open your mouth.

(OLD TENY *does not react.*)

MRS. DAVIS: Please, open your mouth.

(OLD TENY *remains immobile.*)

MRS. DAVIS: (*Gently pulls* OLD TENY's *chin, opens her mouth and puts the thermometer in. Checks her pulse and the blood pressure and records them on a chart. Takes the thermometer out, checks the temperature.*) Good, you don't have a fever. Is there anyone you want us to get in touch with?

(OLD TENY *does not answer.*)

MRS. DAVIS: Let me see your head wound (*Checks the back of* OLD TENY's *head.*) Does it hurt?

(OLD TENY *does not answer.*)

MRS. DAVIS: Good, the wound is healing. (*Records and leaves the chart on her desk. Crosses to stage right and looks off.*) What a beautiful spring! Flowers have bloomed. You know, you have the best view of the garden. (*Crosses to the wheelchair and moves* OLD TENY *to stage right.*) In the morning you'll hear birds playing and singing. Last year they made a nest by this window. *(To* OLD TENY*)* Do you like birds?

(OLD TENY *does not answer.*)

MRS. DAVIS: I do. (*Points outside.*) Oh look, my friends the Canadian geese are here. They have made their permanent residence here. You see, patients come and go, but these birds always return. You know, I recognize some of them. I think they recognize me too. I feed them when I go out for my lunch break. (*Moves* OLD TENY *back to stage center and goes stage right.*) Did you know that geese go through a courtship before mating? . . . And they stay together for life? (*Dreamy as if talking to herself*) What devotion, what commitment! I always wonder, what keeps them together? It can't be only physical attraction. It must be more than that. It might be love.

DR. BROWN: (*Enters wearing a white coat, a stethoscope in his pocket, holding a small note pad where he frequently records his observations. An eager and caring individual.*) Good afternoon, Mrs. Davis.

MRS. DAVIS: Good afternoon, Dr. Brown.

DR. BROWN: If you're talking about love, it must be spring.

MRS. DAVIS: It certainly is spring.

DR. BROWN: How is she?

MRS. DAVIS: Her temperature is normal. Her blood pressure is still on the high side.

DR. BROWN: *(To* OLD TENY*)* Good afternoon, Ms. Ross. I'm Dr. Brown. We'll work together to get you well. How are you today?

(OLD TENY *does not answer.*)

DR. BROWN: *(To* MRS. DAVIS*)* Did we get her admission papers?

MRS. DAVIS: Yes, Dr. Brown.

DR. BROWN: May I see the reports, please?

MRS. DAVIS: *(Takes three folders from her desk. Hands one folder to* DR. BROWN*.)* Here's the police report.

DR. BROWN: Thank you. *(Thumbs through, reads as if skipping lines)* Responding to the neighbor's call, arrived at the scene . . . The doors were locked . . . No signs of break-ins . . . She did not respond to the knock on the window . . . Forced the door open . . . She was lying on the floor with a pool of blood around her head . . . Did not respond to questions . . . There was a shopping cart full of food . . . Scattered papers, newspapers, letters on the floor . . . She had a piece of paper clutched in her hand . . . Called the Paramedics immediately . . . *(Closes the folder and gives it back to* MRS. DAVIS*.)*

MRS. DAVIS: This is the Paramedics report. *(Hands another folder to* DR. BROWN*.)*

DR. BROWN: Thanks. *(Thumbs through, reading)* Unconscious . . . Oxygen administered . . . Neck and head immobilized. *(Closes the folder and gives it back to* MRS. DAVIS*.)*

MRS. DAVIS: And this is the Emergency Room report. *(Hands* DR. BROWN *the last folder.)*

DR. BROWN: Thank you. *(Thumbs through and focuses on the important words)* Fluctuations in blood pressure . . . sweating bouts . . . incoherent words. *(To* MRS. DAVIS*)* These sweating bouts, did you notice any fever associated with them?

MRS. DAVIS: No.

DR. BROWN: O.K., let's keep monitoring them. *(To* OLD TENY*)* May I examine you?

(OLD TENY *does not respond. Dr. Brown pricks* OLD TENY*'s upper arm with a needle.* OLD TENY *responds with a sigh signifying pain.*)

DR. BROWN: Very good. *(Pricks* OLD TENY*'s hand with a needle.)*

(OLD TENY *responds by pulling her hand.*)

DR. BROWN: O.K. (*Checks* OLD TENY's *feet. Points to the left foot.*) Ms. Ross, how did you get this scar on your left ankle?

(OLD TENY *does not respond.*)

DR. BROWN: (*To* MRS. DAVIS) May I see that police report again?

MRS. DAVIS: (*Hands* DR. BROWN *the police report.*) Here.

DR. BROWN: (*Looks at the report.*) There is no mention of the scar. (*Hands back the report to* MRS. DAVIS.) Mrs. Davis, could you please get the neighbors' telephone number from the police station?

MRS. DAVIS: (*Hands him a piece of paper.*) Here it is.

DR. BROWN: (*Smiles.*) You knew I would ask for this, right?

MRS. DAVIS: I guess. I called, but the neighbors were not home.

DR. BROWN: (*Disappointed.*) Great! Has she responded to any questions?

MRS. DAVIS: No. But last night she stepped down from her bed and limped around the room. She seemed to be looking for something or somebody.

DR. BROWN: You said she limped? Did we get back her neurological tests?

MRS. DAVIS: (*Hands him a folder.*) Yes.

DR. BROWN: (*Reads the folder.*) Normal . . . normal.. Aha, left foot drop. I wonder what might have caused it. Oh, Mrs. Davis, can you see to it that we get court permission to visit this lady's house?

MRS. DAVIS: I'll do that first thing on Monday morning.

DR. BROWN: Monday morning? (*Checks his watch.*) Of course, it's five o'clock, Friday. (*Checks the chart.*) Where does she live?

MRS. DAVIS: Meadow Park.

(DR. WILLIAMS *enters wearing a white coat. A confident knowledgeable authoritative and well-composed gentleman.*)

DR. BROWN: (*To* MRS. DAVIS) Where is Meadow Park?

DR. WILLIAMS: About half an hour from here.

DR. BROWN: Oh, hi, Joe.

DR. WILLIAMS: Hi, Jim. Good afternoon, Mrs. Davis.

MRS. DAVIS: Good afternoon, Dr. Williams.

DR. WILLIAMS: Well, any leads?

DR. BROWN: Not really. She sweats at times, her heartbeat races. She stepped down from her bed last night and limped around. But she has not responded to questions yet.

DR. WILLIAMS: Did you say she limped?

MRS. DAVIS: Yes, she has a left foot drop and a scar on it. It looks like an old injury.

DR. WILLIAMS: A fall maybe.

DR. BROWN: Maybe.

DR. WILLIAMS: How about her tests?

DR. BROWN: All normal.

DR. WILLIAMS: What's her name?

DR. BROWN: Ms. Ross, Ms. Teny Ross.

DR. WILLIAMS: How did she get here?

MRS. DAVIS: The neighbors had stopped by to say good-bye before going on vacation. They knocked on the door and got no response. They looked through the window and saw her lying on the floor. They called the police and the police called the Paramedics and here we are.

DR. WILLIAMS: What else do we know about her?

DR. BROWN: That's it.

DR. WILLIAMS: *(To* OLD TENY*)* Hello.

(OLD TENY *stares straight ahead without answering.*)

DR. WILLIAMS: How are you?

(OLD TENY *does not answer.*)

DR. WILLIAMS: *(To* DR. BROWN*)* Has she talked at all?

MRS. DAVIS: She hasn't uttered a word since she was admitted. Sometimes she makes sounds, which seem like incoherent words.

DR. WILLIAMS: Maybe a language we don't understand.

DR. BROWN: That's a possibility.

DR. WILLIAMS: *(Holds* OLD TENY'*s hand gently.)* How are you, Ms. Ross?]

(OLD TENY *is silent.*)

DR. WILLIAMS: Do you speak English?

(OLD TENY *is silent.*)

DR. WILLIAMS: Habla Espanol?

(OLD TENY *is silent.*)

DR. WILLIAMS: Como esta usted?

(OLD TENY *is silent.*)

DR. WILLIAMS: What nationality is she?

DR. BROWN: I don't know yet.

DR. WILLIAMS: Has anybody inquired about her?

MRS. DAVIS: No, no record of any contacts.

DR. WILLIAMS: How about the neighbors, has anybody contacted them?

DR. BROWN: Mrs. Davis did.

MRS. DAVIS: I called, they were not home, left a message on their answering machine.

DR. WILLIAMS: Let's keep on trying. Let's find out as much as possible about this lady. Maybe we should contact her other neighbors.

OLD TENY: *(Makes a monotonous high-pitched sigh)* Naaa . . .

MRS. DAVIS: Here she goes.

DR. WILLIAMS: What?

DR. BROWN: *(To DR. WILLIAMS. In a low voice)* Shhhhh.

OLD TENY: Naaa . . . Naaa . . . *(Her voice rises. She starts shivering.)*

DR. BROWN: *(Comes closer and in a comforting voice)* It's all right, it's all right. You can talk. Do you want to say something, Ms. Ross?

OLD TENY: Naaa . . . Naaa . . .

MRS. DAVIS: There, you heard what I've been hearing all night long.

DR. BROWN: *(Takes a tissue and wipes OLD TENY's forehead. In an encouraging tone)* Can I get you something? Water? Mrs. Davis, please get a glass of water.

(MRS. DAVIS hands a glass of water to DR. BROWN who in turn gives it to OLD TENY. She does not respond. He gives the glass back to MRS. DAVIS.)

OLD TENY: Naaa . . . *(Calms down gradually.)*

DR. BROWN: *(To DR. WILLIAMS)* If only I could make her go beyond that sound. *(To OLD TENY)* I'm trying to help you get well, but I need your help. *(In a friendly gesture holds both her hands.)*

OLD TENY: *(Frees her hands.)* Don't hold me. Let me go! Let me go!

DR. BROWN: *(Excited)* She speaks English! *(To OLD TENY)* Where do you want to go, Ms. Ross?

(OLD TENY is silent.)

DR. BROWN: Do you want to go out for a walk? Do you want to go home?

(OLD TENY is silent.)

DR. BROWN: Ms. Ross, say something.

(OLD TENY is silent.)

DR. BROWN: Do you know where you are?

(OLD TENY is silent.)

DR. WILLIAMS: Jim, She may have spoken as a reaction to something. What do you think she reacted to?

DR. BROWN: *(Realizes)* But of course. She reacted to my holding her hands. *(Slowly tries to hold both of* OLD TENY's *hands again.)*

OLD TENY: *(Loud)* Don't touch me!

*(*DR. BROWN *attempts to hold her hands again.)*

DR. WILLIAMS: Is it wise to put her through this?

DR. BROWN: This is the only clue I've had so far. *(Holds both of* OLD TENY's *hands firmly.)*

OLD TENY: *(Frees her hands.)* Let me go! Let me go! *(Loudly)* The scissors. The scissors. Where are my scissors? *(Steps down from her wheelchair, limps around looking for something on the floor. Calms down. Bends and strokes the floor.)* Tarragon . . . It's grown . . . *(Points offstage, terrified.)* Over there . . . they're waiting . . . Look out! Look out! They are approaching . . . *Yegan, yegan!* Get down, get down . . . O.K. I'll put the mud on my face . . . Hold on to my hand. Don't let go . . . *(Shouts)* No . . . no . . . no . . . *(starts crying.)*

DR. BROWN: *(Approaches* OLD TENY *and tries to comfort her.)* It's O.K. *(Takes a tissue and gently wipes her tears.)* It's O.K. *(Holds both her hands.)*

OLD TENY: *(Loud)* Let me go!

DR. BROWN: *(Releases her hands. Pauses attentively. Looks at his hands, then* OLD TENY's. *Extends one hand only and helps her stand up. Brings her back to her wheelchair, strokes her forehead very gently.)* It's O.K., it's O.K.

*(*OLD TENY *calms down gradually.* MRS. DAVIS *walks to her desk, sits down and starts writing.)*

DR. WILLIAMS: Well, Jim, what do you make of this?

DR. BROWN: I don't know; it seems a chaotic world.

DR. WILLIAMS: Waiting to be unraveled.

DR. BROWN: If only I had a clue, then I would understand it.

DR. WILLIAMS: I'm sure you will.

DR. BROWN: I'll try, I'll try, that's if she lets me.

DR. WILLIAMS: *(Walks towards the exit.)* You've always succeeded in the past.

DR. BROWN: Yes, I have.

DR. WILLIAMS: *(Stops and turns.)* By the way, Jim, I didn't see you at the weekly conference this morning.

DR. BROWN: Oh, my God, I forgot all about it.

DR. WILLIAMS: You know you're needed there. The residents missed you. This case has really captivated your entire attention.

DR. BROWN: Well, it's quite an unusual case.

DR. WILLIAMS: Unusual cases demand . . .

DR. BROWN: Crazy psychiatrists.

DR. WILLIAMS: I was going to say . . .

DR. BROWN: Crazy psychiatrists. Come on Joe, say it. Everyone else is saying it.

DR. WILLIAMS: *(Smiles.)* Well, this case is right up your alley. You know what I mean. Let me know if I can be of any help.

DR. BROWN: I need all the help I can get.

DR. WILLIAMS: I'll be there.

DR. BROWN: I'll be in touch with you.

DR. WILLIAMS: Good luck.

DR. BROWN: I'll need more than good luck.

DR. WILLIAMS: *(Referring to* DR. BROWN's *writing pad.)* Are you writing another article?

DR. BROWN: Maybe.

DR. WILLIAMS: If it's anything like your last one, you'll be on the frontiers of psychiatric thinking again.

DR. BROWN: Oh, come on, Joe.

DR. WILLIAMS: No, really. That last article was a mind boggler. My belated congratulations.

DR. BROWN: Thanks.

DR. WILLIAMS: What a catchy title, "The Non-existent Past"! I can't say I understood the entire article. As a matter of fact, I still have difficulty with your concept of "letting the non-existent go." *(Pauses.)* If something doesn't exist, how can you let it go? One of these days, when you have more time, we can talk about it.

DR. BROWN: Sure.

DR. WILLIAMS: Well, let me leave you with her.

DR. BROWN: I'm really glad you called me for this case. Thanks, Joe.

DR. WILLIAMS: You're welcome. See you. *(Exits.)*

DR. BROWN: *(Thinking aloud)* What I need now is this woman's help. *(To* MRS. DAVIS*)* Mrs. Davis.

MRS. DAVIS: Yes, Dr. Brown.

DR. BROWN: I want this patient watched very closely. Please videotape everything she does, and I mean everything.

MRS. DAVIS: Yes, Dr. Brown.

DR. BROWN: I've prescribed a mild sedative, all right?

MRS. DAVIS: I'll make sure she takes it.

DR. BROWN: Thanks. Have a nice weekend. *(Walks toward the exit.)*

MRS. DAVIS: You too, Dr. Brown. *(Walks to her desk. Suddenly.)* Oh, Dr. Brown.

DR. BROWN: Yes, Mrs. Davis.

MRS. DAVIS: *(Takes out a folded piece of paper and extends it to* DR. BROWN.*)* Here's the map.

DR. BROWN: What map?

MRS. DAVIS: The map to her house.

DR. BROWN: How did you know I was going to take a ride there? Am I that transparent?

MRS. DAVIS: No, it's only ten years of working with you.

DR. BROWN: Thank you.

MRS. DAVIS: You're welcome. Have a nice weekend.

DR. BROWN: You too. You know you can call me if you see anything unusual.

MRS. DAVIS: That I know too well.

DR. BROWN: Boy, I *am* transparent. See you. *(Exits.)*

MRS. DAVIS: *(To* OLD TENY*)* Can I get you anything, Ms. Ross?

*(*OLD TENY *is silent.)*

MRS. DAVIS: Now you can rest. *(Turns off the light and exits.)*

(The lights dim slowly.)

SCENE THREE

(Same place. Some of the columns have been rotated in the dark to display the mirrored sides It is evening. The music of Delé Yaman is heard.)

OLD TENY: *(Shows some signs of discomfort and starts her high-pitched sigh)* Naaa . . . Naaa . . . *(She shivers, then quiets down.)*

*(*YOUNG TENY *enters upstage left and in a dreamlike walk crosses the stage slowly diagonally.)*

OLD TENY: *(To* YOUNG TENY, *smiling)* You're here, how nice.

*(*YOUNG TENY *doesn't respond and moves on and exits downstage right.)*

OLD TENY: *(Steps down from her wheelchair and follows* YOUNG TENY. *Looks offstage where* YOUNG TENY *has disappeared. Joyfully.)* Everyone's here. I'm not alone. *(Addressing offstage)* Yes Mama, I'll do Maro's hair. No Mama, I haven't forgotten the tarragon. I don't have flowers but I'll pick some when I go to the fields today.

(The mirrored columns rotate to display the gray sides.)

*(*MARY *enters carrying a flower. She is dressed very neatly in a flower-patterned dress. Her hair is groomed nicely. She recites every word clearly.)*

OLD TENY: *(Turns and looks at Mary.)* Oh, here you are.

MARY: Hi, I'm Mary. Dr. Brown told me you're new here. *(Extends the flower to Old Teny.)* Here, you're welcome. I mean . . . not that I want you to be in the hospital . . . I mean . . . I guess you know what I mean . . .

OLD TENY: *(Smiles.)* How nice, Maro, you brought me a flower. I didn't have time to get any myself.

MARY: You like flowers?

OLD TENY: Let me take a look at you. What a beautiful dress.

MARY: I sewed it myself.

OLD TENY: Look at the design of the flowers, they look exactly like the untouched wild flowers in the fields. Let me take a look at your hair. What have you done to your hair?

MARY: I just put it up.

OLD TENY: Maro, you shouldn't have. Mama says girls should wear their hair long.

MARY: Why?

OLD TENY: Mama says men like girls with long hair. *(She lets MARY's hair down)* Look how beautiful you look. When you get married, I'll fix your hair.

MARY: Married?

OLD TENY: I know you're still young, but you'll be the most beautiful bride in the world when the time comes.

MARY: M-m-married?

OLD TENY: Well, every girl in our village gets married. *(Looks at MARY.)* And you will be so beautiful.

MARY: Dr. Brown tells me that I was . . .

OLD TENY: But Maro, you have to wait your turn, you are my younger sister. I have to get married first. That is our tradition.

MARY: But I was . . .

OLD TENY: Hush, little sister. Now, go and help Mama make dinner. I have to go to the fields, otherwise Mama will be angry with me.

MARY: *(Walks towards the exit.)* I'll come to visit you again.

OLD TENY: Yes, yes, we'll talk. I am going to tell you a secret. But you have to promise not to tell anyone, O.K.?

MARY: A secret?

OLD TENY: Maro, you go now. Mama will be angry if I don't get the tarragon.

MARY: *(Defiant.)* My name is . . . *(Confused.)* Mary? *(Looks at OLD TENY and exits.)*

(OLD TENY looks stage right where YOUNG TENY had exited earlier and limps to her wheel chair.)

(Several columns turn to the mirrored side.)

(Joyful Armenian dancing music is heard. It is bright spring morning downstage. There is the sound of birds chirping.)

(YOUNG TENY *enters, carrying a basket. She is wearing colorful villagers dress and a hat. Has long braided hair. She dances to the music. Takes out a pair of scissors from the basket and starts as if cutting tarragon leaves on the ground. Bends down to wash her face in an imaginary stream.*)

GARO: (*Enters in shepherd attire with a hat—a "pappakh." Throughout the scene, he looks around cautiously checking for danger. Watches* YOUNG TENY *from a distance.* YOUNG TENY *does not notice him.*) Pahrev . . . Hi.

YOUNG TENY: (*Stands up scared. Looks at* GARO.) Pahrev, Hi. You startled me.

GARO: Sorry, I didn't mean to.

YOUNG TENY: I came to pick tarragon for my mother. She dries it for the winter. This area has the best tarragon in the whole wide world.

GARO: How do you know it's the best tarragon in the whole wide world?

YOUNG TENY: I just know. I always pick it here. You see this tree? The tarragon grows right around it. This is my special place. No one else knows about it. I always come here in the spring for tarragon.

GARO: I know.

YOUNG TENY: You pick tarragon here, too?

GARO: No, but I see you when you come to your . . . private place.

YOUNG TENY: Now you are going to tell everyone.

GARO: No, I won't. If you tell me why the tarragon here is the best.

YOUNG TENY: Last summer, my father came back from a far-away country, where he had gone to find work to support us. You should have seen the tarragon he brought back! It was terrible! We gave it to our dog, but he wouldn't eat it.

GARO: I didn't know dogs eat tarragon.

YOUNG TENY: Our dog does . . . if it's good tarragon.

GARO: You must have a smart dog.

YOUNG TENY: The smartest in the whole wide world. Oh, please, don't tell anyone that I come here.

GARO: I won't.

YOUNG TENY: Promise?

GARO: Promise.

YOUNG TENY: How?

GARO: I just gave you my word.

YOUNG TENY: That's not enough.

GARO: What else?

(YOUNG TENY *motions for* GARO *to come closer.* GARO *comes closer.* YOUNG TENY *motions for* GARO *to sit next to her.* GARO *sits down next to her.*)

YOUNG TENY: Put your hand on your heart.

GARO: Why on my heart?

YOUNG TENY: Because the heart knows when you lie.

GARO: So what if it does?

YOUNG TENY: Then it stops and you . . .

GARO: Die?

YOUNG TENY: Well . . . just put your hand on your heart.

GARO: *(Playfully seeks his heart's location then puts his hand on his heart.)* Here it is. What now?

YOUNG TENY: Repeat after me. If I tell anyone . . . *(Looks at* GARO *who is silent.)* Come on, repeat after me. If I tell anyone . . .

GARO: If I tell anyone . . .

YOUNG TENY: About your secret . . .

GARO: About your secret . . .

YOUNG TENY: Then . . . *(Looks at* GARO *again who is silent. Louder.)* Then . . .

GARO: Then . . .

YOUNG TENY: May God burn my path with bolts of fire.

GARO: Don't you think that's a bit too much just for this tarragon?

YOUNG TENY: This is not about tarragon. It is about *my* secret . . . I mean my secret territory.

GARO: What's so secret about your secret territory?

YOUNG TENY: Because no one knows about this place. It's so secluded, so serene. When I come here, I'm all alone with myself. I think, I dream . . . I dream beautiful dreams . . .

GARO: What kind of dreams?

YOUNG TENY: If I told you, they wouldn't be secret anymore.

GARO: All right, then. *(Places his hand over his heart.)* May God burn my path with bolts of fire.

YOUNG TENY: *(Terrified.)* Oh no, may God never do that to you!

GARO: Isn't that what you wanted me to say?

YOUNG TENY: I just tested you to see if you respected my secret.

GARO: Well, did I pass the test?

YOUNG TENY: With flying colors. Now, this place is your secret place too. You too can pick tarragon here.

GARO: Gee, thanks. *(Pauses, then with a serious tone.)* May I tell you something?

YOUNG TENY: You have a secret too?

GARO: You shouldn't come to the fields all by yourself. It's not safe.

YOUNG TENY: Why? I'm only a holler's distance away from our village. If I yell "help," the entire village will come to my aid.

GARO: Don't be so sure. People are busy, you know.

YOUNG TENY: But our villagers . . .

GARO: *(Interrupting.)* I know, they have the best hearing in the whole wide world.

YOUNG TENY: Hey, don't mock my villagers. They are the best people in the . . . *(Pauses.)* Well, they are. Besides, I'm not afraid of the enemy. My father tells me . . . do you see these mountains? My father tells me these mountains protect us from the enemy.

GARO: How could mountains protect you from the enemy?

YOUNG TENY: My father says *(looks around and in a low voice)* that our *fedayees*, our freedom fighters are in these mountains. They protect us from the enemy. My father also says that you can't recognize the *fedayees* when you see them. They look like ordinary people but they are the strongest people in the . . . *(emphasizing)* the whole wide world. They carry weapons, *(in a low voice)* concealed weapons, just in case the enemy . . .

GARO: Your father's right. The *fedayees* do look after people like you. They want people to enjoy their God-given rights, be free to say what they think, enjoy the fruits of their labor, protect their heritage, and practice their religious rights without persecution. This is *our* land. Our ancestors have lived here for thousands of years. It's our right to live on this land to enjoy life here and prosper. We are a minority in this society. Being a minority here is like a curse.

This country has laws . . . what a joke. The rulers, who are supposed to uphold these laws, are the first to bend them to their liking and cause suffering to innocent people like you. I don't want you to suffer. *(Softly.)* A beautiful girl like you should never suffer.

(YOUNG TENY embarrassed, lowers her head.)

GARO: Come now; give me your most beautiful smile, the best in the whole wide world.

YOUNG TENY: *(Smiles.)* My father says . . .

GARO: Yes?

YOUNG TENY: *(Hesitating)* That . . . you are a *fedayee* . . . and . . . you are always in these areas . . . You'll protect me, won't you?

GARO: *(Touches YOUNG TENY's hair tenderly.)* Oh, dearest. If it were up to me, no one in this world would get hurt. *(Gets ready to move away.)* It's almost sundown. Soon it'll be dark. Please go home. *(Walks towards the exit.)* I'll be up in the mountains.

YOUNG TENY: I'll be here tomorrow.

(GARO looks affectionately and exits upstage left.)

YOUNG TENY: May God shower your path with the most beautiful flowers in the world. *(Goes to pick up her basket.)*

(The sound of marching gendarmes is heard.)

(YOUNG TENY, frightened, leaves her basket and the scissors and hides behind OLD TENY's wheelchair.)

OLD TENY: *(Fearful.)* The scissors! The scissors!

(YOUNG TENY *runs downstage, grabs the scissors. The sound of marching gendarmes gets louder. She runs to hide behind the wheelchair holding the scissors in a defensive gesture.*)

(GENDARME *enters upstage right, notices* YOUNG TENY's *basket. Comes close and looks at the basket, looks around, picks up the basket, looks in it. Laughs. Dumps the imaginary content, throws the basket on the floor and exits.*)

(YOUNG TENY *looks around. Makes sure the* GENDARME *is gone, runs and picks up her basket and tries to put the tarragon leaves back in it.*)

TENY'S MOTHER: (*Shouting offstage.*) Varteny, Varteny. (*Enters with an apron on. Shouts.*) Varteny, Varteny, *oor es,* where is that girl?
YOUNG TENY: (*Runs to her mother.*) Yes, Mama.
MOTHER: *Aghchee, oor menatseer?* Girl, where have you been?
YOUNG TENY: I was in the fields, Mama, picking parsley, dill and tarragon.
MOTHER: Let me see the basket.

(YOUNG TENY *extends the basket.*)

MOTHER: There is no parsley, no dill and hardly any tarragon. Is this all you got in four hours?
YOUNG TENY: But Mama, I had to look and choose only the best.
MOTHER: What did you do the rest of the time, dance in the fields? How many times do I have to tell you it is dangerous to come here all alone. Why didn't you bring your brother Armenag with you?
YOUNG TENY: Armenag was playing with his friends in the yard. Besides, Papa says the freedom fighters the *fedayees* will protect us.
MOTHER: Yes, they will, but . . .
YOUNG TENY: And Mama, I met one of them.
MOTHER: What are you saying, *aghchee,* girl?
YOUNG TENY: I saw Garo the shepherd. He is a freedom fighter.
MOTHER: Come to your senses, Varteny.
YOUNG TENY: Honest, Mama. He said he'd be looking after me.
MOTHER: Quiet, child. If your father hears that you have talked to a man in the fields, he'll kill you . . . and he'll kill me too for letting you come out here all alone. You've become a woman. You can't wander around and meet men in the fields. Now, tell me the truth, child, what happened?
YOUNG TENY: Nothing, Mama, we just talked.
MOTHER: What kind of talk?
YOUNG TENY: Plain talk.
MOTHER: What kind of plain talk?
YOUNG TENY: Plain, plain talk.

MOTHER: What else?

(YOUNG TENY *hangs her head.*)

MOTHER: Girl, I asked what else?

YOUNG TENY: He said . . .

MOTHER: Yes?

YOUNG TENY: That I have the most beautiful smile in the whole wide world.

MOTHER: *(Makes the sign of the Cross.)* Oh, my God. What else?

YOUNG TENY: He touched my hair.

MOTHER: *(Makes the sign of the Cross.)* Oh, my God.

YOUNG TENY: Mama, I said, my hair.

MOTHER: *(Extends her hands to the heavens.)* Mary, Mother of God, please protect
    your innocent lamb from the ills of the world. What else?

YOUNG TENY: Nothing.

MOTHER: *(Kneels as she makes the sign of the Cross.)* Oh, my God.

YOUNG TENY: Mama, I said, "nothing."

MOTHER: I heard you. That's worse.

YOUNG TENY: Why is it worse?

MOTHER: Because we don't know what he's thinking. Is he interested in marrying
    you? Is he ready to start a family? Has he talked to his parents about you?

YOUNG TENY: Mama, I'm only sixteen.

MOTHER: I was thirteen when I married your father. By sixteen, I already had you
    and your brother Armenag. What am I going to tell your father?

YOUNG TENY: *(Upset.)* Nothing, Mama. Nothing happened.

MOTHER: Child, innocence is like a crystal, it doesn't just break, it shatters.
    (Touches YOUNG TENY's *face with her hands.)* My love, my innocent baby. I see
    spring has flourished within you. *(Kisses her.)* Let me take a good look at you.
    (They rise.) Turn around.

(YOUNG TENY *turns around slowly.*)

MOTHER: When did you grow so fast?

YOUNG TENY: It took sixteen years, Mama.

MOTHER: *(Pulls* YOUNG TENY *to her chest. Hugs her tightly.)* My baby, my love.

YOUNG TENY: Mama, I'm choking, can't breathe.

(MOTHER *lets* YOUNG TENY *go.*)

YOUNG TENY: *(Pauses. Softly.)* Mama, I'm always thinking about Garo.

MOTHER: *(Pulls* YOUNG TENY *back to her chest and hugs her tightly again.)* I
    should've choked you. *(Releases her.)* Now, let's go, there's work to be done at
    home.

(YOUNG TENY *walks toward stage left.*)

MOTHER: (*Slowly walks backwards looking at* YOUNG TENY.) Varteny, thoughts are like winds, my dearest, they carry us to worlds unknown. Don't let those thoughts carry you. (*Exits stage right.*)

(YOUNG TENY *exits stage left.*)

(*Columns rotate to display gray hospital walls.*)

OLD TENY: (*Gets off her wheelchair, walks towards* MOTHER*'s exit.*) Mama, Mama.
DR. BROWN: (*Runs in.*) It's O.K., it's O.K. Ms. Ross, can you tell me what happened, please?
OLD TENY: Mama, mama, I love him.
DR. BROWN: Whom do you love, Ms. Ross?
OLD TENY: I do, Mama, I really do love Garo.
DR. BROWN: Where is Garo, Ms. Ross? Who is Garo?

(OLD TENY *returns to her wheelchair and sits down.*)

DR. BROWN: Please, Ms. Ross, say something, where are they? And who is this Maro you told a patient of mine about.

(OLD TENY *does not answer.*)

DR. BROWN: Where is Garo? Where is Maro? (*Frustrated*) Oh, God . . . Just when I thought I had a clue, she gives up on me. (*He ponders.*) Maro, Garo . . . What a web, what a web!

(*Lights dim slowly.*)

SCENE FOUR

(*Same place. It is morning.*)

(OLD TENY *in her wheelchair.* DR. BROWN *sitting next to her wheelchair, dozing.*)

DR. WILLIAMS: (*Enters.*) I thought I'd find you here.
DR. BROWN: (*Startled.*) What did I miss now, another conference?
DR. WILLIAMS: Since you asked, you missed an interview with an upcoming resident as well as a departmental conference.

DR. BROWN: I'm really sorry, Joe.

DR. WILLIAMS: So, I have arranged for you to give a talk about your new . . . venture, "The letting go of the non-existent past."

DR. BROWN: And when is that?

DR. WILLIAMS: This Friday afternoon.

DR. BROWN: Joe, be realistic, how can I?

DR. WILLIAMS: Well, you know everything about the subject.

DR. BROWN: You're not serious, are you?

DR. WILLIAMS: I am dead serious. You wrote the paper and it's published. You're surely prepared.

DR. BROWN: But this woman.

DR. WILLIAMS: Well, that's something else I want to talk to you about. I called your home last night you weren't there. Your wife told me you haven't been home for three days. Jim, this room has become your living quarters again and *that* scares me.

DR. BROWN: Don't worry, Joe, I'll be fine.

DR. WILLIAMS: I've heard that before. Jim, I've known you for a long time. I respect your knowledge and conviction tremendously. Whenever you handle unusual cases, you get so obsessed that I wonder what truly drives you. I've come to the realization that the basis of this obsession is *your* own search.

DR. BROWN: What do you mean?

DR. WILLIAMS: You really haven't given up your personal search, have you?

(DR. BROWN *doesn't answer.*)

DR. WILLIAMS: Any progress?

DR. BROWN: Well, she has . . .

DR. WILLIAMS: *(Interrupting.)* I mean about *you.*

DR. BROWN: Joe, right now, this case is more important. The other one . . . *me,* some other time.

DR. WILLIAMS: I'll take a rain check on your story.

DR. BROWN: O.K. Anyway, about this case, all we get are the same few signs: shivers, sweating and those moaning sounds: Na . . . na . . .

DR. WILLIAMS: Painful memories?

DR. BROWN: I guess.

DR. WILLIAMS: Abused childhood? Locked closets? Incest?

DR. BROWN: I don't know. Anything is possible. Abused childhood, incest, rape . . . God knows what else, but definitely a deep affection for her mother. I was watching her movements as she was limping around. At the end she uttered "mama" in an affectionate, clinging manner, "mama, mama" . . .

(OLD TENY *smiles.*)

DR. BROWN: Look, she is smiling. *(Approaches* OLD TENY, *gently strokes her fore-head.)*

OLD TENY: *(Euphorically. Faces right where she imagines her mother.)* Mama, Garon desa, I saw Garo again. *(Pauses. Faces left when imagining Garo.)* My garden has bloomed, Garo. Yes, it's our garden now. No one knows about this place. It's our secret. *(Faces right.)* Mama, Garo told me he loves me. I love him too, Mama. No, no, I didn't tell him that I love him. I know, I know it's not appropriate. *(Faces left.)* Did I call you Garo? Oh, my God, this is the first time I say your name aloud. Of course I've said it many, many times . . . in your absence . . . to myself . . . in my prayers.

DR. BROWN: *(Holds* OLD TENY's *both hands.)* Where is Garo, Ms. Ross?

OLD TENY: *(Pushes* DR. BROWN's *hands away and shouts.)* Don't touch me! Go away . . . Go away . . . *(Stares aimlessly in silence.)*

DR. WILLIAMS: Who's she pushing away?

DR. BROWN: I don't know. She is guarding her private world so tightly. I wish I knew how to get in there.

DR. WILLIAMS: Is she remembering her past?

DR. BROWN: No, I think she is *living* her past. There's nothing about the present. As a matter of fact, there's a total denial of it.

DR. WILLIAMS: Are you thinking what I'm thinking?

DR. BROWN: Yes.

DR. WILLIAMS: Anterograde amnesia.

DR. BROWN: Exactly. Something must have triggered it.

DR. WILLIAMS: Like what?

DR. BROWN: I don't know. Whatever it is, it has caused her past to be her present. She has totally wiped out her present.

DR. WILLIAMS: But why?

DR. BROWN: I don't know. People remember their past, I mean those who do have a past, but they're able to put it back where it belongs. For most people, parting with an existing past is an easy process.

DR. WILLIAMS: How about parting with *your* "non-existent past"?

DR. BROWN: My "non-existent past" is like a black hole. It's as if someone took an eraser and wiped out my past and a part of me. I can never be a complete person. It's the wiped out piece that I need to complete myself. It is painful to have part of you missing.

DR. WILLIAMS: How's your search about your childhood progressing?

DR. BROWN: I thought I had reached back to the edge of nowhere. To the Big Nothing.

You see, Joe, you people with a known past are truly fortunate. You can talk about all phases of your lives. In all likelihood, your parents kept baby books where they recorded in detail the first time you smiled or uttered "mama" or "papa." You may be able to draw your family tree back to . . . oh, I don't know how many generations. My past is me as is. My past begins with me. You have a recorded and documented past, my past is a blank.

All my life I have tried to find out about my birth. My first adoptive parents, the Browns, lost their lives in a fire and all the adoption records were lost. My second adoptive parents told me that the Browns had picked me up from an orphanage and brought me over to this country.

To stop the search and let go of my "non-existent" past was . . . *is* painful. That means I will never find out about a part of me. For a long time I didn't want to give up. That meant defeat. It was more than that. It meant killing part of me.

I had come close to accepting myself from the point of my first adoptive parents, but something stops me now: a faint light, a new hope. This patient prevents me from pulling the trigger that would kill my "non-existent past." This might sound silly, but I envy this woman . . . for having a vivid past.

Joe, you don't know how lucky you are to have all phases of your life.

Well, Dr. Williams, does the article "Non-Existent Past" make sense?

DR. WILLIAMS: *(Patting Dr. Brown on the shoulder.)* The article does, but I'm worried.

DR. BROWN: Worried, why?

DR. WILLIAMS: You, this woman, your unusual attachment to this case, and your neglect of everything else. Do you think you'll see the light you've been waiting for?

DR. BROWN: I don't know, but I sincerely hope so.

DR. WILLIAMS: I hope that light will help you find your complete self and release you from your entrapment.

DR. BROWN: Nicely put, Joe. When and if I find the light, you'll be the first to know. Thanks my friend.

DR. WILLIAMS: I'll send you my bill.

DR. BROWN: At this stage, I'm more concerned about this woman than myself.

DR. WILLIAMS: Any new information?

(MRS. DAVIS enters and goes to her desk and starts writing.)

DR. BROWN: Her neighbors told me she's Armenian.

DR. WILLIAMS: Armenian? With a name like Ross? Don't Armenian last names rhyme with the word "Armenian"?

DR. BROWN: I guess she must have changed it. She came to this country in the twenties after the Armenian Genocide. One and a half million Armenians were brutally massacred by the Ottoman Turks during the First World War and yet not too many people know about it.

DR. WILLIAMS: Yes, I am aware of that inhuman calamity. Jim, I was wondering about the Ross matter. Did you get court permission to enter her house?

DR. BROWN: Yes, I did.

DR. WILLIAMS: Did you find anything relevant?

DR. BROWN: Yes, I did find something quite interesting: a photo album. There was a picture of a group of children in an orphanage. There was an arrow pointing to a little girl. It must have been Ms. Ross. I also spoke with the neighbors. They told me she lived alone, worked and supported herself. Was not married. Seldom spoke about her life, and when she did, she shivered like a terrified child.

      The neighbors also told me her name is Teny. She went to an Armenian church regularly. I called her priest. He told me her name is *(Takes a notebook and spells out)* V-a-r-t-e-n-y, Varteny.

DR. WILLIAMS: Varteny?

(OLD TENY moves.)

DR. BROWN: She heard you. *(Holds OLD TENY's one hand.)* Varteny?

(OLD TENY moves her head to the side.)

DR. BROWN: *(Stands on the side of the wheelchair and whispers in OLD TENY's ears.)* Varteny, Varteny . . .

(OLD TENY holds Doctor Brown's wrists very strongly and pulls herself into an upright position staring straight ahead.)

(Loud screeching music begins as a few of the columns rotate so the mirrors face the audience. The lights turn violet and blue. As the screeching music subsides, joyful dancing music from scene three is heard again.)

(YOUNG TENY enters wearing the same villager's dress with her basket. Circles the stage. Takes out a pair of scissors and starts cutting imaginary tarragon leaves.)

(During the following lines YOUNG TENY's actions reflect OLD TENY's words.)

OLD TENY: This tarragon is so beautiful. Mama will be so happy when she sees me with a basket full of tarragon.

(YOUNG TENY looks around as if waiting for someone.)

OLD TENY: He's late. He told me he'd be here before sundown.

(YOUNG TENY takes out a long woven white scarf from the basket, wraps it around her neck.)

OLD TENY: My own knitting for my first and only love. This'll keep him warm in the mountains. And he'll always feel my touch. I'll surprise him with it.

YOUNG TENY: *(Puts the scarf in the basket.)* I miss you. *(She bends as if to wash her face in a stream.)*

(DR. BROWN takes notes.)

(GENDARME enters, approaches YOUNG TENY and stands behind her, then touches her hair.)

YOUNG TENY: *(Without looking.)* Garo?

(GENDARME strokes YOUNG TENY's hair.)

YOUNG TENY: *(Without looking.)* Garo, last night I told my mother that your mother is going to ask for my hand in marriage. She cried. She said, "My little girl is going to be a bride." I think she's going to tell my father about us tonight. *(Blushing, takes out the white scarf, extends it to the GENDARME without looking.)* This is for you. I knit it with my very own hands. It's the best wool in the country. It came from our own lambs. It'll keep you warm in the mountains.

(GENDARME takes the scarf and wraps it around his neck.)

YOUNG TENY: How does it feel?

(GENDARME is silent.)

YOUNG TENY: Garo, say something. Do you like it?

(GENDARME strokes YOUNG TENY's hair.)

YOUNG TENY: You liked it. Let me see. *(Turns, sees the GENDARME, shouts.)* Garo! *(Pushes GENDARME's hand away and tries to escape.)*

OLD TENY: Run, run, it's the Gendarme!

(GENDARME laughs loudly and cuts her off.)

OLD TENY: The scissors, the scissors . . .

(DRS. BROWN, WILLIAMS, and MRS. DAVIS watch OLD TENY attentively.)

(YOUNG TENY runs for her pair of scissors and picks them up. Holds them in a defensive gesture.)

OLD TENY: Don't come near me, I'll kill you! I'll kill you!

(GENDARME *laughs loudly and gets closer.*)

OLD TENY: Don't touch me!

(YOUNG TENY *makes a stabbing move.* GENDARME *holds both of* YOUNG TENY's *wrists.*)

YOUNG AND OLD TENY: *(Scream together.)* Help! Help!

(OLD TENY *has clutched both of her hands.*)

YOUNG AND OLD TENY: *(Together.)* Let me go! Let me go!

(GENDARME *throws* YOUNG TENY *forcefully to the ground. He looks at her and starts untying his belt.*)

(*Loud screeching music begins. Blackout.*)

OLD TENY: *(At the top of her lungs.)* No . . . no . . . no . . . !

(*The music ends in total darkness.*)
(*The columns turn to hospital walls.*)

SCENE FIVE

(*Next morning.*)

(OLD TENY *in a wheelchair center stage.* DRS. WILLIAMS AND BROWN *enter.*)

DR. WILLIAMS: All night long I thought about Mrs. Ross.
DR. BROWN: Et tu?
DR. WILLIAMS: What an agonizing experience. What could have triggered her anterograde?
DR. BROWN: Wait a minute.
DR. WILLIAMS: What?
DR. BROWN: *(Addressing offstage.)* Mrs. Davis.
MRS. DAVIS: *(Enters.)* Yes, Dr. Brown?
DR. BROWN: Where are Ms. Ross's belongings?
MRS. DAVIS: *(Picks up the bag.)* Here. *(Looks inside.)* There's a purse and some clothes.

DR. BROWN: Anything else?

MRS. DAVIS: No.

DR. BROWN: What's in her purse?

MRS. DAVIS: A few dollars and some change.

DR. BROWN: What else?

MRS. DAVIS: *(Looks inside the purse, takes out a piece of crumpled paper.)* This.

DR. BROWN: *(Takes it, looks at it.)* What is this? Joe, can you make anything out of this writing?

DR. WILLIAMS: *(Looks at it.)* No. It's a foreign alphabet.

DR. BROWN: Of course.

DR. WILLIAMS: What now?

MRS. DAVIS: The police report said that she had a piece of paper clutched in her hand. This is it. The E.R. nurse must have put it in her purse.

DR. WILLIAMS: I wonder what it says?

DR. BROWN: It could be something important, whatever it is.

DR. WILLIAMS: Yes, if she didn't let go of it.

DR. BROWN: That's right. I'm going . . . *(Gets ready to go.)*

DR. WILLIAMS: Where to, Jim?

DR. BROWN: To her church. I'm going to take this paper to her priest to read it for me. This is my last hope.

DR. WILLIAMS: You might be right.

DR. BROWN: I know I am, otherwise . . .

DR. WILLIAMS: Otherwise what, Jim? You'd better be sure, damn it. I don't want another hellish experience in my department.

DR. BROWN: Joe, you won't . . .

DR. WILLIAMS: Only if you promise.

(DR. BROWN is silent.)

DR. WILLIAMS: Jim, let me remind you . . . no, let me tell you. No more experimental drugs in this department. The Medical Board banned you from using that drug. *(In a firm tone.)* No experimental drugs. Is that clear, Jim? You know what will happen to you this time.

DR. BROWN: I'm not the issue here.

DR. WILLIAMS: Yes, you are. Your probation is still in effect. I'm supposed to be overseeing your treatments. Honestly, if I didn't think you were a brilliant psychiatrist, I would have fired you long time ago. I defended you with all my power. I jeopardized my position and career for you. You promised me never to use that drug again.

DR. BROWN: Yes, I promised you. But I have to be honest with myself. I can't sacrifice scientific truth for prestige.

DR. WILLIAMS: You didn't hear a word I said, did you?

DR. BROWN: I heard you. But let me say this. If, that is *if* I have to use that drug again, I'll take all the responsibility, I'll leave this hospital and save you the embarrassment, regardless of whether she gets well or not.

DR. WILLIAMS: She won't get well, Jim.

DR. BROWN: *(In a burst of anger.)* How do you know that? *(Pauses.)* Trust me, please.

DR. WILLIAMS: The last time I trusted you the patient died, Jim.

DR. BROWN: The cause of death of that patient was *not* the drug, Joe.

DR. WILLIAMS: No one accepted your hypothesis then and no one will accept it now.

DR. BROWN: But I have proof of my hypothesis now.

DR. WILLIAMS: What are you saying?

DR. BROWN: I'm telling you; the patient didn't die because of that drug. I have solid proof. I'll tell you when I come back. Can you wait?

DR. WILLIAMS: *(Angry)* No, I can't wait.

DR. BROWN: *(Angry)* Two more hours? *(Apologizing.)* I'm sorry, Joe. Let me run now. *(Walks toward the exit, remembering something.)* I guess I'll be missing yet another conference. Joe, I'll catch up, don't worry. Trust me, I won't let you down. *(Exits.)*

DR. WILLIAMS: *(Looking after* DR. BROWN, *shaking his head.)* You son of a bitch.

MRS. DAVIS: *(Astonished.)* Dr. Williams, I've never heard *you* swear.

DR. WILLIAMS: This is not swearing. Well, yes it is. Doctors swear too, you know.

MRS. DAVIS: May I say something, sir?

DR. WILLIAMS: Go ahead.

MRS. DAVIS: I'm really glad you stuck up for him. He won't let you down. Besides he's terrific, we can't afford losing him.

DR. WILLIAMS: That son of a . . . I couldn't agree with you more.

OLD TENY: There . . . I want to go there . . .

DR. WILLIAMS: Where, Ms. Ross, where?

OLD TENY: There . . . I want to go there . . .

DR. WILLIAMS: *(Comforting.)* You'll get there. You'll get there. Once you get well, you can go anywhere you desire. Now, you can rest. *(To* MRS. DAVIS.*)* Please let that . . . Jim know about this. That son of a gun, he knows I have a soft spot for him. My protégé, my pride. I'll see him tomorrow. *(Walks towards the exit.)*

MRS. DAVIS: *(Happily saluting.)* Yes, sir.

DR. WILLIAMS: *(Looks at* MRS. DAVIS.*)* Mrs. Davis, I didn't know you had been in the military.

MRS. DAVIS: I haven't, sir . . . Dr. Williams. It was . . . instead of a hug . . . I guess . . . sir.

DR. WILLIAMS: *(Smiles.)* The hug is accepted. *(Salutes back and exits.)*

OLD TENY: There . . . I want to go there . . .

MRS. DAVIS: I'm sure you'll get there, Ms. Ross, you'll get there.

(Lights dim slowly.)

SCENE SIX

(The same place. Late morning.)

MARY: *(Enters. She is dressed nicely. Groomed neatly. Walks toward* OLD TENY.*)* Hi, I'm Mary. I think I told you that, but you kept on calling me something else, I don't remember what.

*(*OLD TENY *is silent.)*

MARY: I'm told you don't have any family. Apparently I do. They used to visit me, but they've stopped. Well, you see, I've been here for two months now. They've told Dr. Brown that they're busy. I think they're lying. They're cheap. They don't want to bring me roses. Only cheap flowers. You see, I love roses. Roses are beautiful, full of life. But I understand them, my family I mean. Who wants to waste time visiting patients like us? No one. We are a bunch of pathetic people. They throw us into these institutions and forget about us. Does anyone visit you?

*(*OLD TENY *is silent.)*

MARY: Oh, I forgot, you don't have a family. Don't worry I'll visit you. Here, I brought you a flower. I really didn't buy it. I don't have money. It was given to me. You don't mind if we share it, do you?

*(*OLD TENY *does not answer.)*

MARY: You know why I came to the hospital? I lost my memory. I look in the mirror and it's like I'm looking at someone else. I don't remember anything from my past. The doctor tells me I'll get it back one day. I don't know what kind of a past I had. Only one woman visits me now. They tell me she's my sister. Poor girl, she tries so hard to convince me that she is my sister. *(In a low voice.)* You know I pretend that I believe her, but I really don't. For all I know, you could be my sister.

(Few of the columns rotate to have the mirrors face the audience.)

OLD TENY: Sister.
MARY: You have a sister?
OLD TENY: Sister . . . Do you remember the war?
MARY: The war? What war?
OLD TENY: The war, Maro, when we were walking through the fields.
MARY: The fields?
OLD TENY: Try sister, try hard, how can you forget that night?

MARY: What night?

OLD TENY: That awful night. Come on, let's go. (*Gets out of the wheelchair, holds* MARY's *hand and leads her around the stage.*)

(OLD TENY's *pounding heartbeat is heard, followed by the sounds of gunshots and rushing water.*)

OLD TENY: It was dark. The enemy was behind us. We came to a river and we had to cross it. Our brothers and sisters were holding hands together. (*Holds* MARY's *hand tightly.*) Come on, let's go.

(*Thunderous gunshots.*)

OLD TENY: Get down! Get down, Maro. Watch out, the enemy's approaching. (OLD TENY *is holding* MARY's *hand and taking her around the stage.*) We have to cross the river before the enemy catches up to us. *Tserkus perné*, hold on tight. We have to cross the river, or else we'll drown. Move against the waves. Hold on, little sister. I'll take care of you. We'll get there. Hold on tight, Maro.

(MARY *follows without resisting. She is confused.*)

OLD TENY: Now, you see? We crossed the river. *Hashvé*, count our brothers and sisters. Is every one here? (*She looks around and calls names.*) Apraham, Noono, Manoog . . . Where is Armenag? Oh, my God . . . Where's Armenag? He's missing. Let's go, little sister, let's go and look for him. I can't walk. *Vodkus*, my foot, my foot hurts so much. (*Touches her foot.*) Maro, I'm shot. I can't walk. (*Calls loudly.*) Armenag . . . *Oor es?* Where are you? (*Lets go of* MARY's *hand.*) I'm tired. I'm really tired. (*Limps back to her wheelchair.*) Go, go and look in the river, see if you can find him.

MARY: (*Walks away. Looks around.*) Find him? Find who? (*Walks back to* OLD TENY *and speaks gently.*) I'll look for . . . (*in confusion*) him . . . in the river . . . (*Walks downstage. Looks around.*) Him? The river?

(*Columns rotate to display the hospital room.*)

(DR. BROWN *enters.*)

MARY: (*Notices* DR. BROWN.) I did what you told me, Dr. Brown.

DR. BROWN: Thanks, Mary.

MARY: She called me Maro like I told you last time. She called me sister again. Is she my sister?

DR. BROWN: (*Writes down in his pad.*) I don't think she is your biological sister, Mary.

MARY: But she called me sister. Doesn't she know who her sister is?

DR. BROWN: Yes she does, Mary. It is kind of complicated. You must have come at a time when she was reliving her past.

MARY: So, she does remember her past.

DR. BROWN: Not only does she remember her past, she's engulfed in her past.

MARY: She's lucky. I want my past, Doctor.

DR. BROWN: And you'll get it, Mary.

MARY: I don't want to live without a past.

DR. BROWN: I fully understand.

MARY: *(To* OLD TENY*)* You understand too, right? We can't be whole if a part of us is missing! And . . . if we're not whole, then we can't be happy! This is not hard to understand, right? *(Bends over* OLD TENY *and gently strokes her arms.)*

DR. BROWN: *(Takes out his notebook and writes.)* Title: "The Self: The Sea of Tranquility." *(Looks at* MARY *and* OLD TENY*.)* What an intricate, pathetic trio: Teny is living in her past, Mary has forgotten her existing past, and I . . . am searching for my non-existent past. When will this labyrinthine search for tranquility come to an end?

MARY: *(To* DR. BROWN*)* You know, it felt good to be her sister. Doc, she was so concerned and caring. This is the kind of sister I wish I could have. And you know something else, Doc?

DR. BROWN: What, Mary? *(Stops writing and looks at* MARY*.)*

MARY: For a moment I felt that I really was her sister. Doc, she was talking about wars and rivers . . . *(pauses.* DR. BROWN *resumes writing)* and running away. She thought she was shot in the foot. Then she got tired and went and sat down. Poor soul.

(Approaches OLD TENY *and whispers in her ear.)* One day, when I remember my past, I really wish you'll be part of it. Good night, sister. Good night, Dr. Brown.

DR. BROWN: Good night, Mary.

*(*MARY *exits.)*

DR. BROWN: *(Looks after* MARY *then goes and sits by* OLD TENY, *holds her hand, strokes it gently.)* Teny, I need to get into your past and to do that, I need your help. Do you understand me? *(Takes out an audio cassette and a portable tape player from his briefcase. Puts the tape in the tape player.)* Teny, I want you to go to your home, the home you love so much. Your priest told me you liked this music. *(Plays the tape. It is "Delé Yaman," the song.)* Do you know this song?

OLD TENY: Yes. My mother sang this song to my sisters and brothers.

DR. BROWN: How many sisters and brothers did you have?

OLD TENY: I had three sisters and two brothers.

DR. BROWN: Where are your brothers and sisters now?

(OLD TENY *starts crying.*)

DR. BROWN: Varteny, please answer me if you can. Where are your brothers and sisters now?
OLD TENY: They are dead.
DR. BROWN: All of them?
OLD TENY: Except for my younger brother Armenag who got lost, all the rest died.
DR. BROWN: How did they die?
OLD TENY: *(Slowly.)* The gendarmes . . .
DR. BROWN: The gendarmes?
OLD TENY: Yes, the Turkish gendarmes. Vicious, terrible and cruel men with guns and swords. The swords, sharp and shining.

The gendarmes came to our village, gathered all the men and lined them up and shot them one by one.

They tied my father to a water mill and turned him round and round all night long till he was drowned.

And then, and then, they brought my uncle's pregnant wife to the village square and stripped her of her clothes and gambled on the sex of the baby she was carrying. Then . . . they cut her open with their swords . . .

That same day, they burned our village. *(Steps down from her wheelchair and limps upstage to one of the panels that has been turned to the mirrored side. Terrified.)* It was chaos. Everyone was running to escape death.

My mother strapped my newborn brother on her back. We left everything behind and ran away . . .

(DR. BROWN *follows* OLD TENY *and stands next to her, watching her moves.*)

(*Some more columns rotate and mirrors face the audience. Red is the dominant color on the stage.*)

YOUNG TENY: *(Enters running. She is out of breath. Looks back to where she came from.)* Mama, mama, hurry up . . .
MOTHER: *(Enters. She is out of breath too. Has a baby strapped to her back.)* Varteny, Varteny.
YOUNG TENY: Yes, Mama.
MOTHER: Come dear. God knows what's going to happen. I branded your sisters and brothers. In case we get lost, all of you will have the same mark. Open up your shoulder, my dearest. *(She takes a small knife from her belt.)* This is going to hurt, Varteny, but it is going to be a permanent scar. Close your eyes and think of beautiful things. *(She makes a small cut in Teny's shoulder.)*
YOUNG TENY: *(Clenches her teeth bearing the pain.)* Mama, let's hurry, let's catch up with the rest of the villagers.
MOTHER: *(Tries to walk, collapses.)* Varteny, let me put this mud on your face. *(She

puts streaks of mud on Teny's face.) You should look ugly, otherwise the gendarmes will take you. Let's run, child, the enemy's getting close. *(Tries to get up and collapses from exhaustion.)*

YOUNG TENY: Mama, let me carry the baby. You are weak, you can't even walk, you just gave birth yesterday.

MOTHER: Girl, let's go. There's no time, the enemy is getting closer, let's run. *(She can hardly walk.)*

YOUNG TENY: Mama, let me help you. Mama, lean on me.

(Gunshots.)

(MOTHER and YOUNG TENY both duck until the gunshots subside.)

MOTHER: *(Looks up.)* Varteny, are you all right?

YOUNG TENY: Yes, Mama, how about you?

MOTHER: Let's run.

YOUNG TENY: Yes, Mama.

MOTHER: Varteny.

YOUNG TENY: What, Mama?

MOTHER: What's the wetness on my back?

YOUNG TENY: *(Checks her mother's back. Yells.)* Mama!

MOTHER: What, child?

(YOUNG TENY sobbing.)

MOTHER: How's the baby?

YOUNG TENY: Mama, he's shot. I think he's dead. *(Makes the sign of the Cross.)*

MOTHER: *(Makes the sign of the Cross. Her first hand movement to her forehead is out of habit. For the next movement, she clenches her fingers into a fist, and makes the sign of the Cross with obvious anger.)* My baby. *(Anxious.)* Varteny, you run. Run and be saved. I'll catch up with you later.

YOUNG TENY: No, Mama. I'll stay with you.

MOTHER: No, child, listen to me. The enemy is almost here. Run, run, I tell you.

YOUNG TENY: But, Mama . . .

MOTHER: Run, my dearest, run. I want to rest for a while. I'll join you later.

YOUNG TENY: *(Starts to leave, stops, runs back and hugs her mother.)* Mama, you'll catch up with me, won't you? *(Exits.)*

MOTHER: *(Drags herself after YOUNG TENY shouting.)* Run, run, *azadeer* . . . be saved. *(Exits.)*

(Columns rotate back to gray walls.)

OLD TENY: *(Looks offstage where her mother disappeared, then turns to* DR. BROWN.*)* My baby brother was shot on my mother's back. That was the last time I saw my mother. *(Limps back to her wheelchair.)*
No one survived from my family. They are all dead. I don't know what happened to my younger brother Armenag. I'm so tired.
DR. BROWN: I understand. Rest now.
OLD TENY: I can't rest. That nightmare. The gendarme. He has me in a web. I can't get out . . .
DR. BROWN: You can get out of the web if you let me help you.
OLD TENY: Really?

*(*MRS. DAVIS *enters.)*

DR. BROWN: *(Opens his briefcase, looks at* MRS. DAVIS, *takes out a syringe.)* Now, you are going to encounter your biggest horror. You'll be all alone and it's up to you, Teny, to stay or get out of that web of horror. *(Injects the drug into* OLD TENY*'s vein.)*

*(*OLD TENY *goes into convulsions, and then quiets down.)*

DR. BROWN: *(Puts the syringe in his briefcase. To* MRS. DAVIS.*)* Are you ready to be part of her emotional perception?
MRS. DAVIS: Yes, I am.
DR. BROWN: *(Takes out a white veil and hands it to* MRS. DAVIS.*)* Here, cover yourself completely. *(Takes out a black veil and exits stage left.)*

*(*MRS. DAVIS *exits stage right.)*

(Lights dim slowly and fade to scene seven.)

SCENE SEVEN

(The scene is dimly lit with blue lighting on the background. The screeching music starts.)

(A few columns rotate and mirrors face the audience.)

*(*OLD TENY *starts shivering.* YOUNG TENY *enters from stage right. Covered with a white veil totally. Her face cannot be seen. Only her silhouette is visible.* GENDARME *enters from stage left fully covered in black. His face is obscured. Only his silhouette is visible.)*

OLD TENY: It's him. It's him. The gendarme. He's here.

(GENDARME *approaches* YOUNG TENY.)

OLD TENY: (*Shouts.*) Don't touch me!

(*Gendarme gets closer to* YOUNG TENY.)

(YOUNG TENY *tries to get away.*)

(GENDARME *cuts her off. Holds her hands and throws her on the ground.*)

OLD TENY: (*Shouts.*) Don't touch me! (*Gets out of the wheelchair, limps toward the* GENDARME *and stabs him in the back as if she had a knife. With every stab she cries out distinctly.*) This is for my mother. This is for my father. This is for my family. And *this* is for *me*, for *me*, for *me* . . .

(GENDARME *falls.* YOUNG TENY *stands up, looks at* OLD TENY.)

OLD TENY: (*Looks at* YOUNG TENY.) He is dead. He is dead. I killed him. I killed him. You are free. (*Cries in happiness and limps back to her wheelchair.*)

(*Blackout.*)

(*Columns rotate to gray walls.*)

SCENE EIGHT

(*The same place. Evening.*)

(OLD TENY *sits in the wheelchair.* DR. BROWN *and* MRS. DAVIS *enter from stage right.*)

DR. BROWN: Mrs. Davis.
MRS. DAVIS: Yes, Dr. Brown.
DR. BROWN: Thank you for helping her.
MRS. DAVIS: Thanks for giving me a chance to be part of her imagination.
DR. BROWN: It worked. You were great as Teny.
MRS. DAVIS: And you played a great *vicious* gendarme, Dr. Brown.
OLD TENY: (*Content.*) I killed him, Doc.

(DR. BROWN *hugs her affectionately.*)

OLD TENY: No more nightmares. The gendarme can't hurt me anymore.

DR. BROWN: No, Varteny, he can't.

OLD TENY: *(To* MRS. DAVIS*)* He is finally dead and I'm free.

MRS. DAVIS: That's wonderful, Varteny, now both of us can go to the garden, watch the birds, and feed the geese. *(Walks to her desk.)*

OLD TENY: Doc, you know, although I'm relieved, I'm very sad.

DR. BROWN: We take a step at a time, *Vart.*

OLD TENY: What did you call me?

DR. BROWN: Vart.

OLD TENY: My little brother Armenag used to call me Vart, it means rose.

DR. BROWN: I know.

OLD TENY: How do you know, Dr. Brown?

DR. BROWN: I read the letter your brother Armenag had sent you.

OLD TENY: You read Armenian?

DR. BROWN: *(Laughs)* No, I don't. Your priest read it to me.

OLD TENY: Then it's not a dream? I didn't imagine it? The letter is real?

DR. BROWN: Varteny, it's real. Your brother Armenag is alive.

OLD TENY: In his letter he says he has six children. He has named them after us and has kept the family name Bedrossian. My last name was changed to Ross when I came to the States. I want to go there . . . to Armenia . . . to see my brother and his family.

DR. BROWN: I'm sure you will go there.

*(*DR. WILLIAMS *enters.)*

OLD TENY: I searched for him . . . for fifty years . . . I got in touch with every search agency but to no avail. I finally gave up and accepted his loss. And all of a sudden from nowhere I receive this letter and he comes to life. Now I blame myself for giving up.

DR. BROWN: I understand.

DR. WILLIAMS: *(To* DR. BROWN*)* Good morning, Jim.

DR. BROWN: Good morning, Joe. Teny, this is Dr. Williams.

DR. WILLIAMS: Good morning Ms. Ross, you look *wonderful.*

OLD TENY: Thanks to Dr. Brown, I *feel* wonderful.

DR. WILLIAMS: I'm glad to hear that.

DR. BROWN: Teny, Dr. Williams was the one who assigned me to your case.

OLD TENY: He must be a great doctor to have chosen you.

DR. BROWN: That he is.

DR. WILLIAMS: Not as great as Dr. Brown.

DR. BROWN: Joe, it works. It really does. The drug works. *(Pauses.)* Now you can fire me.

(During the following conversation, DR. WILLIAMS *and* MRS. DAVIS *turn several*

panels so that the mirrored sides face the audience. They do not turn the three center panels.)

DR. WILLIAMS: Fire you? And go down in history as the greatest fool of them all? We still have a long path together. *(Walks to stage right and turns two of the panels to the mirrored side.)* By the way, Jim, your lecture, the one about . . .

DR. BROWN: I know, it is this afternoon. I'll be there.

DR. WILLIAMS: *(Turns one more panel to the mirrored side. Stands by it.)* We have a new case, Jim.

DR. BROWN: A new case?

DR. WILLIAMS: This one is *mine*. It will be the challenge of *my* life, the acme of my career. We'll discuss it later. See you at the lecture.

DR. BROWN: Thanks, Joe.

DR. WILLIAMS: For what?

DR. BROWN: For everything.

(MRS. DAVIS turns other panels to the mirrored side.)

DR. WILLIAMS: Don't thank me *yet*. *(To* OLD TENY*)* Now, you stay well, Ms. Ross. A whole new exciting life is awaiting you.

OLD TENY: Thanks, Dr. Williams.

DR. WILLIAMS: You're most welcome. *(Exits.)*

(MRS. DAVIS exits after DR. WILLIAMS.)

DR. BROWN: Teny, I'm really glad that you came out of your grief.

OLD TENY: This whole thing is so confusing. I can't understand it at all.

DR. BROWN: It's not easy.

OLD TENY: Dr. Brown, why am I so fragmented?

DR. BROWN: We are all fragmented, only in different dimensions.

OLD TENY: Dr. Brown?

DR. BROWN: Yes, Teny.

OLD TENY: Give me your hand.

DR. BROWN: *(Smiling.)* One or both hands?

OLD TENY: Both. It doesn't matter anymore.

DR. BROWN: *(Extends his hands.)* Here.

OLD TENY: *(Grabs them affectionately.)* Thanks.

DR. BROWN: Thank you.

OLD TENY: *(Looks at Dr. Brown's wrist.)* What is this scar on your wrist?

DR. BROWN: Oh, that. My adoptive parents told me I had it when they adopted me.

OLD TENY: I thought you too were branded.

DR. BROWN: Branded?

OLD TENY: Yeah, like me. (*Shows the scar on her shoulder.*) See? My brother Armenag has one too. That's what he says in his letter, right?

DR. BROWN: Right.

OLD TENY: Dr. Brown, does your past visit you like mine?

DR. BROWN: (*Pauses, looks at the scar on his wrist.*) I wish it would, Varteny, I wish it would.

OLD TENY: Dr. Brown, my loved ones, will they visit me again?

DR. BROWN: They'll always visit you. They are part of your life, part of your memory. (*Hangs his head and holds it in his hands.*)

(*The lights change to blue. The music of "Delé Yaman" begins and continues until the end.*)

(MOTHER *enters downstage right and crosses the stage. Walks to one of the three center panels. Turns the left panel to the mirrored side and exits through the turn.*)

OLD TENY: Mama . . . Mama.

DR. BROWN: (*Raises his head and whispers.*) Mama.

(GARO *enters downstage left and crosses the stage. Walks to one of the three center panels. Turns the right panel to the mirrored side and exits through the turn.*)

OLD TENY: Garo, my love.

(YOUNG TENY *enters, wearing the same white dress as in scene two.*)

OLD TENY: It's you. It *is* you. It's *always* been you.

(YOUNG TENY *walks upstage center, turns the last panel to the mirrored side and exits through the turn. All of the panels now have their mirrored sides facing the audience.*)

(OLD TENY *moves her wheelchair to where* YOUNG TENY *exited. Faces the mirrors with her back to the audience.*)

DR. BROWN: (*Looks at* TENY. *Gathers his papers. Takes his briefcase. Walks toward the exit. Turns and looks at* TENY.) Let them rest, Varteny. Let them rest. (*Pauses.*) You too, Varteny. Rest. (*Exits.*)

(*Lights dim slowly to a single light on* OLD TENY. *Then blackout. "Delé Yaman" continues in the dark.*)

The End

DELÉ YAMAN

An authentic Armenian love song from the region of Van. Transcribed by Komitas.
The musical notes are from Vaghinak Chakmishian, *Song Book* (Yerevan, Armenia: Anahid Press, 1992). Transliterated into English and loosely translated.

> *Delé yaman—Oh my heart,*
> *Mer toon, tser tan dimats, dimats—In the house across the way.,*
> *Delé yaman—Oh my heart,*
> *Herik anes achcov imats—Enough of flirting with your eyes,*
> *Yaman, yaman, yar—Dearest, dearest love.*
> *Delé yaman—Oh my heart,*
> *Arev dipav Masis sarin—Like sun rays reflecting Ararat's snow.*
> *Delé yaman—Oh my heart,*
> *Karot munatsi yes im yarin—I yearn with love for you,*
> *Yaman, yaman, yar—Dearest, dearest love.*

WILLIAM ROLLERI AND
ANNA ANTARAMIAN

THE ARMENIAN QUESTION

A Play in Two Acts

PREFACE: THE DEVELOPMENT OF THE ARMENIAN QUESTION

The Voices of the Children

Early in 1977, when the young, talented director Anna Antaramian asked me if I wanted to collaborate on a play about the Turkish genocide against the Armenian people, my immediate reaction was typical of most Americans: What genocide? Thus began my education in historical events that would overwhelm me. They still do.

Anna had been asked by then Archbishop Torkom Manoogian, Primate of the Diocese of the Armenian Church of America (Eastern) at Saint Vartan's Cahtedral in New York (now Patriarch of Jerusalem) if she would team up with a playwright to mount a theatrical production for commemoration of Martyrs Week, coming within two months. Time was a problem. But the enticement for me was the inescapable sense of injustice being inflicted on Armenians. Nothing attracts a playwright as does injustice, and there is no injustice that can compare to the scale and enormity of genocide.

We developed a fictional "container" in which much of the world's population was starving and threatened with extinction due to a global drought engendered by humankind's compulsion to destroy its own living environment. Thus we worked within a scenario in which the government of Turkey is supplicant to a United Nations agency for famine relief and is confronted by Armenian genocide survivors in the Diaspora demanding justice for food. But even before pen touched paper, Anna was recruiting actors. She operated on the principle: "Build it, and they will come." They came even before it was built: Anahid, Lynne Cherry, John P. Clark, Glenn R. Czako, Anita Khanzadian, Joseph Ragno, Jane Roberts, Ed Setrakian, Richard Sisk, Paul Tankersley, and Martin Zurla.

Then came the genocide survivors. Anna had put out the word in the community that we wanted to interview them. We wanted them to tell us their *childhood* stories of torture, mass atrocity, and murder. These "children" came as people bent by age and infirmity, some who could not walk very well but who would have crawled up marble staircases to sit before a tape recorder and tell their stories for generations they would never meet.

Pathos and rage possessed us. Actors turned away in tears as the old people struggled with their stories. We realized then that numbers on paper would not convey that sense of outrage to audiences. Only these epic horror stories could do that. Even as a non-Armenian, there is an inner place that still pangs when I conjure up those haunted faces recounting the unthinkable, courageous souls who took those memories to bed with them every night of their lives and woke up with them every morning.

Anna and I set to work synthesizing the experiences of these "children" into mature theatrical characters, and even though we did our best to lend a sense of authenticity to the theatrical "container" of a courtroom environment, their stories and the depth of their emotions created a heartbeat for this play that persists to this day. As co-authors, Anna and I must acknowledge that the original production was truly a collaborative work of theatre artists and seekers of justice, and not the least of these were the "children."

The 1977 Equity Showcase of the play in NYC was quite successful, playing to sold-out audiences at several houses located in the West Village, including the art colony at Westbeth. But there was no question that the original script "played to the chorus." The script was therefore "retired" and spent almost twenty-five years on a shelf.

It was in the wake of the 9/11 tragedy that Ed Shockley, artistic director of the American Concert Theatre (as well as the Philadelphia Dramatists Center) chose to mount staged readings of the original script, the first of these at the Community Education Center in Philadelphia in October 2001. The "team" was joined by veteran theatrical producer Lee Pucklis at that time. Almost at the same time, publicity efforts attracted the attention of noted dramatist and professor of theatre Dr. Nishan Parlakian, who for many years served as artistic director of the N.Y. Diocese, and he offered to include the play in this anthology.

Subsequent readings and staged readings took place at the Playground of the Adrienne Theatre (October 2002) and the New Freedom Theatre (March 2003) and at Saint Vartan Cathedral in New York City (May 2003). Each of these experiences resulted in significant revisions under the guiding hand of dramaturg Ed Shockley (who also directed). Co-authors Rolleri and Antaramian coordinated revisions in cyberspace. Critical feedback was also provided by the InterAct Theatre Writers' Group under the direction of InterAct Theatre (Philadelphia) Literary Manager Larry Loebell.

It was due to the heroic efforts of Sam Azadian with the cooperation of Hirant Gulian, both of the Mid-Atlantic Chapter of the Knights of Vartan, that interest in hosting the New York event was generated. Plans are currently underway for the next staged reading to be hosted by the Knights of Vartan, this one on 19 October 2003 at Holy Trinity Armenian Apostolic Church in Cheltenham, Penn., coordinated by Harry Andonian with the cooperation of Dr. Andre Garabedian, Chairman of the Inter-Communal Committee.

The events of September 11, 2001, do not belong solely to Americans, nor do the nightmare years of the Holocaust belong solely to Jews. All civilized people everywhere own these historic happenings, and they are universally, though sadly, acknowledged. Most of the enlightened nations on earth have also acknowledged the Turkish genocide of Armenians during World War I and in so doing prevail upon the Turkish government to cease the hypocrisy of denial. However, American presidents, be they politically left or right, have resisted repeated congressional resolutions to do the right thing. We applaud such recent works as *Nine Armenians*, *Beast on the Moon*, and *Ararat*, as well as the authors of works contained in this volume—since we are firm in the conviction that the arts must amplify The Voices of the Children so that they will be heard.

WILLIAM ROLLERI

ABOUT THE AUTHORS

William Rolleri authored a number of dramas produced off-off-Broadway in New York City where he served as managing director of the Raft Theatre (late 1970s, early 1980s) after studying under Israel Horowitz at the City University of New York (1973–1976). By 1998, he enrolled as a graduate student at the University of Delaware, joined the Philadelphia Dramatists Center (PDC) in 1999 and resumed playwriting, co-authoring *Maggie's Stand*, the first part of a trilogy, which won a statewide community theater competition the same year. The second part of the trilogy, *Eight Ball, Wrong Pocket*, followed quickly. His *Brothers Flanagan* won finalist status in the InterAct Theatre New Play Festival in Philadelphia during 2001–2002 season and was given a reading at the Hedgerow Theatre in Media, Penn. (May 2002) with a view to another reading at the Abingdon Theatre in New York City. In various stages of development are full-length works such as *Random Selection*, *Tooth of the Lion*, *Bless Me Father*, and *Cassandra*. The *Armenian Question*—written in collaboration with director Anna Antaramian was first produced in New York City in 1977 and was revised for the American Concert Theatre and the PDC for staging in the spring of 2003 in Philadelphia and for inclusion in this anthology.

Anna Antaramian spent considerable time and effort in the late 1970s and early 1980s establishing the Armenian Repertory Theatre (ART) which produced a series of readings of new plays as well as performances of classic Armenian folktales scripted by her and her husband Patrick McGuire. She directed several plays at Raft Theatre in Westbeth at the same time. She left for the Midwest in 1986, and between then and now she has become professor of theatre at Northeastern Illinois University in Chicago, where she has directed numerous plays and a musical. At Northeastern Illinois, she has been director of theater (both artistic and managing) for the university's theatre season. In 1998, she received a grant from Northeastern Illinois to do theatre research in Ireland and, in 2002, she was granted a sabbatical to do research on Hallie Flanagan and the Federal Theatre Project in Washington, D.C., and New York City. In 1996 she was elected president of the Illinois Theatre Association and has been on the ITA board for ten years. In 2001, she received the ITA award for exceptional work in the University/ College Theatre division. She has directed a musical for the Rocky Mountain Repertory Theatre each summer since 1995. She lives in Wisconsin with her husband and their five children.

THE ARMENIAN QUESTION

A Play in Two Acts

WILLIAM ROLLERI AND ANNA ANTARAMIAN

TIME

1977

PLACE

Municipal Hall, Paris

CHARACTERS

JENNIFER GOLDSMITH, UNFRA Committee Chair, 30s/40s

RENE PENSAR, UNFRA Committee Member, late 40s

ERIC HEINMAN, UNFRA Committee Member, late 50s

WALTER FREEMAN, attorney for the Armenians, African American, 40s

KAZIM YUCELEN, Turkish GENERAL, 60s

ARMIN WEGNER, advocate for justice, 91

ANAHID SIROONIAN, Armenian Witness/Activist, 70s,

ARPINE GARABEDIAN, Armenian Witness, 80s

GERARD MOURADIAN, Armenian Advocate, 80s

Members of the PRESS, including photographers with flash attachments

ACT ONE

Lights up. Large hall or courtroom. Large wall sign: UNITED NATIONS FOOD REDISTRIBUTION AGENCY (UNFRA). Three separate tables and chairs set out with pads, pencils, carafes, and glasses to accommodate a Turkish General, three judges or committee members, and FREEMAN *with* ANAHID; *witness chair. Several other empty chairs placed about. Books and files already in place on the three conference tables. Most of the actors enter with audience, stand about chatting with them "in character." The Turkish table is vacant. Slide projector and screen in place. Much milling about, hum of conversation. The judges enter, chat among themselves, arrange their files and papers.* GOLDSMITH *sits at center, surveys the crowd, raises the gavel and taps for attention.* FREEMAN *and* ANAHID *continue to confer.)*

GOLDSMITH: *(Taps gavel again.)* Mister Freeman, we will begin now with or without the pleasure of your company.

*(*FREEMAN *hurries to his table.* ANAHID *follows.)*

HEINMAN: *(Holds up note.)* I have a note here that . . .
FREEMAN: *(Sits.* ANAHID *does the same.)* Yes, ma'am.
GOLDSMITH: Last Friday we had the Ambassador from Turkey here. Please someone tell me he is not late this morning.
HEINMAN: *(Holds up a note.)* I picked up this note on the way in, Dr. Goldsmith. It appears . . .
PENSAR: What note? Where was it?
HEINMAN: From the Turkish Consulate. It says . . .
PENSAR: The Ambassador? That note was intended for Dr. Goldsmith, *n'est-ce pas?*
GOLDSMITH: Dr. Heinman, you picked up a note that was addressed to me? From the Turkish Consulate?

*(*GOLDSMITH *and* PENSAR *stare at* HEINMAN. HEINMAN *places the note in front of* GOLDSMITH. GOLDSMITH *picks up the note and reads it in silence.)*

HEINMAN: In future, I shall leave notes where I find them.
GOLDSMITH: *(Drops the note in front of* PENSAR.*)* Food poisoning. Of all things.
PENSAR: *(Picks up the note.)* Pardon?
GOLDSMITH: The Ambassador returned to Turkey to confer with his superiors and it appears he came down with food poisoning and . . .
PENSAR: *(Returns note to* GOLDSMITH.*)* He did not fly Air France.
GOLDSMITH: He will be replaced by General Kazim Yucelen, Deputy Prime Minister.

PENSAR: *(Noting the vacant conference table.)* Who is late? I suggest we begin. We can . . .

HEINMAN: It would be inappropriate to start without the General . . .

PENSAR: I believe Dr. Goldsmith is Chair of this Committee.

HEINMAN: He probably flew in this morning, I suggest we . . .

GOLDSMITH: *(Blinks at camera flashes. They cease.)* Thank you. And thanks to Mister Freeman, we have with us today more members of the press than usual. *(Beat. She checks her notes.)* For the sake of those new faces, it makes sense to clarify the role of this agency. You all know that we are in the midst of a catastrophic global drought. Famine runs rampant in many parts of the world. Canada, the U.S., and Mexico have placed their grain surpluses at the disposal of UNFRA. The United Nations Food Redistribution Agency. Our mission is to assure that surplus grain gets where it is most needed. While we are running out of grain and time, we are not running out of starving nations. Last Friday the Turkish Ambassador delivered his country's most recent census report to document the nutritional needs of his country.

PENSAR: Business as usual.

GOLDSMITH: But something else happened last Friday that is not business as usual. An American trial attorney, Mister Walter Freeman . . .

(Photographers' camera flashes as FREEMAN rises, waves, smiles.)

GOLDSMITH: *(Cont'd.—Annoyed by flashes. To fotogs.)* That will do. *(Flashes stop.)* Mr. Freeman came here with some of his fellow citizens requesting that they be heard as witnesses. At the discretion of this committee and . . .

HEINMAN: And so long as the testimony is relevant to the nutritional needs of Turkey. We can ask Mister Freeman to explain how his clients . . .

PENSAR: We can listen to the witnesses for ourselves, *n'est-ce pas?*

GOLDSMITH: We can stop bickering, *n'est-ce pas? (To PRESS.)* The Turkish Ambassador agreed to these conditions last Friday. He asked us to give him the weekend to confer with his government in Ankara. Now he has fallen ill. He has been replaced by Turkey's Deputy Prime Minister, Mister, General?—Kazim Yucelen, is that General?

HEINMAN: *(To the press.)* Yes, General, he prefers to be called . . .

PENSAR: *(To HEINMAN.)* He is a friend of yours?

FREEMAN: *(Stands)* Dr. Goldsmith . . . can we proceed with the first witness please?

PENSAR: Of course, it is time.

HEINMAN: *(To GOLDSMITH.)* We should wait for the General. While this is not a court of law . . .

GOLDSMITH: *(To PRESS.)* It is nevertheless a formal hearing.

FREEMAN: My first witness is Miss Anahid Siroonian. Just to be ready whenever you . . .

PENSAR: *(To the* PRESS.*)* Also we are not judges. I teach Philosophy at the Sorbonne. Dr. Goldsmith is a leader of the feminist movement in America. *(Points at* HEINMAN.*)* He's the only lawyer here.

*(*GENERAL *enters, a striking man, conservative civilian clothes, military bearing. He makes his way forward.)*

HEINMAN: I plead guilty as charged.
PENSAR: *(Sees the* GENERAL.*)* These military professionals march while the rest of us merely walk. Jennifer?

*(*GOLDSMITH *gets the message, motions to the* GENERAL *to come forward and sit.* ANAHID *to witness chair.* HEINMAN *offers Bible; "swearing in" is inaudible.)*

HEINMAN: Uh—do you swear to tell the truth . . .

(The GENERAL *bows to* GOLDSMITH *, turns to pose for several more photos.)*

ANAHID: My name is Anahid Siroonian. I was born in Sivas, Turkey . . . perhaps I should wait until the General is finished posing.
GOLDSMITH: *(Acknowledges the remark.)* Good morning, General. Please have a seat and . . .
GENERAL: Good morning, Dr. Goldsmith, my abject apologies for my late arrival, but . . .
GOLDSMITH: *(To fotogs.)* If your cameras are a disturbance, I will bar them. *(To* ANAHID.*)* Madame, please go on, briefly.
GENERAL: *(Removes leather folder from attaché case.)* Ah, Dr. Goldsmith, if I may, before we, ah . . . I have here an official statement from my government, may I . . .
GOLDSMITH: All in due time, General. Right now we have a witness on . . .
ANAHID: We lived on a farm. I was one of five children, we were a very large family of . . .
GENERAL: *(Puts down leather folder.)* I do beg your pardon but, with all due respect, the witness, Ms. Siroonian, certainly, given her age, she must be treated with respect, but . . .
FREEMAN: She said later.
GENERAL: In all sincerity, I ask if it is prudent to assume that everyone is here for humanitarian reasons? She is a lifelong political activist and I am obliged to question the relevance . . .
HEINMAN: I join the General in raising that question, Dr. Goldsmith.
FREEMAN: She has not even begun to . . .
PENSAR: I suggest that the sooner we hear what these people have to say, the sooner we can . . .

GENERAL: Truthfully, Dr. Goldsmith, it was most disheartening to learn that you would be taking testimony from Armenians when the rightful concern of . . .

PENSAR: General, your Ambassador agreed to . . .

GENERAL: Yes, a good man, a very fine man, David Havig, I have known him for years, highly respected, but, ah, I must say, he simply should not have authorized this.

PENSAR: Nevertheless he did agree.

GENERAL: Yes, and his word will be honored, but we implore you to reconsider your decision to . . .

PENSAR: General, the charter of this agency allows for testimony from any source and provides discretionary authority to . . . *(Begins to rise.)* I have a copy here for . . .

HEINMAN: I'm confident the General already knows . . .

GOLDSMITH: *(Touches* PENSAR's *arm.)* Rene, please. *(He sits.)*

PENSAR: The Ambassador was quite articulate in conveying his lack of joy at the prospect of . . .

FREEMAN: Dr. Goldsmith, I have a witness on the . . .

GOLDSMITH: General Yucelen, our decision has been made. It will not be reversed.

GENERAL: All the same, we are not persuaded that the Ambassador was sufficiently assertive regarding the severity of—I dread to think of the Turkish people who died of starvation in the last two days simply because . . . and that is to say nothing of all the other nations in dire need of relief that has been delayed by this . . . this lawyer who . . . well . . . There are other nations in great need. They are waiting on line, so to speak, no?

PENSAR: *(To* GOLDSMITH.*)* Perhaps we can postpone this hearing to attend those other nations?

GENERAL: Good heavens, I have simply made a point of order.

FREEMAN: Madame.

GENERAL: In view of the suffering in my country even as we speak, I must . . .

FREEMAN: Madame, this woman traveled all the way from California to be here today, and . . .

GENERAL: Yes we know of her, and I must question the credibility of her . . .

MOURADIAN: *(On his feet, waves cane.)* No, she not lie! You lie!

GENERAL: *(Points at* MOURADIAN.*)* Aha! You see, Madame? This old man, he . . .

GOLDSMITH: *(Gavel.)*: Mr. Freeman, does he belong with you?

ANAHID: Gerard! Sit down!

ANAHID: *(To* GOLDSMITH.*)* He is a friend, he is . . . Armenian, but he is not going to . . .

MOURADIAN: *(Sits.)* He lies. *(Mumbles.)* That one over there, he lies.

GENERAL: *(Rises.)* Madame, you see here, this old man, a remnant of the past from a time of . . .

MOURADIAN: Yah? Me? What he say?

GENERAL: This old man is tragically the essence of what is Armenia today: Hatred for Turkey.

ANAHID: We hate no one.

GENERAL: *(To* MOURADIAN.*)* I assure you, Sir, we hold no hatred for you, only sorrow. *(To* GOLDSMITH.*)* And please believe me, I do not question their sincerity. But they have been led to believe that terrible inhumanities were committed by my government against . . .

GOLDSMITH: General, please be seated.

PENSAR: Unless you wish to postpone?

GENERAL: *(Sits.)* I wish to remind us all that we are here to relieve the suffering of starving people, not . . .

FREEMAN: Miss Siroonian, what can you tell us about that year 1915, in Turkey? The government?

ANAHID: The government?

GENERAL: Of course, at that age, ten were you, how could you know about . . .

ANAHID: I know everything was peaceful and loving before they . . . We were not wealthy, but there was always enough food, warm clothing, shoes. Then the Turks came, with their guns. They said the men had to leave right away to join the Turkish Army. They were waving this piece of paper, and they kept on saying that our three men had to come immediately.

GENERAL: It was the war. My own father was given four hours' notice. One week later he was at the Russian border with a rifle and six bullets. A month later he was . . .

ANAHID: My father and my uncles, they protested.

GENERAL: My father has no grave.

ANAHID: They said what are you doing? You can't just take us away like this, we have family . . .

GENERAL: Please, in all fairness, do consider the inequity of discussing these matters without acknowledging the revolution at a time, of profound international pressure on Turkey in 1915. Armenians, most unfortunately were traitors, there is no way to soften the word, and . . .

FREEMAN: *(To* GOLDSMITH.*)* There was no revolution.

GENERAL: And the sovereign government was forced to suppress a revolutionary uprising in which thousands of innocent Muslims were slain . . . and you, Sir, are far too young to speak authoritatively of the revolution of 1915.

(Only elderly Armenians respond to FREEMAN*'s following requests.)*

FREEMAN: Excellent point, Sir, which applies to you as well. *(To* GOLDSMITH.*)* Madame Chair, with your permission . . . *(To all)* May I see a show of hands of people present today who are old enough to remember the year 1915 in

Turkey? (*A number of elderly people raise their hands.*) Now, General, how much would you like to bet that most of them are Armenian survivors of the bloodbath you . . .

HEINMAN: This is certainly out of order.

GOLDSMITH: (*Slams gavel. To the people.*)Put your hands down! (*To* FREEMAN.) That was a mistake, Sir, one that I trust you will not repeat. Miss Siroonian, we don't have much time.

ANAHID: The Turks forced the men to get ready. We protested . . . began to cry. My father . . . he picked me up and held me. I can still . . . he said not to worry. God would protect them.

FREEMAN: And—at gunpoint—the Turkish soldiers took them away?

ANAHID: I never saw my father again. One week later, Turkish soldiers came again. They rounded up all the older boys, ten years and older. They tied their wrists to each other. Then they marched them out of town. Into the fields, about 200 yards away . . .

GENERAL: Is it not reasonable to ask if a ten-year-old can judge 200 yards?

ANAHID: We heard gunfire! We climbed up onto the rooftops. We could see . . . we could see them! Shooting right into the boys. They were falling down, bouncing on the ground, writhing. The soldiers stood over them, shooting. Then they didn't move anymore. Two of them were my brothers, Gabi, eleven, Hirant, twelve!

GENERAL: Yes, tragic. So young, so . . . but Madame, we must acknowledge that youngsters have been soldiers in all wars, and that is the true tragedy. Korea, Vietnam. The Americans used them in Vietnam, did they not, Lieutenant Freeman, yes?

FREEMAN: I don't know what you're talking about.

GENERAL: But you must have seen this, I did.

FREEMAN: The Turks did not fight in Nam.

GENERAL: Ah, those operations are still highly classified, very understandable, Delta Force, was it?

FREEMAN: Anahid, your brothers . . .

GENERAL: Yes, the world should know the things the Americans did, yes, I was there and . . .

PENSAR: But that is not why we are here.

FREEMAN: (*To Anahid.*) Your brothers, Anahid. How many Turks did they kill?

ANAHID: They did not kill anyone. (*Beat.*) The Turks ordered us to get ready to leave. Babies, old people, young girls. Some had ox carts. We packed as much food and clothing as we could. They drove us out onto the road. I never saw my home again. There were beautiful flowers in the front garden, my mother called it her rainbow, she made me a beautiful red and yellow dress and we called it my rainbow dress and . . .

FREEMAN: Anahid? What happened after. After you left . . .

ANAHID: We were on the road . . . the soldiers stopped us near a town. They let the people come and take everything. The ox carts, our food, clothing. The people beat us with clubs and stoned us. They took the young girls, they . . .

FREEMAN: Your family?

ANAHID: One of my aunts had a gold watch. A wedding present. She wouldn't let a soldier have it, so he just put a gun to her chest and pulled the trigger.

GENERAL: *(Holds up a file.)* War is a wild beast. *(To* PENSAR.*)* Sir, you were a resistance fighter in France . . . a courageous boy, just fifteen. You know the horror, one cannot control random acts of cruelty. Without question . . . *(To* ANAHID.*)* this woman lost her beloved aunt in a terrifying manner, a deeply painful experience that cannot be . . .

PENSAR: *(Notes file.)* Tres bien, your files, you know so much. Do you know that I was born in Le Chambon? A beautiful little village in southern France? When the Nazis came they . . .

HEINMAN: What benefit in digging up old . . .   GOLDSMITH: Rene . . . must you?

PENSAR: Yes, the Nazis. We saved the lives of 5,000 Jews by taking them into our homes. For this, people were shot. The little boy who lived in my basement for two years. In the darkness. Can you tell me what happened to my little friend, Andre? Do you have also a file on my friend Andre? My mother? My father? Do you . . .

GENERAL: *(Holds up file.)* No, we do not know everything, Professor. But we do know that Dr. Heinman was a tank commander in a Panzer Division. Your enemy.

FREEMAN: May I finish with this witness, or . . . ?

GENERAL: Your enemy, yet you serve together now, that is all in the past, just as it should be. Sergeant Eric Heinman, highly decorated, for valor. Not what one would call a Nazi.

HEINMAN: I was a simple soldier. I fought for my country, that is all.

GOLDSMITH: We stray, gentlemen.

GENERAL: *(To* PENSAR.*)* And there is hardly anything in the human experience that is more of a wild beast than starvation. *(He picks up Turkish paper and holds it aloft.)* My people are dying in frightening numbers, they . . . I have statistics. Time is . . .

PENSAR: We cannot read Turkish. And Mr. Freeman would like to . . .

GENERAL: *(Lowers newspaper. To* GOLDSMITH.*)* You yourself have two young children in Chicago, Dr. Goldsmith. Have they ever . . .

GOLDSMITH: My children?

GENERAL: *(To* GOLDSMITH.*)* Madame, have you ever gone hungry? We become less human when we are starving. I have seen parents eat while their children died. Unimaginable? Yes. I appeal to your best nature as a human . . .

FREEMAN: *(Stands.)* Is he finished?

GOLDSMITH: Mister Freeman, the point is that lost time could be lost lives.

ANAHID: *(To FREEMAN.)* We do not wish to see innocent people suffer, least of all the children . . .

FREEMAN: On the road, Anahid. Anahid? How did they keep you moving on the . . .

ANAHID: Bayonets. Clubs. Stragglers were shot, even children. Yes, even the children. My infant brother, Adon. I screamed at one of the beasts and he laughed at me. He said, "If you survive this, little girl, you will tell people about it till the day you die. But nobody will ever believe you." Nobody.

FREEMAN: You told me there were 2,000 people in your group when you left. Six months later . . .

GENERAL: Again, a ten-year-old who can count that high?

ANAHID: Two hundred arrived in Aleppo. *(Beat.)* Out of 2,000.

GENERAL: *(Picks up the leather-bound folder.)* Dr. Goldsmith, I truly wish you would permit me to present this official statement of policy, a formal pronouncement by my prime minister and . . .

FREEMAN: Is my client to be continually interrupted?

GENERAL: I do apologize, Mr. Freeman, if the situation were not so desperate . . .

HEINMAN: This hearing allows for informality, Sir, if the statement is . . .

GENERAL: Thank you, yes, did Armenians suffer? Did they die? Yes, as did the many thousands of Muslims who died at the hands of the traitors. It is merely a matter of historical fact that the government had to relocate some 400,000 people, you can imagine . . .

FREEMAN: The number of deportations we have is 2 million.

GENERAL: The logistical challenge, to move 400,000 people over major highways, through cities and towns where people feared them, even despised them for what their friends and relatives were doing to innocent Muslims.

ANAHID: We did nothing to Muslims. Our people were attacked by the Turks in all the major cities in the east, they tried to protect themselves.

GENERAL: Our soldiers tried to protect the Armenians from angry citizens and Russian artillery during this massive relocation, but 15,000 perished on the road from . . .

ANAHID: More.

GENERAL: Disease took another 25,000, even our own troops were without medical . . .

ANAHID. Many more.

GENERAL: Only 40,000 out of 400,000 died. That is why this woman's statistics are false. Based on the facts, if 2,000 people left Sivas, 1,800 arrived in Aleppo. Unharmed and protected.

FREEMAN: We'll be more than happy to play the numbers game a little later, right now I would like to continue with . . . Anahid, please just tell your . . .

GOLDSMITH: General, let's finish with this witness now. And then . . .

GENERAL: Did he say game?

ANAHID: Before we passed out of Sivas, I was sold to an Arab as a slave. My cousin told the Arab we had wealthy relatives in Marsovan, and he could . . .

GENERAL: This is no game, Sir, this . . . may I question this woman?

ANAHID: He could make a lot of money by taking me there. He sold me to my Uncle Raffi. I got word later in Fresno . . .

GENERAL: (Rises.) I see you wear a cross, do you go to church on Sundays as a rule?

ANAHID: Crucifix. (Beat.) Every Sunday. Except when . . .

GENERAL: (Approaches her.) Except when you're ill, wonderful, every Sunday, my mother was very religious as well, also my wife, you do this even when you travel? Away from home, you . . .

ANAHID: Yes.

GENERAL: So, you were in church just yesterday, no? Here in Paris? There is a church . . . ?

ANAHID: Saint Marie's.

GENERAL: (Stands close to her.) Good, very good. Perhaps you can tell me how many people were in the church with you. Just twenty-four hours ago, remember now, God is listening, so how many people . . .

FREEMAN: God might agree it's a dumb question.

GENERAL: How many?

ANAHID: I don't know. Maybe . . .

GENERAL: (Stands over her.) I would like to most respectfully remind you, Madame, you took an oath here, you . . .

ANAHID: When I am in church I pray, I do not count people!

GENERAL: You called God as your witness and you . . .

FREEMAN: No need to badger the witness, General.

GENERAL: You can smear the good name of Turkey, but we are not permitted to make a point? I must ask: (To ANAHID.) Why this man?

ANAHID: He's an attorney.

GENERAL: (Picks up another file.) And his clients? The highly regarded leaders of the civil rights movement? No. They are the dope peddlers of New York, the scum of the . . . he collects his fees from people who keep their entire estates in their socks, he has often faced ethics charges . . .

FREEMAN: I was cleared of all such charges.

ANAHID: It's true he may have set criminals free, he is very . . .

FREEMAN: It's called due process. Presumed innocence? We find that more humane than wiping out an entire culture just because . . .

GENERAL: How much are you stealing from these Armenians?

ANAHID: Nothing.

GENERAL: Ah, pro bono? Altruism? You are here on principle? Because in your own country your kind are oppressed by those in power?

GOLDSMITH: General, that is not germane.

GENERAL: Good law school, top of the class, why was he rejected by all the prestigious law firms? I apologize, Madame, but no reputable attorney would have accepted this assignment. All he wants is his name in the newspapers.

ANAHID: He defends the indefensible. And he wins.

GENERAL: Are you saying your own cause is indefensible?

ANAHID: No. Yours is.

GENERAL: (To FREEMAN.) You advance your career over the bodies of dying children, and you put their blood on the hands of your clients. (To ANAHID.) I ask you to answer from your heart now: If you thought for one moment that you were killing little children, would you leave here? (Pause.) I said would you . . .

ANAHID: Yes!   FREEMAN: No! That is not . . .

GENERAL: (To ANAHID.) Believe me, Madame, you get what you pay for, and you pay for what you get. Tragically, he does not care one whit about the suffering children of Turkey.

ANAHID: Tell him he's wrong.

GOLDSMITH: You will all get back to the matter at hand or . . .

GENERAL: (To GOLDSMITH.) Of course, Madame. Were there tragic events in Turkey in 1915? Undeniably, it's in all our history books. The Young Turks, before the war. Talaat, Enver, and Jemal, Talaat chief among them. Young. Idealistic. They wanted religious and ethnic equality for all. At a time when black Americans were being hanged from trees just for trying to . . .

FREEMAN: This is not about American history.

GENERAL: Quite so, but there was a festering hatred among the Armenians because they had not been well treated, historically. Can you blame them for feeling like second-class citizens? I do not. But their hatred was so deeply rooted that when Talaat held out the hand of compassion, the opportunity for a better life in a more unified nation . . .

FREEMAN: The home of the free and the brave.

GENERAL: (Picks up Turkish newspaper.) Before those hatreds could be resolved, we were at war. The opportunity fell from our hands. (To GOLDSMITH.) And now you have an opportunity that may slip through your fingers. In Turkey eighty dead every day. (Drops the newspaper near ANAHID.) And how many of them do you think are innocent Muslim children? I beg of you, with every ounce of my heart and soul, do not let the children continue to suffer.

ANAHID: We mean no harm to any child, Muslim or Christian.

PENSAR: Nor does anyone here.

FREEMAN: Madame, we are supposed to be hearing from this witness about . . .

GENERAL: (To ANAHID.) And for what purpose? In the name of Allah, why are you here, what do you want?

ANAHID: Justice!

GENERAL: And what do you call justice?

FREEMAN: The concept is both simple and universal.

GENERAL: Regrettably, your client mistakes vengeance for justice, and you encourage her.

HEINMAN: Mr. Freeman, again, will you please make the necessary connections now.

GOLDSMITH: Mr. Freeman, do you understand?

FREEMAN: Dr. Heinman, it is as an attorney that I appeal to you, that I ask your forbearance . . . I will make those connections, but please permit me to . . . uh . . .

GENERAL: To bury children.

GOLDSMITH: I caution you, Sir. You will not use this agency to achieve unrelated political . . .

FREEMAN: Madame, I just need a little time to structure that sense of relevance Dr. Heinman requires, I need to bring us all to a place where . . .

PENSAR: Ah, Dr. Goldsmith, perhaps he wishes merely to lay the, uh, foundation. The, uh . . .

FREEMAN: Exactly.

PENSAR: *(To colleagues.)* Perhaps we can be patient for a while.

HEINMAN: That no longer works for me. *(To GOLDSMITH.)* It's your choice.

PENSAR: Jennifer, a few minutes, ça va?

GOLDSMITH: *(To FREEMAN.)* You realize that we are bending over backwards to be fair.

FREEMAN: Anahid, you were taken to Marso . . . ?

ANAHID: Marsovan. My uncle owned a factory there, they needed him to run it. Also, at about this time, the deportations out of Marsovan stopped. The Turks . . .

FREEMAN: Why did the deportations stop?

ANAHID: The shops were closing, places of work were shutting down. You see, Turkish men only know how to serve in the army or in government jobs, they don't know how to do anything useful, so they needed Armenians to . . .

GENERAL: *(To Committee.)* Now that is both unfair and untrue. Can't you see what they are doing?

FREEMAN: *(To GENERAL)* Perhaps you can tell us why the deportations stopped.

ANAHID: They stopped because the Armenians were the light of the city. The Turks discovered they were putting that light out. This was . . .

GENERAL: They stopped simply because the insurrectionists had been identified, apprehended, and deported to holding camps. To contain them. Very simple.

FREEMAN: *(To ANAHID.)* So, life went back to normal in Marsovan? Almost? No?

ANAHID: General Kahlil Bey. He brought his army through, killing all the Armenians in his path . . .

GENERAL: This child could not have known by her own eyes that Kahlil Bey was killing all Armenians in his . . . please admit someone put that idea in your head. Admit that . . .

ANAHID: *(Drifts into her own thoughts.)* Horrible things were done to people.

Unimaginable things were . . . old, young, women, men, little ones . . . children . . . we can't harm the little . . .

GENERAL: One particular little child?

FREEMAN: What?

(ANAHID *is silent. She stares at* FREEMAN.)

GENERAL: Yes? What happened to this little girl? Was she unusually pretty? With golden curls and rosy cheeks? A plaything? Little girls can be quite coquettish, isn't that true? Did you twirl for him, in your pretty red and yellow dress, your . . .

ANAHID: My rainbow dress . . . my mother gave me that dress for my tenth birthday. It was covered with blood.

GENERAL: Grown men, away from their wives, evil thoughts . . .

ANAHID: It was torn to shreds . . .

GENERAL: Men who normally would never dream of . . .

ANAHID: It started to rain.

GENERAL: Oh, please do say it aloud, Madame.

ANAHID: I died there in the rain in that . . .

GENERAL: So I can deal with it.

MOURADIAN: She died.

GENERAL: Say it!

ANAHID: No!

GENERAL: Now!

ANAHID: It was a clear night. I was in the street, lost. Alone, I don't know why. I couldn't scream. He . . . the stars were shimmering . . . heaven was trying to catch her breath, I lay there wondering if God . . . if God even cared. The blood was inside me. My life was over sixty years ago! I have no children. I never married.

GENERAL: Wartime. Beastly acts. But what of men who commit atrocities in peacetime? The wanton murder of the Turkish Ambassador to Austria just a few years ago? And then the First Secretary of our embassy in Beirut is killed at his own dining room table. And last February, the Turkish Ambassador to the Vatican is torn apart by automatic gunfire on the steps of the embassy. All atrocities, all in peacetime. Yanikian?

ANAHID: What?

GENERAL: You know that name? (*Beat.*) No answer. It all started with Yanikian, did it not, these killings, this wave of terrorism. Five years ago in Los Angeles?

FREEMAN: What is this, who are you . . .

GENERAL: That name rings a bell, yes? This terrorist sends word to our Consul General that he wishes to make a gift. A rare painting of one of our revered leaders. And when he comes for his gift, it is a bullet. Beware of Armenians bearing gifts. We know you were his friend. Did you know of his plan? Justice you say? No. Revenge. Because your life ended in some alleyway sixty years ago.

FREEMAN: *(To* ANAHID.*)* What is he talking about?

GENERAL: Did you know of his plan?

ANAHID: He was my friend, but I never . . .

FREEMAN: You will not accuse my witness of complicity in . . .

ANAHID: I didn't know!

GENERAL: You did not know he was going to commit murder? A close friend?

ANAHID: I had nothing to do with any of this!

PENSAR: Sir, what honor is there in suggesting that an old woman is responsible for killing . . .

GENERAL: Let me ask you, what honor is there in permitting outrageous lies to be entered into an official record, to be reported to the world by . . .

HEINMAN: There is no question of honor here, or lack of it.

GENERAL: *(To* HEINMAN.*)* You know of honor, Sir, you were awarded the Iron Cross. Heroism under intense enemy fire. So indeed I bow to your judgment on this point.

HEINMAN: That was a long time ago, Sir. Again I was only a . . . I was not a hero.

GENERAL: I am reminded that heroes are modest. My point . . .

GOLDSMITH: As Dr. Heinman suggests, it is time, Mr. Freeman. In fact, I have begun to question the prudence of my decision to permit your witnesses to testify at all. You will now make that all-important connection or terminate further . . .

FREEMAN: *(As* ANAHID *leaves witness chair.)* But I told these people that according to the very bylaws of your charter they would be permitted to testify, under oath, that . . .

HEINMAN: Subject to our discretion, those bylaws are quite explicit, subject to . . .

GENERAL: *(Holds up leather folder.)* I assume that at some point in this process I will be permitted to finish the official policy statement of my government. So far . . .

HEINMAN: I suggest we permit the General to do so, Dr. Goldsmith. It will give Mr. Freeman time to mull over what you have requested of him.

FREEMAN: Wait a minute.

GOLDSMITH: That's fine. Take a seat, Mr. Freeman.

PENSAR: Dr. Goldsmith . . .   FREEMAN: Madame, please . . . I told them . . .

GOLDSMITH: *(To* FREEMAN.*)* This committee is not bound by commitments you made. Ponder that. General.

*(*FREEMAN *sits and motions* ANAHID *off the witness stand. She resumes her seat next to* FREEMAN.*)*

PENSAR: How many more witnesses are here?

MOURADIAN: Millions, all dead, yah.

GOLDSMITH: That does not matter, Rene.

HEINMAN: I must agree.

PENSAR: *(Points at* MOURADIAN.*)* The old man, is he . . .

GENERAL: In the name of humanity, please, no more witnesses!

PENSAR: *(To* GENERAL.*)* You are not dictating to this committee, Sir!

GENERAL: Please do not force me to caution you, Sir, that . . .

PENSAR: You caution me?

GENERAL: How many innocents will die while you enjoy mythology? Can you hear their cries? The old, the sick, the children . . . especially the . . .

ANAHID: *(To* FREEMAN.*)* Tell them.

GOLDSMITH: Tell us what?

FREEMAN: I have no idea.

ANAHID: Tell them.

GENERAL: *(To* FREEMAN.*)* Yes. Tell us.

FREEMAN: *(To* GOLDSMITH.*)* It's nothing. *(To* ANAHID.*)* You don't win by advertising your weaknesses.

PENSAR: If you refuse to let at least one more of these people speak, I will take them out into the hallway and listen to every word they have to say.

ANAHID: *(Stands.)* Then I will.

PENSAR: *(Stands to address front row.)* And I invite the members of the press to come with me!

FREEMAN: *(Rising, to* ANAHID.*)* Don't do that.

ANAHID: Our attorney has been given explicit instructions.

FREEMAN: *(Takes* ANAHID*'s arm.)* Please!

PENSAR: *(To the* PRESS.*)* Will you come with me?

ANAHID: *(Pulls loose of* FREEMAN.*)* No children are to be jeopardized!

GOLDSMITH: *(Gavel.)* Everyone! Sit down! *(To cameras.)* Stop that! *(Flashes stop, they all sit.)* No one is going anywhere! Dr. Pensar, remember where you are.

PENSAR: *(Calming.)* I apologize. Indeed, I . . . but please . . . perhaps just one more. For the sake of fair . . . fair . . .

FREEMAN: Play.

PENSAR: *Oui, merci,* fair play.

HEINMAN: And what of fairness to Turkey?

GENERAL: Exactly.

GOLDSMITH: That is why we are here. *(To* FREEMAN.*)* One more. Do you understand?

FREEMAN: Oh, yes, ma'am.

(FREEMAN and ANAHID review the list. They turn to look at one woman.)

FREEMAN: Madame. Madame, will you please take the stand? *(The woman does not*

298 WILLIAM ROLLERI AND ANNA ANTARAMIAN

move.) We absolutely need you to come and take the stand. *(Beat.)* I call Mrs. Arpine Garabedian. *(Pause.)* And if she does not come forward . . .

GOLDSMITH: There is no going back.

GENERAL: Perhaps the clever lawyer from New York has outfoxed himself.

FREEMAN: *(To ARPINE.)* Has the clever lawyer from New York outfoxed himself? It has cost a great deal of money to bring us all here.

MOURADIAN: *(Stands.)* Yah. All my money. Arpine . . .

ANAHID: Gerard, no.

(ARPINE frozen. MOURADIAN moves toward the witness chair.)

ANAHID: Gerard   FREEMAN: Mr. Moura-   HEINMAN: Sir?
                     dian, don't . . .

(MOURADIAN ignores everyone, goes to the witness chair and sits.)

MOURADIAN: I pay. I speak.

GOLDSMITH: Am I to understand this old man has financed this whole . . .

ANAHID: Everything.

GENERAL: Quite believable, he's a madman. Senile.

ANAHID: *(Rises, goes to MOURADIAN.)* He is not mad. He is . . . broken. Gerard. Come.

(MOURADIAN rises, lets himself be led out of the witness chair by Anahid. She speaks to him, inaudible, He looks at Arpine. Anahid returns to her seat.)

GENERAL: Very well, then. Can we move along now?

(MOURADIAN moves toward ARPINE.)

MOURADIAN: Yah. Move along, yah.

FREEMAN: *(Picks up file.)* Yes, we can. I would like to . . .

GENERAL: You are finished, Sir.

GOLDSMITH: Mr. Freeman, there is something about "no more witnesses" that baffles you?

FREEMAN: *(Holds up a letter.)* This is not a witness, Madame. It's . . .

(MOURADIAN, stands before ARPINE, speaks to her, inaudible)

GENERAL: *(On his feet.)* Madame, have we not had enough of this Mr. Freeman?

HEINMAN: In view of the critical nature of the famine in Turkey . . .

PENSAR: *Au contraire*, in view of the famine throughout the world . . .

HEINMAN: In view of the boorishness of philosophy professors . . .

PENSAR: In view of the hauteur of German attorneys . . .

GOLDSMITH: *(To her colleagues.)* Gentlemen! This is not a struggle for male dominance, we are here to make decisions . . .

GENERAL: Most respectfully, decisions that will be heard round the world, yes.

GOLDSMITH: Meaning? Sir? Please say what you are saying, General.

GENERAL: Meaning only that this is the most significant humanitarian initiative in the history of . . .

PENSAR: I believe he is making reference to your appointment to your President's . . .

GOLDSMITH: I have no appointment to my President's cabinet.

GENERAL: It's true, the American secretary of education is quite ill but I had no intention of . . .

GOLDSMITH: Yes, I am under consideration as his replacement, along with several others. That's personal, it has nothing to do with this hearing, General.

GENERAL: I believe that, Madame, but you are also a highly regarded figure in the feminist movement in your country, and you wrote a book that . . .

PENSAR: That is also personal.

GENERAL: For this you are to be greatly admired, but your book, Madame . . . it does not treat kindly of woman's role in Muslim societies and even though I have not finished reading . . .

GOLDSMITH: Finish the book, Sir. It does not treat kindly of woman's role in the Judeo-Christian culture that presupposes God is of the male gender. But you are suggesting I have a bias?

(FREEMAN holds up a piece of paper to get GOLDSMITH's attention as MOURADIAN struggles to his knees before ARPINE. She reaches out to steady him.)

GENERAL: Madame, relations between your country and mine are excellent and I would regret to see . . . we should . . . I just wish to clear the air on anything that might . . .

GOLDSMITH: *(To GENERAL.)* I'm greatly relieved to hear that. *(To FREEMAN.)* Will you please stop . . . what is that?

FREEMAN: *(Holds up the document.)* This is what the General asked for. By lamenting the lack of documentation, he . . .

GENERAL: I lament only dishonesty . . . and your presence.

(ARPINE rises, helps MOURADIAN to his feet.)

FREEMAN: Documentation that something other than an insurrection took place. Something like a . . .

(ARPINE and MOURADIAN cross.)

GOLDSMITH: As Dr. Heinman has made clear, this committee will base decisions on . . . *(Sees* ARPINE.*)* Oh. It appears you have a choice. Mr. Freeman . . . your last witness or your document.

GENERAL: Must we?

MOURADIAN: Yah. We must, yah.

FREEMAN: *(To* ARPINE.*)* Thank you, ma'am. *(Puts down the document.)* We can wait on this.

PENSAR: May I see that?

FREEMAN: *(Takes document to* PENSAR.*)* Absolutely.

*(*HEINMAN *quietly swears in* ARPINE; PENSAR *studies document.)*

GENERAL: One hopes to hear a different story from this witness, perhaps a story about a compassionate Turk who gave a dying Armenian a sip of water, a piece of bread, a . . .

FREEMAN: Yes, one can always hope. I'll be happy to sit down and be quiet if . . .

GENERAL: That would be greatly appreciated.

FREEMAN: *(To* GENERAL.*)* But only if you acknowledge the genocide. *(Pause.)*

GENERAL: Only if there are icicles in hell, Sir.

GOLDSMITH: General, I will limit Mr. Freeman's time, but please let us go forward now.

FREEMAN: Yes, Ma'am. I would like to make the point that Mrs. Garabedian was an adult in 1915, well into her twenties. The General was quite adept at minimizing Mrs. Siroonian's testimony because she was so young, but Mrs. Garabedian, you were already . . . ?

ARPINE: I was married. I already had my own little . . .

MOURADIAN: Yah! I know her then, I am little boy.

ARPINE: My little princess.

PENSAR: Eh, *bien.* There you are, please do continue.

FREEMAN: Where were you and your family living in 1915 and what happened to you at that time?

ARPINE: Dibrik. My father was a successful merchant, he held important positions in the community, so did my husband. They helped a lot of poor people to . . .

GENERAL: To buy guns?

ARPINE: They were both fine, upstanding men . . . and they were hanged.

GENERAL: *(File in hand.)* Madame, was your father an insurrectionist? *(To* GOLDSMITH.*)* I'm obliged to ask this woman what were the roles of her father and husband in the insurrection. *(Beat.)* Regrettably, they were found guilty of treason during a time of . . .

ARPINE: My husband was a very gentle man. He was very well educated, a Yerospoghan, like a Senator in the United States, if you needed money for something . . .

GENERAL: For guns that killed so many innocent Muslims and brought the blind hand of justice down upon your own people. Did you know that your father confessed to . . .

ARPINE: That is not true.

FREEMAN: You have a signed confession here?

GENERAL: Many authentic documents are en route and that may well be among them. Oh, and yes, perhaps you did not know that it was your father who implicated your husband. He . . .

FREEMAN: Mrs. Garabedian, what was the first indication of something, well, out of the . . .

ARPINE: Turkish soldiers came like a tidal wave . . . it was insane. Killing, looting, burning homes. The whole city was crying. You could hear it, the wailing of the young women at night, it was like a thousand broken bee hives. At the same time, we heard that all Armenians in the Turkish army were stripped of their guns, they were being used as common laborers, digging ditches and . . .

GENERAL: I myself have dug many ditches.

FREEMAN: And graves. *(Beat.)* You told us about the armory? Before?

ARPINE: Armory? Oh, yes, later, they herded us into a huge wooden armory. They brought dry hay. Soon smoke is everywhere . We hold onto each other, screaming . . . praying. *(Pause.)* Our prayers were answered. A military doctor. Put out that fire, he screamed at the soldiers. And then he said: They will stink up the city for weeks, you must stop burning people to death and then he screamed: Kill them differently!

GENERAL: Please, you were inside this huge armory with so many people praying and screaming and this military doctor was out in the street, how could you hear him say . . .

ARPINE: *Oldermek farkli! Oldermek farkli!* Those words will echo in my tomb. Kill different.

GOLDSMITH: Mrs. Garabedian? *(Pause.)* Do you wish to stop?

GENERAL: This is too much for her that would be best for all . . .

ARPINE: I did not want to come here at all.

FREEMAN: You're doing fine.   MOURADIAN: You do good, yah, she do good.

ARPINE: They took all the old men into a high school. I stand out in the street with the others. We listen to the screams. We can hear the sound of the whipping and the bastinado, we . . .

GOLDSMITH: Bastinado? . . . Madame?

FREEMAN: *(To* GOLDSMITH.*)* You don't   GENERAL: It's immaterial. We . . .
know? Shall I explain?

GENERAL: We cannot even be certain it was employed! Madame, I suggest . . .

FREEMAN: Oh, I hear it's quite popular in Turkish prisons even today. The ankles of the victim are secured or lashed to a pole . . . Madame, please, I . . .

GENERAL: *(To* GOLDSMITH.*)* I can only ask that you consider the inflammatory nature . . .

GOLDSMITH: I will hear this, General. *(To* FREEMAN.*)* Up to a point.

FREEMAN: And the pole is held horizontally by two men, one at each end. When they lift it, the bottom of the victim's feet are exposed to the executioner. The shoes of . . .

GENERAL: This is not an execution!

FREEMAN: They will often leave the victim's shoes on for this little number. The executioner . . . (FREEMAN *approaches* MOURADIAN, *reaches for his cane.)* Excuse me, Sir, may I?

MOURADIAN: *(Clutches cane.)* You give back, yah?

FREEMAN: *(Takes the cane.)* Trust me. *(Holds up the cane.)* The executioner employs something like this, this length and shape, but probably made out of metal, for weight, make a better swing.

(FREEMAN *stands near the* GENERAL *and takes a practice baseball swing.)*

FREEMAN: *(Cont'd.)* The executioner then swings the rod with great power and whips it across the bottom of the victim's feet. The pain is terrible to begin with but as the whipping proceeds, with blow after blow . . .

(FREEMAN *leans against the* GENERAL's *conference table and begins to tap the cane against the bottom of one his own feet, in synch with his words.)*

FREEMAN: *(Cont'd.)* . . . the pain *(Tap.)* gets worse because the feet are being damaged, you see. *(Tap.)* And now the feet begin to swell from the constant beating. *(Tap.)* But they can't, because they are trapped inside the shoes, remember? And the beating goes on. *(Tap.)* And on. *(Tap.)* And on. The beating goes on . . . *(Tap.)* until the feet eventually burst.

PENSAR: They burst?

FREEMAN: Burst.

PENSAR: Grotesque!

FREEMAN: *(Returns cane to* MOURADIAN.*)* Throughout this process, the victim continues to scream. The sound of the bastinado is unmistakable. The screaming is maddening.

GENERAL: *(To* FREEMAN.*)* There were things done to the Vietnamese by Americans that would turn the stomach of any civilized human being, and you know that, you . . .

FREEMAN: *(To* ARPINE.*)* I think you were saying, the women were standing outside, listening . . .

ARPINE: There is a blacksmith shop next to the high school. Soldiers take all the horseshoes, all the horseshoe nails. They pile them up next to the hearth. They force the blacksmith to pump the bellows. They aim a gun at him, and he pumps . . . he cries, the poor man, but he pumps, he pumps. Heating the horseshoes red hot.

GENERAL: Can we stop this?

ARPINE: Red hot they glow. They bring the men out. They have already been through a nightmare, naked, covered with blood that pours from toothless mouths, dirt, down onto their bellies in the dirt.

GENERAL: Incredible . . .

ARPINE: Soldiers hold their feet up so they can . . . and they . . . they . . .

GENERAL: I think it would be best for her if . . .

ARPINE: They nailed them!

GENERAL: Will someone please stop this.

ARPINE: They nailed those red-hot horseshoes into the bleeding feet of those men! You will all burn in hell for that! Oh, my God, I can still hear that scorching sound when the metal was pressed into their flesh, I can still . . . can you . . . can you smell that?

GENERAL: Smell?

HEINMAN: *(To* GOLDSMITH.*)* Has this gone far enough?

FREEMAN: Ma'am, you mentioned you already had your first baby, can you . . .

ARPINE: Baby? Yes. Zabel. My princess. I was holding her. A soldier tickled her. She giggled. I remember thinking maybe he has a little baby at home, and he . . . he asked if he could hold her. I told him she would cry, and then she did just that, she started to cry and he told her to stop crying, why are you crying, little one, do you think the big, bad Turk would harm you, no, no, no, stop crying, little one, I said stop . . .

FREEMAN: Go on, please.

ARPINE: He took my little princess in one hand by the ankles, he wrenched her away from me, he swung her around singing some insane Turkish song and then he bashed her brains out against a rock. There, he said, she has stopped crying. She has stopped . . .

(ARPINE *drifts off, cradles her arms, hums lullaby to imaginary baby.*)

GENERAL: What is going on here?

FREEMAN: Mrs. Garabedian?

ARPINE. *(To* FREEMAN.*)* Don't you think she's beautiful

FREEMAN: Uh . . . yeah, I, uh . . .

ARPINE: Maybe just to me she's . . . she does have her father's ears. Such big ears my baby has, but to me. . . she looks like an angel who just left the arms of God, an angel He sent to us . . .

GENERAL: The woman is lost . . .

ANAHID: We should let her go.

FREEMAN: Arpine? Mrs. Garabedian?

ARPINE: *(Holds baby forth to* FREEMAN.*)* My little baby girl. Just twenty days old. Isn't she beautiful?

PENSAR: *Mon Dieu.*

GENERAL: Madame, the poor woman is hallucinating. She's repeating herself, rambling on and . . . She should be excused, she is not even here. *(Beat.)*

FREEMAN: She'll be all right.

ANAHID: Are you blind? Look at her.

GENERAL: Mrs. Garabedian, do you know where you are? See? That look in her eyes?

ARPINE: He sends these little angels to teach us how to love.

ANAHID: *(To* FREEMAN.*)* Can't you see what's happening?

GENERAL: This is impossible. *(To* GOLDSMITH.*)* Madame, most humbly, may I suggest . . . I sincerely do not want to question this woman, she is . . .

ANAHID: Arpine, you can leave, you . . .

FREEMAN: Leave her alone. She's just . . .

GOLDSMITH: *(To* ARPINE.*)* Madame?

FREEMAN: Just a little emotional, we . . .

ANAHID: He will destroy her as he tried to do me. She is old, frail, she is . . .

FREEMAN: *(Stands.)* We have come this far. If you insist . . .

ANAHID: If I insist?

*(*FREEMAN *begins to jam files and papers back into his attaché case.)*

ANAHID: *(Cont'd. —rises, goes to* ARPINE.*)* We cannot let him do this.

GENERAL: My last word, that woman is in no condition to be in that witness chair. *(Beat.)* Please. If you do not have this woman stand down, I am obligated to . . .

ANAHID: *(Behind* ARPINE, *hands on her shoulders.)* I'm here. *(To* GOLDSMITH.*)* Madame . . .

GOLDSMITH: You chose to be here.

GENERAL: Very well. Mrs. Garabedian. A tragic story, despair is a common experience during . . .

ARPINE: No, you do not speak to me of despair.

GENERAL: I could not help but think of my own daughter when she was just a little . . .

ARPINE: I saw an old woman.

GENERAL: Our princess.

ARPINE: Rags. Filthy.

GENERAL: I beg your . . . oh.

ARPINE: Stinking for lack of bathing. She had fallen. She could not get up. She knew, we all knew, the Turks were leaving the dead on the roadside, leaving them in the streets where they dropped. She began to dig in the dirt. Her fingernails were broken. I helped her. Her fingers were bleeding, but she did not make a sound. When the hole was big enough, she rolled her body into it and began to pull the dirt in on top of her. I helped her. When all that was show-ing was her face, she looked at me. She smiled. I put her shawl across her face. I covered it with dirt, patted it down. She didn't want the wild dogs to mutilate her flesh. She wanted to meet God with . . . God forgive me, I helped her.

GENERAL: You were without blame, and it pains us to watch you relive this tragic memory. (To FREEMAN.) In fact, we deplore those who require that you endure this . . .

ARPINE: I still lay awake with her smile in the darkness. You do not speak to me of despair.

GENERAL: I truly wish it were not so. I wish also that I did not have to ask . . . your name—Garabedian—it is well known in Turkey, your ancestors, doctors, lawyers, teachers . . . my task is not an easy one, I . . . Madame, you still have relatives living in Turkey?

FREEMAN: He's threatening her? (To GOLDSMITH.) Madame, he's . . .

GENERAL: I knew this would happen, I had hoped, a foolish hope no doubt, that Mr. Freeman would relent even for one moment, but no, I was hoping we could come together for one precious moment to agree on what might be done to protect those people, but, no, not . . .

ARPINE: Protect, my brother, his wife? The children? I don't . . .

GENERAL: With Allah as my witness, I threaten no one, my concern is for the wel-fare of your . . . (To FREEMAN.) You had to do this, didn't you? (To ARPINE.) Madame, this man does not care about you or your loved ones, he knew that by having you testify you would jeopardize them and he . . .

FREEMAN: That is not true! That's . . .

GENERAL: They live among Muslim families who now watch their own children suffer, what can you expect of them? I will ask the local authorities to protect your family, but how long . . . how long can we . . . (To FREEMAN.) And you, Sir do not give a damn.

ANAHID: Let her be.

FREEMAN: None of this would be necessary if you would just admit that . . .

GENERAL: Will you admit that you prompted this poor woman, you filled her head with terrifying distortions, you rehearsed this entire scene knowing . . .

ANAHID: Can't you see . . .

GENERAL: Knowing full well what the consequences would be for her and her loved ones and then you dragged her in here and . . .

ANAHID: She's suffering!

GENERAL: You would crucify this woman, you would sacrifice all of them just to win.

(ARPINE clutches her belongings and rises.)

ARPINE: You leave them alone! Damn you!

MOURADIAN: *(Rises, waves cane.)* No! Do not go!

ANAHID: Let her go!

GENERAL: *(To* ARPINE.*)* Speak the truth, Madame, they told you to tell these lies!

ARPINE: *(Tries to run out.)* Yes, yes, all lies!

MOURADIAN: *(Blocks her path.)* Do not let them drive you out again!

ARPINE: Let me go!

MOURADIAN: No! You will not run away! We do not run. No more, yah?

*(*ARPINE, *blocked, puts face in hands.* MOURADIAN *takes her to a seat.)*

GOLDSMITH: Mr. Freeman, have you had enough of this?

FREEMAN: *(Folder in hand.)* Enough?

GOLDSMITH: Is that a question? Yes, enough. I am not an attorney, but it's obvious you're willing to delay our decisions in order to achieve your objectives yet you keep those objectives a secret. To me, that is heartless and uncaring in view of the . . .

FREEMAN: And if the cause is just? We have heard from only two survivors and they account for many who died under decidedly questionable circum . . .

GENERAL: I believe that by any sensible standard of judgment their testimony has been worthless in view of the fact that we are supposed to be here to help starving people.

FREEMAN: Speaking of starving people . . . *(Holds up file of photos.)* I have here a small sample of photographs that will horrify anyone with a grain of human decency or com—

HEINMAN: One moment.   PENSAR: Photographs?

GENERAL: Wonderful, he has photographs. Please, the Armenians have been circulating bogus, unauthenticated inflammatory literature and yes, photographs, for years now and . . .

FREEMAN: *(Advances on Committee.)* I'll show you . . .

HEINMAN: Wait! You will halt right   PENSAR: May I . . .
there.

GOLDSMITH: *(Rises, gavel.)* Did you hear Dr. Heinman?

HEINMAN: Those photos are authentic? Mister Freeman? Can you prove . . .

FREEMAN: Someone said this is not a court of law.

HEINMAN: And I say we are attempting to be a court of reason. Dr. Goldsmith?

GOLDSMITH: Put them away.

FREEMAN: But, Madame, we . . .

GOLDSMITH: Now.

FREEMAN: *(Puts down the folder.)* Would you question the authenticity of a report provided by Professor Anthony Merlino of Columbia University who until recently was a member of the UNFRA Committee holding these hearings in London. *(Holds up report jacket.)* I believe you know him?

GOLDSMITH: Don't be coy, Mr. Freeman.

FREEMAN: *(To GENERAL.)* I meant you. General? You know this man? Merlino? Advanced degrees in history, sociology, a recognized authority on population trends . . .

PENSAR: Very highly regarded, yes.

GENERAL: Scholars can be bought.

PENSAR: I beg your pardon?

FREEMAN: They can also be destroyed.

GENERAL: He is apparently on Mr. Freeman's payroll, perhaps they hired him as a propagandist.

FREEMAN: I asked Dr. Merlino—on the basis of what was known of the Armenian population before the war—if they had never been touched or disturbed in any way, if they had been permitted to reproduce in a normal manner—I asked how many of them would be living in Turkey. I submit this report as evidence . . .

GENERAL: You cannot put that report under oath, can you? No. Produce this Merlino so we can . . .

FREEMAN: Professor Merlino was recalled. He's back at Columbia trying to defend his job, thanks to the influence of the Turkish government. But of course, you know nothing of that.

GENERAL: We wish him well.

FREEMAN: Yeah, right, but his work will not have been in vain because on the basis of this report and on behalf of my clients, I contend that those dead people, those murdered Armenians, and all the babies and grandchildren that would have come from them in the last sixty-plus years, if they had been permitted to live . . . nine million, that's the magic number . . .

GENERAL: Absolutely without foundation! Dr. Goldsmith!

(FREEMAN snatches the census report off GOLDSMITH's conference table.)

FREEMAN: Nine million of the dead and never-born!

(He slams the census report down onto the GENERAL's table.)

FREEMAN: *(Cont'd.—To GENERAL.)* They're all in here, aren't they?

GOLDSMITH: Freeman, there are limits to my patience!

FREEMAN: You put them in here, the dead and the unborn.

HEINMAN: That is slander!

GENERAL: I am not on trial here! Turkey is not on trial here!

GOLDSMITH: *(Gavel. To FREEMAN.)* You have overstayed your welcome here!

(FREEMAN brings the census report back to place it squarely in front of HEINMAN.)

FREEMAN: We ask that those dead and unborn Armenians be deducted from the 49 million population claimed by the Turkish Government in this bogus document.

HEINMAN: Out of the question, this is not . . .

PENSAR: I find the idea interesting . . . After all, if the census is inaccurate . . .

GENERAL: Interesting? Fascinating. Mr. Freeman knows full well that if I accede to his suggestion that would amount to my government's official acknowledgement of a genocide that never took place.

FREEMAN: *(To HEINMAN.)* You demanded relevance? I gave you relevance.

HEINMAN: *(To GOLDSMITH.)* Relevance is not proof. Jennifer, please.

GOLDSMITH: Mr. Freeman, you are finished here.

ANAHID: *(Approaches Committee.)* No, please.

PENSAR: *(Holds up document.)* Dr. Goldsmith . . .

GOLDSMITH: Not a word, Rene.

FREEMAN: Madame, please bear with   PENSAR: Dr. Goldsmith . . .
me for a . . .

GOLDSMITH: *(To FREEMAN.)* One more word of contention and I will lodge an official complaint with your ethics committee. You have just flown too close to the flame, Sir, and now you can . . .

(ANAHID rushes to PENSAR and picks up the document.)

ANAHID: *(Offers document to GOLDSMITH.)* Madame, please.

GOLDSMITH: *(Pushes document away.)* Ms. Siroonian, you will please . . .

ANAHID: We need Mr. Freeman . . .

GOLDSMITH: *(To FREEMAN.)* Your objectives have now become a matter of utter indifference to me, Sir, and . . .

ANAHID: *(Stops center.)* No! If we lose him . . .

FREEMAN: Madame, please . . .

ANAHID: *(Addresses the PRESS.)* We will be alone again.

GOLDSMITH: Miss Siroonian, sit down or . . .

ANAHID: *(To the PRESS.)* May I read this to you?

GENERAL: What is she doing?

ANAHID: I will read this to you.

GOLDSMITH: You will not read anything here unless I . . .

ANAHID: This is an official letter from the minister of the interior to the governor of Aleppo.

GENERAL: Can you stop her?

ANAHID: September 15th, 1915.

GENERAL: Where fact ends . . .

ANAHID: "It was first communicated to you . . .

GENERAL: And fiction begins.

ANAHID: ". . . that the Ottoman Government . . ."

HEINMAN: *(To* ANAHID.) Madame.

ANAHID: ". . . has decided to destroy completely . . ."

GENERAL: She is out of order!

ANAHID: ". . . all Armenians living in Turkey. An end . . ."

GENERAL: I do not want to hear this!

PENSAR: Be quiet!

ANAHID: "An end must be put to their existence, however criminal the measures taken. No regard must be paid to age, sex or conscientious scruple. Those who oppose us cannot remain on the official staff of the Empire. They are to be arrested." The letter is signed Minister of the Interior, Talaat.

(Silence. ANAHID *turns to face the Committee. She holds forth the document.* GOLDSMITH *stands, does not reach out for the document.)*

ANAHID: However criminal the measures taken . . .

GENERAL: This is unpardonable. *(Pause.)* Madame, I respectfully request that profanity be deleted from the record of this hearing, and without any further waste of time . . .

ANAHID: *(Hands the document to* PENSAR) However criminal . . .

GENERAL: And without any further damage to the relationship between my country and the international community.

FREEMAN: Meaning the United States.

GENERAL: I did not say that!

GOLDSMITH: Mr. Freeman, are you implying that my candidacy for a cabinet position may impair my objectivity? *(To* GENERAL.) Does anyone imply that?

GENERAL: Sincerely, Madame, no such intimation was . . .

GOLDSMITH: And my performance here may impair my chances of a cabinet position? I say this publicly because I need to acknowledge how important that appointment is to me.

GENERAL: Quite understandable, of course, but . . .

GOLDSMITH: Please understand this: The first American woman to hold a cabinet position was Frances Perkins, Secretary of Labor under President Roosevelt. She created our Social Security System. She was my grandmother. We were very close. I learned a great deal from her.

HEINMAN: Dr. Goldsmith, may I ask where this is going?

GOLDSMITH: She has disappeared between the lines of history books because history is written by frightened men. She taught me to try very hard to do the right thing. I cannot tell you how much that has cost me. I may well have to pay that price again today.

HEINMAN: Jennifer . . .

GOLDSMITH: Where is this going? It is going toward a recess, which I am calling to discuss . . .

GENERAL: Recess?

GOLDSMITH: We will discuss the question of whether or not that census report is accurate.

GENERAL: It is absolutely . . .

GOLDSMITH: *(To* ANAHID *and* FREEMAN.) And we will do this with the full knowledge that while we talk, children are dying. We may also ask ourselves, are we human?

PENSAR: *(Reads from the document.)* However criminal . . .

GOLDSMITH: *(Gavel. Moves away.)* Eric. Rene. Now, please.

PENSAR: *(Still reading.)* No regard for age or sex.

(HEINMAN *and* GOLDSMITH *stop when they see that* PENSAR *has not moved.)*

GOLDSMITH: Professor Pensar.

PENSAR: *(Holds forth the document.)* Have you read this?

GOLDSMITH: I said we have to talk.

PENSAR: My question, Madame.

(PENSAR *does not move or respond.* GOLDSMITH *returns to snatch the document out of* PENSAR's *hand.* PENSAR *stands to follow her.)*

GENERAL: *(Stands abruptly.)* Madame! That document is not worth the . . .

GOLDSMITH: *(As she leaves.)* We are in recess. *(Points at* FREEMAN.) And we will decide your fate, Mr. Freeman.

(They exit. All still. ANAHID *looks throughout the audience, then goes to* MOURADIAN.)

ANAHID: Is he here yet?

MOURADIAN: He will come.

GENERAL: Who?

(ANAHID, MOURADIAN, *and* FREEMAN *all stare at the* GENERAL, *but they do not answer him. Lights down, lights out.*)

End of act one.

ACT TWO

One hour later.

(*Lights up. All present as before as* HEINMAN *and* PENSAR *enter and sit.* GOLDSMITH *enters, takes center "space" and remains standing in her territory.*)

GOLDSMITH: General, you made earlier reference to my president?
GENERAL: Merely that our two nations are very close and . . .
GOLDSMITH: (*Holds up paper*). Very strange that during our recess I picked up a telegram at the communications desk. It's from my Secretary of State. I will read it, in part: "I am authorized to convey to you the President's personal request that you bring to fair and equitable conclusion the hearing on the Turkish application for famine relief." (*To* GENERAL.) Comment?
GENERAL: I assure you, Madame, this is the first I have heard of that telegram.
GOLDSMITH: I am now offering to recuse myself from this hearing.

(*She sits.* HEINMAN *and* PENSAR, *perplexed, stare at her.*)

PENSAR: You are serious, Jennifer? You could have told us this during the recess?
GOLDSMITH: I'm telling you now.
HEINMAN: At least we would have had the opportunity to discuss it and . . .
GOLDSMITH: You can discuss it now.
ANAHID: If you do that, Dr. Goldsmith, your colleagues will never agree.
PENSAR: We will have to postpone.

GENERAL: We cannot postpone,   ANAHID: No.
    please . . .

GENERAL: Another delay . . . my countrymen . . . Madame, I ask that you stay in place, or . . .
ANAHID: (*Points at* GENERAL.) And he will blame us for those who die.
GOLDSMITH: (*To* ANAHID) And perhaps my government will blame me. What do you have to lose?
ANAHID: Madame, you must . . .
GOLDSMITH: (*Motions toward* HEINMAN, PENSAR.) It's up to them. Eric? Rene?
HEINMAN: I ask that you remain in place as Chair of this Committee.

GOLDSMITH: Reason.

HEINMAN: As someone has said, people are dying. And I trust you.

GOLDSMITH: Rene.

PENSAR: I have absolute confidence in your impartiality, *mais* . . . but if we are to proceed, I would like to know along what lines we can . . .

GOLDSMITH: I plan to deal with facts, simple enough.

GENERAL: Yes, substantiated facts.

PENSAR: *(To* GOLDSMITH.) With a little more clarity? How do you . . .

GOLDSMITH: *(Holds up* ANAHID's *document.)* A very serious allegation has been made. We are in the global spotlight. The jackals are coming, Walter Cronkite is packing a bag right now. We cannot so lightly dismiss this allegation. Clearly, I plan to deal with the facts.

FREEMAN: Thank you.

GOLDSMITH: There will be no more anecdotal testimony here.

GENERAL: I thank you.

GOLDSMITH: And I plan to place a time limit on all proceedings.

HEINMAN: Provable facts.

PENSAR: Or what we believe to be true?

GOLDSMITH: We are aware that some terrible things happened to people in 1915, there is no need to . . .

GENERAL: Because of the war, yes.

GOLDSMITH: Because of the war, diplomatic breakdown, political arrogance, ethnic hatred and/or because of Haley's Comet, it was not a good year, all right? Nevertheless, we need to make some decisions today.

PENSAR: You are serious, Dr. Goldsmith? You would leave?

GOLDSMITH: *(Begins to gather personal stuff.)* Make a decision, Rene—today.

PENSAR: May I first ask General Yucelen and Mr. Freeman what their intentions are?

GENERAL: *(Stands, places hand on the carton.)* Very well, then, I am pleased to inform this committee that I have received from Ankara many documents that will prove beyond even the limits of Mr. Freeman's cynicism that there was no genocide in Turkey. Ever. Pure myth and I intend to . . .

FREEMAN: And I intend to call a witness.

GENERAL: What's that?   HEINMAN: You wish what?

FREEMAN: I think it only proper that you put the General under oath.

HEINMAN: The General?

PENSAR: That makes sense.

GENERAL: Ridiculous!

FREEMAN: If the Turkish government would lie about the historical fact of the genocide . . .

GENERAL: You are the liar here!

GOLDSMITH: All attorneys lie, Sir.

HEINMAN: The trick is to catch them.

GENERAL: *(Holds up leather folder.)* This is the official position of my government with the signature of my prime minister.

FREEMAN: And you are his official representative.

GENERAL: It absolutely documents the fact that no genocide took place in Turkey in 1915, not then and not since.

HEINMAN: And since he is not here to take the oath himself . . .

PENSAR: But the General is here.

GENERAL: I am an instrument of state.

PENSAR: General . . .

FREEMAN: *(To* HEINMAN.*)* I put it to you, Sir, that if the General does not take the oath, then all of the uncorroborated documents I have submitted should be acceptable.

GENERAL: That is unacceptable!

PENSAR: All this screaming, may I . . .

FREEMAN: Then you can take your official statement and . . .

GOLDSMITH: That is enough! *(They all fall silent.)* Rene.

PENSAR: General, to put it rather bluntly, if you do not take the oath, I am sorely tempted to accept Dr. Goldsmith's offer.

GENERAL: That is blackmail.

PENSAR: Yes.

GENERAL: In the presence of the world press.

PENSAR: I will be famous.

GOLDSMITH: The decision is yours, General.

GENERAL: *(Stands, points at the Bible.)* That is not the Koran.

HEINMAN: You may consider yourself under oath, General.

FREEMAN: Which means Allah will be listening, General.

GENERAL: Is that slide projector operable? And the screen?

PENSAR: *(Waves stage manager forward)* Of course.

*(*GENERAL *takes several slides to the stage manager, then goes to screen.)*

GOLDSMITH: Rene?

PENSAR: *Oui?* Yes?

HEINMAN: He vexes me. Professor Pensar, do you want Dr. Goldsmith to remain as chair of this

PENSAR: Ah, *ça va sans dire, n'est-ce pas?*

GOLDSMITH: No, Professor, it does not go without saying. *Oui ou non?*

PENSAR: I wish for you stay with us.

MOURADIAN: Yah. We all stay.

GENERAL: *(To the screen with pointer.)* Perhaps we can have the lights lowered? *(Lights lower.)* Thank you. First slide please.

(Image appears, large map of Turkey. He uses pointer.)

Yes, Turkey. France and Britain to the west, Russia to the east, winter 1915. We are at war with all three of these powerful nations, Germany and Austria our allies. Surrounded. Next slide, please. *(Closer image of Turkey's eastern border.)* The Russian front. Our eastern border a shambles . . . 300,000 well-equipped fighting men reduced to 15,000 ragged patriots counting their bullets, all that stood between our heartland and the Russian barbarians. Which included 50,000 Armenians in Russian uniforms.

ANAHID: They were Russian, not Turkish.

GENERAL: Deserters.

ANAHID: Armenians who had been driven out of Turkey by . . .

HEINMAN: I recommend we show the General the courtesy of letting him finish.

GENERAL: *(Pointer.)* The city of Van. Here, Bitlis, here Erzerum. Cities teeming with well-armed Armenian insurrectionists, fanatical haters of Turks and Muslims. The Russian barbarians are pouring over those eastern borders, slaughtering, destroying. And that is when the insurrectionists attacked from the rear with all the ferocity of raging savages. Many soldiers, many innocent Muslims died. This is historical fact. It was imperative that the Armenian population be moved away from proximity to the Russian front, to new homes where good Armenians would not have to suffer because of the disloyalty of traitors.

FREEMAN: And where are those good Armenians?

GENERAL: That is why we did our utmost to get them out of harm's way while our armed forces from the interior rushed forward to quell the insurrectionists and meet the enemy.

PENSAR: Allow me. *(To ANAHID.)* To your knowledge, Miss Siroonian, were there Armenian revolutionaries at that time? Sivas, was it?

ANAHID: Only those trying to protect their families from being murdered in their beds.

GENERAL: Traitors, Madame.

FREEMAN: May I? *(Beat.)* How far is it from Sivas to the Russian front? It looks like quite a . . .

GENERAL: *(Points at Sivas.)* Ah, yes, where this woman's family lived? Excellent question, why indeed move people out of Sivas? *(Points.)* You see these lines? Major roads to the front over which traveled truck convoys. Food, munitions, medical supplies for our soldiers. Roving bands of Armenian rebels were tearing up these roads, destroying the convoys, killing men who are trying to help their suffering comrades, the same in areas such as Cilicia, Urfa . . .

MOURADIAN: Yah, me Urfa!

GENERAL: Yah, you Urfa. Now you can see how the things that happened sixty-two years ago have absolutely nothing to do with this hearing.

(GENERAL takes the leather folder to GOLDSMITH's table. He lays it on top of the Turkish census report. Lights up. He proceeds toward his own table.)

GENERAL: *(Cont'd.—As he heads toward his seat.)* And now you understand how the enemies of Turkey were able to create the fiction that a genocide was underway. And how these tragically misguided souls have tried to perpetuate that myth. Thank you.

FREEMAN: Ah, excuse me, General.

PENSAR: General?

GENERAL: *(To PENSAR.)* Sir?

FREEMAN: *(Points to the witness chair.)* Over there.

PENSAR: *(Points to the witness chair.)* S'il vous plaît.

GENERAL: *(Hesitates, but goes.)* Very well.

GOLDSMITH: *(Checks her watch.)* You're on notice, Mr. Freeman, you have ten minutes.

FREEMAN: *(Points at box of files.)* General, you say all that came from Ankara this morning. Did anything else come to you from Ankara this morning? Hmm?

GENERAL: Can this man be asked to be more specific?

GOLDSMITH: That would help.

FREEMAN: All right, last Friday your Ambassador to France, David Havig, he came here and . . .

GENERAL: Yes, and you—how do you say?—you blind-sided him.

FREEMAN: And so he returned to Ankara to confer with his superiors. Was that you?

GENERAL: Yes, yes, and he became ill, what is the point of . . .

FREEMAN: *(Crosses, offers telegram to GOLDSMITH.)* I, too, received a telegram. I found it at the communications desk in the lobby this . . .

GENERAL: I will answer questions about the nutritional needs of Turkey, nothing more and . . .

GOLDSMITH: *(Reads telegram, gives it to HEINMAN.)* Who sent this?

FREEMAN: A personal friend. He works on the foreign news desk at the *New York Times.*

HEINMAN: *(Holds up the telegram.)* General? *(Pause.)* I will read it. "Word from our bureau in Ankara, David Havig, Ambassador to France who was recalled there last Friday, found dead in his home Sunday night, gunshot wound to the head. Walter, is this the Turk version of food poisoning?" That's not my question, it was in this . . .

GOLDSMITH: Your friend is not amusing, Mr. Freeman.

FREEMAN: But the question is, what happened to the Ambassador? I mean, first it was food poisoning. Now it's a bullet in the head. I'm confused.

GENERAL: It is not my responsibility to alleviate your confusion, Mr. Freeman.

FREEMAN: Well, the General claims that I am desperate . . . what is . . .

GENERAL: You are desperate, and you cannot afford the price of failure, can you?

FREEMAN: Good point. What's the price of failure in your government?

GENERAL: I don't know what you mean.

FREEMAN: Failure? The way your Ambassador failed? What did he have to pay?

HEINMAN: Mr. Freeman!

FREEMAN: A bullet in the head!?

HEINMAN: Mr. Freeman, you are out of order. Significantly.

FREEMAN: So who is desperate to win, and how many lies will he . . .

GENERAL: A bullet in the head is not the price of failure in my government, it is the result of deep depression, and profound sadness for what is happening to one's country, that so many must suffer for . . . in your country, Mr. Freeman, what is the price of unethical behavior?

FREEMAN: *(To* GENERAL.*)* What d'you mean? *(Pause.)* I'm posing a question, you refuse to answer?

PENSAR: General, will you please explain whatever you meant by . . .

GENERAL: One of my subordinates made contact with the Ethics Commission of the Bar Association of New York to . . . well, I had nothing to do with it, they . . .

PENSAR: This is serious?

FREEMAN: Only if I want to feed my kids.

GENERAL: We meant no harm, of course. We wanted to know more about his background and, of course, they would not disclose anything unless we explained who we are and why we . . . your Mr. McCauley is it?

FREEMAN: McCauley. He's a bit of a louse, actually.

PENSAR: General, your government has filed a complaint against Mr. Freeman on behalf of . . . ?

GENERAL: These naive people believe he can achieve goals for them that are attainable only through deceit and fraud. He will give them nothing but great anguish.

ANAHID: We can bear anguish.

FREEMAN: Fraud? And I suppose if I pack up and get out of here, you will withdraw that complaint.

PENSAR: If he goes home, you will forgive him? You will call off the pigs?

HEINMAN: Dogs.

PENSAR: Dogs, cats, pigs.

GOLDSMITH: *(Holds up her watch.)* Mr. Freeman. Eight minutes.

FREEMAN: General, your census claims more than 49 million people in Turkey, which . . .

GENERAL: Yes, 49 million, 248 thousand, men, women, children, all ages, all sexes, Turk, Kurd, Christian, Armenian, Jew, girl, boy, everybody. *(To* FREEMAN.*)* No dogs.

FREEMAN: Which of course we've established is a false number, so . . .

HEINMAN: Sir, you have established no such thing.

GENERAL: We have established that Turkey is a free and open society. All religions, all . . .

FREEMAN: Muslim. Islam? State religion, no?

GENERAL: There is no state religion, Sir. We are secularized.

FREEMAN: Really, since when? Long after World War I, maybe even the beginning of the Cold War? When you began to see economic advantage in renting your country to my country as a land base in case we went to war with the Soviets?

HEINMAN: That is not the concern of this committee!

FREEMAN: *(To HEINMAN.)* Yessir, you are absolutely right. But there were three million Christians in Turkey before that war, so how could you secularize? No, you had to wait until there were only a few.

GOLDSMITH: Mr. Freeman, stop right there. We did not ask the General to take the stand so you could play political advocate.

FREEMAN: Yes, ma'am, let me hop right over to virginity control in Turkey. Islam places a high priority on the virginity of . . .

HEINMAN: What was that? What . . .

FREEMAN: What? Oh, yes, Sir, forced virginity control. See, when women are arrested in Turkey even for political reasons they have to undergo gynecological exams to make certain . . .

GOLDSMITH: They're virgins? Is that true, General?

FREEMAN: Since the prisons are state institutions, this policy would tend to substantiate that . . .

GOLDSMITH: General?

FREEMAN: That he's lying about separation of church and state, and if he would lie about that, he . . .

GOLDSMITH: Freeman, be quiet! *(To GENERAL.)* Sir?

GENERAL: I am not an authority on penal systems, Madame, but I have heard that this is a precautionary procedure to protect females against rape while in the custody of the . . .

FREEMAN: Oh, that's very good.

GENERAL: *(Begins to rise.)* I thought you would like that. Madame, if there are no valid questions from . . .

PENSAR: Ah, *oui*, perhaps, General, you can tell us just how you went about taking this census.

GENERAL: *(Sits back down.)* How? The census was taken the way a census is taken.

PENSAR: Yes, of course, but I too would like to know how . . . I mean, in your country, how . . .

GENERAL: Turkey is a highly modern civilization, sir. We had the very best equipment and highly sophisticated systems of, uh, we have IBM printouts of all data. It is organized by a highly sophisticated computer program. This program accounts for population density by

PENSAR: Yes, yes, yes, I understand this but . . .

Yes, yes, yes, quite . . . quite sophisticated . . .

The size of this census . . .

census tract, the size of each cen- Yes, but how . . .
sus tract determined by that den-
sity. The . . .

PENSAR: General, how did you acquire the original numbers? The raw . . .

GENERAL: Yes. Well our census headquarters, you see, were established some years ago in Istanbul. During the census, we set up temporary regional offices as information input centers.

PENSAR: This is an answer?

HEINMAN: *(To PENSAR.)* What exactly is it you wish to know?

PENSAR: I wish to know how the raw data was collected before it was sent to . . .

GENERAL: Ah. I see. For example, a man will go to a door. He will simply knock on that door.

PENSAR: Yes, yes . . . a man goes to the door and knocks. Then what happens?

GENERAL: Someone answers the door. The census-taker asks certain questions. The answers to these questions constitute what you refer to as the raw data.

PENSAR: Questions like, ah, how many people in your family? Their ages, sexes, occupation of the head of household, family income, all questions like that, is that right?

GENERAL: Yes. Standard questions.

PENSAR: And if no one is at home?

GENERAL: Nobody home?

PENSAR: General, the census-taker knocks. *(Raps his knuckles on the table, pauses.)* He knocks again. *(Knocks harder.)* No answer. *(Pause.)* What I am asking is, what does the . . .

GENERAL: He guesses.

(Pause. Awkward.)

PENSAR: He guesses. You say he guesses?

GENERAL: The system is quite reliable, I assure you.

FREEMAN: *(Rises.)* Reliable, sure, but . . . *(Beat.)* I only have eight minutes, so . . .

GOLDSMITH: Seven.

FREEMAN: Moving along then. General, in your culture, do you distinguish between killing a Muslim and killing a Christian?

GENERAL: I make a distinction between killing a human being and killing a lower form of animal life. *(Beat.)* I hope that's clear enough for you.

FREEMAN: Patently. General, in Turkey, what would you say the quality of the officer training was? High standards, medium, low, whatever . . .

GENERAL: Very high standards.

FREEMAN: In the field of study such as   GENERAL: Very high, Sir. To be or not
mathematics? How about biology?   to be . . .

GENERAL: Schubert. Bobby Darin.

FREEMAN: Yes, amusing, and history, Sir?

GENERAL: Certainly. Santayana. Those who forget history are doomed to . . .

FREEMAN: Would you therefore tell this Committee everything you know about the genocidal massacre of one and one-half million . . .

HEINMAN: Dr. Goldsmith, really, I . . .   GOLDSMITH: Mr. Freeman.

GENERAL: *(Interrupting.)* No, please.

(Rises, goes to carton on his conference table, brings it back to the witness chair and withdraws a thick bound document. He places this before HEINMAN, *sits.)*

GENERAL: *(Cont'd.)* We have here documentation that repudiates the credibility of this repugnant accusation. Abstracts from the old census reports. These prove it was utterly impossible for 1.5 million Armenians to die in Turkey because the entire Armenian population was far less than that to begin with. There were more Armenians living in a large community east of the Turkish border, in Russia actually and . . .

PENSAR: And how many Armenians did die in Turkey during the . . .

GENERAL: *(Removing another file from the box.)* The credible figures indicate that perhaps 300,000 Armenians died in the same time frame that 2.5 million Muslims perished under the Russian sword. But only 40,000 died as a result of the relocation effort, the rest were casualties of war and . . .

HEINMAN: And how do we span the gap between 1.5 million and a mere 40,000?

GENERAL: In my culture, one needless death is a tragedy. I personally have never seen a shred of evidence to support the myth that even one Armenian was mistreated by . . . you bring one vaguely worded and counterfeit letter into this hearing and you call that proof of . . .

FREEMAN: *(Holds up a file.)* You don't like that one? I have others here and . . .

GENERAL: More forgeries?

*(*FREEMAN *moves files from his table to the committee's, creating some disorder.)*

FREEMAN: Let me take a moment to show you these, General, see if you recognize any of them. Just some old telegrams and letters, will you accept these as proof, General? Will you accept these, they're all authentic, all dated and signed, what more can you ask? Signatures in blood? A notary public?

GENERAL: I don't know what this is, but . . .

HEINMAN: Stop that.

GOLDSMITH: Mr. Freeman, this . . .

PENSAR: *(Reaching.)* May I see those?

FREEMAN: They're not in any particular order, I'll just read a few and then . . .

PENSAR: . . . then pass them along so we can . . .

FREEMAN: *(Selects one.)* This came from the archives in Berlin, a German national who was living in Syria he traveled in Turkey often, he . . . his name is deleted from the document, he lived in fear of his life. He saw thousands of Armenians laying dead by the side of the railway between Anatolia and Syria.	GENERAL: His name? How convenient. Enough. That's enough!

FREEMAN: Oh. I'm sorry. You were saying?

GENERAL: I say nothing. *(To GOLDSMITH.)* I am shocked that you permit this . . .

HEINMAN: In the absence of someone to give corroborative testimony, Mr. Freeman, what value do you suggest we place on those documents?

GOLDSMITH: Mr. Freeman?

(FREEMAN *begins to thumb through papers in another file jacket.*)

ANAHID: *(To FREEMAN. Offers file.)* The Ten Commandments.

FREEMAN: Huh? (ANAHID *offers him a file.*) Oh. Yes, all right, thank you.

GENERAL: Wait. That is a term of contempt.

FREEMAN: Will the General contest the fact that there was, in late December 1914, January 1915, a special meeting of, uh . . .

GENERAL: These were tactics for the waging of war and we never used such disrespectful expressions.

GOLDSMITH: Meeting of who?

GENERAL: Muslims are reverential of all religions, we never . . .

ANAHID: The Young Turks.

FREEMAN: Yes, the leadership, Talaat's cabinet so to speak, these were the decision makers at the highest level of government, it was Talaat Pasha who called them together to . . .

GENERAL: There were many such meetings, strategy sessions, you cannot wage war without . . .

FREEMAN: This was, according to both the British and German archives, the first meeting at which official reference was made to genocidal measures. Talaat announced the Ten Commandments of . . . they're very brief. *(Motions to Anahid.)* Anahid, will you . . . ?

GOLDSMITH: If you are going to read those tactics, you will not refer to them as commandments.

ANAHID: *(Rises, file in hand. Reads.)*

First, shut down all Armenian organizations, march members into the countryside, and wipe them out on the road.

GENERAL: It was critical to deal quickly with the insurrection leaders. They were killing innocent people, that is clear enough. This woman is not an attorney, how can she . . .

ANAHID: Collect all arms. Use military forces to provoke organized massacres by Muslim civilians. Exterminate all males under the age of 50, leave girls to be. . . Cut all familes off from all food and water.

GENERAL: Of course, disarm them. Now come the lies.

GENERAL: Turk soldiers were dying for lack of food and water!

ANAHID: Expel and execute all Armenians who hold governments posts and . . .

GENERAL: Only the traitors!

ANAHID: Kill all—all—Armenian members of the Turkish military. All action to begin simultaneously, leave no time for preparation of defensive measures. Finally, Commandment Number Ten, treat these instructions with the greatest confidentiality and deny everything. Deny everything. Deny . . .

GENERAL: A vast conspiracy of lies.

(FREEMAN stands as ANAHID returns to her place.)

FREEMAN: And as if these commandments were not clear enough, Talaat ended this meeting with a special message to his subordinates: "Do not give in to your compassion, do not indulge in pity, or it will be the end of Turkey." His words. Any response, General?

GENERAL: Forgeries. How can one respond to such things? Authentic documents? No.

GOLDSMITH: *(Holds up single piece of paper.)* This was recently typed, Mr. Freeman.

HEINMAN: *(Holds up another document.)* Where are the originals? This isn't actual evidence, it's

FREEMAN: *(Holds up a book.)* How about the American Ambassador to Turkey? Henry Morganthau? He wrote a . . .

GENERAL: A work of fiction.

FREEMAN: *(Drops book in front of GOLDSMITH.)* The man practically got down on his knees and begged Talaat to stop the carnage, he . . .

GENERAL: How can I account for Morganthau's agenda? This is not evidence!

FREEMAN: *(Producing a new file page.)* Okay, let's try this, a telegram, American archives, okay? July 31, 1915, from Henry Morganthau to President Wilson: "The president of the German-Orient Mission which maintains six Armenian orphan asylums in Turkey . . ."

GENERAL: Again, is that the actual docu . . .

FREEMAN: ". . . reports that Armenians, mostly women and children deported from Erzerum have been massacred en route to Karput. Very few . . ."

HEINMAN: Is it?

FREEMAN: "Very few deportees actually reach their so-called destinations. Please advise."

GENERAL: Obviously not.

FREEMAN: *(Places paper before* GOLDSMITH.*)* All of this can be corroborated and . . .

HEINMAN: But not by us here and not by us now and . . .

GOLDSMITH: And not in the next four minutes.

FREEMAN: *(To* GOLDSMITH.*)* For God's sake, our own ambassador.

GENERAL: *(Produces another file.)* Yes, your own ambassador. May I take a moment here? *(To* GOLDSMITH.*)* I have hesitated to speak with cold candor about Morganthau because, frankly, I did not want to alienate you. *(Opens file.)* It was common knowledge he had been assigned as Ambassador to Turkey with political aims rather than those of diplomacy.

FREEMAN: Can you prove that?

GENERAL: *(Passes file to* HEINMAN.*)* So long as you accept copies, here are copies of Morganthau's telegrams to President Wilson. They prove he provided false information to the Americans to ignite the passions of misguided justice. Please note that he refers to the Turkish people as "inferior blood."

FREEMAN: I doubt that there is any such reference made in Morganthau's book, and . . .

GENERAL: Yes, inferior blood. You doubt? Have you even read the book, Sir? Cover to cover, word for word? Have you seen all his telegrams, his letters?

HEINMAN: *(Reading from file.)* It says "inferior blood." *(Passes to* GOLDSMITH.*)* And you're losing time, Mr. Freeman.

FREEMAN: How about an article in the *New York Times*, all the news that's fit to print, right?

GENERAL: A socialist propaganda vehicle if there ever was one, but by all means . . .

FREEMAN: The article speaks of an official appeal by the United States to the Turkish government to halt the massacre of innocent Armenians, this appeal delivered personally to Talaat.

GENERAL: *(Removes documents from box.)* I sincerely hope that this Committee has grown tired of looking at forgeries and copies of mythical documents. *(Holds up documents.)* What I have here are actual documents. Originals from the official archives, they are both irrefutable and irreplaceable. The Russians lied, they told President Wilson we were committing these atrocities. Their strategy was to weaken our war effort by turning the Americans against us. Here, official documents, not copies, actual documents proving Talaat took every possible humanitarian precaution to . . .

FREEMAN: *(Holds up page from a file.)* May 29, 1915, from the French government warning the Young Turks they would be held personally responsible for their crimes against humanity, specifically the wholesale massacre of innocent Armenians.

GENERAL: *(Holds up file again.)* Again, propaganda designed to create tensions between Turkey and the United States.

FREEMAN: *(Holds up another document.)* This is a copy of a memo from the Austrian Ambassador Pallavicini to his superiors, dated January 20, 1917, it says "The anti-Armenian measures in Turkey aim at the extermination of the Armenian population." Can't call him a windbag.

GENERAL: Pallavicini was a politician who saw which way the winds of war were blowing. He wanted butter on both sides of Austria's bread, he . . .

FREEMAN: *(Holds up another page.)* How about your great ally, this one is from the German Ambassador—Hans von Waggenheim?

GENERAL: Yes, all right then, Waggenheim.

FREEMAN: Yes, Waggenheim, to his superior in Germany, July 17, 1915: "The Turks have now begun deportations of Armenians from areas not threatened by invasion."

GENERAL: I explained all that, the attacks on the roads, the convoys, the . . .

FREEMAN: "The manner in which the relocation is being carried out demonstrates that the government is really pursuing the aim of destroying the Armenian race in Turkey."

GENERAL: That telegram never existed. *(Produces a document.)* This is the original document . . . same date, from Ambassador Waggenheim to Talaat Pasha. "We understand and concur in the need to relocate Armenian families from the proximity of roads over which war supplies travel to the Russian front, and endorse your beneficent measures to protect them en route to safer regions. We ask if there is any further humanitarian assistance we . . ."

FREEMAN: *(To GOLDSMITH.)* Ma'am, please, on the one hand he can deny the validity of every piece of evidence I put forth. On the other, there's my client, who fears more for the welfare of Turkish children than she does her own cause. If I lose I lose, if I win I lose, how can I . . . ?

GENERAL: Life is not fair, is it?

HEINMAN: Your complaint belongs in a higher court.

FREEMAN: *(To all.)* Very well I have here a series of telegrams by Talaat.

HEINMAN: Are they also copies? Where are the originals?

GENERAL: I've already said they do not exist.

FREEMAN: These were sent in 1915. August 12, this first one says . . .

HEINMAN: *(Stands.)* May I see that document?

FREEMAN: May I read it?

HEINMAN: May I see it? First.

FREEMAN: *(Hands it over.)* All right.

HEINMAN: Also typewritten. When? Yesterday? And the original? *(Beat.)* Dr. Goldsmith, even though this is not a court of law . . .

GOLDSMITH: Reality rears its ugly head, Mr. Freeman, your time is up.

FREEMAN: *(Holds up a book.)* Madame, just one . . .

GOLDSMITH: No more documents unless you can establish authenticity, Mr. Freeman. This agency will not become your media conduit to discredit the government of Turkey. You will . . .

FREEMAN: *(Rushes files to GOLDSMITH's table.)* These are eyewitness reports, Dr. Goldsmith . . .

HEINMAN: *(He pushes files away.)* Stop that.

FREEMAN: *(Continues to push files.)* Reports from missionaries and scholars, not Armenians, people like . . .

GENERAL: Are they here? Can we put them under oath?

FREEMAN: Johannes Lepsius.

GENERAL: He's dead. Are you calling him to testify?

FREEMAN: Dr. Clarence Usher.

GENERAL: Also dead.

FREEMAN: Armin Wegner. Are these men . . .

GENERAL: Long dead, and good riddance, he was a traitor and a liar!

ANAHID: *(Stands.)* Armin Wegner was not a liar! He saw! He saw everything! He was a German officer in 1915, highly decorated, he was assigned as an aide to a high-ranking German officer in Turkey and he . . .

GENERAL: He disobeyed direct orders, he should have been . . .

ANAHID: He traveled in parts of Turkey that were forbidden except to those on official business. The death marches, the death camps, yes.

GENERAL: There were no death marches, no . . .

ANAHID: And he wrote about it after the war, he told the truth but his work was suppressed . . .

GENERAL: Because he was a liar!

GOLDSMITH: If they are all dead, please stop wasting time!

FREEMAN: But are they all liars!? How about a world renowned and highly credible historian whose work verifies the Morganthau claims? Arnold Toynbee? Is he a liar?

GOLDSMITH: That's enough!

FREEMAN: They must all be liars!

GOLDSMITH: Mr. Freeman, you will clean up this chaos.

(FREEMAN returns, gathers papers. PENSAR assists, but he picks up the Turkish archive documents, slips them into the leather portfolio and puts them aside.)

HEINMAN: General? You may return to your . . .

(WEGNER, *seated in the audience, raises his hand. No one notices.*)

GENERAL: *(To* GOLDSMITH.*)* Madame, once again, the only piece of reliable evidence before you is that census report. If you base your decision on anything else, the entire world will know that you were duped by a tainted New York attorney and a political activist of questionable reputation. Whereas the documents I have provided here . . . where? Where are they?

PENSAR: Where is what?

GENERAL: *(Stands, approaches.)* The official documents from the Turkish archives. They are irreplaceable.

(GENERAL *pokes among the papers and files on the judges' table while* PENSAR *and* HEINMAN *attempt to put things back where they were before he moved them. Same time,* ANAHID *has* MOURADIAN's *attention, nods toward* WEGNER)

GENERAL: *(Bumps* FREEMAN.*)* Yes, but I put them right there . . .

GOLDSMITH: *(Holds down papers.)* Please stop that.

GENERAL: Someone has taken them.

GOLDSMITH: They were here a minute ago.

HEINMAN: General, please.

(MOURADIAN *rises, makes his way toward* WEGNER.)

GENERAL: . . . they are authentic originals, not copies . . .

HEINMAN: Please, General, we will find them when . . .

GENERAL: *(Turns on* FREEMAN.*)* You took them.

(ANAHID *half-rises to see as Mouradian reaches* WEGNER. *They shake hands.*)

FREEMAN: Me?

GENERAL: You.

FREEMAN: *(Crosses his heart.)* Cross my heart.

(MOURADIAN *helps* WEGNER *to his feet, they fumble with the slide carousel box.*)

GENERAL: Where are they?

FREEMAN: I should know?

GENERAL: Return those documents now!

GOLDSMITH: *(Gavel.)* General!

(*The two old men drop the box.* MOURADIAN *retrieves it, hands it to* WEGNER. *As the search for the document goes on, they make their way forward.*)

HEINMAN: We will most certainly find your documents, General, but I suggest we get on with . . .

GOLDSMITH: *(Notices the old men.)* What is going on?

(WEGNER gives box to FREEMAN who opens it as ANAHID whispers to him.)

GENERAL: Please, it is an official document, it was signed personally by my Prime Minister late last night in Ankara and it was in . . .

PENSAR: *(Stands, leather folder in hand.)* Voila! I have them here. *(Hands it to the General.)* They somehow ended up inside this . . . and who is that?

(MOURADIAN begins to move WEGNER toward the witness chair.)

GOLDSMITH: Mr. Freeman, what is that man doing?

(HEINMAN recognizes WEGNER, stands motionless.)

FREEMAN: I don't . . . Anahid?

ANAHID: Dr. Goldsmith, I must apologize . . . to Mr. Freeman as well . . . I . . . we did not know if he would be able to be here to . . . he came from Italy . . .

GOLDSMITH: Mr. Freeman, is this some kind of ploy?

FREEMAN: Madame, I swear . . .

GENERAL: I've warned you all, he is a hoaxster. A circus huckster.

FREEMAN: Barker. I swear, I don't . . .

ANAHID: He knows nothing of this. The man is here as an eye witness, he . . .

(HEINMAN bows to WEGNER; WEGNER acknowledges.)

GOLDSMITH: He is Armenian? I have already ruled there will be no further . . .

HEINMAN: I know him.

GOLDSMITH: Yes?   PENSAR: You know him?

HEINMAN: *(Remains standing.)* He is German. His name is Armin Wegner.

GENERAL: *(To WEGNER.)* Who? *(Looks closely at the old man.)* I thought you were dead.

WEGNER: *(To General.)* Many times. Next time maybe will do the trick.

GOLDSMITH: Eric.

GENERAL: Madame, we have already established, the man is a liar and a traitor, he betrayed his own . . . and if he is not dead he must be senile by now.

WEGNER: If I am still breathing in two months, I will be ninety-one years of age. Someone should tell me I look young for my age.

MOURADIAN: Yah! I say that!

WEGNER: Danke, Gerard, you lie, but danke.

GENERAL: He hates Turks, who is he to be here?

WEGNER: *(To General.)* I mean no harm to your people, *ach, mein Gott,* the Turk-ish people, they are wonderful, no, no, we cannot blame them for what their government does. Who am I? Why am I here? I am here because I have to be, same as you.

GOLDSMITH: The question is, Sir, do you stay here?

ANAHID: *(Holds up page of notes.)* I have already told, you, he was there. He saw everything. *(To* WEGNER.*)* Tell them . . .

PENSAR: You were there when . . .

WEGNER: Yes. I will never forget their eyes, they will go with me to the grave.

GENERAL: This is an opera? Where is the music?

WEGNER: You like Wagner?

GENERAL: You realize people in my country are dying while you sit there and . . .

WEGNER: Oh, people are always dying, General, you cannot stop them. Just in my short time on this planet, millions have been tortured, butchered, brutalized, murdered, they did not need a famine, one calamity following the other as the child comes forth from the mother and then becomes the mother of the next monster, and so it goes, and so it goes.

GENERAL: Madame, the man proves himself to be incompetent, he should be dis-missed and . . .

HEINMAN: No.

GENERAL: No, you say, Herr Heinman?

HEINMAN: He should be heard.

GOLDSMITH: Eric?

HEINMAN: Dr. Goldsmith, in our country Herr Wegner is somewhat of a leg-end, to some he is a great hero of human rights, to others, yes, a traitor, but to so many he is a myth.

WEGNER: Ah!

A living hero, no? In the flesh, *ja?* A traitor too?

HEINMAN: In our country, Dr. Wegner achieved high status as a great writer, as a doctor of law, a man of great stature and promise. In 1933 he threw it all away by protesting the treatment of the Jews by Adolph Hitler. He was arrested and tortured by the Gestapo.

WEGNER: It was Turkey all over again, what they were doing to the Jews. My beau-tiful wife was Jewish, you see, and . . . she is gone now.

HEINMAN: They put him in a concentration camp to let him die. Instead, he es-caped to Italy. A traitor? Perhaps a magnificent traitor. Perhaps many things, a soldier, a true hero, a poet, a teacher, a dock worker, husband, father, socialist, priest, rabbi. A mystery. But he is a good man. And we are running out of good men. Yes, I think he stays here.

GOLDSMITH: All well and good, Eric, but . . .

HEINMAN: I ask you as a personal favor. He is neither Turk nor Armenian, he is without prejudice, he knows what happened and he will . . .

GENERAL: *(To HEINMAN.)* And you did not know what was happening to the Jews at the hands of the Nazis? Perhaps. Even so, how could one man standing alone . . . of course, we understand. I know what it is to be duty bound, yes, of course, you were a good soldier, a . . .

PENSAR: What is the General talking about?

HEINMAN: He is talking about me. Sir, you have browbeaten two old women, you have berated members of this committee, you have destroyed the career of an attorney at law, and now you intimidate me. And in my humble judgment you did not have to do any of that to get your way, you did not have to . . .

GENERAL: And you did not have to join the Nazi Party, did you? There is always a choice, yes?

PENSAR: What? You were a Nazi?

WEGNER: *(To GENERAL.)* On this we agree. The fork in the road. You go this way, go with the crowd, *ja*, at least they will not beat you, put you in prison, pull out your teeth with pliers, set your beard on fire, destroy your family and steal your shoes. Or you can . . .

GENERAL: *(To GOLDSMITH.)* Obviously demented. I beseech you . . .

(GOLDSMITH holds up her hand to silence GENERAL.)

WEGNER: Or you can go that way. Where you are often alone on the path, quite alone. And always frightened, *ja*, frightened almost to death. And lonely.

HEINMAN: It would be a lie to say that I did not fear the Nazis. I was paralyzed. What they would do. My mother and father, my sisters, we all knew. I wrote my name down on a piece of paper. I said some words. And then I kept silent. That one moment, I . . .

WEGNER: *Keine antwort ist auch eine antwort.*

HEINMAN: *Ja*, silence gives consent. I ponder that moment every day of my life. I look back and try to make it different. I cannot. You see, I am not a hero, I am merely a man.

PENSAR: *(To GOLDSMITH.)* You could have told me I would be sitting so close to a Nazi.

WEGNER: As my Italian friends say, *Meglio un giorno de leone che cento dapecora:*

PENSAR: Better one day as a lion than a hundred as a sheep.

WEGNER: *(Almost to himself.)* Who pays more, the lion or the sheep? Always there is a price, yes, always a . . .

FREEMAN: Dr. Wegner, in the time you spent in Turkey during the First World War, can you . . .

GENERAL: This is quite pointless.

WEGNER: Ah, exactly, you understand. I would look at what was being done to those people and I would say, what is the point? There was no point, and that is a very important thing to understand about the affairs of humans. *(Beat.)* It's their eyes that stay with you. More than sixty years now and I still see . . .

GENERAL: No point?

WEGNER: This God. He, She, It gave us many religions, *nein?* Many races, black, white, brown, red, many races, many nationalities, Adam and Eve.

GOLDSMITH: Men and women.

WEGNER: *Ja*, but what did He have in mind? Perhaps that we would find joy in our differences? Instead we are alienated from one another. Do you realize, General, that we are the only species on this planet that hates itself?

GENERAL: He's quite insane, you know.

WEGNER: *(To* HEINMAN.*)* Have you mentioned the *staatsprezess* here? You know? In Berlin? The . . .

HEINMAN: The trial.

WEGNER: *Ja*, 1921 it was. Talaat was living in Berlin. Living quite openly. A young man walked up to him one day and shot a *kugel*, a bullet, through his head. *Au revoir*, Talaat.

GENERAL: A flagrant act of terrorism.

WEGNER: An act of terrorism or an act of honor, who knows? But Talaat is kaput and the young man is arrested, Solomon Tehlirian. The trial made very big headlines, murder was less acceptable than war. When it started the question was: Is Tehlirian guilty as charged? By noon the question had become: Is Talaat guilty of mass murder? And much evidence was presented that Talaat was the driving force behind the plan to destroy the Armenians.

GENERAL: This has never been proven! Never!

WEGNER: *Jawhol*. Sadly, *jawohl*.

*(*WEGNER *produces a tissue-wrapped package. He unwraps carefully.)*

ANAHID: *(Rises, approaches.)* Can I help you?

WEGNER: *(Hands package to* ANAHID.*)* It would be most uncivil to turn down an offer from such a lovely *maidchen. Danke*

*(*ANAHID *unwraps it with the same delicacy* WEGNER *demonstrated.)*

WEGNER: *(Cont'd.) Ja*, with care. They are quite old. I have difficulty reading these days, so . . . so if you would be kind enough to read the one on top? *Ach*, first,

I should tell you, these are telegrams that were sent to Jemal Bey, one of the Young Turks, in 1915 and 1916. He was second in command to Talaat and was headquartered in Aleppo where was situated one of the largest death camps. I think the earliest one is dated March 15th, there were earlier messages, but I do not have these. Can you . . . March 15th?

ANAHID: *(Reading.)* It says, "It is the duty of all of us to effect on the broadest lines the realization of the noble project of wiping out of Armenians who have for centuries been a barrier to the empire's progress in civilization." Signed Talaat.

GENERAL: Talaat was referring to Russian Armenians, soldiers who. . . .

WEGNER: You know, General, I never thought of that. This old brain, you know? Anahid?

ANAHID: April 19: "We are obliged to resort to very bloody methods . . . our political opposition has called upon us to be merciful. This is nothing short of stupidi- ty." Signed Talaat

GENERAL: War is always bloody.

ANAHID: September 3, 1915: "Submit the women and children also to the tactics which have been previously prescribed as to be applied to the adults." October 21 . . .

WEGNER: Ah, yes, this is the one about the little ones.

ANAHID: "Collect and keep only those orphans who cannot remember the terrors to which their parents have been subjected. Send the rest away with the cara- vans." Talaat.

FREEMAN: The children.

WEGNER: *Ja*, the little ones with the big eyes.

ANAHID: Dec. 11: "We learn that some individuals are obtaining photographs and letters which represent tragic events . . . have these dangerous persons arrested . . ." Talaat.

WEGNER: That's me, I was a very dangerous person.

ANAHID: December 29: "Foreign officers are photographing Armenian corpses along the road. It is essential to have these corpses buried at once, do not leave them out in the open."

FREEMAN: Neatness counts.

GENERAL: You are enjoying this, Mr. Freeman? Madame, I think you will agree that I have tolerated this demonstration with patience and self restraint. I wish to point out that these pieces of paper—they are all bogus frauds created as part and parcel of an international scheme of propaganda and incitement to terrorism—and they should be disregarded as such.

WEGNER: The telegrams are authentic.

GENERAL: They are so blatantly incriminating, Jemal would have destroyed them and . . .

WEGNER: It was Jemal who preserved them. He did not trust Talaat. He knew the war was lost. He also knew of his own reputation as the butcher. He wanted to be able to prove that Talaat owned the butcher shop.

GENERAL: Very well, how did you come by them?

WEGNER: The German officers on Jemal's staff. If you turn them over, they were signed by those officers. Brave men, they knew they could be killed for this. These are just a few, there were many others that now reside in the Turkish archives. Of course you know that, but your government refuses to let anyone see them. Thank God these few were preserved.

GENERAL: And by whom were they preserved?

WEGNER: By he who smuggled them out of Turkey. Me, I am the thief. *Jawohl*, I did that. I had duplicates made and it was I who provided those copies to the defense attorney at the trial of Talaat's assassin. Those copies have resided in the German archives since 1924. It is in my will that these originals will go there as well. Soon maybe.

HEINMAN: Dr. Wegner, can you tell us what you, ah, as a witness, what . . .

WEGNER: Yes, you want to know what I saw there. Personally. In Turkey. What they did to the Armenians. As civilized people, you have always suspected, *ja*? The truth?

PENSAR: *Oui, c'est vrai.*

WEGNER: We don't ask, we are afraid to know.

PENSAR: This also is true.

WEGNER: Why? Are we so heartless? *(Beat.)* Maybe, if we know, we are afraid we will have to do something about it. And we are afraid that we will not have the courage to do what must be done. We fear our own cowardice. God forgive us.

HEINMAN: Dr. Wegner, you say you saw the death marches?

WEGNER: I saw. I watched the Armenians walk into the dessert and never return, leaving their dead along the way, dropping them like a rag picker tossing garbage off the side of his wagon.

GENERAL: He is writing more fiction now, can't you . . .

WEGNER: They took a part of me, they gave me a part of themselves. We were both on journeys that had no end. They changed my life. They changed who I was. *Immer.*

HEINMAN: Forever.

WEGNER: Forever. *(Beat.)* Ja, I saw.

HEINMAN: You were alone?

WEGNER: *Ach*, I could not ask a fellow soldier to come with me, it was too dangerous.

GENERAL: You disobeyed orders. In wartime . . .

WEGNER: I could not tell anyone what I was doing or   kaput. So I wrote to my mother, *ja*. I asked her, "Do I still have the right to breathe . . . when all about me are the eyes of the dead?" She told me: "Now you live only to bear witness. So you must stay alive." And I have tried to bear witness. Who would listen?

HEINMAN: The world was indifferent?

WEGNER: Indifference, an evil word. In German it even sounds evil, *ja*? *Gleichgultigkeit*. But my country was dying. She was being torn apart. You could not blame the people. Then came the Turkish denials. They foretold a future that could make God tremble. (*Beat.*) You see, if they could get you to believe it never happened, it could happen again. This was perhaps the greater evil. This Armenian tragedy, it was the *eingang*, the . . .

HEINMAN: The doorway.

WEGNER: And the door was off its hinges. You cannot walk away from history. It will . . . *pirsch?*

HEINMAN: Stalk.

WEGNER: Stalk you, it will haunt you into your grave . . . as millions go into graves without markers. Forgiveness? A future? Go forward? Nein. We must have the courage to go back, to see that we are stuck in time. Years later, when the Gestapo strapped me naked to the table and used the whips, I had one clear thought. I was not being tortured. I was being christened. I was an Armenian. I would later be a Jew. That's when I knew that these people had given me the most precious gift I would ever . . .

GENERAL: Dr. Goldsmith, please . . . I think you would agree that this man has nothing to offer.

HEINMAN: You are the last one to judge that.

GENERAL: What then can you offer us, Herr Wegner?

WEGNER: Photographs?

GENERAL: We have already rebuffed Mr. Freeman's insidious effort to introduce staged photographs as valid evidence of . . .

WEGNER: Staged?

GENERAL: Spurious. Fraudulent photographs that have been floating around for years and . . .

WEGNER: I took them.

GENERAL: No one knows who, what, where or how they . . .

WEGNER: I said I took them.

PENSAR: You took them?

WEGNER: Most of them. Others also. German officers who were horrified at what they saw. They gave me their negatives. I kept them hidden in my belt, I was skinny then.

PENSAR: You have the photographs in that box?

FREEMAN: (*Removes carousel, holds it up.*) Slides.

GENERAL: I must point out that if Turkish officers had seen the Germans making photographs of supposedly incriminating activities, they would have put a stop to . . .

WEGNER: No, it was required by Talaat himself, *ja*. Photos were taken and sent to Talaat as proof that his orders were being followed. He did not trust the people in the field, he wanted the photos taken by German and Austrian officers, photographic proof . . .

GENERAL: If this is true, which it is not, then the photos would have been in Talaat's possession. Were he such a monstrously diabolical criminal, he would have destroyed them.

WEGNER: More photos were taken than were sent.

PENSAR: Since the General was kind enough to have a screen set up, and the projector . . .

FREEMAN: An excellent idea, Professor. *(To judges.)* May we continue?

GENERAL: Dr. Heinman!

HEINMAN: Would you call this a moment of choice, General?

GOLDSMITH: Eric?

HEINMAN: Yes.

GENERAL: Dr. Goldsmith, a moment, please consider . . . showing the kind of photos that always emerge in the aftermath of bloody battle . . .

WEGNER: No battles. Only the killing, the suffering, the dying . . . each photograph authenticated by the supervising Austrian or German officer. These officers were also required to provide an accompanying letter of verification. They gave me their copies. In the box.

(FREEMAN lifts out of the box a handful of pages. ANAHID takes them. FREEMAN takes the carousel to the slide projector, fidgets.)

GENERAL: No, stop this. Dr. Heinman. Dr. Goldsmith, you must . . . I am obligated to give you official notification that I intend to file a complaint with your governing body at the United Nations and take immediate steps to . . . to . . .

PENSAR: Yes?

GENERAL: Yes, to have each and every member of this Committee removed from this . . .

GOLDSMITH: General, you do yourself a disservice. Threats? Especially with the news media here? What else? Are you going to make a personal call to my president to tell him how I lost control of this hearing? Are you going to use Turkey's influence to rob me of my future? What else? A forced virginity exam?

GENERAL: You have certainly given the press something to write about. I fear your president may . . .

GOLDSMITH: I share that fear. I told you that I learned a lot from my Grandmother, Frances Perkins. She told me everyone in this world is afraid of losing something. Something very dear to them, a loved one, a position, a house a fortune, a way of life, something. They are afraid that if they lose this thing, they will not know who they are anymore. When I was quite young, she said to me, if you are in great fear of losing something, then lose it. The fear will go away, but you will not. Mr. Freeman, your witness.

GENERAL: I refuse to sit here while this outrageous spectacle takes place!

PENSAR: Then leave, Sir! Leave now! *(Beat. Calls out.)* Can we have the lights lowered?

(Lights dim. FREEMAN *has installed the carousel, flicks on the projector light.)*

FREEMAN: Dr. Wegner, would you let me know when to start and when to, uh . . .
WEGNER: *Ja.* First slide, *bitte.*

(The images on the screen change consistent with the descriptions provided.)

WEGNER: *(Cont'd.)* Hanged without a trial after . . .
GENERAL: Military tribunal during a time of war. This man was . . .
WEGNER: *(Shares document with Anahid.)* The official directive is an order issued
    February 27, 1915, by Talaat. Right here, Anahid, it should read, "The Imperial
    Ottoman Empire . . . uh . . ."
GENERAL: The white gown, it . . .
ANAHID: *(Reads.)* ". . . Ottoman Empire issued an order for the extermination of
    the Armenian race. All Armenians are to be taken out of the towns and slaugh-
    tered. Even babes in the cradle are not to be spared."
GENERAL: That white gown signifies this man was found guilty of a capital crime.
    This was the lawful execution of a . . .
WEGNER: Next slide.

(Image is similar to prior one, but the victims are not wearing white gowns.)

WEGNER: *(Cont'd.)* No white gowns. The crime was just to be Armenian, Chris-
    tian. Next.
PENSAR: Even so: Why should a photograph like that disturb the General, eh?

(The second slide appears on the screen. MOURADIAN *rises.)*

WEGNER: This is a group of deported Armenians, south of Aleppo.
PENSAR: There must be thousands of them.
MOURADIAN: *(Approaches for better view.)* Yah.
WEGNER: They are walking into the Arabian Desert. Next. *(Beat.)* They will not
    come back. Next.

PENSAR: Just taking a Sunday afternoon   GOLDSMITH: Professor, please.
    nap. Nothing disturbing in that, is
    there?

MOURADIAN: *(Points at image with his cane.)* Yah, me. There. Little boy.
PENSAR: Just a stroll in the sunshine.
WEGNER: Next slide please. *(Slide change. An image of dead body on a roadside.)*
    You recall the telegram in which Talaat criticized the local authorities for leav-

ing dead bodies in full view at the roadside. This is what he meant. Just a bit too incriminating. Next.

(Slide change. Image of murdered parents, child with distended belly.)

FREEMAN: Just a little kid.
PENSAR: The child, where is his mother?
MOURADIAN: *(In Armenian.)* Mother?
PENSAR: Where is this child now, Mr. Ambassador? Bouncing his grandchild on his knee?
WEGNER: Next.
GOLDSMITH: *(Motions toward MOURADIAN.)* The old man.

(Image depicts children in a long line; malnutrition and fear.)

FREEMAN: More kids.
GENERAL: Get him out of here.
WEGNER: This photo is in response to order no. 603, November 5, 1915: "We are informed that the little ones are adopted by certain Muslim families and protected as servants. You are to collect all such children and . . ." Gerard?
MOURADIAN: Yah, kill them.
WEGNER: Does that sound familiar?
GOLDSMITH: *(Nudges HEINMAN, nods at MOURADIAN.)* Eric, please.
PENSAR: Perhaps they are just taking a sun bath, General?
MOURADIAN: Sun bath?

(HEINMAN rises, goes to MOURADIAN, touches his arm gently.)

FREEMAN: *(To GENERAL.)* I think he's talking to you.

(HEINMAN speaks inaudibly to MOURADIAN.)

GENERAL: I am steadfast, Sir. I maintain that these photographs could have been . . .

(HEINMAN gently leads MOURADIAN toward his seat.)

WEGNER: I assure you they are quite authentic. Next slide.

(The image of a pile of human bones explodes onto the screen.)

PENSAR: *(Rises.)* What in God's name is that? Is that pile of human bones, that rubble?

GOLDSMITH: *(Her hand on* PENSAR's *arm.)* Please sit down, Rene.

GENERAL: That is obscene! Stop this now!

ANAHID: January 18: "It has been ascertained that there are about 5000 people from the said provinces under our jurisdiction."

PENSAR: Can you explain all this, General?

ANAHID: ". . . most of these are women and children."

PENSAR: *(Leaves his place.)* General?

ANAHID: ". . . these women and children have been sent under Turkish guard with the understanding that . . ."

PENSAR: *(Advances toward* GENERAL.*)* How many were children?

GENERAL: *(Rises. To* GOLDSMITH.*)* Madame.

ANAHID: ". . . that they are never to return."

PENSAR: What did you do to them?

GOLDSMITH: *(Taps gavel.)* Rene.

*(*HEINMAN *has not persuaded* MOURADIAN *to take his seat, but commotion gets his attention and he turns to see* PENSAR *advancing toward the* GENERAL.*)*

PENSAR: *(Advances.)* They look like leftovers after a hearty meal! Did you eat them, General? Did you eat all those Armenians?

*(*PENSAR *has advanced to the point that he is a physical threat to* GENERAL.*)*

PENSAR: *(Cont'd)* Did you eat my little friend André as well, and my mother and father!?

*(*GOLDSMITH *rises, slams her gavel.* HEINMAN *starts back toward* PENSAR.*)*

GOLDSMITH: Dr. Heinman!

GENERAL: That man is mad!

PENSAR: *(Leaps at the* GENERAL.*)* Did you eat those Armenians!

HEINMAN: *(Grabs* PENSAR.*)* Rene, stop!

GOLDSMITH: Stop the projector! Freeman!

GENERAL: *(To* FREEMAN.*)* Stop it now!

*(*HEINMAN *and* PENSAR *struggle.* MOURADIAN *begins to approach them.)*

PENSAR: You claim to be civilized!

GOLDSMITH: *(On her feet, slamming gavel.)* Stop that projector now!

PENSAR: You are animals!

FREEMAN: *(Fidgets with projector.)* I'm trying!
GENERAL: Damn you, Freeman!

(PENSAR strikes HEINMAN, who staggers. At the same time, the projector stops. PENSAR becomes aware of himself, covers his face with his hands.)

GOLDSMITH: *(Pounds the gavel.)* That is enough! *(Beat. To all.)* Everyone! You will remain where you are. Eric. *(Points at PENSAR.)* Bring him.

(HEINMAN gently leads PENSAR out as they follow GOLDSMITH.)

GOLDSMITH: *(Cont'd.—To all.)* You will all excuse us for a moment. That is not a request.

(GOLDSMITH, HEINMAN, PENSAR exit. MOURADIAN up center.)

MOURADIAN: Yah. Me Mouradian. I speak now.
GENERAL: Get him out of here.
FREEMAN: He's just an old man.
ANAHID: He means no harm.
GENERAL: He does not belong here.
FREEMAN: Mr. Mouradian? You'll have to . . . take a seat . . .

(MOURADIAN picks up the Bible kisses it.)

MOURADIAN: I do. Yah. You ask, I answer. I live in Urfa. They come, the soldiers come. *(Points at GENERAL.)* Like that one. They take us out of Ourfa. Shoot the men.
GENERAL: Sit down and be quiet, old man.
MOURADIAN: Twenty-six days we walk, many die. Old people first. The women kill their babies, yah, they do that, I see it.
WEGNER: Gerard, you distress yourself.

MOURADIAN: We got to cross the river. They got boats there. Some fall in the river, so they shoot them. They shoot them in the river. They laughing while they shooting. I am 12 years old, bodies float in the river, women, children, babies . . . floating away forever.

GENERAL: *(To FREEMAN.)* Mr. Freeman, you are responsible. Can you silence this man?

Can you please . . .
If he were not pathetic he would be . . .

GENERAL: He would be amusing. But . . .

MOURADIAN: I amuse you? You laugh at me? I understand. I crazy, not stupid. You want me to go away, yah?

GENERAL: Yah, go . . .

MOURADIAN: Never. You go home to your family, I am there, me, Mouradian. Your sun comes up tomorrow, I am there. Touch your wife, kiss your children, go to meetings with important men, kneel to pray to your God, I, Mouradian, I will be there always. Always.

GENERAL: Get that man out of here!

MOURADIAN: (To audience.) What is this? Hah? You. Look at you. (He surveys audience members.) What are you all doing here? You are listening to sad stories? Do you enjoy that? You do nothing but listen to sad stories, is that it? I want to know who you are. Me. I am Armenia. I will always be Armenia.

GENERAL: (To all.) Will someone please come and take this lunatic?

MOURADIAN: (Points cane at ANAHID.) She is Armenia. Yah. Me too, yah, I am Armenia. Look on me.

GENERAL: You are insane.

MOURADIAN: (Advances to GENERAL, who stands) Yah, crazy. You are clever, no? You rob my mind and then you call me crazy. Yah, that is clever. If you cannot murder me, if you cannot do that, then you drive me away. That is clever, too . . . yah?

(MOURADIAN taps his cane against GENERAL's chest. GOLDSMITH and HEINMAN enter, but freeze when they see MOURADIAN and GENERAL.)

MOURADIAN: (Cont'd.) Smile at crazy man, yah. I am crazy, smile. Clever people smile good, no? (Beat.) Give me back my mind, you animal!

(GENERAL does not retreat, stands at attention.)

MOURADIAN: (Cont'd.) You lost something too, Turk. And you will never get it back!

(MOURADIAN winds up the cane, it appears he is going to strike the GENERAL, but he brings the cane down onto the GENERAL's files several times as ANAHID and FREEMAN rush to restrain him.)

MOURADIAN: (Cont'd.) Never, never, never!

(The GENERAL wrenches the cane from MOURADIAN and yanks him across the table. He raises the cane as if to strike the old man across the back.)

GENERAL: (Cane raised.) Damn you, will you never die!?

(Cameras flashing, ANAHID *quickly shields* MOURADIAN *with her own body as* HEINMAN *rushes center.* GOLDSMITH *stunned, remains frozen.)*

HEINMAN: General!   FREEMAN: Hey!

MOURADIAN: *(Looking up at* GENERAL.) Yah? Yah?
GOLDSMITH: General!

*(*GENERAL *hears* GOLDSMITH, *becomes aware of the cameras. He throws down the cane, sits.* MOURADIAN *upright,* ANAHID *recovers the cane for him.)*

GOLDSMITH: *(Crosses, to* MOURADIAN.) Sir, you will leave this place now.
MOURADIAN: All right. Yah, my time to go. I go.
WEGNER: *(Rises, reaches toward* MOURADIAN.) Gerard. Come.

(It is now WEGNER *who helps* MOURADIAN *toward exit as* GOLDSMITH *takes her place at Committee table.)*

WEGNER: *(Cont'd. — as they exit.)* You think maybe we're getting too old for this sort
    of thing? *(They exit.)*
FREEMAN: *(Watches* MOURADIAN *and* WEGNER *leave.)* There goes the twentieth
    century.
GENERAL: I must now remind you, Madame, that your president has made known
    his wishes.
GOLDSMITH: And I will remind you, General, that I serve the United Nations here,
    not . . .
GENERAL: I can only suggest that you comply with those . . .
GOLDSMITH: That would seem the intelligent thing to do. But Dr. Heinman, Pro-
    fessor Pensar and I have come to the decision that . . .

(The GENERAL *leaps to his feet, grabs the census report takes it to* GOLDSMITH'S *table and slams it down there.)*

GENERAL: No. This is your decision. You and you alone.
HEINMAN: We are together.
GOLDSMITH: *(Gavel.)* Our decision. We lack sufficient and credible documenta-
    tion of the nutritional needs of your nation to render an evaluation that is fair
    and equitable to other applicant nations.
GENERAL: That is unacceptable, Madame.
ANAHID: What is she saying?
GOLDSMITH: We therefore require that a new census be taken in Turkey under the
    direct supervision of United Nations officials who will attest to its accuracy.

GENERAL: Do you realize what you do?

GOLDSMITH: If your government declines to accept these conditions, Sir, no grain will be released to Turkey at this time based on this hearing.

GENERAL: This cannot be.

GOLDSMITH: You can file an appeal today.

ANAHID: Mr. Freeman, what . . .

FREEMAN: I'm not sure. Wait a . . .

GOLDSMITH: Your appeal will be given priority attention. *(Reaches for the gavel.)* This hearing is . . .

GENERAL: Madame!

ANAHID: *(On her feet.)* No! This hearing is not closed! Not while children starve!

FREEMAN: *(Grabs* ANAHID's *arm.)* Anahid!

ANAHID: *(To* GOLDSMITH.) Please listen to me for one moment, I . . .

GOLDSMITH: *(Hesitates.)* We have already listened to you, this hearing . . .

ANAHID: This decision, Madame . . . people will . . . children will . . . this will bring shame to our cause, you make us all bear a terrible guilt.

GOLDSMITH: That is not my cause, Madame, and it is not my shame.

ANAHID: Please, listen, listen to me: We all stand here. We are all adults. It is the adults who make important decisions about what will be and what will not be. But who pays?

HEINMAN: We all pay.

ANAHID: We pay nothing. Infants. The old and the sick. They will be the first to die. Please, not again. I appeal to the mother in you. The mother I could never be. Do you feel nothing?

GOLDSMITH: Do I feel? Yes, I feel. I feel that I was doing a service to humanity by accepting the offer to chair this committee. I feel that it was in the interest of world peace that I left my children and my career behind. I feel that by doing the right thing here today I have jeopardized my future and the security of my family. And I feel that the food stolen in the name of the children of one nation is death to the children of another nation

HEINMAN: That is true.

GOLDSMITH: I have answered your question and now I will ask mine: Do you think that anyone here today has won anything? Anyone? Anything? Who? No one. Nothing. We have all lost. And that is what happens when you inflict one terrible injustice as remedy for another.

ANAHID: What choice did we have!? Where can we go?

FREEMAN: *(Rises.)* Dr. Goldsmith, perhaps . . .

GOLDSMITH: Yes? What else do you have to lose, Mr. Freeman? What say you?

FREEMAN: I stand with my client.

GOLDSMITH: And what say you, General? Last call.

GENERAL: Our Ambassador to the United Nations will take this matter up with the Security . . .

GOLDSMITH: *(Drops the gavel.)* This hearing is closed. *(Exits. Camera flashes cease)*

(The GENERAL *is left standing, stunned. Stunned also are* FREEMAN *and* ANAHID. *All in silence for a moment. They turn to gather their belongings.* HEINMAN *hesitates, then approaches* FREEMAN.*)*

HEINMAN: You will have a different kind of hearing to deal with when you return home.

FREEMAN: Yeah.

HEINMAN: If there is anything I can do . . .

FREEMAN: I think I'm on my own.

HEINMAN: *Ja.* As with all of us.

FREEMAN: But thanks.

(As HEINMAN *exits,* FREEMAN *turns to see* ANAHID *slumped in her chair, the* GENERAL *packing his case.)*

FREEMAN: *(Cont'd. —To the* GENERAL.*)* Give up the lie, man. All you have to do . . .

GENERAL: Yes. You Americans love easy answers.

*(*FREEMAN *sits to rest, gather his things.* ANAHID *rises as the* GENERAL *starts to leave. She stands center, he senses her eyes on his back. He stops, turns.)*

GENERAL: Madame?

ANAHID: You have the power to change everything.

GENERAL: Would it do any good at all to tell you that I'm sorry?

ANAHID: You have the power to free the world from the past. And the world has to stay where it is if you fail to use that power.

*(*FREEMAN *stops packing to watch, listen.)*

GENERAL: You really think that?

ANAHID: I know. I know you are afraid. You are a very brave man, but you are afraid. I ask you to live in your courage, not in your fear. Let the dead be buried now. Speak the truth.

GENERAL: Madame, I truly regret what happened to you. I hope you return home with some peace of mind that you have . . .

ANAHID: I have done nothing.

GENERAL: Yes, I fear you have spent your life on a futile quest. Remember what that soldier told you. *(In Turkish.)* "One generation after another . . ." *(In English.)* "One generation after another . . ."

(GENERAL exits. ANAHID alone down center. FREEMAN, seated, watches as she stares after the GENERAL

ANAHID: "One generation after another, you will cry out to the world . . . nobody will believe you."

(Lights down. Lights out)

The end.

JOYCE VAN DYKE

A GIRL'S WAR

A Play in Two Acts

THE PLAYWRIGHT

Joyce Van Dyke's *A Girl's War*, received its world premiere at New Repertory Theatre, opening 17 September 2003. Previously, as a workshop production at Playwrights' Theatre in 2001, the play had been named one of the "Top Ten" productions of the year by *The Boston Globe*. It has also won a number of awards, including the 2001 John Gassner Memorial Playwriting Award (NETC), the 2001 Provincetown Theater Company Playwriting Competition, and designation as a finalist for the 2003 Jane Chambers Award.

The playwright is the recipient of a 2001 Massachusetts Cultural Council Playwriting Finalist Grant and a graduate of Boston University's playwriting program. Her previous full-length play, *Love in the Gulf*, was produced by Boston Playwrights' Theatre in 1996. A lecturer on Shakespeare and lyric poetry at Harvard University Extension School for the past fourteen years, she also taught at Wellesley College for four years and has published articles on literature and drama in *Virginia Quarterly Review*, *Shakespeare Survey*, *Studies in English Literature*, and *The Women's Review of Books*, among other publications. Before moving to Boston, she worked as an independent speechwriter for presidential appointees in the Departments of Labor and Justice and as a researcher and writer for members of Congress in Washington, D.C. She holds degrees in English literature (B.A., Stanford University;

M.A., Brandeis University; Ph.D., University of Virginia) and in creative writing (M.A. in creative writing, Boston University).

A member of the Dramatists Guild and Stage Source, she made her playwriting debut in 1991 at MCI—Framingham, the Massachusetts prison for women, with *The Scarlet Letter*, an adaptation of the novel performed by and for the women in prison. Other plays include *The Perfect Man* (staged reading, Harvard University, 1993) and *National Guilt Festival* (Underground Theatre Workshop, Boston, 1995).

She lives in the Boston area with her husband and two sons.

ABOUT WRITING *A GIRL'S WAR*

The germ of A *Girl's War* was a speculative conversation over lunch with a friend about what it might feel like to be a model (neither of us had any experience): how would it affect your self-consciousness to be continually looked at, continually photographed? Afterwards I kept thinking about it, and these musings began to coalesce into a someone, a model—a "girl" as they're called—but it wasn't until months later, when I imagined this model coming from Karabakh, that the idea for the play was born. She had come to New York—why? What would make her go back home to Karabakh? And what would happen to her when she did? Eventually, Karabakh and the war ended up taking over the play, while the model business and the issues related to it (including a New York subplot with a character from Argentina) receded substantially, to be postponed to a subsequent play.

The obvious question is *why* did she—this model—come from Karabakh? It satisfied a dramatic need. What more unlikely conjunction could there be? There aren't many Armenians in the fashion industry—perhaps none from Karabakh. The incongruity appealed to me, the radical extremes of the two worlds in every respect—New York fashion and the culture of mountainous Karabakh, half a world distant and in some ways a century or more in the past.

But it is not by chance that this eastern/western model came from Karabakh. I am half Armenian; my maternal grandparents came from Kharpert; and my grandmother was a survivor of the deportations of 1915. Although the character of Arshaluis, the mother in the play, is not based on my grandmother, some of her lines are things I heard my grandmother say. I do know that as I was working on this play, I had a physical sensation I've never had before, that I was excavating something real and whole. Whatever it was that I was uncovering, I felt I had to treat it with the utmost care and accuracy, and I have attempted to do so in depicting the heartbreaking and enormously complex situation in Karabakh. I also knew that I did not want to write a play about the Armenian genocide—or I didn't feel able to do so. But to write a play about the war in Karabakh was a way of exploring a particular war zone that had some analogies to what I knew about the genocide. Certainly, I wasn't aware while writing of all the connections between these stories. It's hard for me to believe now, but it didn't occur to me until after the play was written that the character of Seryosha in A Girl's War had something to do with my uncle, my grandmother's son—a boy who disappeared during the 1915 death march and many years later was miraculously found, and who had become a shepherd and a flute-player.

So, the characters in the play are fictional—all of them—but living in a situation that I have tried to make as close to present-day reality as I could. Of course, the situation of the play resonates far beyond Karabakh and its unresolved conflict; there are so many wars, in many cultures, that could be the basis for a story like this one.

JOYCE VAN DYKE

A GIRL'S WAR

A Play in Two Acts

JOYCE VAN DYKE

CHARACTERS

ANAHID SARKISIAN (called ANNA), 31, a model

ARSHALUIS SARKISIAN, 55, her mother; now, a
 sniper in the Karabakh army.

SERGEI SARKISIAN (called SERYOZHA), 21, a shepherd; ANNA's younger brother.

STEPHEN WELLINGTON, 50, a photographer

TITO UCCELLO, 22, his assistant

ILYAS ALIZADE, 22, a refugee and deserter from the
 Azerbaijani army

SETTING

*The action takes place in the present in a mountain
village near the Karabakh–Azerbaijan front, and also
in a photographer's studio in New York City. The
main location is the central room of the Sarkisian
house in the village of Matarash in Karabakh.* It is
an old (nineteenth-century) stone house built on the
mountainside. A main wing of the house was ruined
by bombs eight years earlier and has never been rebuilt. A heavy plastic sheet is nailed over the crumbling opening to the ruined wing; over the years, duct
tape has repaired tears in the plastic. The house is
sparsely furnished, although everything is kept
scrupulously clean. The one exception to the otherwise
shabby furnishings is the "martyr's corner," with a
small table that holds two large framed photographs
of Anna's brothers, as well as a Bible and a crucifix.*

*Karabakh—also known as Nagorno–Karabakh—is a small Armenian-populated enclave in the southern Caucasus Mountains. During the Soviet regime, when Karabakh was an autonomous region within the Soviet republic of Azerbaijan, it had a mixed population of ethnic Armenians (about three-quarters) and Azerbaijanis (about one-quarter). In 1988, Karabakh became the first territory in the USSR to demand independence and unification with the neighboring Soviet republic of Armenia, their ethnic kin. "Ethnic cleansing" followed, leading to full-scale civil war between Armenians and Azerbaijanis after the 1991 collapse of the Soviet Union. In 1994 a cease-fire went into effect, but the political situation remains unresolved, and border skirmishes and deaths continue to occur. More than a million people, both Azerbaijanis and Armenians, were displaced or made refugees by the conflict; nearly a decade after the cease-fire, many Azerbaijani refugees still live in refugee camps in Azerbaijan.

The Karabakh village of Matarash (its Armenian name) or Madariz (its Azerbaijani name), where most of the action of the play occurs, is fictional.

ACT ONE

Scene One

(In the dark, a strobe flashes on ANNA in a sequence of different postures, being photographed by STEPHEN. Lights come up on a photography studio, New York City, afternoon. TITO is alone, arranging strobes and reflectors on the set.)

STEPHEN: (off; calling.) Tito? You ready to go?
TITO: She's not out yet.

(ANNA enters, oblivious, and hurries across the stage carrying a book.)

    Anna?
(ANNA exits.) Sure thing.

(STEPHEN enters with a camera with a Polaroid back.)

STEPHEN: I'm not happy, Tito!
TITO: She'll be out in a sec. Supposed to be a nice weekend. You going out to the beach?
STEPHEN: Is she reading in there? (Calling.) Anna!
ANNA: (off) Tito, tell him I'm not ready!

(TITO "passes" this remark to STEPHEN.)

STEPHEN: C'mon, c'mon—(*indicating he wants* TITO *to pose for him on the set.*)

(TITO *turns his good side toward the camera, smoothes his "dress."*)

TITO: Or, you could just go with me.
STEPHEN: I'm tempted.

(STEPHEN *takes a Polaroid of* TITO. *He paces as he waits for the Polaroid to develop.*)

What the hell is she—(*directed off at* ANNA.)
TITO: It's makeup . . . Hey, that building you were talking about, with the court-
    yard –
STEPHEN: Yeah?
TITO: —I stopped by this morning on my way down and—
STEPHEN: What'd you think? You go into the courtyard?
TITO: Yeah, I felt—(*putting a hand on his solar plexus*)—I felt it. Must be some nu-
    merical thing, huh?—the proportions—like the golden ratio—

(ANNA *enters, still carrying her book.*)

    (*Admiring* ANNA.) Hey! Wow!
STEPHEN: Let's go, let's go! Make my life worth living, Tito! Is that too much to ask?
    Can't we make some Italian light? I thought you were supposed to be Italian.

(STEPHEN *prepares to take a Polaroid of* ANNA. *She stands on the set half reading her
book.*)

    No, no, no, no, no, no—give me a better angle, Anna!

(*She turns, without looking up from her book.*)

STEPHEN: (*cont.*) Turn. More. Turn. More! Hey Anna, you know we kicked your
    pay rate up to Model Occasionally Lifts Her Eyes From The Page.

(ANNA *looks up.* STEPHEN *takes the Polaroid.*)

    (*To* ANNA.) Many thanks.

(STEPHEN *waits for the Polaroid to develop,* ANNA *reads.*)

    (*To* TITO.) So why don't you find out how we can shoot there? See who we
    need to talk to. (*Watching the Polaroid develop, addressing the air.*) I don't
    think I'm happy!

(He looks at the Polaroid, sticks it in his pocket. He prepares to take another picture.)

Turn, Anna. Turn. More.

(STEPHEN takes another Polaroid.)

Tito—.

(STEPHEN moves upstage with TITO to discuss some pictures. ANNA, still holding her book, goes into a daydream . . . and with change in lighting ARSHALUIS enters carrying a large crockery bowl of madzoon [yogurt] and a spoon.)

ARSHALUIS: Taste.

ANNA: It's so hot.

ARSHALUIS: Taste, I say!

ANNA: It's too hot to eat.

ARSHALUIS: Not too hot for *madzoon!* Come taste! *(Indicating ANNA's book.)* What is that?

ANNA: "Poems of the English Socialists." William Blake. Percy Shelley.

ARSHALUIS: Da, Shelley. We learned in school. "I fall upon the thorns of life, I bleed." "Ode to the West Wind," composed 1819. Poetry is good, but history is more important. Come, sit and taste!

(ARSHALUIS spoons madzoon into ANNA's mouth. With every statement comes a spoonful.)

Very sweet, eh? That time, I was telling before, Armenia had empire—you remember? Long long ago. Before Jesus Christ. Empire that touched three seas.

(Spoonful.)

Armenia is first nation in all the world to become Christian. First nation in all the world to translate Bible into our own language.

(Spoonful.)

Last Armenian kingdom was 1375. After that time, Armenians ruled by many other peoples . . . Persians . . . Russians . . . but especially Ottoman Turks. Mohammedans. They like to do their Satan minds, persecuting Armenians in all their dominions.

(Spoonful.)

1895—Turks massacre Armenians.

(Spoonful.)

1905—again they massacre.

(Spoonful.)

1915! Vy, Astvadz *[Oh, God]*, 1915! Astvadz, we cry to you—why have you for-saken us?

(Spoonful.)

1915 we can never forget. Turks kill one and a half million Armenians.

(Spoonful.)

They kill. They rape.

(Spoonful.)

They torture.

(Spoonful, which ANNA refuses.)

ANNA: Ma. Ma. Ma. Ma—I know the English word for *madzoon*.
ARSHALUIS: English people no eat *madzoon*.
ANNA: Yes they do. They call it yogurt.
ARSHALUIS: That is Turkish word.
ANNA: But that's what they call it in America.
ARSHALUIS: America friends with Turkey. They like to use Turkish word.
ANNA: Yogurt is the same thing as *madzoon*. The words are different but the thing is the same.
ARSHALUIS: Not the same.
ANNA: Why not?
ARSHALUIS: Not the same.
ANNA: Do the Turks make it differently? Don't they use milk?
ARSHALUIS: They use.
ANNA: And starter?
ARSHALUIS: They use.
ANNA: You mean they add other ingredients?
ARSHALUIS: No. I don't think so. I never watch them.

ANNA: So it is the same. *Madzoon* and yogurt are the same thing.

ARSHALUIS: No! Not the same! Anahid, listen what I telling. What Turk is doing, what Turk is saying, is never the same as Armenian!

ANNA: But why isn't it?

ARSHALUIS: Different, I say! Down to the center of the earth!

ANNA: But if it's made the same way—how is it different? I don't understand.

ARSHALUIS: Who can understand? How, why—we can't understand. Only we know what is history. Never forget history. Most important thing in all the world happened 2000 years ago. Easter Day, resurrection of Jesus Christ our Lord. O lamb of God . . . that takest away the sins of the world . . . have mercy upon us.

(STEPHEN *exits.* TITO *comes downstage with* STEPHEN's *camera, as lights change and* ARSHALUIS *exits.* TITO *replaces the Polaroid back with a regular one and checks the light with a light meter, during the following.*)

TITO: Can I get you a tea or anything?

(ANNA *shakes her head.*)

TITO: *(cont.)* How're you doing?

(ANNA *strikes a pose.* TITO *laughs.*)

ANNA: Where is he?

TITO: He stepped out.

ANNA: That was about me, wasn't it.

TITO: What? No—really. It was technical stuff. Really.

ANNA: He didn't tell you about me?

TITO: Oh yeah. I mean. Before you came.

ANNA: What did he tell you?

TITO: Just . . . he said that you used to be together.

ANNA: *(Prompting him.)* And . . .

TITO: Uh . . . that it's been a long time—three years?—Since you . . . He doesn't, you know. Tell me intimate stuff.

ANNA: You're so nice, Tito.

(ANNA *kisses him. He gets nervous.*)

ANNA: *(cont.)* What, are you going to get in trouble? Stephen looks a lot older. Don't tell him I said that.

TITO: I won't.

ANNA: What're you doing in this business? You should be a vet or something.

TITO: I like cameras. I like beautiful women. What are *you* doing in this business, then?

ANNA: Oh, I'm not. I'm not in it. "You put your right foot in, you put your right foot out . . ."

(TITO *laughs.* STEPHEN *enters and takes the camera from Tito.*)

STEPHEN: *(To* TITO.*)* Go tell them to see if they can get the new girl for tomorrow—the new girl, uh . . . they'll know her name. But find out if she has any tattoos. I don't want tattoos anywhere. No marks. No history. And then come right back.

(TITO *exits.*)

OK, let's see if we can get the shot this time, huh?

(STEPHEN *begins photographing* ANNA *continuously.*)

You know, insolence is my favorite quality in a girl. But you know that, don't you, Anna. When you do that I can see that top clamp. Don't give me a cliche. You're very quiet. What's on your mind, Anna?

ANNA: Nothing.

STEPHEN: You want to know why I booked you, after all this time.

ANNA: No.

STEPHEN: Bullshit. *(As he shoots:)* Nice. I've been waiting all day for you to ask and you just stand there, not asking. I'll give you a hint: it's not what you think.

ANNA: What do I think?

STEPHEN: Come on, come on—you were dying to come. You had to see for yourself.

ANNA: I don't know what you're talking about.

STEPHEN: Photographer Obsessed With Former Model. Creative Drive Blocked For Years. Lost Without His Muse—

ANNA: Shut up, Stephen!

STEPHEN: *(Delighted, laughs.)* Every girl who comes in here—

ANNA: *(Interrupting.)* Don't call me that.

STEPHEN: Every girl who comes in here is . . . a girl, you're no different.

ANNA: You're an asshole.

STEPHEN: Well—I've heard it suggested. But it's never been proven. Want me to tell you why I called? We go on sabbatical in a few months—and big changes since your time, we go for four weeks now, and we take the whole crew—no models, we don't do any fashion, we do . . . explorations, we do—last year in Egypt we did a series on beggars, some great stuff. We're going to Istanbul this year.

ANNA: How nice.

STEPHEN: Turkey.

ANNA: I got that. So what?

STEPHEN: Want to come?

ANNA: What?

STEPHEN: Nice. Do you want to come?

ANNA: Is this a joke? Or an insult? I don't get it.

STEPHEN: I thought of it as an invitation.

ANNA: You haven't seen me in three years. And you invite me to Turkey, off the cuff? You just told me you don't take models anymore.

STEPHEN: We wouldn't be taking you as a model, more as a . . .

ANNA: I don't speak Turkish.

STEPHEN: Who does?

ANNA: This is ridiculous!

STEPHEN: Nice.

ANNA: Oh my God!

STEPHEN: Yes!

ANNA: You said all that just to get the shot! Didn't you! You did it for the shot!

STEPHEN: Would you have considered going?

ANNA: I'm not speaking to you. For the rest of the day.

STEPHEN: Yeah, all my best stuff is coming out of sabbaticals these days. Got to get outside to . . . life and death . . . well, sex and death. Every now and then a girl in the studio . . . has it . . . but then it's usually someone too ruined to work. But the others bore me. That's nice.

(TITO *reenters.*)

Tito! Just reminiscing about old times. You know those old pictures of Anna — the boulder series —

TITO: Oh yeah, sure — where she's lying — yeah, they're legendary. When was that, when you did those?

STEPHEN: It was about — . It was — . No, it was ten years ago. Jesus.

(STEPHEN *stops shooting.*)

TITO: I love those pictures. Well, who doesn't.

ANNA: I don't

STEPHEN: Fuck.

ANNA: I've done much better things since then.

STEPHEN: It was April. The light on the water was —

(ANNA *walks aside and takes off her shoes.*)

Where are you going? You just had a rest. Tito, bring her a tea.

ANNA: I don't want a tea! Thank you.

STEPHEN: My pleasure. Get back on the set.

ANNA: You're embarrassing Tito.

STEPHEN: Am I? No, two years here—poor Tito's seen it all. We're wasting time. Tito—go stand behind Anna.

TITO: Me in the frame?

STEPHEN: *(Starting to shoot again.)* I'll take care of it. Tito, pull her arms behind her, she likes that. Tighter. Hold her tighter. Good. Good. Yes! I love your dirty looks, Anna, that's all I want, I don't know why I have to work so hard to get them. Yes—yes—yes—

(ANNA wrenches herself free from TITO's grasp.)

What are you doing? I'm not done! I haven't finished!

ANNA: *(Shrieking, in Armenian.)* I'm finished! I'm finished! I'm finished!

(ANNA messes up her hair and starts to tear off the clamps on her dress, continuing to cry out in Armenian, "I'm finished!")

STEPHEN: Anna! Anna! *(To TITO.)* Hold on to her—Don't let her wreck anything—

(ANNA is struggling with TITO.)

STEPHEN: *(cont.)* God I could kill you for doing that!

(He grabs the camera and starts shooting her as TITO tries to pull her away.)

You fucking have to—*(Continuing to shoot.)* Tito! Hold her! Hold onto her! I'm gonna—goddammit—

(He continues to shoot.)

ANNA: Go on, kill me! Go on! Take everything!

TITO: *(Seizing ANNA.)* Stephen! No! No! Stop it! Stephen! Both of you! Stop it! Both of you!

(TITO separates them. ANNA and STEPHEN facing each other, breathing hard. ANNA turns suddenly and exits.)

STEPHEN: *(To TITO.)* Go call her agency. Call her booker. Go on, Tito!

(TITO exits. STEPHEN kicks the wall. Hearing ANNA approach, he turns to study a con-

tact sheet from another job. ANNA *enters, putting on a shirt. She buttons it in silence.* STEPHEN *ignores her.)*

ANNA: I'm tired. This is my third continent in four days.

STEPHEN: If you don't want to do the job, quit.

ANNA: You can get "the new girl."

STEPHEN: That's right. You're free to go.

ANNA: Free to go! Thanks to you, I'm free to go! Where am I free to go?

STEPHEN: Anywhere, what the fuck do I care.

ANNA: I've been there already.

STEPHEN: Then go home. I've got work to do.

ANNA: "Work"! You mean abusing people so you can—

STEPHEN: *(Interrupting.)* Oh Christ.

ANNA: It's your fault! You provoked this! Whipping everyone into this fake frenzy— fake emotion—it's all you can do—because you don't have any real feelings!

STEPHEN: Because you refused to give me anything, that's why! You refused to give me a goddam thing all day! You stand there like a stone!

ANNA: I hate you. You're such an appalling waste of life.

STEPHEN: Listen to you. The pot calls the kettle a whore.

ANNA: At least I don't glorify what I'm doing! "Sabbaticals!" "Life and death!"

STEPHEN: You're a model—

ANNA: No, I'm not! I'm quitting! I'm getting out of the business!

STEPHEN: Yeah, well, you're thirty-one.

ANNA: That's not why. I don't want to be old and bitter, like you.

STEPHEN: You were old and bitter when you were nineteen. Now, you're—like a lot of other girls.

ANNA: That's a lie! You're a liar! Acting like the past never happened. Like you've forgotten . . . what I was.

STEPHEN: That's life, isn't it.

(ANNA *turns to leave.)*

By the way, you can tell your booker if she wants the voucher for today she can come downtown and duel me for it.

(ANNA *is on the point of exiting when* TITO *enters with a phone.)*

TITO: Excuse me—Anna? I'm sorry, it's your agency. They said it couldn't wait.

ANNA: *(To phone.)* Hello?

(ANNA *listens.)*

I'm here. I'm leaving now. 'Bye. Yes. 'Bye.

(She puts the phone down.)

STEPHEN: Anna?
ANNA: My brother. Seryozha.
STEPHEN: What happened?
ANNA: They killed him. Soldiers.

(ANNA presses a hand to her forehead, hard.)

ANNA: *(cont.)* My head!
STEPHEN: *(Touching her, trying to hold her.)* Anna. Anna . . .

(ANNA is oblivious and does not respond to him.)

ANNA: *(To herself.)* I have to go.

(She goes out.)

TITO: Stephen? Do you know—
STEPHEN: Her brother—it must be her younger brother. There was another one—
    he was older—he was killed a few years ago.
TITO: Where is this?—a war?
STEPHEN: Karabakh. Where she's from. Run after her, Tito, make sure she gets a
    cab.

(TITO exits.)

Scene Two

*(Three months later, Karabakh. ARSHALUIS is dressed in black. We hear the repeated
clanking of pipes offstage.)*

ARSHALUIS: *(In Armenian, on the phone.)* Babu Sarah? Babu Sarah? Can you hear
    me? Babu Sarah, can you hear me? Babu Sarah—

(Sound of clanking pipes. ARSHALUIS hangs up the phone.)

ANNA: *(off; calling.)* Ma? Does she have water?
ARSHALUIS: Who knows? Phone is died.

(ANNA enters. She goes to the door, opens it, and looks down the mountainside.)

ANNA: I think I can see her down there. There's a speck of blue moving around. I'll just walk down and ask her.

ARSHALUIS: What use? If she has water, we still don't have. After, we bring more from spring. Now come, work.

(ANNA *kneels down and begins to wash the floor.*)

This is how you wash the floor?! Amahn!

(ARSHALUIS *demonstrates the correct technique.*)

(*In Armenian.*) Watch me. Make arcs. Make arcs. You understand?

(ANNA *tries it.* ARSHALUIS *is still dissatisfied.*)

ANNA: Ma, it's a floor.

ARSHALUIS: (*In English.*) Clean the right way. Watch me. *Big*. Make *big*. Like this. Ahmot [*shameful*]! My English is better than your Armenian. Thank God, now we have independence, they teach Armenian in the schools. (*Continuing to wash the floor.*) Yesterday I saw your English teacher. Arkady Minassian. He is talking about you. Talking, talking. He is widower now.

ANNA: I know, Ma. He told me.

ARSHALUIS: He has three children by this second wife. Now she died, last year. Breast cancer.

(ANNA *washes the floor.*)

ARSHALUIS: (*cont.*) You admire him. Intelligent, handsome man.

(ANNA *washes the floor.*)

Now is three months since you came back.

ANNA: And not married yet!

ARSHALUIS: Yes! Time is gliding!

ANNA: I didn't come back to get married.

ARSHALUIS: Why you came back?

ANNA: How can you say that?

ARSHALUIS: Fifteen years you don't come back. Fifteen years. When Andranik is killed in 1992, you don't come back.

ANNA: Don't start, Ma.

ARSHALUIS: Anahid, you listen. Now you are here three months already. Time is gliding. Time to work, time to take husband. What you do? This is you, every day, walk around Matarash, taking picture. You see fence, you take picture! You see clothesline, you take picture! What use? Work! Why you stop? Work!

ANNA: My hand. I hurt it on that faucet.

ARSHALUIS: *(Dismissively.)* From Alizades' time. Alizades put the flosset when we lived. Stepanakert.

ANNA: It's just a bad design.

ARSHALUIS: What can you expect? Alizades are Turk people. Bad work. Bad quality.

ANNA: Ma. They weren't Turks. They were Azerbaijanis.

ARSHALUIS: Turk, Azeri—same thing.

ANNA: They're not the same, Ma. They're different.

ARSHALUIS: Turks, I say! Alizades are just Turks! Robbers! Those people take everything. Yesterday you look for samovar? Gone! They take samovar. They take all precious things—rugs, lamps, silverware, candelabra—even my *doshag [cushioned sleeping mat]* they took. All looted.

ANNA: You don't know it was them.

ARSHALUIS: Why you like to take their side! I let them live here free, my house, for four years—and they repay by looting. When we come back from Stepanakert, everything gone. Even they unscrew light fixtures out from the ceilings! Ahmot! When I hear those Alizades died in refugee camp, I think—now, all our house is gone . . . All things robbed, looted, pass from hand to hand, disappeared . . . all is scattered and lost.

ANNA: They put in the plumbing, didn't they? The Alizades put in the plumbing.

ARSHALUIS: I surprise they don't take that too! I surprise they leave the flosset!

ANNA: At least we have running water now.

ARSHALUIS: Running? Ha! *(She laughs.)* Water comes like fart, once, twice—*(she makes the noise)*—all finished.

ANNA: Your English is improving. Look, what if I went down to Stepanakert tomorrow? Maybe I could find a faucet.

ARSHALUIS: Ah! *(Dismissive gesture.)* Throw money away. Throw, throw—this is American style. Everything is money. We have flosset, we don't need.

ANNA: It's *faucet*, not *flosset*.

ARSHALUIS: We need pipe, not flosset. Andranik telling I should buy new water pipe. Too much rust the water. Vy, Andranik! Where I get the money?

ANNA: I'll give you the money, Ma! Why do you talk to Andranik? He can't help you!

ARSHALUIS: Many years you were not here, he helped me. All those years.

ANNA: Oh, and Seryozha, does he help you now too? They help you more than I do, right? Do they tell you to go out on duty every night? I thought it was shameful for a woman to leave the house at night! That's what you taught me!

ARSHALUIS: Why you come back? To spy on us?

ANNA: Why wouldn't you tell me where you were going every night?! I had to find out my mother is a sniper! Every night! This is supposed to be a cease-fire!

ARSHALUIS: Cease-fire? If there is cease-fire, why they kill Seryozha? No, we have no peace!

ANNA: Because no one will stop fighting!

ARSHALUIS: What are you talking—standing there? Why you don't help? Why you don't do something?!

ANNA: It's not my war!

ARSHALUIS: I say that is lie! You are Karabakhtsi. Fifteen years in America—for what? You don't marry, you don't have children—why you don't have children? In all New York you can't find husband?

ANNA: I don't want your kind of life, Ma! That's why I left!

ARSHALUIS: Who wants?! You think we ask for this kind life?! Please God, send us hard, hard life! Take away our joys, take away our food, take our beloved ones, fill our mouths with dust, make happen that we cry until no more tears can come!

ANNA: And you want me to have children? That's insane.

ARSHALUIS: I want you should help!

ANNA: You mean join the war! I will never do that!

ARSHALUIS: Already you joined. Already you paid for weapons.

ANNA: You know I was sending that money for you and Seryozha! If I'd known what you were using it for—

ARSHALUIS: We use it to survive!

ANNA: This isn't life.

ARSHALUIS: You like to defeat us then? Is this why you come back?

ANNA: No, I came back to say, Onward, Christian soldiers!

ARSHALUIS: You don't respect God! You have no right!

ANNA: Who respects God?

ARSHALUIS: Amahn!

ANNA: You pray to the God of Battles! The God of Armies, the Lord of Hosts!

ARSHALUIS: (In Armenian.) Disgraceful girl!

ANNA: "Saul has killed his thousands, And David his ten thousands." That's your religion. I've never met a Christian in my life!

ARSHALUIS: Ahmot! You are not worthy to be Armenian!

ANNA: I don't want to be Armenian! I never wanted to be!

(ANNA *exits.* ARSHALUIS *straightens the objects on the martyrs' table. She wipes off a speck of dust. She picks up* SERYOZHA's *picture, kisses his forehead, and makes the sign of the Cross.*)

ARSHALUIS: (In Armenian.) In the name of the Father, the Son, and the Holy Ghost. Amen.

(ARSHALUIS *puts the picture back in its place on the table. Light change.* SERYOZHA *enters with a clarinet. We hear clarinet music, although* SERYOZHA *does not hold the instrument to his mouth.* ARSHALUIS *does not look at him.*)

ARSHALUIS: *(cont.; in Armenian.)* Seryozha, darling. How sweetly you play, Seryozha. What a musician you are, Seryozha.

(At the sound of a grenade exploding, the music stops.)

(In Armenian.) Stay, darling, stay. Stay, Seryozha, stay.

(SERYOZHA *exits with lighting change.* ARSHALUIS *gets down and scrubs the floor, reciting the Psalm.*)

> *(In English.)* The Lord is my shepherd, I shall not want.
> He makes me lie down in green pastures.
> He leads me beside the still waters.
> (Another grenade explosion.)
> He restores my soul.
> He leads me in paths of righteousness for his name's sake.
> Even though I walk through the valley of the shadow of death,
> I fear no evil,

(Another grenade explosion.)

> For thou art with me,
> Thy rod and thy staff, they comfort me.
> Thou prepares! a table before me

(A series of grenade explosions close together.)

> The Lord is my shepherd, I shall not want.
> He makes me lie down in green pastures.
> He makes me lie down in green pastures.
> The Lord is my shepherd.
> The Lord is my shepherd.
> The Lord is my shepherd.
> The Lord is my shepherd.

(ARSHALUIS *leans over and rests her head on the floor. When she gets up, she puts the rags in the bucket. But when she wrings them out, they are full of blood; the bucket is full of blood. She gives a cry of fear; she carries the bucket to the door, goes outside*

with it, and closes the door. At the sound of the door closing, Lighting to normal.
ANNA *calls from offstage.)*

ANNA: *(off)* Ma?

(ANNA enters.)

   Ma?

(She opens the door, looks out and calls.)

   Ma, where are you! Ma! Ma!

(ANNA turns back into the room. After a moment, ARSHALUIS re–enters.)

   (Casually.) Where did you go?
ARSHALUIS: I dump blood on the garden.
ANNA: Blood? Ma?
ARSHALUIS: Head aches.
ANNA: Did you say blood?
ARSHALUIS: Bucket, from floor.
ANNA: Ma. I'm sorry.

(ANNA embraces her and pulls her to sit down.)

   Ma. It doesn't have to be like this. We could go somewhere.
ARSHALUIS: Go? Where?
ANNA: Anywhere! We could move to Yerevan.
ARSHALUIS: I never leave Karabakh.
ANNA: OK, we could move down to Stepanakert. Get a nice house in town.
ARSHALUIS: What I do in big city?
ANNA: Stepanakert's a small town! You could do something with your training, you
   could get another engineering job. I'm just saying you don't have to go on liv-
   ing here. What if something happened? What if you stepped on a mine like
   that girl in Berdzor?
ARSHALUIS: Who can hurt me? All things taken from me already.
ANNA: I heard that company in Stepanakert was looking for people, they pay
   well—
ARSHALUIS: Money, pah! You are just American.
ANNA: No I'm not. Don't tell me what I am.
ARSHALUIS: You are Anahid Sarkisian, born Matarash village, Karabakh. Mother,
   Arshaluis Sarkisian, father, Levon Sarkisian *(crossing herself)*. Flesh and blood,
   eh?

(ARSHALUIS *strikes her on the upper arm with the back of her hand.*)

You like to disagree? You are somebody else? Vy, Anahid!

ANNA: Did you know that in Russia, women go and take their sons *out* of the war?

ARSHALUIS: What are you talking?

ANNA: In Chechnya! Russian women, they go to the military bases, they pay bribes—

ARSHALUIS: Russians don't fight for their own land!

ANNA: —the mothers say NO! to the generals, they do things no man would dare to do—

ARSHALUIS: I tell you Russians don't fight for their own land! They are sent to fight in Chechnya, they don't fight for their own land!

ANNA: And land is more important than living! Land is more important than life!

ARSHALUIS: Yes! Yes! Of course more important! We are glad to give our lives!

ANNA: For what? A government of thieves and killers? Why should we die for them? I will never give my life! I will never be a picture on the martyr's table in this house!

ARSHALUIS: No, you like to be picture in magazine!

ANNA: Yes! Yes I do!

ARSHALUIS: Showing your body! Shame, shame, shame!

ANNA: This is the shame, the way you live here. This is the shame!

ARSHALUIS: No shame to be poor. Shame is to do evil.

ANNA: And all the evil is done by the Azeris and the Turks!

ARSHALUIS: They are Satan on earth.

ANNA: What about what the Armenians did in Khojali?

ARSHALUIS: We have to protect ourselves!

ANNA: Protect? It was a massacre! What about all the Azeri refugees from this war—half a million people, children—

ARSHALUIS: Don't tell me Azeri refugees! Why you don't tell about Armenian refugees!

ANNA: People we knew! Our neighbors!

ARSHALUIS: I say Armenian refugees! How many Armenian refugees from this war? Hundreds of thousands! And before this war, how many years Azeris try to bury us little by little! Even our language is not allowed! Why you telling me Azeri refugees? Why I feel sorry for them?

ANNA: (*Quietly.*) I don't know, Ma. Why should anyone feel anything for anyone? All I know is, when I left, the Alizades were our neighbors. They were our friends. Olga was your good friend. What about her son, Ilyas? Ilyas and Seryozha— you used to say Ilyas and Seryozha were like David and Jonathan in the Bible. Don't you remember?

ARSHALUIS: No.

ANNA: You only remember the terrible things.

ARSHALUIS: We can't forget what they have done to us. Twenty-one years old. My Seryozha. Mine, but everyone loved.

ANNA: Ma.

ARSHALUIS: Andranik they kill in battle, but Seryozha—

ANNA: Ma!

ARSHALUIS: He was shepherd. They torture, then they kill.

ANNA: Ma!

ARSHALUIS: They cut off his head.

ANNA: Stop it!

ARSHALUIS: They put clarinet the mouth—

(ANNA *puts her hands over her ears.*)

ANNA: (*Screaming.*) Ma!

ARSHALUIS: Who can do this thing? To a child?

ANNA: Ma. Stop. Listen. I have to tell you something. I'm going to go back for awhile. To New York.

ARSHALUIS: This is joke?

ANNA: No.

ARSHALUIS: You say, now you will stay in Karabakh.

ANNA: I never said that. I didn't say it.

ARSHALUIS: How you can go?

ANNA: It's already arranged.

ARSHALUIS: Arranged?

ANNA: I got a campaign.

ARSHALUIS: Arranged?

ANNA: My booker got it for me. A contract. Totally out of the blue, but it's really—

ARSHALUIS: How arranged?

ANNA: I have a plane ticket. In a week.

ARSHALUIS: Vy, Astvadz!

ANNA: It's a lot of money! We could rebuild the house. We could put in a water system for the whole village. I have to go.

ARSHALUIS: You like to go! You like to go back to that Satan world! You were Judas before. Still Judas.

ANNA: I'm Judas.

ARSHALUIS: Betrayer. Kiss, and then kill

ANNA: That makes you Jesus Christ.

ARSHALUIS: Not only me you betray. Everybody in Matarash. Now we see, this is why you come back. To betray. Go. Go.

(ARSHALUIS *exits.*)

Scene Three

(Later that night The room is dark. A basket of clean laundry on the floor. ILYAS *opens the door, slips inside and looks around the room, taking it in. He sees the photos on the martyr's table, picks up the picture of* SERYOZHA *and studies it. He notices the laundry basket and rummages through it. He finds* ANNA's *shirt—the same one she put on in scene one—takes off his own shirt and puts hers on. He searches for pants in the basket but finds none he can wear.* ANNA *enters and sees* ILYAS *holding a gun on her.)*

ANNA: Is that my shirt?

ILYAS: I need pants.

ANNA: OK. Good. Yes. I'll get you—there's some on the clothesline—right outside—

(She moves toward the door, and he blocks her exit.)

ILYAS: No. Who are you? I said, who are you?

ANNA: *(Flashing him a winning smile.)* Your English is very good.

ILYAS: Are you Armenian?

ANNA: No.

ILYAS: American?

ANNA: No. I'm a visitor. There are some pants—

ILYAS: *(Dismissing the laundry basket.)* Too small.

ANNA: Not those. My brother's.

ILYAS: Whose?

ANNA: My brother's.

ILYAS: Your brother's.

ANNA: Yes.

ILYAS: Your brother's.

ANNA: Yes, my brother's.

ILYAS: *(Picking up* SERYOZHA's *picture.)* This is your brother.

ANNA: Yes. *(Referring to both photographs on the table.)* Both of them.

ILYAS: What is his name?

ANNA: Seryozha.

ILYAS: When did he die?

ANNA: Three months ago. I'll get the pants.

ILYAS: Where were you when he died?

ANNA: New York. I'll get the pants.

ILYAS: No. Not his. You will make me some pants. New pants.

ANNA: I don't know how.

ILYAS: You know how to sew.

ANNA: I can *sew*, I can sew on buttons and—

ILYAS: Begin.

ANNA: I've never made a pair of pants. I've seen it done—

ILYAS: Where? Where have you seen it?

ANNA: In New York.

ILYAS: For which man?

ANNA: Which man? A model, he was—

ILYAS: (Interrupting.) Your husband?

ANNA: No.

ILYAS: Why not?

ANNA: I'm not married.

ILYAS: Why not?

ANNA: Because I don't want to be.

ILYAS: You don't like my questions? I have more.

ANNA: So do I.

ILYAS: But I have the gun.

(ANNA makes a break for the door. ILYAS seizes her, but without threatening her with the gun.)

Don't leave.

ANNA: The house down there, our neighbor, I know they've got pants, there's a man living there, I mean he's not there right now—I'll get them for you. It's just the next house, it won't take a minute—

ILYAS: No. I could have done that. I won't kill you.

(ILYAS empties the gun into his palm. He holds the bullets out to her. She takes them.)

ANNA: I want the gun too.

ILYAS: No. You keep those, I'll keep this. Anahid. You don't remember me.

ANNA: What did you say?

ILYAS: I used to live in Madariz. I used to live here.

ANNA: When?

ILYAS: In this house.

ANNA: This house.

ILYAS: You were gone.

ANNA: What?

ILYAS: You went to New York. I knew Seryozha.

ANNA: When? When did you?

ILYAS: When we were young.

ANNA: He's dead.

ILYAS: I was his friend. I'm Ilyas.

ANNA: He's dead. Who?

ILYAS: Ilyas Alizade.

ANNA: No, they died in Saatli, the whole family. The Alizades. During the war.

ILYAS: No. It isn't true. Who told you this?

ANNA: You're not dead.

ILYAS: Not yet.

ANNA: I don't understand.

ILYAS: You remember?

ANNA: I don't know. You're so tall.

ILYAS: How old are you now?

ANNA: Thirty-one.

ILYAS: Old.

ANNA: How did this happen? You're—you're—. You must be . . . twenty–two?

ILYAS: Yes.

ANNA: You're Ilyas? Are you really Ilyas? My God, how did this happen?

ILYAS: I deserted.

ANNA: From the Azeri army? You deserted from the Azeri army?

ILYAS: Yes.

ANNA: Oh thank God! You deserted! *When?* When did you desert?

ILYAS: Now. Tonight.

ANNA: Now? And you came *here*? Why did you come here? How did you cross the border?

ILYAS: In the back of a vegetable truck. Under a lot of melons.

ANNA: An Armenian truck? And the driver didn't know? You're lucky!

ILYAS: I've always been lucky.

ANNA: Where did you get out of the truck?

ILYAS: Behind the church. He stopped for cigarettes.

ANNA: But you're crazy to come here! To Matarash. It's so dangerous for you.

ILYAS: For you too.

ANNA: But I'm not the enemy!

ILYAS: Neither am I. I am like you. A visitor.

ANNA: Other people won't see it like that.

ILYAS: There are no other people. There is only you.

ANNA: But you won't be able to stay here—in Matarash. I mean—Madariz.

ILYAS: I know. Your mother—she is still living?

ANNA: Yes. She's in the army now—a sniper. She'll be out all night. On duty. You're lucky you came when she was gone.

ILYAS: You don't mind to be alone with a man in the house?

ANNA: Oh for God's sake! Are you OK? You're not injured? What are you going to do now?

ILYAS: I would like to sit down.

ANNA: Yes! Sit! Sit!

ILYAS: If it is OK.

ANNA: Oh, who cares! Let them cry shame if they want to! We'll get drunk and crazy. We'll give them something to cry shame about.

(He sits. She brings over the vodka bottle and two shot glasses, and pours drinks.)

To deserting!

(They drink.)

ANNA: *(cont.)* Ilyas! I can't believe it's really you. Why is your English so good? You don't talk like someone who grew up in a refugee camp.
ILYAS: I was in Baku.
ANNA: Baku? And then you went into the army? What about your family? your little sisters—they're not little any more—What happened in '92? God, Ilyas! How did you live?
ILYAS: These questions cannot be answered now. I am tired.

(SERYOZHA enters with light change. ANNA jumps up.)

ANNA: *(To SERYOZHA.)* You're so grown up.
SERYOZHA: Not really.
ILYAS: *(Jumping up.)* Where are you going!
ANNA: *(To ILYAS.)* I'll get you something to eat.
ILYAS: No!
ANNA: OK.
ILYAS: Don't go!
SERYOZHA: *(To ANNA.)* You remember the day I found you and that guy? in the field, lying down in the poppies.

(ANNA sits back down, ILYAS does too.)

ILYAS: That was a nice smile you gave me.
SERYOZHA: I was little and you were so mad at me, you twisted my arm so hard—
ANNA: What else shall we drink to?
SERYOZHA: and you gave me a look—like you were on fire, and I was in the way.

(ANNA refills their glasses.)

ANNA: To . . . melons! To all the melons that brought you here!

(They drink, as SERYOZHA exits. Light change)

ILYAS: *(Picking up the vodka bottle.)* If you're going to toast the fruits and vegetables, I better be *tamadah.*

(ANNA laughs. He refills their glasses.)

To life . . . within life.
ANNA: *(Toasting.)* To life within life! What does that mean?
ILYAS: The *within.* Where the life is.

(They drink.)

Where no one can touch you.
ANNA: Life is in the mountains. Life is in the Motherland!

(ANNA begins to sing the Soviet national anthem. ILYAS joins in.)

ANNA AND ILYAS: *(In Russian.)* Unbreakable Union of freeborn Republics
Great Russia has welded forever to stand.
Created in struggle by will of the people,
United and mighty, our Soviet land!

(They laugh.)

ANNA: Were you in Komsomol?

(ILYAS nods. They laugh.)

ILYAS: When did you come back here?
ANNA: Three months ago. Oh God, Ilyas! I'm sorry, I'm going back to New York.

(Long pause.)

I came back because of Seryozha. Now there's no one—my mother—I could
never live here again.
ILYAS: When?
ANNA: In a few days.
ILYAS: Yes.
ANNA: You'll be gone by then. You'll have to be.
ILYAS: Of course. Definitively, I will.

(He gets up.)

May I keep this? *(indicating her shirt.)*

ANNA: Are you leaving?

ILYAS: I'll go up to the caves.

ANNA: Don't go.

ILYAS: I'll leave Madariz tomorrow night. May I? *(indicating the shirt.)*

ANNA: Yes, keep it. But you don't have to go yet! You just got here! Ilyas! *(Holding his arm.)* I want to see you again.

ILYAS: No. Your mother is here.

ANNA: I could come up to the caves. No one would know! There's so much to talk about!

ILYAS: What?

ANNA: Everything! What happened to everybody—the old days—Seryozha—.

ILYAS: I don't really remember him.

ANNA: What? What do you mean?!

ILYAS: I remember he had a bicycle. He promised he would leave it for me when they moved to Stepanakert. But he didn't.

ANNA: Wait!

(ILYAS opens the door.)

ILYAS: Don't tell anyone you saw me.

ANNA: You can't just walk away!

ILYAS: It doesn't matter where I go.

(ILYAS exits.)

Scene Four

(Three nights later, Karabakh. ARSHALUIS is at her sniper's post. She has a rifle with a night-vision sight. She scans her target area, finds nothing, lays the rifle down. She takes prayer beads from her pocket and whispers the prayers, as she passes the beads through her fingers. Light change. SERYOZHA enters.)

SERYOZHA: Mama, this fight with Anahid.

ARSHALUIS: *(Whispering.)* Seryozha . . .

SERYOZHA: You want her to go back to New York and never come home again? Three days now you haven't spoken to her! Man, you're stubborn. The two of you! She did something so terrible you can't talk to her for three days? I'm going to give you some advice.

ARSHALUIS: *(Whispering.)* Vy, Seryozha.

SERYOZHA: When you go home, you make something nice for dinner, make *kufta*, and give Anahid your blessing. You've seen her the last few days—like a different person—working very quiet, like a nice girl, all the time she's thinking.

Thinking about what you said. You're going to win. Blood's thicker . . . our blood's in this ground. She'll come back, she'll have children—

ARSHALUIS: *(Whispering.)* Vy, Seryozha, vy—

SERYOZHA: I give you strength, don't I? I help you aim. Didn't I help you with that lieutenant, the one who was carrying bread to his men? I'm proud of you, Mama.

(ARSHALUIS picks up her rifle and scans. There is nothing. ARSHALUIS puts down the rifle again.)

ARSHALUIS: *(Whispering.)* Seryozha-djan.

(SERYOZHA seems to sense another presence.)

SERYOZHA: Down there . . . by the river . . .

(ARSHALUIS swings the rifle into position. ARSHALUIS and SERYOZHA simultaneously focus on someone, ARSHALUIS gazing through her rifle-sight.)

I see him. Coming down to the water, I see him. He's carrying . . . it's just a hat. Wait, wait, let him come down to drink. Look, he's young. And stupid. That's where they caught me. At the river. I came down to the river and they saw me. First they shot me in the foot so I couldn't run.

(SERYOZHA cries out for help.)

Mama! Mama!

(ARSHALUIS lowers the rifle. SERYOZHA disappears. Light change.)

ARSHALUIS: *(Crying out.)* Seryozha!

(Her cry echoes against the mountains. Distant sounds of splashing and someone scrambling over rocks. ARSHALUIS picks up her rifle and tries frantically to find the target, but she has lost it.)

(In Armenian.) My son, my son! Seryozha, my son! My son!

Scene Five

(That same night. A battered old tin bathtub in the middle of the floor, partly filled with water. ANNA is taking a bath. Next to the tub is ILYAS's shirt which she has just

taken off. She uses a small metal bowl to pour water over herself. After a moment, the door opens and ILYAS *is on the threshold. He wears a shepherd's clothes, which are wet all along on one side, and he carries a hat full of mulberries.)*

ANNA: *(Grabbing his shirt and holding it up for protection.)* What are you—I'm taking a bath!

(ILYAS *steps into the room.)*

   I thought you were gone! You can't come in.
ILYAS: Where is your mother?
ANNA: You can't come in! Go away!
ILYAS: Is your mother here?
ANNA: I'm taking a bath—that's why!
ILYAS: Is she on duty?
ANNA: Yes! Where were you? I thought you were gone.
ILYAS: I stayed in the caves.
ANNA: For three days? Why didn't you come back?
ILYAS: You might have decided to turn me in. *(Noticing the shirt.)* Are you washing my shirt?
ANNA: No! I thought you'd left. I mean—. Go outside. Please go outside!
ILYAS: So you can call the authorities.
ANNA: No! So I can get out. Go.

(ILYAS *lights a cigarette.)*

   How dare you!
ILYAS: Who did you tell about me?
ANNA: No one!
ILYAS: Your mother.
ANNA: No! I didn't tell her anything!
ILYAS: You didn't betray me? You protected me? How can I believe that?
ANNA: I didn't say a word. I swear! I'm not part of this war.
ILYAS: That's easy to say. For a rich American. A tourist.
ANNA: That's not what I am!
ILYAS: You're an Armenian girl.

(ANNA *stands up in the tub. A long moment of silence.)*

ANNA: You're supposed to say something.
ILYAS: What?

(She pulls a robe on quickly.)

ANNA: Why did you come back?

(ILYAS *holds out the hat full of mulberries.*)

ILYAS: I brought this for you.
ANNA: You're soaking wet!
ILYAS: I slipped. In the river.
ANNA: Mulberries?
ILYAS: I've been eating them for three days.
ANNA: What were you doing all this time?
ILYAS: Visiting. I visited places in Madariz.
ANNA: When?
ILYAS: At night.
ANNA: Why didn't you come see me?
ILYAS: Do people in New York ask so many questions?
ANNA: Yes. Yes they do.
ILYAS: I don't like questions.
ANNA: Or answers! I only have three more days before my flight.
ILYAS: Good.
ANNA: Good? You're glad?
ILYAS: No. Could I have some vodka?

(ANNA *pours glasses for both of them.*)

ANNA: You're running a huge risk staying in Matarash. How much longer are you
    going to stay?
ILYAS: Three more days.

(ANNA *drinks, he follows suit.*)

ANNA: Where'd you get those clothes?
ILYAS: I found them in one of the shepherds' caves. I put holes, stains. For disguise.
    What do you think it is like, to be in love?

(*Long silence.*)

    People in New York don't ask this?
ANNA: No, they do. Sometimes. It isn't easy to answer.
ILYAS: (*Holding out his glass.*) Could I have some more?
ANNA: (*Pouring him a drink.*) You must be hungry.
ILYAS: No. I'd like a bath. I smell like sheep.
ANNA: There's no more water. This is the last of the water.
ILYAS: I can use this water.

ANNA: No. You can't. It's not right. My mother isn't here.
ILYAS: You said you didn't care . . .

(He takes the shirt off while she is looking at him, so he is wearing only his shorts. She turns to leave.)

. . . about what is improper.
ANNA: It's her house.

(He squats down and swirls his hand in the water. She looks down at him.)

ILYAS: Will you give me a bath? I took baths in this house when I was a boy.

(He lifts his wet hand and brushes his head with it.)

ANNA: A woman is supposed to wash her father-in-law's feet. That's what my mother used to do.
ILYAS: I don't want to be your father-in-law.
ANNA: I'll turn on the kettle. There's one kettle of water left.
ILYAS: You are kind.
ANNA: You think so? My mother would kill me. I don't care.

(ANNA goes off, to the kitchen, and he takes off his shoes, socks, and trousers. She reenters in time to see that he is still wearing her shirt, under the other clothes. It has a large stain on it.)

Is that blood?
ILYAS: No. Mulberries.

(He takes the shirt off while she is looking at him, so he is wearing only his shorts. She turns to leave.)

You don't like me?
ANNA: Look! This is not what happens, is it!
ILYAS: You don't want to look at me?
ANNA: I can look at you.

(She turns back to look at him. He slips off his shorts.)

ILYAS: You don't say anything either.

(He gets into the bath.)

The bathhouses below the spring are gone.

ANNA: They were bombed. They never got rebuilt. I don't know if anyone will re-build them now. More people are putting in plumbing.

ILYAS: I remember, the towels there used to smell of *camfora (saying the word in Russian)*. I don't know the English.

ANNA: Yes! You're right! Camphor. I'd forgotten all about that.

ILYAS: Since I came back to Madariz, I remember more and more.

(ANNA pours them more drinks, and they toast.)

ILYAS: To water.

ANNA: To water.

(They drink.)

ILYAS: I should have been a water animal. My soul was made to live in the water. But all my life I've been on land. Looking for water.

ANNA: Till now.

ILYAS: Yes.

(The kettle whistles in the kitchen. ANNA goes off, and returns with it. She pours it slowly into the bath.)

Do you know the story about the two peasants who are arguing about whose land it is?

ANNA: No.

ILYAS: There are two peasants. Having an argument. The first peasant says, "This land you are standing on belongs to me!" The second one says, "I despise you and your family! This land belongs to *me*!" The first man says, "You lying bas-tard, I spit on your wife, your children and your parents! This is *my* land!" The second one says, "I will grind the bones of all your ancestors into dust till they are washed out of the mountains and into the sea! I tell you, this land belongs to me!" Then a third peasant comes along and listens to the two of them. After a while, he kneels down and puts his ear on the ground. The first two both cry out, "What are you doing!" And the third man says, "Sshhhh! I can't hear what the earth is saying." "Well?! What does the earth say?" ask the first two. The third man puts his ear to the ground again, and he says: "The earth is saying: both of you belong to me."

ANNA: And then what happens?

ILYAS: Probably the two men start fighting again. I didn't want to go in the army.

ANNA: Why don't you want to kill the Armenians? Why don't you hate them?

ILYAS: You don't hate the Azeris.

ANNA: I might, if I lived here. But I'm not Armenian.

ILYAS: What are you then?

ANNA: Why does it have to be a country?

ILYAS: I don't say that.

ANNA: Why should someone die for a country? Why should that be who you are?

ILYAS: I met an old man from Thailand. He said, "Be a water."

ANNA: A water?

ILYAS: Yes. *(Pause.)* In the Azeri quarter, everything is gone. There are no ruins even.

(ANNA nods.)

Our old house—there is nothing there. Except the pomegranate tree. Not one stone.

ANNA: After the cease-fire, people took the stones—from there—to rebuild. To repair their houses.

ILYAS: Armenian houses.

ANNA: Ilyas. Where are your sisters now? Elizaveta, and the little ones . . . What happened to your family, are they in Baku?

ILYAS: No.

ANNA: They're not still in Saatli?

ILYAS: No.

ANNA: They got out? Did you get separated? Are they—Ilyas. Are you the only one . . . I'm sorry. I'm sorry. Your mother too?

ILYAS: They died in Saatli. My sisters. And my mother. They had cholera.

ANNA: Your father too?

ILYAS: No. Here. In Madariz. In the fighting. We could not bury him before we left. They had his body.

(She fills the bowl with water and pours it over him repeatedly.)

All my mother ever talked about in Saatli was Madariz. When would we come back . . . "Madariz, Madariz." When she died we carried her on a board. There was a pile of bodies. I remember the smell. We had to tip the board and when she slid off her dress tore. I wanted to stay and look at her but the smell was so bad. She just lay there. Her hair was blowing. It must have been windy.

ANNA: How long were you in Saatli?

ILYAS: I don't remember.

ANNA: What was it like in the camp?

ILYAS: I don't remember much. One day someone came from Baku. I went to Baku with her.

ANNA: With her? As . . . to do what? To go to school, or—? You mean someone adopted you?

ILYAS: Not exactly.

ANNA: How old were you at the time?

ILYAS: Seventeen.

ANNA: And you lived with her? for how long?

ILYAS: Five years.

ANNA: What's her name?

ILYAS: Lydia.

ANNA: Lydia. She's Russian?

ILYAS: No. She is American. She works for Exxon. In Baku.

ANNA: So when was the last time you saw her?

ILYAS: It is two months.

ANNA: Did you have a job too? other jobs? I mean—

ILYAS: Many jobs. I can do anything. Pipe fitter, translator, taxi driver, also I worked at Hyatt Regency.

ANNA: But why didn't she keep you out of the army? Why didn't she pay to keep you out?

ILYAS: Is there more vodka?

ANNA: I'll get you a towel.

(She brings him one.)

It doesn't smell of camphor.

ILYAS: I hated that smell.

(ANNA laughs. He wraps the towel around his waist.)

I hope I don't smell like a sheep anymore.

ANNA: No. I'm sure.

(ANNA suddenly picks up her camera and starts taking pictures of him.)

Do you like being a model?

ILYAS: I don't know how to do it.

ANNA: You just stand there.

ILYAS: What else?

ANNA: That's all.

ILYAS: No. There's more. Anahid. Stop. Anahid.

ANNA: *(Lowering the camera.)* What is it?

ILYAS: I think you know.

(Pause.)

Say my name. I want you to say my name to me.

ANNA: I can say it.

ILYAS: Say it to me.

ANNA: I am saying it.

ILYAS: In your mouth.

ANNA: It's not—it's—

ILYAS: Every mulberry I picked, I said your name. Every one I ate, I said your name.

ANNA: Oh Jesus.

(They kiss.)

Ilyas. Ilyas.

(Kissing.)

(end of act one)

ACT TWO

Scene One

(The next night, Karabakh. A CD player, with CDs scattered around.)

ILYAS: *(Calling off.)* Anna? Where is the CD you played for me last night? Anna?

(He puts on a CD. Clarinet solo. After a moment with a change in lighting SERYOZHA *enters.)*

SERYOZHA: You filth. Dogface. Shit-eater. You dishonored my sister, you son of a whore. May you weep blood. May your veins fill with sewage, till they burst open and pour your stinking secrets onto the ground.

(He approaches ILYAS.*)*

You think you can have anything you want, don't you. You got out.

(He sits down next to ILYAS.*)*

I wanted to get out. I wanted to play in a club. In Yerevan—or Moscow. Jazz. American jazz. I never liked this traditional stuff. They sent me to the conservatory in Shushi anyway. But they should've given me a gun—not a clarinet. They gave the clarinet back to my mother—along with my head, the Azeri butchers. Inhuman dogs. The rest of my body was scattered and smeared all over a pile of exploded sheep. It was a thousand times stronger than coming, a thousand times—the hate that got born then. It filled the whole pasture, like shock waves. I wish I were still alive. I wish I could go out and plant mines like you're doing. In Baku—I'd like to mine every street. I'd like to blast every Azeri pig-dog to kingdom come. But it won't change anything. You think it's going to, but it won't. It feels good at first but it won't last. You can blow up the whole village but it won't last. You know what will last? You and me. We were born here. Nothing can change that.

(SERYOZHA *exits with light change.*)

ILYAS: Anna! Anna!

(ANNA *enters.*)

You went out. I was calling you.
ANNA: I didn't go out.
ILYAS: How do I know that?
ANNA: How do you know? Because I told you. Ilyas—
ILYAS: You should not go out.
ANNA: I was trying to reach that guy with a car. We can always take the bus from Stepanakert if we have to. Don't worry, I'll get us out of here.
ILYAS: Are you a god?
ANNA: Yes.
ILYAS: You can do anything. You can change anything.
ANNA: That's right.
ILYAS: What do you want to do with me?
ANNA: I'd like to take you apart. I want to make you lose control.
ILYAS: Would I like that?
ANNA: I want to mark you. Burn you, or scar you. I don't want to be just some episode in your life! "Anahid? Anahid? I don't really remember her." I want to be remembered forever. I'm making you nervous.
ILYAS: No.
ANNA: Liar.
ILYAS: What about you? Will you remember me forever?

(*Knocking at the door.*)

STEPHEN: (*off*) Anna? Hello? Anna? Are you there?
ANNA: What? What in the world—
STEPHEN: (*off; knocking.*) Hello? Hello?

(*She opens the door.*)

Anna.

ANNA: My God.

(STEPHEN *grabs her in a hug.*)

STEPHEN: While you're collecting yourself, let me explain.

ANNA: No!

STEPHEN: Your booker told us how to find you.

ANNA: Lea?

STEPHEN: Tito winkled it out of her. Women like him, for some reason.

ANNA: I don't believe it.

STEPHEN: You look well, Anna.

(*He moves to kiss her but she evades it.*)

We had a hell of a time getting up here—my God, these roads!

ANNA: Who is we?

STEPHEN: Tito's in the Jeep, with the cameras. I see you already have company, Anna.

ANNA: Who else is out there?

STEPHEN: Just Tito. The crew is back in Yerevan.

ANNA: Yerevan! I thought you were going to Turkey!

STEPHEN: Well, we ended up taking a side trip to Armenia. Then Tito and I took a sidetrip up here. If the mountain won't come to Mohammed—

ANNA: I don't believe this. I don't believe this.

STEPHEN: Amazing mountains, Anna, like you said—were those pomegranate orchards we passed?

ANNA: Stop calling me Anna!

STEPHEN: Look, I don't want to leave Tito out there in the Jeep—

ANNA: Shsht! Shsht!

STEPHEN: Is that Armenian for come in and have a drink? I know this is impromptu, but we come to you as a refuge, an ever-present help in time of trouble.

ANNA: What trouble!

STEPHEN: Well—a misunderstanding in Turkey. I'll let Tito give you the gory details, blood actually was involved. Let's just say it seemed like a good time to cross the border, see Armenia. But let's not spoil the present with bygones. Won't you introduce me to your friend, Anna?

ANNA: No. You can't stay.

STEPHEN: Of course we wouldn't dream of imposing. Though a drink would be just the thing, if the bar's not closed. We could all use a pick-me-up—poor Tito especially. He was arrested in Turkey.

ANNA: Arrested!

STEPHEN: He's fine, he's fine. Now. (*To* ILYAS.) Hello—I'm Stephen.

ANNA: I hate you.

STEPHEN: Darling, let's not talk shop.

(STEPHEN *kisses* ANNA.)

ANNA: You have an incredible nerve.
STEPHEN: What's the etiquette—you don't say hello to strangers here?
ANNA: *(To* ILYAS.*)* This is Stephen, he's from New York. This is Ilyas. Ilyas Alizade.
STEPHEN: *(To* ILYAS.*)* Enchanté. *(To* ANNA.*)* Shall I just tell Tito you're going to revive us and then we'll head for a hotel?
ANNA: There's no hotel here. Not in the village. You'll have to go back down to Stepanakert.
STEPHEN: So be it. I'll go help Tito.

(STEPHEN *exits.*)

ILYAS: Anahid. Who is this man?
ANNA: He's a photographer. I worked with him in New York. I worked with him a lot at one time. You're the one I want.
ILYAS: I want to be alone with you. Like last night.
ANNA: I won't let them stay, don't worry.
ILYAS: You make me hard.

(She kisses him.)

    Did you feel me? I'm going to stay like that till they go.

(TITO *enters carrying one light bag and the keys.* STEPHEN *follows carrying all the heavy bags.* TITO'*s head is bandaged.*)

ANNA: *(Kissing him on both cheeks.)* Tito. How are you?
TITO: Hey, Anna.
ANNA: Are you all right?
STEPHEN: He drove us up here!
ANNA: *(To* TITO, *indicating the bandage.)* What happened?
TITO: A cut.
STEPHEN: So this is where you grew up, Anna? In this house?
TITO: *(To* ILYAS.*)* Hello. I'm Tito.

(STEPHEN *walks around the room, and looks at the photographs. He picks up the picture of Andranik.*)

STEPHEN: Are these your brothers, Anna?
ANNA: That's Andranik. He was a *fedayee.* That's like, a guerilla.

STEPHEN: Look at the hand on the bandolier. Look at the eyes. And he died *(looking at* ANNA*)*—

ANNA: Eight years ago.

*(*STEPHEN *puts down Andranik's picture and picks up the picture of* SERYOZHA *and studies it.* ANNA *watches him looking at it.)*

Well. We have vodka, and vodka.

STEPHEN: That sounds ideal.

*(*ANNA *passes out glasses.)*

They say people in these parts are renowned for their hospitality.

ANNA: They say that in every backward country in the world. Where do they talk about people renowned for their inhospitality?

STEPHEN: New York, I believe.

*(*ANNA *hands* TITO *a drink. He looks at the drink.)*

ANNA: Is something wrong?

TITO: No.

ANNA: I can take your coat—

TITO: That's OK. I'm a little cold.

STEPHEN: *(Pointing to the plastic curtain.)* Anna—what happened?

ANNA: The house was hit by a missile. In 1992.

STEPHEN: What's behind the curtain?

ANNA: Ruins. There's nothing there. *(To* TITO.*)* Tell me what happened.

TITO: Oh no. Not right now. What is this? *(referring to the drink.)*

ANNA: Vodka.

*(*TITO *smells it.* ANNA *approaches* STEPHEN.*)*

Stephen.

STEPHEN: You OK, Tito?

*(*TITO *nods. He sips his drink.)*

ANNA: *(To* STEPHEN.*)* What happened?

STEPHEN: *(Trying to keep it a private conversation.)* We'd been at a soccer game. Coming back, we got on the wrong road. There were soldiers, a dozen of them, outside this village. I should have quit shooting after the first roll, but it was addictive—those guys—their faces, their eyes—their attitude . . . everything as tight as wires. Anyway, it was a misunderstanding. As we later figured

it, they were there to clear out a Kurdish village. Ethnic cleansing. They didn't
want any photographers around!

ANNA: What happened? Did they take you in?

STEPHEN: Look, all in good time—but not right now, OK? *(indicating* TITO.*)* So
when are you coming back to New York, Anna?

ANNA: I'm not.

(ANNA puts on a CD, then goes to sit next to ILYAS.*)*

STEPHEN: Lea said that you got—

ANNA: *(Interrupting.)* Lea's wrong. I changed my mind.

(ANNA kisses ILYAS. STEPHEN *shoots them as they kiss.)*

STEPHEN: Can we see you tomorrow, Anna? I mean, what's your schedule
here?

ANNA: Booked. Very booked.

STEPHEN: I'm happy for you.

(STEPHEN moves in closer to shoot ANNA. ANNA *gets up to get the vodka bottle and*
STEPHEN *follows her, shooting.* ILYAS *watches her every move. She dances with the*
vodka bottle as STEPHEN *shoots her.)*

(To ANNA.*)* Actually maybe you could advise us. We thought we'd stay in
Karabakh a couple days, but we don't want to get too close to the front. Stay
away from soldiers.

ILYAS: Anna!

ANNA: *(To* STEPHEN.*)* You looking for wrinkled faces and broken teeth?

STEPHEN: Not necessarily.

(Eventually ANNA *dances within range of* ILYAS *and he grabs her by the wrist. She*
kisses him.)

ILYAS: You forget me.

ANNA: *(Laughing.)* You're crazy.

(STEPHEN moves in to focus on ILYAS, *dividing him from* ANNA.*)*

STEPHEN: *(To* ILYAS.*)* You know, you have a quality . . . intense privacy.

ILYAS: You can photograph this?

STEPHEN: Oh yes, I think so. Stand over here. Do you mind?

(ILYAS moves, STEPHEN *keeps shooting.)*

Nice. I like that. How you seem to show yourself but I can tell at the same time you're not really showing me . . . you're holding everything back.

(ANNA *watches from across the room, drinking with* TITO.)

Walk. Walk over there. Go slow. Lean against the wall a little. Tense your leg, just put your foot against the wall and press it. A little lower. Push up the shirt a little,

TITO: Stephen's working hard.

STEPHEN: Put your hand inside the top of your pants, just inside the top. Push the pants down an inch, and pull up the shirt, can you do that? Up a little. That shirt is still—

(ILYAS *takes off the shirt.*)

You're not one of those innocent shepherd boys, are you.

ANNA: Shepherds aren't innocent! They herd animals.

(*She pulls* TITO *into a close dance, watched by* ILYAS *as* STEPHEN *continues to shoot him.*)

STEPHEN: (*To* ILYAS.) You ever think of modeling? Is that something you'd like to try?

ILYAS: Where?

STEPHEN: Anywhere—New York—

(TITO *falters.*)

TITO: The vodka.

ANNA: You hardly had any.

TITO: Your boyfriend's jealous.

ANNA: He's not my boyfriend.

TITO: Well—your cousin, then.

STEPHEN: (*To* ILYAS.) Do you have a button-down shirt? You know? A shirt that buttons, like this?

ILYAS: Anahid. A button shirt?

STEPHEN: Does he have a button-down shirt? Never mind, there's one in the bag. Tito?

(TITO *goes to their bags and pulls out an army shirt. He tosses it to* STEPHEN, *who then hands it to* ILYAS.)

ANNA: Where'd you get that?

STEPHEN: We picked it up in Turkey.

(ILYAS *puts on the shirt.*)

  I know you're not a soldier, but you can—
ILYAS: *(Interrupting.)* I am a soldier. I was. I deserted.
STEPHEN: You deserted, how marvelous! Don't button it. And when did you desert?
ILYAS: A few days ago.
STEPHEN: And when did you meet Anna?
ILYAS: I knew Anahid when we were children.
STEPHEN: I wish we had a gun.
ILYAS: I have one.

(*He pulls out his gun.*)

  It's not loaded.
STEPHEN: Yes, but just show me please? "Safety on the set."

(ILYAS *shows him the gun is empty.*)

  OK, hold it out at arm's length.

(ILYAS *lets the gun hang off the end of his hand languidly, not aiming it.*)

  More tension. Aim it. Tense, tense. Hey, Tito, can you give me a hand?
TITO: Stephen—
STEPHEN: Just for a sec, Tito—take the gun and move away. Ilyas. Look at it, you want it, he has it. OK, walk toward him, Tito.
TITO: Who are we?
STEPHEN: You're people who hate each other. Now get close. Get very close.
TITO: We're on opposite sides?
ANNA: You have to hate the person on the other side. It's the rule.
TITO: I want to kill him.
STEPHEN: And he wants to kill you.
ILYAS: These are stupid games.

(ILYAS *grabs* TITO's *arm with the gun and tries to get it away from him.* TITO *struggles.* STEPHEN *shoots pictures.* ILYAS *gets* TITO *down on the ground, wrestling, straddling him. The fight is real.* TITO *cries out.*)

STEPHEN: OK, break it up! Ilyas! Tito! Break it up. Hey! Ilyas—

(As STEPHEN *tries to separate* ILYAS *and* TITO, ARSHALUIS *enters. She is returning from duty, unarmed.*)

ANNA: Get up off the floor!

(As they scramble to their feet, ILYAS *shoves* TITO.)

ARSHALUIS: Anahid! (In Armenian.) What's going on here!
ANNA: Ma, it's OK. It's OK. Stephen, this is my mother. Arshaluis Sarkisian. This is Stephen. From New York. And his crew. He's a photographer. We used to work together. I didn't expect you.
STEPHEN: How do you do?
ANNA: They just came from New York. They just got here. I had no idea they were coming.
STEPHEN: I hope we didn't alarm you. I was just taking pictures. It wasn't a real fight.
ARSHALUIS: Gun is not real?
ANNA: It wasn't loaded.
ARSHALUIS: You like to make pictures of fight?
STEPHEN: Exactly.
ARSHALUIS: Why?
STEPHEN: It makes great pictures. Interesting pictures. That people like to look at.
ARSHALUIS: (To ILYAS *and* TITO.) You are models?
TITO: Uh—yes.
ARSHALUIS: Ahmot! You are men! Shame!
TITO: I also help Stephen, I'm his assistant. My name's Tito, how do you do.
ARSHALUIS: (To TITO.) What happened your head?
TITO: I had an accident.
ARSHALUIS: (To ILYAS.) Where you take this shirt? Where you find this?
ANNA: They brought it with them.
ARSHALUIS: What place they come from?
STEPHEN: From Turkey.
ARSHALUIS: Turkey? Amahn!
ANNA: Ma, it's OK. They're going to stay in Stepanakert tonight.
ARSHALUIS: Stepanakert? (To STEPHEN.) You have Armenian friends?
STEPHEN: I do—yes. Actually, in New York, too, I have a friend who's Armenian, he's famous.
ARSHALUIS: Who?
STEPHEN: He cuts hair, his name is John—
ARSHALUIS: (Waving this away dismissively.) You know Kirk Kerkorian?
STEPHEN: I'm afraid not.

ARSHALUIS: He is billionaire. Armenian American. Owns MGM movie company. He paid for new highway in Karabakh.

STEPHEN: Did he? Good for him.

ARSHALUIS: Many many rich are not like that.

STEPHEN: I'm afraid that's true.

ARSHALUIS: Who are your friends in Stepanakert?

ANNA: Ma, they're going to the hotel—

ARSHALUIS: Hotel? Why hotel? Friends are not home?

ANNA: They want to, Ma.

ARSHALUIS: Hotel is not nice. We have *vermags*. We can put. *(Indicating the floor.)*

ANNA: Ma, it's what people in New York do. They'd rather go to a hotel.

ARSHALUIS: OK. I don't understand. If you say, OK. *(To* ILYAS.*)* What is your name?

STEPHEN: This is Ilyas.

ARSHALUIS: You are New York too?

*(*ILYAS *nods.)*

ARSHALUIS: *(cont.)* You offer them to drink, Anahid? You brought food?

ANNA: They didn't want to eat anything, Ma. They ate before they got here.

ARSHALUIS: Amahn! Everybody like to eat. What kind hospitality is this? Anahid, go, bring what we have.

ANNA: They were just about to leave, Ma.

ARSHALUIS: First, eat something. Go, Anahid. Go, I say.

*(*ANNA *exits to the kitchen.)*

Sit. Sit. I apologize I have no any nice places for guests to sit. Once I had beautiful things. Now all are gone.

STEPHEN: Anna said your house was hit.

ARSHALUIS: Yes. But also we had many things stolen by Azerbaijani family who lived here during war.

STEPHEN: How terrible.

ARSHALUIS: I will tell you. During war, from 1988 to 1992, Azeris drove all Armenians out of Matarash. So we went to live Stepanakert. When we have to go, I tell our neighbors, Azeri family, you come live my house, take care. Better you live here than strangers. Their house also was bombed, worse than ours. They were nice people. I thought. But when I come back in '92, my house is ruin. They take everything—everything! Even my *doshag* with needlepoint my mother made for me, they take.

ILYAS: That's not true.

ARSHALUIS: Not true? You know my story?

(ANNA *enters with a tray of food.*)

What means "not true"? Why you say "not true"? Your name is Ilyas? Where are you born? where are you born?

ANNA: Ma!

ARSHALUIS: I think you are Azeri? You sound like Azeri.

ANNA: Ma! Stop this! He's a guest—

ARSHALUIS: You look like Azeri. Where are you born? Where are you born, I say?

ILYAS: I was born here. The same as you.

ARSHALUIS: Amahn! How many lies you tell? Anahid! You know where this one comes from?

ANNA: Ma. Ma. Listen to me. I think you should sit down, and listen.

ARSHALUIS: Why?

ANNA: Sit down first.

ARSHALUIS: No. I stand.

ANNA: Stephen and Tito—they're from New York.

ARSHALUIS: And this one?

ANNA: No. He's not. He's from Matarash. Ma—this is Ilyas.

ARSHALUIS: Who?

ANNA: Ilyas. Ilyas Alizade. Do you recognize him? Seryozha's Ilyas. He remembers everything, it's really him—

ARSHALUIS: No.

ANNA: He didn't die in Saatli! He came back.

ARSHALUIS: Ilyas Alizade died.

ANNA: No, Ma. It's really him.

ARSHALUIS: I tell you, he died! This is ghost.

(ANNA *takes her mother's hand and places it on* ILYAS's *body, moving it from place to place.* ARSHALUIS *touches him. She examines his face, convinced that this is not* ILYAS. *She turns his profile. A stab of recognition. She studies his face searchingly.*)

(*In Armenian.*) My son. Seryozha, my son, my son.

(*She moves her hands over him, touching him.*)

(*In Armenian.*) My son, my son. Is this Ilyas? Is this Ilyas? I see Olga here (*indicating his eyes.*) (*In English.*) I see your mother, I see Olga here (*indicating his eyes.*) Vy, Olga, vy! This is Ilyas? How handsome you are grown. Vy, Ilyas, vy! You are too late for Seryozha.

ILYAS: I know.

ARSHALUIS: (*In Armenian.*) My son, my son, Seryozha, my son. (*In English.*) This is miracle. This is Ilyas. (*Taking his hands.*) Look, you have a man's hand. (*To*

ANNA.) Anahid—cognac! *(To* ILYAS.) How tall you are grown! Look how many tall children are in my house. Anahid, hurry. Bring cognac, bring vodka, apricots, figs, string cheese is in yellow bowl, bring almonds, jam—bring everything.

Scene Two

(The next day. ARSHALUIS *and* ANNA *are cracking walnuts with a hammer and cleaning them.)*

ARSHALUIS: But this truck—who it belongs to? How he can sneak inside this truck at border? No, like this.

(She demonstrates to ANNA *how to crack the walnut open efficiently.)*

You say he arrive Matarash last night.
ANNA: Yes.
ARSHALUIS: And New York people too.
ANNA: They came a little bit later.
ARSHALUIS: You were alone with him.
ANNA: For God's sake, Ma—
ARSHALUIS: Not for long, eh? Where he is now?
ANNA: He's still asleep in the cowshed.
ARSHALUIS: Why you let him sleep there? Ahmot! Why you don't put a *vermag* [quilt] for him in the house?
ANNA: He wanted to sleep there.
ARSHALUIS: Amahn! Why you don't put the right place?
ANNA: Why do I never do anything "the right way," Ma?
ARSHALUIS: I don't know. This is riddle?
ANNA: No.
ARSHALUIS: I told you, plenty times, but you don't listen.
ANNA: Told, told, told, told, told, told, told!—what I am, what I have to know, what I have to say, what I have to do, what I have to believe, what I have to feel . . . That's all there ever was. I never existed. Just who I was supposed to be . . .

(ARSHALUIS *grunts.)*

And when he—*(she breaks off).*
ARSHALUIS: Why he came here? This boy?
ANNA: He wanted to see Matarash.
ARSHALUIS: He doesn't want to see anything.
ANNA: Maybe he wanted to see you.

ARSHALUIS: Oh yes, boys like to visit old ladies. Why he takes risk to come here? Nothing here for him. No Seryozha. You are not his friend, eh?

ANNA: He used to live here. He was born here. What other life does he have?

ARSHALUIS: Wild life in Baku.

ANNA: What does that mean, "wild"?

ARSHALUIS: Baku. Like New York. I warn you about him. You are not melons from the same vine.

ANNA: I thought you were glad he came! You hugged him—last night—you were singing—

ARSHALUIS: I don't trust. Don't trust boy.

ANNA: You don't believe him? You think that was a lie, that they locked the house when they left?

ARSHALUIS: I don't know.

ANNA: How could they have taken everything? They were in a panic, they didn't even have time to bury his father's body. Ma, come on!

ARSHALUIS: Why you never marry in New York?

ANNA: What?! Are you starting that again? I am not going to marry Arkady Minassian! I will never marry an Armenian. "What do I have in common with the Armenians? I don't even have anything in common with myself."

ARSHALUIS: What is that?

ANNA: Kafka said that.

ARSHALUIS: Kafka? Kafka was Armenian?

ANNA: No, Ma, he was a Jew. He said "what do I have in common with the Jews?" Same difference.

ARSHALUIS: Never mind. You listen what I telling. You watch this boy. Stay with him. You understand me? Pick the vegetables for *kufta [stuffed meatballs]*, let him help you. I go buy the meat and come right back.

(ILYAS *enters with a pail of milk.*)

ILYAS: I milked the cows. Was that OK?

ARSHALUIS: Sure! Thank you. After I come back I make *madzoon*. I make *kufta* for dinner. I remember, I think you like *kufta*, Ilyas?

ILYAS: I like your *kufta*. Yours is the best.

ARSHALUIS: Vy, *deghah [boy]*, vy. (*Picking up the milk pail.*) Anahid, I come back right away.

(ARSHALUIS *exits. They wait to hear the door close. As soon as it bangs shut, they are kissing.*)

ILYAS: Let's go back to the cowshed.

ANNA: There isn't time.

ILYAS: I want to eat you like a melon.

ANNA: Why did you milk the cows?

ILYAS: I had to do something. I knew she was in here and I wouldn't be able to touch you. What did they say about the car?

ANNA: Tomorrow.

ILYAS: It's better if we go early. Don't tell your mother.

ANNA: I can't just disappear.

ILYAS: Yes you can. I wish I could weld your body to mine.

ANNA: Ilyas—

ILYAS: Yes—

ANNA: Why are you here? In Matarash? Tell me the truth.

ILYAS: Because of you.

ANNA: But you didn't know I was here.

ILYAS: I told you. I deserted.

ANNA: Yes, but when? How long before you came to the house? How long before you saw me? How many days before? How many hours before?

ILYAS: It was after I saw you.

ANNA: What? What do you mean? It had to be . . . what about the vegetable truck? Crossing the border? That didn't happen?

ILYAS: It might have happened. If I'd thought of it sooner.

ANNA: What happened!

ILYAS: Many things happen at once. Many possibilities occur at the same time. I could have come in the back of a truck.

ANNA: But you didn't? You didn't?

ILYAS: Why does this matter now? It didn't matter before. Everything is different now.

ANNA: If you didn't desert, why were you here? Why were you in Matarash? If you didn't desert, you were still in the army. You must have come here to do something—what were you doing?

ILYAS: I was trying to get out.

ANNA: Of the army?

ILYAS: Yes. And—everywhere. Everywhere I've been.

ANNA: You were sent here. What for? Spying? Covert operations?

ILYAS: When I saw you, I didn't think about other things.

ANNA: You think you can flatter me?! Are there other Azeris in the village? Are you alone? Are there others in the village?

ILYAS: No. No one else. I don't flatter you. When I saw you something happened.

ANNA: You deserted? You really deserted?

ILYAS: Yes.

ANNA: How do I know you're not making that up?

ILYAS: You don't.

(They stare at each other.)

ANNA: I feel like your hands are on me right now.

ILYAS: Me too. It's hard to think about anything else. There's nothing I can do about it.

ANNA: About what?

ILYAS: You. It's too late.

ARSHALUIS: *(off; calling.)* Anahid! Anahid!

ANNA: Go outside, go out to the vegetable garden. Here *(handing him a basket.)* No, not that way, go out the back. I'll come out in a minute. Pick the tomatoes, pick them all, we need a lot.

(She kisses him and pushes him out. ARSHALUIS *enters.)*

ARSHALUIS: Where he is?

ANNA: Picking the vegetables.

ARSHALUIS: How you know he came to Matarash last night?

ANNA: Why? What's wrong?

ARSHALUIS: Arkady was killed.

ANNA: *What?!*

ARSHALUIS: It was landmine. In Fizuli Street.

ANNA: Arkady! He's dead?

ARSHALUIS: Happened last night. After midnight. While we have party here, Arkady is killed. Everybody talking. They think we already know.

ANNA: How could there be a mine? You said they'd all been cleared!

ARSHALUIS: Yes.

ANNA: Arkady!

ARSHALUIS: This was new mine. They cleared all mines, two years ago. Cleared all streets in village. This was new mine. Hundred times people have walked on that corner of Fizuli Street since deminers were here. This was new mine. Where it comes from?

ANNA: You think it's Ilyas!

ARSHALUIS: You know him one night!

ANNA: He couldn't have. There must be some explanation.

ARSHALUIS: He puts mines, then he comes to eat and drink here! You go now and tell him to come in. Don't tell what happened! Tempt him inside, say sweet things to him.

ANNA: What are you going to do?

ARSHALUIS: I tell Captain Mikoyan we have him.

ANNA: No! Ma! Just because he's Azeri you assume he's guilty. They'll take him away!

ARSHALUIS: They will find the truth. *(She looks out toward the vegetable garden.)* Where he is?

*(*ANNA *looks out.)*

ANNA: He's gone.

Scene 3

(Late that night. STEPHEN *and* ANNA *are drinking vodka.* TITO *is wearing his coat. He's not drinking. There are some photographs spread out in front of them.)*

ANNA: I should be at the wake too. Arkady was—a remarkable person. I think I went to America because of him. He thought that things could change. I just saw him two days ago, he—

TITO: Anna—excuse me. I gotta use the john. You think it's safe to go out there?

ANNA: Tito.

*(*TITO *exits.)*

You have to tell me what happened. In Turkey.

STEPHEN: Yeah, well. It was—At the police station. They did take us in. And then the questioning went nowhere—obviously, since we knew fuck-all. After a while they told me I could wire for money. It looked like they were going to let us go—and then some of them started jeering at Tito, and they took him—downstairs . . . and they—apparently they forced him to drink something first that . . . I will tell you. I promise. When we get back to New York.

ANNA: No, now.

STEPHEN: Anna. When we got out, when we walked out into the light . . . I said, that's it: I'm going to find you. Poor Tito thought I meant you were in Istanbul. Anna.

ANNA: Please. I can't—*(She picks up a photograph at random.)* Who's this guy?

STEPHEN: An arms dealer—a free-lance arms dealer. He chatted us up in Stepanakert.

ANNA: What did he say.

STEPHEN: He's Russian—Anna. He told us he grew up in the Moscow slums—

ANNA: What time is it?

STEPHEN: One-thirty.

ANNA: What else? What else did he say?

STEPHEN: He told us about his car. He's got a Mercedes, he said it was "color of champagne." I asked who he sells arms to, he said "people who have cash." He gets stuff from Russian army officers—whatever they can grab—they sell to him, he sells to the Armenians, the Azeris, the Abkhazians, the Kurds, the Chechens, whoever. He pulled out his palm pilot and showed us some of his inventory. He lists stuff on the Web, he's got a Web site. But he told us he wasn't "Big Bizniss" yet. I said what's Big Business, he said nuclear parts. He showed us his wooden leg—

ANNA: His wooden leg?

STEPHEN: That's what he called it. Said it was better than any prosthesis you can get in the Caucasus. Apparently there are huge waiting lists, years sometimes. He went to New York, Mt. Sinai. Wouldn't let me take a picture of it though. He said it would be bad luck, I think he meant the evil eye, if anybody saw the picture. Where the hell is Tito?

(ANNA *suddenly sees a picture of* ILYAS *in the pile, and grabs it.*)

ANNA: Why didn't you tell me you got Ilyas's developed?

(ANNA *seizes the rest of* ILYAS*'s pictures and looks through them.*)

STEPHEN: Anna, for God's sake, what are you doing here? You can't stay here.
ANNA: Where would you recommend?
STEPHEN: Anywhere! Anywhere in the world! Christ, you come back here and im-
    molate yourself—you live like a nun—
ANNA: I'm not living like a nun.
STEPHEN: Yeah, well, take him back to New York! If you're so keen on him.
ANNA: When did you become so altruistic?
STEPHEN: Last week. You look awful.
ANNA: That's how you like it, isn't it.
STEPHEN: No.

(ANNA *puts her face in her hands.* STEPHEN *pulls them away and kisses her. A tight embrace.*)

    It isn't even safe here.
ANNA: I wish I could go back. I wish I could.

(STEPHEN *kisses the palm of her hand.*)

STEPHEN: Come with me.
ANNA: Even if he comes back—He's—He's a ruin. He's blown to pieces inside.
STEPHEN: You can't save everybody.
ANNA: I never saved anyone.
STEPHEN: Anna, Anna, Anna!
ANNA: Help me! Stephen, please! Help me get him out of here! Take him with
    you! You could get him work in New York—
STEPHEN: Are you crazy?
ANNA: You can save him!

(ARSHALUIS *enters.*)

ANNA: *(To* ARSHALUIS.) Ma! I was worried.

ARSHALUIS: He didn't come?

ANNA: Not yet.

ARSHALUIS: People ask for you. I say you are sick.

ANNA: How was it?

ARSHALUIS: Too many children, Arkady had. Too many.

ANNA: Were they all there?

ARSHALUIS: Sure. They bring food, they help. Four children, orphans now. You know how many orphans we have in Karabakh? Even in Matarash only? You Americans don't know. Four orphans—not important for TV news, but this is history. Lasts for eternity. What somebody did thousand years ago touching us today.

STEPHEN: That's what makes it hard for the peace negotiators, isn't it.

ARSHALUIS: Peace? You know about peace? Amahn! Everybody telling us how to make peace. NATO, Madeleine Albright, Minsk peace process—how kind, how thoughtful nations, they like to solve our problem. I tell them how to solve, you like to know? First, change history. Change the past. Then give us money. Plenty money to Armenians and to Azeris. Everybody here poor, except mafia. There is Armenian saying: "When your neighbor is poor, you are in trouble." This was our problem with Azeris. Armenian villages nicer than Azeri villages. Armenians have bigger houses. So Azeris like to take our properties, our villages. Now everybody poor. Now big rich nations, now maybe you will be in trouble, eh? Big nations like to take oil out of Caspian Sea, but now everybody afraid of poor people in Karabakh. Everybody afraid of more war in Karabakh. Maybe West is going to be in trouble now.

STEPHEN: That's a very cogent analysis.

(The sound of a mine explosion in the distance.)

ARSHALUIS: Amahn!

ANNA: What was that?

ARSHALUIS: Land mine.

ANNA: A mine?!

(Another explosion.)

Oh God!

ARSHALUIS: Near church.

STEPHEN: Where the fuck is Tito?

ARSHALUIS: *(To STEPHEN.)* You will sleep here tonight. Not safe to leave. You go bring your bundles from Jeep. Go now and bring, I say!

STEPHEN: I don't know where Tito went!

ANNA: *(To* STEPHEN.*)* Where are you going?

*(*STEPHEN *exits.)*

Stephen! Stephen! *(To* ARSHALUIS.*)* What's going on? What's happening?

ARSHALUIS: I go find out.

ANNA: No! Ma! No!

ARSHALUIS: Maybe somebody is hurt. Maybe dying.

ANNA: Please. There are already people there by now. Neighbors.

ARSHALUIS: I am needed, I say!

ANNA: Ma, wait! What if I need you? Stay with me. Till we know it's safe. Please, Ma. Please.

ARSHALUIS: Babu Sarah made very nice *yalanchi* for Arkady's. She puts dill. I never put dill.

ANNA: I'm sorry I wasn't there.

ARSHALUIS: How many times. How many times.

(The lights change and SERYOZHA *enters.* ANNA *holds her mother.* ARSHALUIS *strokes* ANNA'*s hair.)*

ANNA: I just saw him . . .

ARSHALUIS: Who?

ANNA: Arkady.

ARSHALUIS: *Sirem, sirem.* We remember. This is our task. We remember. How my mind is full! How many dead are living here! *(Pointing to her head.)* Living here!

ANNA: Vy, Seryozha, vy.

ARSHALUIS: We remember. This is our task.

ANNA: I left when he was only seven.

ARSHALUIS: How he liked to sing with you. You remember?

*(*ANNA *starts to cry.)*

ANNA: It's hard.

ARSHALUIS: Sure, hard. This is hardest work.

ANNA: I remember him—catching lizards. Stuff like that. I can't think about—I don't know what to do.

ARSHALUIS: Remember. Forget is death. While we live, remember. Remember gives life.
Lift up your heads, O gates!
And be lifted up, O ancient doors!
That the King of glory may come in.

Who is this King of glory?
The Lord of hosts,
He is the King of glory!
ANNA: "Who is this King of glory?"

Scene Four

(Later that night. It is still dark, but during the course of the scene, dawn begins to lighten. ANNA stands alone at the window.)

ANNA: *(Whispering.)* Seryozha . . .

(STEPHEN enters.)

STEPHEN: I found him, Anna!
ANNA: You did?
STEPHEN: He's packing the Jeep.
ANNA: Oh! Tito.
STEPHEN: He got lost. He climbed up a hill to look at the stars—he must've come down in the wrong direction. He's fine.
ANNA: I'm glad.
STEPHEN: I never saw so many stars.
ANNA: I know.
STEPHEN: You heard nobody got hurt? Those mines?

(ANNA nods.)

They're saying the road is safe. Look—Anna—it's not our fight.
ANNA: No.
STEPHEN: If you knew the whole story . . . When Tito . . . They tortured him.

(ANNA turns away.)

I couldn't stop them. They raped him. Anna. I'll see you before I go. *(STEPHEN exits.)*
ANNA: Tito, poor Tito! Seryozha! Seryozha!

(ANNA is in tears. ILYAS appears in the doorway. She rushes to him. A tight embrace.)

Where were you?
ILYAS: I have to talk to you.

(She kisses him.)

ANNA: I was calling your name, over and over, did you hear me?
ILYAS: Yes.
ANNA: Where were you? Someone was killed!
ILYAS: What?
ANNA: A mine in the village—Arkady Minassian—did you know him?
ILYAS: No.
ANNA: He was our friend.
ILYAS: Can we get out of here? Now?
ANNA: Did you hear what I said? Didn't you hear the explosions a while ago?

*(*ARSHALUIS *enters with her rifle.)*

Ma! No!

*(*ILYAS *backs away with his hands up.)*

She thinks you laid the mines! Ma, stop! There's an explanation!
ILYAS: *(To* ANNA.*)* You betrayed me.
ANNA: No! I didn't do this!
ARSHALUIS: *(To* ILYAS.*)* You. Sit down, there.
ANNA: Ilyas, please, listen to her.
ILYAS: So you can turn me in.
ANNA: No! So you can explain! So you can defend yourself! Ilyas, please!
ARSHALUIS: You lay mines in our village. Then you come eat and drink my house.
    While we have party here, our friend Arkady is killed. Four children he
    had!
ANNA: Ilyas, tell her! Tell her! You didn't do it.
ILYAS: I didn't do it. It wasn't me.
ANNA: Ma—
ARSHALUIS: You believe what Turk is saying.
ANNA: Ma, there's an explanation—just because you don't know what it is yet—it
    couldn't have been Ilyas!
ARSHALUIS: *(To* ILYAS.*)* Why you come to Matarash? Why you are here?
ILYAS: Because of Anahid.
ARSHALUIS: Anahn! You don't know Anahid! This is lie.
ILYAS: No.
ANNA: It's true, Ma, it's because of me—
ARSHALUIS: *(Scoffing.)* He knows you are here? He remembers you? *(To* ILYAS.*)*
    You say you deserted!
ILYAS: Yes.

ARSHALUIS: You are lying. How many stories can you tell? You come because of Anahid, you come because you desert—Why you come to Matarash if you desert? You are not stupid. I think you are sent here to lay mines. You know the village. So they choose you.

ILYAS: I want to talk to Anahid alone.

ARSHALUIS: Ai! The devil is bold! You think I leave my daughter with a Turk?!

ANNA: Ma!

ILYAS: She's an old woman.

ANNA: Everybody sit down. Ma. Sit down.

(ANNA *pulls her mother to sit down next to her.* ANNA *sits between* ARSHALUIS *and* ILYAS.)

Let's be calm. Let's be calm. Let's not do anything wild. Give him a chance to explain. He's Seryozha's friend, Ma—remember? Remember all the times— remember when you used to take us on picnics by the river and we—

ARSHALUIS: *(Interrupting.)* That's enough.

ANNA: She just came from the wake. For Arkady. You have to understand. We are in shock. He was—a good friend. He was my teacher. I loved him.

ARSHALUIS: *(Keening.)* Vy, Arkady, vy! Vy, Anahid!

ILYAS: I see.

ANNA: It wasn't like that. He was a great man.

(Silence.)

You—you could say you're sorry.

ILYAS: I don't know him. This great man.

ANNA: No, but—

ILYAS: Are you sorry for Mr. Mamedov?

ANNA: Who is Mr. Mamedov?

ILYAS: He was in Saatli too. His daughter drowned in a water hole. Afterwards he stole one of the bulldozers they used for burying the bodies, and he filled in the water hole. They killed him for it—the people in the camp. Because there was so little water. Are you sorry?

ARSHALUIS: Amahn!

ANNA: Of course I am. Who wouldn't be.

ILYAS: You would be surprised.

ARSHALUIS: Never mind those people now. We are waiting. Why you don't speak? You owe us explanation.

ILYAS: I owe you?

ANNA: Ilyas—

ARSHALUIS: This is my house.

ILYAS: We lived here too.

ARSHALUIS: It was my house! Mine! Never yours!

ILYAS: I lived here.

ARSHALUIS: I let your family live here.

ILYAS: Madariz was our village too. Where are the stones from our house? Where are they?

ANNA: Ilyas. Please. She's my mother.

ILYAS: My mother is mud in Saatli.

ARSHALUIS: Terrible! Terrible! We all have terrible thing happen to us.

ILYAS: My sister is a whore.

ARSHALUIS: Amahn!

ANNA: You said your sisters died in Saatli!

ILYAS: The little ones. Not Elizaveta.

ANNA: Elizaveta—

ILYAS: When we got to Saatli they took her away. For prostitution.

ARSHALUIS: Ahmot!

ILYAS: I saw her in Baku six months ago. On the street. She wouldn't speak to me.

(ILYAS *stands up.*)

ANNA: Ilyas! No, no, no, no—

(*He moves toward the door.* ARSHALUIS *picks up the rifle and fires as he is about to cross the threshold, deliberately winging his shoulder. He falls against the door.* ANNA *screams and runs to him.* ARSHALUIS *holds her rifle on him.*)

ARSHALUIS: Put him there (*indicating a chair*). Flesh wound only. Bind it.

STEPHEN: (*off*) Anna!

ANNA: How?

(ANNA *finds a clean towel and a bowl of water. She begins to pull away his shirt and wash and bind the wound.* STEPHEN *comes rushing in, followed by* TITO *with the keys in his hand.*)

STEPHEN: She *shot* him?!

ARSHALUIS: I stop him only. He tried to escape.

STEPHEN: Jesus Christ.

ARSHALUIS: (*To* STEPHEN.) You know our story? Anahid told you? I have two sons—martyrs. You know our story, you will understand. My son, Seryozha— youngest son. He was shepherd. In the mountains, near the border. They take him. Azeris take him. They torture, then they kill.

(TITO *turns to leave.*)

STEPHEN: Tito! Wait! Mrs. Sarkisian—

ARSHALUIS: They kill his sheep, then they kill Seryozha.

STEPHEN: It's terrible but—

ARSHALUIS: No reason. He was shepherd. He didn't have gun. They beat him to death.

STEPHEN: Please Mrs. Sarkisian—

ARSHALUIS: His clarinet—how I had to wash. Keys were stuck like glue with blood, with hair from his head. They cut off his head. Then they put clarinet in the mouth—To play for dead sheep. Why you don't take these pictures? Why you don't show these terrible things? Everybody in Karabakh has terrible thing happen to their family—everybody. People scream and cry when they see these pictures. Even they don't know the people, they are sick when they see this thing. What happens to us when this happen to somebody we love, when we see his—What happens to us, can you imagine?

ANNA: Ilyas. Ilyas. Did you lay the mines?

ILYAS: Yes.

ANNA: Ai! Ai! Ai!

ARSHALUIS: Vy, Astvadz!

ANNA: In Fizuli Street.

ILYAS: Yes.

STEPHEN: Christ.

ARSHALUIS: Amahn, amahn!

ANNA: Oh God! Oh God! Oh, what a fool, what a fool, what a fool! I let you in. I believed you. Oh my God! Was it before? Was it before?

(ARSHALUIS *is holding her gun on* ILYAS.)

ARSHALUIS: Anahid! *(In Armenian.)* That's enough!

ANNA: Was it before?

ILYAS: Before what?

ANNA: Was it before you saw me? Before you came to the house?

ILYAS: Yes.

ANNA: And not after.

ILYAS: Some after.

ANNA: Some after? Some after? Oh God!

STEPHEN: Anna!

ARSHALUIS: I say, no talking to the prisoner!

ANNA: After you'd seen me you went back and laid more?

ILYAS: You were going back to New York.

(ANNA *cries out.*)

ARSHALUIS: Anahid, I say!

(ANNA *begins hitting* ILYAS.)

STEPHEN: Anna—

ANNA: (*Hitting* ILYAS.) Because I was going back to New York? I wasn't leaving for another week! And my mother, you could have killed my mother—

ARSHALUIS: Stop! Nobody talk to the prisoner! Wait for Mikoyan!

STEPHEN: Anna, Anna—

(STEPHEN *attempts to restrain her and pull her away from* ILYAS.)

ANNA: (*To* ILYAS.) I thought, I can see what's in you, waiting to come out—but that was all a delusion. There's nothing there. You're empty. Did you think if you seduced me I would take you back to New York?

ARSHALUIS: Ahmot! What are you talking?

ANNA: I could be the new Lydia! I could be your new American savior! And then Stephen shows up and you even have a choice of saviors! I saw you playing him. You were very cool with him, you were made to order, but that's what you are, isn't it.

ARSHALUIS: (*To* STEPHEN.) You know who is Lydia?

ANNA: (*To* ILYAS.) You don't exist—you don't exist, you just play into every hand that comes along. You'll do anything, won't you.

ILYAS: Anna. I detonated them. The mines.

ANNA: That was you? Setting them off?

ILYAS: Yes.

ANNA: Well, they must be expecting you to report back.

ILYAS: I'm not going back. I wasn't going back. I deserted.

ANNA: So that much is true?

ARSHALUIS: Anahid. When he came here? When he came to Matarash? I say when!

ANNA: I don't know. Five or six days ago.

ARSHALUIS: Amahn! He is here a week? A week? You hide him for a week?

(ANNA *buries her head in her hands.*)

ANNA: You weren't speaking to me.

ARSHALUIS: (*To* STEPHEN.) Amahn, she lied! She lied! He is here a week! She say he comes same night as you people! She lied to me! (*To* ANNA.) Why you don't tell he has come, why? If we know he is here, maybe we can stop him. Amahn, amahn!

ANNA: What have I done?

ARSHALUIS: I am shamed before God. Before God and before my village, I am shamed. I have two sons, holy martyrs—and only daughter is a traitor—a Judas and a whore!

ANNA: What have I done? What have I done?

ARSHALUIS: I tell you. You kill Arkady.

STEPHEN: Mrs. Sarkisian!

ANNA: He was Seryozha's friend! I wasn't part of this war!

ARSHALUIS: *(To STEPHEN.)* You! *(To STEPHEN and TITO.)* You know this girl? You people make her like this! Your Satan world! You seduce my daughter—you kill her. You kill my daughter. Swearing, lying, whoring—this is your life! We are dying while you take picture. You like to take picture now? Why you don't take picture?

(STEPHEN turns away.)

ANNA: *(To ILYAS.)* Why did you do it, why?

ILYAS: You were never going to be with me.

ARSHALUIS: *(To ANNA.)* Amahn, amahn! You love the traitor! You love the enemy!

ANNA: *(To ILYAS.)* I never hurt you.

ILYAS: *(To ANNA.)* Americans—they think they can have everything. I only like Azeri girls.

ARSHALUIS: Please Mikoyan, come soon! Come now!

ANNA: Ma—wait! Don't call him!

ARSHALUIS: Already I called.

ANNA: You called Mikoyan? When?

ARSHALUIS: Before. Soon he will come to take the prisoner.

ILYAS: Anahid! They'll torture me. They'll torture me if they take me.

ANNA: Ma? Is that true? Is it?! Ma!

TITO: *(Loudly wailing.)* Stephen! I have to go!

(TITO darts toward the door. As he does so, ILYAS leaps up and grabs TITO and holds him in front of him. ILYAS pulls a knife and holds it to TITO's throat.)

ILYAS: *(To TITO.)* Give me the keys.

(TITO pulls the keys out of his pocket. ILYAS grabs them and starts to drag TITO toward the door.)

STEPHEN: Tito!

ANNA: No! Ilyas! Stop! Ilyas!

ILYAS: Stay back!

ANNA: Ma! Tell him he can go! Let Tito go! Ilyas, let Tito go! Ma, tell him he can go free!

STEPHEN: Tell him to let Tito go!

ARSHALUIS: Let him go! Let him go, I say!

ANNA: You can go, Ilyas, but let Tito go! Let him go!

ILYAS: *(Hesitating.)* So you can kill me.

ANNA: No! Ma, tell him he can go!

STEPHEN: Tito!

(In hesitating, ILYAS has loosened his grip on TITO and ARSHALUIS sees her chance for a clear shot. She fires. ILYAS staggers, and then buries the knife in TITO. TITO falls. STEPHEN grabs TITO up, giving a great roar.)

STEPHEN: Tito! Tito!

(He shakes him desperately as if to wake him.)

Tito!

(He holds TITO as if he were a child.)

ANNA: Get a doctor! Get a doctor!

(ARSHALUIS rushes to the phone. She can't get through. ILYAS sits down heavily. He is bleeding.)

ILYAS: Anna. Anna.

(ANNA goes to ILYAS.)

I'm sorry. Why was he—He was a kid. Anna.

(He struggles.)

ANNA: Ilyas! Ma! Get a doctor! Get somebody! Call a doctor!

ARSHALUIS: Phone is not working.

(ARSHALUIS heads toward the door. ILYAS is bleeding profusely all over his chest and abdomen. ANNA gets covered with his blood on her hands and body as she tries to stop the bleeding.)

ANNA: *(To ILYAS.)* Where are you hit? Where are you hit? Where are you hit? *(To STEPHEN.)* Is Tito hurt bad? *(Calling to ARSHALUIS as she is leaving to get help.)* Ma! Ma!

(ARSHALUIS turns back.)

ILYAS: Anahid. In Madariz—Madariz—

(ILYAS *dies.* ARSHALUIS *feels for his pulse.*)

ARSHALUIS: Ai! Ai! Ai!
ANNA: No, no, no, no! Ilyas! Ilyas!

(ANNA *collapses on* ILYAS. STEPHEN *holds* TITO.)

    Oh Jesus! Oh God!
STEPHEN: He's dead.
ARSHALUIS: *(In Armenian.)* God have mercy! God have mercy! God have mercy!

Scene Five

(Two days later. SERYOZHA *and* TITO, *specially lit, in a loose white shirts, with backs to the audience.* ANNA, *kneeling, watches* ARSHALUIS *wash the floor.)*

ANNA: I brought more water up.

(As ARSHALUIS *moves,* ANNA *follows on her knees, pushing the bucket toward her mother.)*

ANNA: *(cont.)* I got some bread for you.

(ARSHALUIS *scrubs desperately and does not acknowledge her.)*

    Will you let me help?

(ARSHALUIS *moves further away.)*

    Please.
ARSHALUIS: I told you, go! Go!
ANNA: I want to help you.
ARSHALUIS: When I see you, I see these children.

(ANNA *looks at* SERYOZHA.)

    Why I don't let him go, why? Why, Seryozha, why? Why I don't let him go?

(ANNA *watches her mother helplessly.)*

ANNA: It's my fault. He would've left. He would have gone.

ARSHALUIS: *(In Armenian.)* God forgive me.

ANNA: Both of them would be alive.

ARSHALUIS: *(In Armenian.)* God forgive me.

ANNA: He was thirteen. When they left. For Saatli.

ARSHALUIS: My son too is dead! My son, my son! Why they take my son, why? He was beloved! Why they don't send him back to me? Let them send him back to me, how I would rejoice!

(ANNA tries to hold her mother but ARSHALUIS pushes her away.)

Ai, ai, Jesus, take this cup from me. Take this cup from me. *(To ANNA.)* Why you give me this cup, why?

(ARSHALUIS exits. On her knees, ANNA plunges her hands into the bucket of water and holds them there.)

ANNA: Ilyas. Ilyas.

(She brings her hands up, dripping.)

Tito.

(STEPHEN enters. ANNA remains on her knees in front of the bucket.)

STEPHEN: Anna. Hello. I just wanted to say, the flight's all set. Tomorrow at 8:00.

ANNA: They'll take . . .

(STEPHEN nods.)

STEPHEN: His parents will meet the plane. I came by before to tell you, but you were out.

ANNA: We buried Ilyas. In the Azeri cemetery.

STEPHEN: I was—I don't know what I was—*(Remembering.)* I wanted to see you. We came because I wanted to—When I look back . . . nothing looks real. It's small. I have to head down to Yerevan. Where are you going to go?

ANNA: The thing I can't—I just stood there.

STEPHEN: *(Gently.)* Bye, Anna.

(STEPHEN exits.)

ANNA: *(The lights change, SERYOZHA by himself.)* To say anything—to them . . . every word is like a boulder!

SERYOZHA: *(Turning around.)* Sing something for me.

ANNA: I can't.

SERYOZHA: You used to sing to me. When you were a girl.

ANNA: I can't sing—not anymore.

SERYOZHA: Everybody can sing.

ANNA: I don't have a good voice.

SERYOZHA: You have a voice. The body is an instrument.

ANNA: An instrument of what?

SERYOZHA: Music.

ANNA: Not just music.

SERYOZHA: No, not just music.

ANNA: Seryozha . . . how could I have twisted your arm and made you cry? I wasn't there—was I?—while you suffered? Behind the curtain . . . the pile of bodies . . . mothers . . . children . . . How did this happen? Were we so different from one another? Were we in the same world at the same time?

The End

DATE DUE

Alliant International University
Los Angeles Campus Library
1000 South Fremont Ave., Unit 5
Alhambra, CA 91803